General Robert E. Lee

ROBERT ·E· LEE

The Complete Man

1861★1870

→≫≫★≪≪←

Sanborn, Margaret
Robert E. Lee

LENDING POLICY

IF YOU DAMAGE OR LOSE LIBRARY
MATERIALS, THEN YOU WILL BE
CHARGED FOR REPLACEMENT. FAIL-
URE TO PAY AFFECTS LIBRARY
PRIVILEGES, GRADES, TRANSCRIPTS,
DIPLOMAS, AND REGISTRATION
PRIVILEGES OR ANY COMBINATION
THEREOF.

By the Same Author

ROBERT E. LEE
A Portrait
1807 ★ 1861

"*. . . and they shall turn their swords into ploughshares
and their spears into sickles.*"
—Isaias 2:4

ROBERT·E·LEE

THE COMPLETE MAN

[1861 ★ 1870]

by Margaret Sanborn

J. B. LIPPINCOTT COMPANY

Philadelphia & New York

FOR

DAVID, CATHERINE, *and* STEPHEN

that they may always find inspiration

in the example of Robert E. Lee

To the Reader

Robert E. Lee, A Portrait: 1807–1861, was not intended as a military biography. Nor is this second volume, covering Lee's remaining years after 1861, meant as such. If the reader expects to find detailed accounts of Lee's battles in this book, it is only fair to warn him that he will be disappointed.

The avowed purpose of this work was to explore Lee the man, to chronicle his moods, thoughts, and reactions even in the midst of battle. Too often Lee has been lost to readers when, in order to report over-all action, historians have moved the focus of attention to other generals in other sectors. In this study we are concerned only and always with Lee. To have recounted in minute detail each action of the Army of Northern Virginia would have meant departing from that intention.

It is not as though the exploits of that noble army are being neglected by this failure to relate them again. The literature on the subject is vast; millions of words have been written about Lee's battles.

Those who wish to read the best accounts (written by the men who fought in the Army of Northern Virginia) should turn to the books by William W. and Charles Minor Blackford, Robert Stiles, George Cary Eggleston, E. Porter Alexander, John Esten Cooke, Fitzhugh Lee, Carlton McCarthy, and Walter H. Taylor. For the most accurate retrospective work on the military movements of Lee's army, the reader should consult Douglas Southall Freeman's four-volume *R. E. Lee*.

M. S.

Acknowledgments

I AM deeply indebted to Mrs. William Hunter deButts and her sister, the late Mrs. Hanson E. Ely, Jr., granddaughters of Robert E. Lee, for permission to study, and quote from, the microfilm of the important R. E. Lee Papers in The Library of Congress. Mrs. deButts also gave permission to read and quote from R. E. Lee's three Memoranda Books in these same archives, and to quote from Lee's letters to Andrew and Harriet Talcott, to John, Eliza, and Margaret Mackay, to Martha Custis Williams, to Margaret and Caroline Stuart, to Jefferson Davis, to James A. Seddon, to John C. Breckinridge, and to J. E. B. Stuart. I am further grateful for Mrs. deButts' ever-courteous responses to many questions.

During the five years of production, I have been frequently sustained by Burke Davis' unwavering faith in this project and his encouragement. I have profited from his critical reading of the manuscript, his perception, and his advice.

Stewart Richardson, of J. B. Lippincott, has never wavered either in his belief that Robert E. Lee the *man* existed, and has counseled and encouraged me with unfailing warmth and thoughtfulness.

Miss Carolyn Blakemore has been a most discerning and sympathetic editor, and a thoroughly delightful person to work with. The book has benefited from her sound judgment.

Over the years, Mrs. Lilla Mills Hawes, Director of the Georgia Historical Society, has been tireless in furnishing prompt and exhaustive written replies to countless questions. With remarkable resourcefulness, she discovered for me little-known and unusual references to R. E. Lee during his many stays in Savannah. I am further grateful for the time she spent in driving me to all places connected with Lee in and around Savannah, and for granting permission to quote from the important material in the Society's collection. Thanks is also due the Colonial Dames of America, Georgia Branch, for permission to quote from copies of the R. E. Lee–Mackay Family letters in their collection, housed in the Georgia Historical Society.

I am also deeply grateful to the following people:

Charles F. Mills of Atherton, California, a great-grandson of Eliza Mackay, for generously giving his time to answer questions concerning Lee's relations with his family, and for supplying copies of all R. E. Lee–Mackay Family letters in his collection, as well as permission to quote from them.

Joseph M. O'Donnell, Chief, Archives and History Section, The United States Military Academy, for painstaking answers to many questions over the years, for providing copies of Lee letters, for his resourcefulness in discovering Mrs. D'Ormieulx's charming "Recollections of West Point in 1853," and for giving permission to quote from it.

Dr. Fred C. Cole, President of Washington and Lee University, for generously giving his time to answer questions and to supply information and pictures. Gene B. Hansley, former Assistant Director of the University's Information Services, for the pains he took to find unusual information. Dr. Ollinger Crenshaw, of the History Department, for supplying much of this material and checking the remainder. Dr. Allen W. Moger, also of the History Department, for permission to quote from R. E. Lee's letters to Jerome Bonaparte and his wife; and Frank A. Parsons, Assistant to the President, for many courtesies.

Admiral Irving T. Duke, Resident Superintendent of Stratford Hall, for answering countless questions by letter; for suggesting sources, providing copies of early Lee inventories; for pictures, and for granting permission to quote from the Gen. Henry Lee Letters in the Robert E. Lee Memorial Foundation, Inc., collection.

Ralston B. Lattimore, Superintendent of Fort Pulaski National Monument, for courteously answering questions by letter; for generously supplying copies of all R. E. Lee–Mackay Family letters in the Fort's collection of originals, and for sharing his own interesting manuscript letter from R. E. Lee to John Mackay.

Lucius S. Ruder of Clearwater, Florida, for also graciously sharing his important manuscript R. E. Lee letter to John Mackay.

Miss Janet Fauntleroy Taylor, of Norfolk, Virginia, a granddaughter of Col. Walter H. Taylor, for her many favors and the warmth of her responses to queries, for providing a picture of her grandfather, and for granting permission to quote from his letters and books.

David C. Mearns, Chief, Manuscript Division, The Library of Congress, for his kindness and cooperation; and Mr. de Porry and the staff of the Manuscript Reading Room, for their interest and help.

Miss Elizabeth J. Dance, Librarian, The Valentine Museum, Richmond, for her interest and help while I was at work in the library, and for patiently answering questions by letter. She also granted permission to quote from Edward V. Valentine's notebook-journal. Miss Lydia Booth Sarvay, of the Museum's staff, for her interest and many favors.

Miss Elizabeth Tindall, former Reference Librarian, Missouri Historical Society, and Mrs. Frances Stadler, Manuscript Librarian for the Society, for many courtesies, and for granting permission to quote both the manuscript and printed R. E. Lee–Henry Kayser letters.

Marshall Gray, Technical Liaison Branch, U. S. Army Engineer Corps, St. Louis, for helpful information about R. E. Lee's work on the Mississippi River.

William J. Van Schreeven, State Archivist, Virginia State Library, for valuable suggestions as to new sources, and permission to quote from the C. C. Lee Papers and from letters from R. E. Lee to Jefferson Davis. Milton C. Russell, Head, Reference and Circulation Section, for promptly and courteously answering so many questions.

Howson W. Cole, Curator of Manuscripts, Virginia Historical Society, for his courtesy and help, and for granting permission to quote from the letters of R. E. Lee to Andrew and Harriet Talcott and to Jefferson Davis.

Mrs. George Bolling Lee of San Francisco, for graciously permitting the use of seven portraits in her collection.

George R. Talcott of Richmond, for his kind permission to use the portrait of Harriet Randolph Talcott.

Dr. Ives Hendrick of Boston, for granting permission to quote from the letter of Samuel Appleton Storrow to his sister, printed in his father's outstanding work, *The Lees of Virginia*, by Burton J. Hendrick.

Mrs. Henry W. Howell, Jr., Librarian, Miss Helen Sanger, Research Librarian, and Miss Mildred Steinbach, Assistant Librarian, all of the Frick Art Reference Library, for their never-failing courtesy and help.

Mrs. Virginia R. Gray, Manuscript Department, Duke University Library, who gave such splendid service in providing copies of R. E. Lee's personal letters, and wartime dispatches and letters. B. E. Powell, Librarian, for granting permission to quote from this material.

Dr. Hugh F. Rankin and Dr. Charles P. Roland, Tulane University, for their interest and help, and Mrs. Connie G. Griffith, Director, Manuscripts Division, Tulane University Library, for her thoughtfulness and aid, and for granting permission to quote from R. E. Lee's letters to Albert Sidney Johnston in the Mrs. Mason Barret Collection.

Herbert Cahoon, Curator of Manuscripts, The Pierpont Morgan Library, New York, for his courtesy and help. Frederick B. Adams, Jr., Director of the Library, for permission to quote from the original R. E. Lee–Martha Custis Williams letters in these archives.

Dr. James J. Heslin, Director, New York Historical Society, for many courtesies.

Miss Eleanor S. Brockenbrough, Assistant Director, Confederate Literary Society, Richmond, for many favors so courteously rendered, and for permission to quote from the letters of Mrs. R. E. Lee to Mrs. Robert H. Chilton.

Mrs. Margaret Moore, Curator of the Lee House, Richmond, for her gracious hospitality.

Mrs. Virginia H. Pinkerton, Norfolk Public Library, for enduring many questions, and for the loan of valuable books.

Mrs. Nancy C. English, Huntington Library Publications, for permission to quote from *"To Markie": The Letters of*

Robert E. Lee to Martha Custis Williams, edited by Avery Craven (Harvard University Press, 1933), and from "To Molly: Five Early Letters from Robert E. Lee to his Wife," by Norma B. Cuthbert, *Huntington Library Quarterly*, May, 1952.

Robert O. Dougan, Librarian, Henry E. Huntington Library and Art Gallery, for his courtesy.

Mrs. Dorothy Thomas, Librarian, Mill Valley Public Library, and staff, for their cooperation. A special note of thanks is due Miss Constance Karla, whose task it was to order and handle the mass of interlibrary loan material; this she did with unfailing cheerfulness and admirable efficiency.

Irenaeus N. Tucker, M.D., who devoted time and thought to the case histories of the mother and wife of R. E. Lee, offering as definite an opinion as is possible to make from the scant information.

Eugene Pike, Reference Section Librarian, The California State Library, and his staff, for responding fully and promptly to all questions concerning sources, and sending countless volumes through interlibrary loan.

I am grateful to Charles Scribner's Sons for permission to quote from *Letters from Lee's Army*, edited by Charles Minor Blackford III (New York, 1947); and from *War Years with Jeb Stuart* by William W. Blackford (New York, 1945); to The Bobbs-Merrill Co. for permission to quote from a letter of Dr. May to Cassius Lee, printed in *Lee of Virginia* by William E. Brooks, copyright 1932 by The Bobbs-Merrill Co., R. 1958 by William E. Brooks, reprinted by permission of the publisher; to Putnam's & Coward-McCann for permission to quote from *Lee's Dispatches: Unpublished Letters of Gen. Robert E. Lee, C.S.A., to Jefferson Davis and the War Department of the Confederate States of America, 1861–1865*, edited by Douglas Southall Freeman (New York, 1957); to Mrs. Douglas Southall Freeman for permission to quote from "Lee and the Ladies" by Douglas Southall Freeman, *Scribner's Magazine*, October, 1925; to The University of North Carolina Press for permission to quote from Henry Kyd Douglas, *I Rode With Stonewall* (Chapel Hill, 1940); and to Houghton Mifflin for permission to quote from Mary Boykin Chesnut, *A Diary from Dixie*, edited by Ben Ames Williams (Boston, 1949).

Last, but by no means least, I want to thank my family for their enduring patience and their encouragement.

Margaret Sanborn

Mill Valley, California
June 30, 1966

Contents

Illustrations

(following page 208)

⇒⇒ I ⇐⇐

In Defense of Virginia

April 19, 1861 ★ *April 9, 1865*

I. In Defense of Virginia

As Lee rode from the Richmond depot to the Spotswood Hotel on the corner of 8th and Main Streets, he saw that the city was in a ferment. The streets were jammed with carriages and hacks, with men on horseback and on foot. Crowds milled on the corners. Every vacant lot resembled a military camp, for tents had been set up to provide shelter for the companies of recruits who were arriving almost hourly and he could see them drilling awkwardly among the weeds. Men were even training in the basement of the Spotswood, and all over town, boys kept their patriotism warm by mock battles of such ferocity that the city council had to stop them.

When Lee called on Governor John Letcher, who had been strongly Union in sympathy until Lincoln called on Virginia for troops, Letcher told him that the state convention, still in secret session, had passed an ordinance providing for a commander in chief of the state's military and naval forces, and that the advisory committee had selected him for the post.

Now the question was: what would Lee do? Without a moment's hesitation, he accepted, and before the night session adjourned, the Governor had submitted his name for confirmation. It was unanimously approved, and the next morning the new Major General opened temporary headquarters and wrote General Order No. 1, announcing acceptance of the command.

He had just finished when a committee of four called to escort him to the capitol to receive his formal notification from the convention. As they waited in the rotunda for the business in hand to be finished, Lee seemed thoughtful. His companions watched him walk over and gaze long at Houdon's masterful statue of George Washington. As he turned away from its contemplation, they overheard him say:

"I hope we have seen the last of secession."

When the convention doors were opened Lee, on the arm of Marmaduke Johnson, the representative from Richmond, entered the chamber. The convention rose, and Johnson paused just inside the door to introduce him to President John Janney on the speaker's rostrum and to the convention at large. Lee bowed, and Janney said:

Major General Lee, in the name of the people of your native State, . . . I bid you a cordial and heartfelt welcome to this Hall, in which we may almost hear the echo of the voices of the statesmen, the soldiers and sages of by-gone days, who have borne your name, and whose blood now flows in your veins. . . . Sir, we have by this unanimous vote, expressed our conviction that you are this day, among living citizens of Virginia, "first in war." We pray God most fervently that you may so conduct the operations committed to your charge, that it will soon be said of you, that you are "first in peace," and when that time comes you will have earned the still prouder distinction of being "first in the hearts of your countrymen.". . .

Lee, it was noted, listened with that "supreme composure, which nothing seemed able to shake," and when thunderous applause and cheering marked the end of Janney's panegyric, he responded:

Mr. President and Gentlemen of the Convention: Profoundly impressed with the solemnity of the occasion, for which I must say I was not prepared, I accept the position assigned me by your partiality. I would have preferred had your choice fallen on an abler man. Trusting to Almighty God, an approving conscience, and the aid of my fellow citizens, I devote myself to the service of my native State, in whose behalf alone will I ever again draw my sword.

The members came forward to shake hands and express their confidence in him, for as Jubal A. Early, the representative from Franklin county, wrote: "Those who . . . saw his manly bearing, and heard the few grave, dignified and impressive words with which he consecrated himself and his sword to the cause of his native State, can never forget that scene. All felt at once that we had a leader worthy of the State and the cause."

As soon as he could graciously free himself, Lee returned to his office to start work. Presumably, there were just twelve

4

days left to complete Virginia's preparations against invasion, since on April 15 Lincoln had announced that the Southern troops would be allowed twenty days of grace to disband and return peaceably to their homes. On May 5, then, or before, the North could be expected to move.

That afternoon, Lee received a message from Alexander H. Stephens, Vice-President of the Confederacy, who had come to Richmond to negotiate for Virginia's alliance with the seceded states. He asked Lee to call at his rooms at the Ballard House, and presented him with a problem in military protocol. The Confederacy was anxious for an alliance with Virginia, he explained, but there was one difficulty: since the army of the Confederacy had no higher rank than brigadier general, Stephens was afraid that the convention, foreseeing friction when Lee found himself under orders from a lower ranking officer, might refuse to join the Confederacy. He wanted to learn Lee's attitude toward such a situation.

As Stephens wrote later: "General Lee did not hesitate one moment . . . he declared that no personal ambition or emolument should be considered or stand in the way. I had admired him in the morning, but I took his hand that night at parting with feelings of respect and almost reverence."

Even this late, Lee received evidence of the people's confidence in his talents as a peacemaker, suggesting again that if he had gone to the convention when it was debating secession, and given his opinion, he might have kept Virginia loyal to the Union. Cassius Lee sent him a letter from a professor at the Alexandria Theological Seminary who had hoped that Robert Lee would use his influence now for peace since "great respect would be shown the judgment and Christian Spirit of one so distinguished as he." In an accompanying note, Cassius wrote that he hoped Robert's connection with the Virginia forces and his friendship with General Scott might "lead to some peaceful settlement of our difficulties." He prayed that God would make Robert "instrumental in saving our land from this dreadful strife."

Up to the end, Lee had clung to tenuous hopes for peace, but now he knew that the time for argument was past. He

5

asked Cassius to thank his friend and tell him "that no earthly act of mine would give me so much pleasure as to restore peace to my country. But I fear now it is out of the power of man & in God alone must be our trust."

Before Lee had come to Richmond, Governor Letcher had made a start at defending Virginia's most vulnerable point, her many navigable rivers. The engineer in charge of these defenses was Andrew Talcott, who had renounced the claims of his Connecticut birth and ancestry, and heeded Virginia's call. Lee was relieved to have such an experienced officer on whom to rely, for as he said: "Good officers are scarce & it will take time to make them." He wrote Andrew on April 30, telling him of his pleasure at being associated with him again, though lamenting "the calamitous times" which had brought them together.

His awareness of this acute shortage of trained officers and men, and the scarcity of munitions and other supplies, led Lee to adopt a defensive policy which was criticized in the press and by the fire-eating politicians who believed that the enemy was ready to drop his gun and fly at the first volley from Southern troops.

"It is important that conflict be not provoked before we are ready," he repeated often.

His most important critic in Richmond was D. G. Duncan, emissary of the Confederate war secretary, L. Pope Walker. In the daily reports he sent his chief at the Confederate capital, then in Montgomery, Alabama, he carped at Lee's extensive preparations and caution, which he saw only as a damper to the people's ardor for war. Because of Lee's condemnation of secession, Duncan even suggested treachery in Virginia.

Lee's stand on secession aroused distrust among South Carolinians also, and the words of one fire-eater from Camden represented their attitude: "At heart Robert E. Lee is against us; that I know." Another suggested that Lee should be tried as a traitor, since he was taking into consideration the possibility of retreat. "To talk of retreat is treason!" he said.

Lee met opposition also from those impractical minds unaware that war calls for systematic preparation. To one man

6

who complained of the poor quality of his company's arms, he said:

"Sir, your people had better write to Mr. Lincoln and ask him to postpone this thing for a few months until you can get ready for him."

No attention was paid to his anticipation of "a prolonged and bloody war," or his recommendation that the volunteers be enlisted for the duration rather than one year. The civil authorities were unable to believe that, with such a craven enemy, there would be any need for an armed force for more than twelve months.

In spite of preoccupation with the most demanding challenge he had ever accepted, he was at times able to lay aside Virginia's problems and interest himself in those of his wife and children. Mary worried him by her refusal to reconcile herself to impending changes and make an effort to find a safer place to live. She was so reluctant to leave her "beautiful home endeared by a thousand associations" that she grasped at every rumor of peace.

Even if war came, Mary believed that, because of their friendship with General Scott, she could stay at Arlington and carry on the old way of life in the midst of the storm. She ignored Robert's advice, though as early as April 26 he had warned:

"War is inevitable, & there is no telling when it will burst around you. Virginia yesterday . . . joined the Confederate States. What policy they may adopt I cannot conjecture. . . . I am very anxious about you. You have to move & make arrangements to go to some point of safety, which you select. The Mount Vernon plate & pictures ought to be secured."

After hearing from her that all was yet at peace, he wrote again on the 30th:

"I fear the latter state will not continue long. . . . I think you had better prepare all things for removal . . . & be prepared at any moment."

And later he cautioned:

Do not go to Berkeley or the Shenandoah Valley, those points are much exposed. But you must not talk of what I write, nor is

Richmond perhaps more out of harm's way. I take it for granted our opponents will do us all the harm they can. They feel their power, & they seem to desire to oppress & distress us. I assume therefore they will do it. Make your preparations quickly. . . . There is no prospect or intention of the government to propose a truce. Do not be deceived by it.

But still she made no effort to leave, and on May 5 wrote General Scott a remarkable letter. She had heard through Orton Williams, who though on Scott's staff still visited at Arlington, that the General's attitude toward Robert was not bitter. Indeed, he had said when he read Lee's resignation that he would rather have had the resignations of *all* his other generals save this one. He continued to show great interest in his favorite lieutenant, and had recently asked to see an account of Lee's reception by the Richmond convention.

This gave Mary an excuse to ask him for the protection that would allow her to stay at Arlington. From the *Richmond Whig* she clipped the article, and enclosed it with her letter.

My dear General, Hearing that you desire to see the account of my husband's reception in Richmond, I have sent it to you. No honours can reconcile us to the fratricidal war which we would have all laid down our lives freely to avert. Whatever may happen, I feel that I may expect from your kindness all the protection you can in honour afford. Nothing can ever make me forget your appreciation of Mr. Lee. If you knew all, you would not think so hardly of me. . . . Oh, that you could command peace to our distracted country!

Yours in sadness & sorrow,
M. C. Lee

General Scott was unable to reply directly, but not long after he had received the letter, Orton rode over to warn the family that Arlington Heights would soon be fortified. Though he could not say so, it was understood that the General had sent him.

This news prodded Mary into action and she began to prepare to leave. But it also did something else: as soon as it was clear that she could not stay in her home, she became embittered and defiant, characteristics that grew more intense with time. They were already evident in a letter written to Mildred the morning after Orton's call:

My dear little girl, I received your amusing letter & am glad that you have the spirits to be happy. We alas are very sad now. We have received information from a friend that the government troops are to take possession of the heights in a few days. . . . Except to relieve your father & brother & leave them free to perform their duty, I would prefer not to stir from this house even if the whole Northern army were to surround us. The zealous patriots who are making their lines to *preserve* the Union founded by Washington might come & take the granddaughter of his wife from her home & desecrate it, for whatever I have thought & even *now* think, of the commencement of this horrible conflict, now our duty is *plain*, to resist unto death. The government has proved itself so false and treacherous that we have nothing to hope. The men who are at the head of it seem to be without honour & without pity & I believe it would give them pleasure to lay waste to our beautiful country.

A few days later, she wrote to Robert telling him that the "wines, stores, pictures & piano" had been sent to Ravensworth, and the silver, personal papers, and other articles of value, shipped to the capital. By this time she was convinced "that Orton was made a tool of by some authorities in Washington to alarm us, either to bring you out to defend your home or get us out of the house. They are anxious at present to keep up appearances & would gladly, I believe, have a pretext to invade."

She was unable to understand Custis' imperturbability at "the possibility of having his early & beautiful home destroyed. . . . He never indulges in invectives or a word of reflection on the cruel course of the Administration. He leaves that for his Mamma & sisters."

When the shipment reached Lee, he sent everything except his box of personal papers to Lexington, Virginia, for safekeeping.

Though Rooney was with the Confederate cavalry at Ashland, Custis was still undecided about his future. He inclined toward leaving the Federal service, but his father had told him not to hurry with his decision, or be influenced by his example. Early in May, the Provisional Army of Virginia appointed Custis a major of engineers—"without any application on my part," his father told the family, adding: "Tell him he is under no obligation to accept."

When Custis decided to take the commission, Lee wrote to ask that he bring "towels, blankets, &c., &c., for both of us for field service. Those Mexican blankets would be useful. Knives, forks, & spoons of some sort will be necessary, & any thing else that could be applied will save their purchase. He had better bring his horse, bridles & saddles. Every thing of that kind you know is lost to me. The supply of such things here I am told is meagre."

Late in March, Charles Anderson of San Antonio sent the baggage and equipment Lee had left there in storage. When it reached New York, McCready, Mott & Co., which ran packets to Indianola and Lavaca, was unable to send it on, and advising Lee, placed it in storage to await his instructions. Before he could arrange for its transfer to Arlington, it was seized and never returned to him.

The frugality that was so natural to Lee was shown at this time, when he asked Mary to take apart his old uniform coat, left at Arlington for one of the servants, in order to "retrieve the eyes or hooks from the shoulders that confined the epaulettes. Will you cut them out & also the loops at the collar. You will have to rip the coat to take them out. . . . Then wrap them up carefully & send them directed to the Spottswood House." Concluding that the whole coat might be of further use, Mary sent it on, too.

On May 11, Mary was still at Arlington, worrying about the disposal of the favorite cat, Tom. But by the sixteenth she had driven over to Ravensworth, where Aunt Maria received her "with open arms."

Each letter to Robert now bore bitter words for those who had forced her from her home, and declarations of her intention to return there soon. Wearily he tried to reason with her:

I sympathise deeply in your feelings at leaving your dear home. I have experienced them often myself, & they are constantly revived. . . . I do not think it prudent or right for you to return there, while the United States troops occupy that country. I have gone over this ground before, & have written Cousin Anna on the subject. . . . I have no time for more. I know & feel the discomfort of your position, but it cannot be helped, & we must bear our trials like Christians.

Lee now moved from his temporary quarters to simply furnished rooms on the top floor of the Mechanics' Hall. His callers were surprised to find no sentinel to mark military headquarters, no "handsomely dressed aides-de-camp or staff officers filling the anteroom," and to observe the General wearing a plain suit without signs of rank. It was noted that although he was fifty-four, he looked exceptionally youthful, and "a model of manly beauty"; and that his erect and muscular frame and firm step gave "ease and grace" to his bearing that belied his years. George Cary Eggleston, who met him for the first time at a dinner in Richmond, was impressed with his "eminent *robustness*, a quality no less marked in his intellect and his character, than in his physical constitution."

Walter Herron Taylor, a capable young man from Norfolk, joined Lee's staff at this time. He had never seen Lee before coming to Richmond, and left an account of his first impressions:

I was at breakfast in the Spotswood Hotel, when he entered the room, and was at once attracted and greatly impressed by his appearance. He was then at the zenith of his physical beauty. Admirably proportioned, of graceful and dignified carriage, with strikingly handsome features, bright and penetrating eyes, his iron-gray hair closely cut, his face cleanly shaven except for a mustache, he appeared every inch a soldier and a man born to command.

Through his work as a Bank of Virginia officer, and as auditor for the Norfolk & Petersburg Railroad, Taylor was familiar with efficiency, punctuality, and attention to detail; but as soon as he saw Lee at work, he admitted:

I can say I have never known a man more thorough and painstaking in meeting all engagements, methodical to the extreme in his way of despatching business, giving close attention to detail—

but not, as is sometimes concomitant, if not the result of this trait, neglectful of the more important matters dependent upon his decision—he seemed to address himself to the accomplishment of every task . . . in a conscientious and deliberate way, as if he himself was directly accountable to some higher power for the manner in which he performed his duty.

Taylor soon discovered that "a scrupulous consideration for the feelings and interests of others" marked Lee's relations with his fellows. He also soon found that Lee's heavy correspondence was a sore trial to him, and that "nothing seemed to tax his amiability so much." Still, he was never satisfied unless, at the close of his office hours, every letter and other matters requiring prompt attention had been taken care of.

In order to get exercise and relaxation, he took daily rides after office hours, going with one or two of his staff to some point of interest around Richmond. "No sculptor or artist can ever produce in marble or bronze the picture of manly grace and beauty that became in those days so familiar to the people in and around Richmond in the person of General Lee on his favorite horse," wrote Taylor, who accompanied him regularly.

The favorite horse at this period was a superb bay stallion given to Lee by several admirers soon after he came to the capital, and called "Richmond" by him. The animal was admired by fanciers of horseflesh, but Lee found him to be "a troublesome fellow, & dislikes to associate with strange horses."

When he returned from these late-afternoon rides, he found further relaxation in the company of the little girls of the neighborhood, to whom he would "talk in the most loving and familiar way."

On May 23, Virginia's Ordinance of Secession was approved at the polls. The official justification for this act was that "Virginia has no grievance. She raises her strong arm to catch the blow aimed at her weaker sisters." The next day Federal troops marched into Alexandria and Lee sent three regiments of reinforcements to Manassas Junction.

On May 28 he went there himself, and though he was much occupied with an examination of the ground and defenses,

12

there was time for a letter to Mary, expressing concern over her presence at Ravensworth, now that the enemy was in Virginia. He had been invited to stay with a cousin while at Manassas, but he refused, establishing a precedent he observed throughout the war:

"I never visit for many reasons. If for no other, to prevent compromising the house, for my visit would certainly be known," he explained.

On the twenty-fifth of May, the life of the Provisional Army of Virginia came to an end after two months of concentrated work on Lee's part. On June 8, her troops were transferred to the Confederate States Army. Lee's genius for organization had produced sixty regiments of infantry and cavalry, and numerous batteries of artillery, a total of fifty thousand, with a large number of other regiments which would soon take to the field. Further, the navy yard at Norfolk had been put into operation again after damage by evacuating Federals; the sunken frigate *Merrimac* had been raised and was being fitted out in dry dock, and a start had been made on salvaging other scuttled ships.

Lee's authority as commander in chief now ended. Although the Confederate Congress had, on May 16, authorized his appointment as one of five generals to its regular army, he was hopeful that if he could be of no more use to Virginia, he would not be called on for further duty. On June 8 he wrote to Mary, who had moved on to Chantilly:

You may be aware that the Confederate Government is established here [Richmond]. Yesterday I turned over to it the command of the military & naval forces of the State. . . . I do not know what my position will be. I should like to retire to private life, if I could be with you & the children, but if I can be of any service to the State or her cause I must continue.

That he did continue was solely because Virginia needed him, and not because of sympathy with the Southern cause. Virginia's physical position, and the Northern policy of war by piecemeal, made her the battleground. When Lee took to the field, he called his command "The Army of Northern Vir-

13

ginia," and his chief concern would always be the defense of his native state.

"I bear no malice, have no animosities to indulge, no selfish purpose to gratify. My only object is to repel the invaders of our peace & the spoilers of our homes. I hope in time they will see the injustice of their course & return to their better nature," was an exposition of his attitude, written at this time.

As Mary said to a friend:

"My husband has wept tears of blood over this terrible war; but he must as a man & as a Virginian, share the destiny of his State, which has solemnly pronounced for independence."

Though he would never have spoken so bluntly, he shared the sentiments of his cousin, Williams C. Wickham, who had been wounded in the fighting near Williamsburg, and said to a friend:

"Blackford, it's a damned shame I should have to suffer so much now and probably be killed tomorrow for a cause of which I do not approve. Remember, Blackford, if I am killed tomorrow it will be for Virginia, the land of my fathers, and not for the damned secession movement."

2

JEFFERSON DAVIS' twenty years in public life had failed to inure him to the slings of cavilers. He was a highly nervous man and so "abnormally sensitive" that "a child's disapproval discomposed him." When he became President of the Confederate States, it was written of him that he noticed "every shade of feeling that crossed the minds of those about him . . . and he could not bear any one to be inimical to him." He seemed more ready than ever to resent criticism and to quarrel with men who crossed him, though he was fiercely loyal to those he counted as friends. He guarded his power jealously, suspecting those about him of contriving to rob him of it. He refused to delegate military authority, choosing to be his own active commander in chief.

Since he was already familiar with Lee's character, and

knew that Robert was neither self-seeking nor disposed to usurp power or glory, he called on him for help. Lee's experience as an engineer and his exact knowledge of conditions in Virginia made him invaluable. Davis retained him as his "constant and trusted adviser," but gave him neither title nor authority to act alone.

Lee respected Davis, and admired him in many ways. He was aware of Davis' peculiarities and adapted himself to them. "Davis required deference, respect, subordination. Lee felt that these were military duties and he was ready to accord them."

Believing that his assignment was temporary, and that he would be shortly sent to the field, Lee did not ask the President to define his exact status. Therefore he remained in ignorance—not knowing "where he was," as he said—until November of that year.

"The Administration at Richmond was of too narrow a mold to understand that a man could be master of more than one thing, and so, recognizing Lee's supreme ability as an organizer, the government seems to have assumed that he was good for very little else, and until the summer of 1862 he was carefully kept out of the way of all military operations," wrote George Cary Eggleston. Actually, Davis was well aware of Lee's military genius, and kept him from the field for personal reasons.

Davis also had a reputation for "military genius of high order," and many believed that he had been chosen to head the Confederacy so that he might command in person. He now had on his hands the one officer above all others whom the Federal government had most regretted losing; the man whom General Scott considered the greatest military genius in America; the man to whom Francis P. Blair had less than three months before offered the command of the entire Union army; the man whom the Virginia Convention had spoken of as "First in war," and likened to the father of his country, a title first applied to Caesar.

The obvious place for Lee was commander in chief, or at least senior general in command of all the armies in the field.

But since Davis had envisioned for himself a role not unlike Napoleon's, he looked on Lee as his most formidable rival. He appreciated the value of Lee's counsel for the direction of military affairs, and believed that there was no better way to profit by Lee's genius and still hold him in check than to keep him in Richmond as his adviser.

His first assignment was an inspection of the batteries and troops on the James and York Rivers. On the way, he stopped to see Charlotte, Annie, and his little grandson whom he found "happy to see his Grd father." He was asked to help select a distinctive insignia for officers, very necessary since those who had been in the old army still wore their blue uniforms. So that the badge might be easily distinguishable, to avoid confusion with the Federals, he suggested "a broad band with a rosette and streams on the left arm above the elbow." But his suggestion was overruled, and a more stylish but less practical insignia was adopted: "A kind of epaulette, not sufficiently distinct enough at a distance I should think," he objected. He predicted that many accidents and deaths would result from the ensuing confusion.

But this was not the sort of duty that brought him satisfaction. As modest as he was, he knew that he could be of more value in the field, and said so. This sense of frustration earned for him the reputation of a "bear" who, "when aroused should be avoided by wise people."

The fact that his daughters refused to regard the times as serious and restrict their summer tours vexed him, and he complained: "I heard the other day that Daughter was at Manassas —for some good object I trust." Agnes was full of projected plans to visit all over the state with Mrs. Warwick, and he grumbled that she talked only "of having pleasant times, as if enjoyment was the order of the day. I hope no other times befall her, but in my opinion these are serious times & our chief pleasure must be what is necessary & proper for the occasion."

Orton Williams' visits to the Lees at last aroused suspicion, and he was sent to Governor's Island and kept there until what information he might have was rendered useless by time. The

16

press dramatized the case, accusing Williams of betraying General Scott's secrets directly to Lee. When Orton was released, he resigned from Scott's staff, changed his allegiance, and became an aide to the "Fighting Bishop," General Leonidas Polk, then with the Confederate army in Tennessee.

Lee regretted that he could not have Williams on his staff, feeling that he might help to curb Orton's recklessness, "but I knew it would have reopened the batteries of the Northern Press, reviving their scandalous assertions."

The slanders about Lee that appeared in the Northern newspapers angered Mary and hurt Markie, each of whom wrote to him of her distress. "The writers for their papers resort to every deception to promote their ends. Do not be surprised at it," he warned Mary. He sent a message to Markie since he could no longer write to her because she lived within Federal lines: "Tell her not to mind the reports she sees in the papers. They are made to injure & occasion distrust. Those who know me will not believe them. Those who do not will not care. . . . I laugh at them."

Though Lee's post kept him in relative obscurity, his reputation was not easily forgotten, especially by Virginians, and there was constant agitation to have him "disinterred" and placed in command of the armies. Rumors that he would be appointed commander in chief were persistent. In July, Mary wrote to him about this possibility, but he dealt with it brusquely:

"I have never heard of the appointment, to which you allude . . . nor have I any expectation or wish for it. President Davis holds that . . . position. Since the transfer of the military operations . . . to the authorities of the Confederate States, I have only the position of a general in that service, with the duties devolved on me by the President." His restiveness caused him to add: "I am very anxious to get to the field, but am detained by matters beyond my control."

The situation in western Virginia was grave. There was widespread sickness among the troops, the terrain was rugged, the roads bad, the rain continual, supplies were short, preparation scant, and above all, there was conflict between commanders in that sector. McClellan had defeated the Confederates in a surprise attack at Rich Mountain, and the Federals, if they chose, could now push into the Shenandoah Valley. It was imperative that someone be sent to advise on the plan of the campaign, promote harmony between the feuding generals, Wise and Floyd, help General W. W. Loring reorganize the forces, and finally, coordinate the divided commands.

Since these were forlorn hopes, Lee was Davis' obvious choice. He was certain that not even Lee's genius for organization could remedy the situation. But his failure would end for all time the agitation that Lee be made commanding general.

All preparations had been made for Robert's departure, but on July 17, General Beauregard telegraphed the War Office that the enemy was advancing toward Manassas Junction. He also wired to Joe Johnston, then at Winchester: "If you will help me, now is the time." Davis, wishing to profit by Lee's counsel, suspended his orders to leave for Staunton, in western Virginia.

Around nine o'clock on the morning of the eighteenth, the Federals attacked at Mitchell's Ford, three miles from Manassas, but they were given a temporary check by the Virginians who "stood with the coolness of veterans, yet fought with the fury of tigers in the charge."

But early on Sunday morning the twenty-first, Beauregard telegraphed the War Department again, warning that the Federals were preparing to attack. The President took a special train to the scene, leaving Lee in Richmond to fret at his inability to "take part in the struggle for my home & neighbourhood" and feel "mortified" at his absence.

It was assumed when Davis left that he would direct the battle in person. When his message: "We have won a glorious though dear-bought victory. Night closed on the enemy in full flight and closely pursued" reached Richmond, it was believed that he was personally responsible for this happy turn of events, and for a matter of hours he was looked on as a hero. But the next day it was learned that the battle had been won and the enemy was already in flight when the President appeared, and that credit for the victory belonged to Beauregard and Johnston.

When Davis came back to the capital, he assured the crowd that clamored for him outside the Spotswood Hotel, where he and his family were staying, that by then the Confederate flag was doubtless floating over Fairfax Court House and would soon be raised in Alexandria. Above the tumultuous cheers, he admonished his listeners: "Never be haughty to the humble, or humble to the haughty!"

"It's all over!" the people said, as they turned homeward. They were satisfied that within a few days their banners would wave over the streets of Washington City, and that "a peace would be consummated on the banks of the Susquehanna or the Schuylkill."

Tales of Manassas drifted into Richmond. It was there on Henry Hill that General Thomas J. Jackson received his sobriquet, "Stonewall." General Bernard Bee, just before he fell mortally wounded in Mrs. Henry's dooryard had, while trying to rally his men, "cried out to them in a voice that the rattle of musketry could not drown, 'Look! There is Jackson's brigade standing behind you like a stone wall!' " Others insisted that Bee had not called him "Stonewall" in admiration but in anger at Jackson's failure to come to his aid, and that he had shouted in rage: "Look! There stands Jackson—like a damned stone wall!"

At Manassas, the unearthly Rebel Yell was first heard. Jackson had told his men to withhold their fire until the enemy was on them, then to fire and give them the bayonet. "And when you charge, yell like furies!" When, heartened by the arrival of reinforcements, they charged, they yelled "like furies," giving voice to a rasping, yipping halloo such as fox hunters use. In face of it, the Federal advance faltered, then broke and ran, shouting to their comrades behind: "Turn back! Turn back! We are whipped!" Panic being contagious, the others broke and fled, too.

Half the population of Washington came out to Manassas to watch the Rebel rout. Congressmen, Cabinet ministers, department clerks, and prominent citizens, all in holiday mood and dress, followed the advancing column closely with their carriages. And "there was not wanting many a hack-load of the *demi-monde* with their admirers to complete the motley crew," one Virginia soldier wrote in disgust.

But when the Federal rout began, the flight of the spectators was compared to a chariot race. All along the road, the pursuit found "parasols and dainty shawls," baskets of lunch half eaten, and hampers of wine, left behind in the stampede.

It proved to be a "dear-bought" victory. Each day more bodies were brought to Richmond to lie in state in the capitol rotunda, and many times a day, the measured tramp of feet and the wail of the dirge was heard through the streets. A woman diarist noted: "Now it seems as if we are never out of the sound of the Dead March in Saul. It comes and it comes until I feel inclined to close my ears and scream."

While Beauregard and Johnston were the men of the hour, lauded and toasted throughout the South as "Eugene" and "Marlborough," there were a few thoughtful enough to realize that if it had not been for the superb organization of Robert E. Lee when he was commander in chief of the Virginia forces, those congressmen, Cabinet ministers, department clerks, and others who had actually ticketed their baggage for Richmond, would have reached their destination.

3

ON Saturday morning, July 27, Lee took the train for Staunton, headed for his mission with the Northwest Army. With him were his two aides, Colonel John Augustine Washington, grandnephew of General Washington and present owner of Mount Vernon, and Walter Taylor, recently promoted to captain. There were also two servants: Perry from Arlington, as factotum, and Meredith from the White House, as the cook. In the baggage car with their tent and camp equipment were Taylor's black mare, Washington's sorrel, and Lee's bay stallion, Richmond.

The morning after their arrival in Staunton, the three men mounted their horses and set out in the rain for Monterey. The road as far as Buffalo Gap was familiar to Lee, for as he told his companions, he had passed over it more than twenty years ago on his way to St. Louis, but had anyone at that time told him the nature of the errand that would take him over it again, he would have thought him insane.

The rain followed them all the way to Huntersville, "a wretched and filthy town," where they found an epidemic of measles and typhoid raging among the troops. The commanding officer, General Loring, had no advance warning of Lee's coming and did not receive him warmly, for he had already planned his next move, was preparing for it now, and did not feel that he needed Lee's counsel.

Loring proposed to march his thirty-five hundred men to the rear of Cheat Mountain, join the advance regiments posted there, and in a surprise attack drive the enemy from his position in the pass. He would then carry the town of Beverly, and open up a rich source of forage and provisions and a vital line of communication. Though the success of his plan lay in its speedy execution, he was disposed "to regard the formation of a depot of supplies at Huntersville and the organization of a supply-train as a matter of first importance," overlooking the fact that "the country along his line abounded in beef and grain," an aide wrote.

The necessity for prompt movement was evident to Lee, but he did not hurry Loring, and when he saw him losing the opportunity for a surprise attack, did not order the plan into immediate operation in spite of Loring, though he has been consistently criticized for not doing so.

It becomes apparent from a conversation Lee had with Davis after his return from western Virginia that, as he understood his verbal instructions (he had no written orders), he was not to supersede any of the generals in that sector by assuming personal command. Although Lee's orders were ambiguous, Davis or someone else took pains to make it clear to the public that Lee was in command.

Lee waited three days for Loring to act; then, knowing

that some other plan would have to be devised since by then all chance for a surprise had passed, he rode (in the rain) to Valley Mountain, taking with him his son Rooney's squadron of cavalry to scout the area. His only recorded comment on Loring's failure to move, was:

"It is so difficult to get our people, unaccustomed to the necessities of war, to comprehend & promptly execute the measures required for the occasion."

On a ridge that overlooked the Tygart River Valley, Lee camped in the rain, sharing his tent with his two aides. Although the simplicity of headquarters impressed young Taylor, accustomed to associate pomp with military rank, he found the austerity "uncomfortable," and to his way of thinking, not entirely necessary. His most strenuous objection was to Lee's tinware—"tin plates, tin cups, tin bowls—everything of tin—and consequently indestructible." During the war this "tin furniture," as Taylor styled it, refused to be lost in spite of the fond hopes of other fastidious staff members, and did service until the final year, when during the siege of Petersburg, a set of china was "surreptitiously introduced" into headquarters baggage. But when "light marching order was resumed," the borrowed china had to be returned, and "the chaste and elaborate *plate*" was again brought out and used until the surrender—and for a time afterward.

At Valley Mountain, there was also much sickness among the troops. The wet weather—"that was the August it rained thirty-two days," an infantryman recalled grimly—the lack of shelter and facilities for proper treatment brought about complications that often proved fatal. By the end of the month, even Lee was complaining:

It rains here all the time, literally. There has not been sunshine enough since my arrival to dry my clothes. . . . But the worst of this rain is that the ground has become so saturated with water, & constant travel on the roads has made them almost impassable, so that I cannot get up sufficient supplies for troops to move. It is raining now. Has been all day, last night, day before, & day before that, &c. . . . It is quite cool, too; I have on all my winter clothes & am writing in my overcoat.

22

Mary was now staying at Audley with the widow of Lorenzo Lewis, the son of Nelly Custis Lewis. From there, she wrote indignantly at the current rumors of their separation, rising, it was said, from incompatibility. Robert wrote at once to reassure her:

"Any one that can reason must see its necessity under present circumstances. They exist only in the imagination of the few. So give them no heed. We both know it cannot be otherwise, & must therefore be content."

She was also angered by the sneering editorials which began to appear in the Richmond papers, referring to Robert as "Granny" Lee and suggesting that he was timorous, over-cautious, and even incompetent, because he had failed to drive the Federal army from its stronghold in the mountains. To his alarm, Mary proposed to refute these statements by sending the newspapers an excerpt from one of his letters:

As to the vile slanders . . . with which you say the papers abound, why concern ourselves [he told her]. I do not see them, & would not mind them. . . . The papers that published them would not put in refutation, so what good would be accomplished. I do not recollect the letter to you or even the part, that you wish to publish. I only know I never write private letters for the public eye. . . . I am content to take no notice of the slanders & to let them die out.

Having neither accurate maps of the area nor a regular engineer officer to reconnoiter, General Loring had to rely on scouts and volunteer citizens for topographical information and reports about the enemy's position and movements. Early in September, Colonel Albert Rust of the Third Arkansas infantry reported to Loring and Lee the results of a reconnaissance on Cheat Mountain. He and a volunteer civilian engineer had reached a point south of the summit from which they could see the enemy's position and were certain it could be easily taken by surprise. The only difficulty was there were no roads, and the terrain was steep and covered with a tangled growth of laurel. But Rust was sanguine, and asked to be allowed to lead the attacking column.

Lee then worked out a plan, and on September 8 issued

orders diplomatically in Loring's name. It was a simple plan: Rust, with about two thousand men, would reach the position he had selected and attack at dawn on September 12, while General Henry R. Jackson, the lawyer-poet from Georgia, would divert the enemy in front. After Rust had carried the pass, Jackson would fall on the Federal rear, General Daniel Donelson would attack his flank along the Lewisburg road, and Loring would come up the main road on the Federal front. Since it was impossible to judge how long it would take Rust to reach his position, his attack would be the signal for the general advance.

"With great effort the troops intended for the surprise reached their destination, having traversed twenty miles of steep, rugged mountain paths; and the last day through a terrible storm which lasted all night & in which they had to stand drenched to the skin in a cold rain," Lee reported to Governor Letcher.

The torrents of water that washed down the slopes that night were like rivers, and would have drowned anyone who might have lain down to sleep, a surgeon wrote.

Toward dawn on the twelfth, the rain turned into a heavy fog. When light came, Lee could barely distinguish the enemy tents (they were "a tempting sight," he wrote) just below him on Valley River. All the provisions had been spoiled, and the troops who had gone without hot supper the night before now had to forego breakfast. Until Rust's signal came, they tightened their belts, soundly cursed the weather, and began to condition their wet guns.

But when dawn passed and all remained quiet, everyone began to ask anxiously: "What has become of Rust? Why don't he attack?" And after still more time had gone by: "What has happened? Rust must have lost his way."

Toward midmorning, the sound of random shots came from the direction of Donelson's lines, and Lee, Taylor, and several volunteers rode down to the Lewisburg road to investigate. They narrowly missed capture as they emerged from the cover of the laurels, for a troop of Federal cavalry, alerted by the firing, thundered past them, then seeing how close they were to Donelson's line, turned and galloped back—"too near to be comfortable," Walter Taylor felt.

Lee and his party then rode into Donelson's camp, where they found, greatly to Lee's annoyance, that a number of men, uneasy about the damp powder in their guns, had fired them to avoid what was known as a "flash in the pan."

By this time it was after ten o'clock and evidently useless to wait any longer for Rust. Lee believed there was still a chance for a successful attack west of the mountain, provided the movement could be undertaken at once. He called his commanders together to propose the action. But morale was low and his officers, with that fine disregard for discipline which characterized the first year of the war, protested that their men were too wet, cold, and hungry, and that the river was too high for fording. Lee ordered the men withdrawn to their former positions to insure their safety.

The next day, it was learned why Rust had not attacked. He reported to Lee that he had been surprised to find, on closer examination, that the enemy's works were more formidable than he had first supposed; he had found a blockhouse along the road, trenches, and an impassable abatis. Believing himself greatly outnumbered, he explained, he had passed the entire day quietly watching the Federals, and toward dark he had quietly withdrawn. What he failed to mention was that his credulity had been imposed on by several Federal pickets he had captured and questioned. They had told him about the great numbers of troops and their strongly fortified position; told him that his presence and plans were already known, and that reinforcements had been sent for and were due shortly.

Rooney, who was now a major of cavalry and the commanding officer on that line, had been working closely with his father during this movement. On the morning of the thirteenth, he was ordered to scout in the direction of the right branch of the Elkwater Fork. Colonel Washington had been anxious for some time to accompany him on such an expedition, but up to now, Lee had not allowed him to go. This day, he gave his permission, and Washington "set off in high spirits."

Late that afternoon, young Lee rode into his father's camp

on Washington's horse. He and his party had met the enemy's pickets, he explained, and at the first volley of Federal fire (which killed Rooney's horse), Colonel Washington had been struck and had fallen to the ground. Under heavy fire, Rooney had managed to jump on the Colonel's horse and escape unharmed.

The next morning, Lee sent a message under a flag of truce to the Federal lines, asking for news of Washington if captured, and the return of his body if dead. On the way, the messenger met a party of Union soldiers carrying Washington's body to the Confederate camp.

Lee was deeply grieved, for as he wrote Washington's daughter, Louisa:

> My intimate association with him for some months has more fully disclosed to me his great worth, than double so many years of ordinary intercourse would have been sufficient to reveal. We have shared the same tent, & morning & evening has his earnest devotion to Almighty God elicited my grateful admiration. . . . May God, in His mercy, my dear child, sustain you, your sisters and brothers under this heavy affliction. My own grief is so great, I will not afflict you further with it.

Walter Taylor "was greatly shocked in the contemplation of my noble companion and friend cold in death." He was facing an aspect of war new to him and asked himself a number of challenging questions concerning the enemy and the conflict as a whole. "As these questions forced themselves upon me, I became embittered; resentment took possession of my heart, and the man on the other side became my enemy," he admitted.

After staying in the Tygart River Valley for three days, Lee was convinced that nothing further could be accomplished there and so returned to his camp on the ridge. His disappointment was keen:

"I cannot tell you my regret & mortification at the untoward events that caused the failure of the plan. I had taken every precaution to ensure success & counted on it," he wrote Mary. He did not blame others as he might easily have done, but looked on the failure as an act of divine intervention: "The

Ruler of the Universe . . . sent a storm to disconcert a well-laid plan, & to destroy my hopes. But we must try again."

The Richmond newspapers now conferred on him the title of "Evacuating" Lee, and seared him with "scathing editorials, abounding in sneers and abuse." Upon him were now heaped "the impractability of the mountains, the hostility of the elements, and the want of harmony of subordinate commanders," an aide wrote. Only a few had the perception to realize that disaster had already befallen the Confederates and the worst had been accomplished before Lee reached western Virginia.

Walter Taylor noted that "no one felt public judgment so keenly as General Lee," yet he characteristically refused to justify his position or come to his own defense. When Taylor called his attention to an especially venal attack, "as unjust in its conclusions as it was untrue in its statements," he asked Lee why he suffered such unwarranted slander in silence.

Lee told him that "while it was very hard to bear, it was perhaps quite natural that such hasty conclusions should be announced, and that it was better not to attempt a justification or defense, but to go steadily on in the discharge of duty to the best of our ability, leaving all else to the calmer judgment of the future and to a kind Providence."

But when writing to Mary, he could not refrain from sarcastic comment: "I am sorry . . . that the movements of the armies cannot keep pace with the expectations of the editors of the papers. I know they can regulate matters satisfactorily to themselves on paper. I wish they would do so in the field. No one wishes them more success than I do & I would be happy to see them have full swing."

In the Kanawha Valley in southwestern Virginia, Generals Floyd and Wise were battling one another over fifty-four sabers that Wise accused Floyd's officers of taking from him; over one field gun that one of Wise's officers was supposed to have abstracted from Floyd; over five wagons Floyd had borrowed from Wise, and not returned; and over Wise's failure to provide Floyd with a cavalry scout. Wise wrote of his senior: "I feel if we remain together, we will unite in more wars than one." Although General Rosecrans was their common enemy, they refused to support each other and took up positions ten miles apart.

Seeing that warfare between these generals was taking precedence over any concerted efforts to hold the enemy, Lee decided to go to the scene and see if he could restore peace.

When he and Taylor arrived (in the pouring rain) at Floyd's encampment at Meadow Bluff, he found the situation even worse than he had imagined. Resentment between soldiers of the two commands ran high, discipline was almost nonexistent, and officers were ignorant of their duties and often negligent in the performance of those they undertook. Lee found his temper sorely tried, and snapped at Lieutenant Morton, who came up to him the first day with questions:

I think it very strange, Lieutenant, that an officer of this command, which has been here a week, should come to me, who am just arrived, and ask who his ordnance officer is and where to find his ammunition. This is in keeping with everything else I find here—no order, no organization, nobody knows where anything is, no one understands his duty!

Lee was soon satisfied that Wise's position on Little Sewell Mountain was the better one, and ordered Floyd's troops forward to that point. Taylor remembered that "no little diplomacy was required . . . to produce harmony and hearty cooperation, where previously had prevailed discord and contention. It will be readily understood that partizans of Floyd at first viewed in no pleasant frame of mind the apparent endorsement of Wise's judgment."

The defenses were just finished when Rosecrans appeared on the opposite height, nearly parallel. Each position was strong, and the Federal commander, observing Lee's formidable preparations, prudently chose not to attack.

When reinforcements from Loring arrived, they made Lee's aggregate strength some eight or nine thousand men, and he had difficulty keeping his officers from taking the offensive, for the men were in fine spirits and eager to attack.

"I know, gentlemen, you could carry the enemy's lines," he told them, "but we cannot spare the brave men who would lose

28

their lives doing it. If Rosecrans does not attack us, we will find a way to reach him that will not cost us so dearly."

It was raining hard at Sewell Mountain, Robert wrote Mary from his camp. This was hardly news, but he was worried because all his men were without shelter. For two nights, Lee himself had slept buttoned up in his overcoat, his only protection from the never-ceasing rain; his wagon had stuck in the mire and was left behind on the approach. Now it had been brought up, and his tent was pitched, but he knew that he would be unable to sleep "thinking of the poor men" lying exposed to the rain—and the cold, for ice had already begun to form on the puddles.

Mary had gone to the Hot Springs with Daughter and Rob. Rob was elated because he carried in his pocket a letter from his father, giving him permission to enter the army. "Ma & Sister are in search of health & myself in search of Pleasure," he wrote.

In her next letter from the Springs, Mary talked again of going home. Wearily, Robert had to repeat: "There is no prospect of you returning to Arlington. . . . You had better select some comfortable place in the Carolinas or Georgia & all board together. If Mildred goes to school at Raleigh, why not go there? It is a good opportunity to try a warmer climate for your rheumatism."

One day while at Sewell Mountain, Lee noticed a fine gray horse. He learned from the young soldier who rode him that he was called "Jeff Davis," was four years old, of the "Gray Eagle" stock, had been raised near Blue Sulphur Springs by the boy's father, Andrew Johnson, and had taken "first premium" for the years 1859–60 at the Lewisburg Fair. Lee offered to buy him, for Richmond and Brown Roan, a horse he had bought at the beginning of the campaign, were breaking down, not being "accustomed to such fare or such treatment," he told a daughter. But Johnson said that the gray was already promised to Captain Joseph Broun as a present for his brother, but if Broun did not buy him, he would let Lee know. The horse was sold to Broun, but as the brother was with the same command, Lee often saw the gray, whose name was changed

29

to "Greenbrier"; and whenever there was a chance, he stopped and talked about "my colt," as he called him. When the campaign closed, Lee saw no more of Greenbrier for a time, but he did not forget him.

Lee now planned to gain the Federal rear. Floyd, who had a knowledge of the area, had reported a practicable route for infantry and artillery, and after dark Lee sent five thousand men to make a dawn attack. But to his bitter disappointment, Rosecrans escaped the trap by a night retreat. Though Lee ordered pursuit, he soon saw the impossibility of overtaking the Federal and bringing him into a successful engagement in the mountainous terrain, and reluctantly allowed his enemy to escape unpunished.

Snow had begun to fall, and several nights were so cold that at bedtime Lee suggested to Taylor they sleep together for warmth. "And so it was vouchsafed to me to occupy very close relations with . . . my commander," Taylor wrote proudly.

Roads that had been impassable sloughs of mud now became slick with ice. There was still much sickness among the men, none of whom had tents, and many were without adequate blankets. It was useless and to Lee's mind, cruel, to carry on active operations under such conditions, so he brought the campaign to a close.

Since the Federals were still in possession of a large portion of western Virginia, the operation was pronounced a failure. Because no battles had been fought, the exponents of aggressive warfare interpreted it as a confession of cowardice, which they refused to tolerate from their positions far from the scene of action. The Richmond editors relished this opportunity for a display of their superior military knowledge. They pointed out all the errors of the campaign and informed their readers how it should have been conducted. They laid the blame for its failure on Lee, whom they now referred to sneeringly as "the President's pet." A Richmond diarist made the best exposition of Lee's position at this time when he wrote:

"Give a great man a field worthy of his powers, and he can demonstrate the extent of his abilities; but dwarf him in an insignificant position, and the veriest fool will look upon him with contempt."

In view of this sharp decline in prestige, Lee must have wondered, as he went to call on the President the morning after his return to Richmond, just what the future held for him. But as Davis resented unsolicited advice and did not tolerate criticism, he defied those who urged Lee's removal by stubbornly keeping him in his old post of adviser.

Lee had prepared no written report, since he would have to include in it an account of Loring's delay, Rust's blunder, and the feud between Floyd and Wise. Davis found him reluctant even to report verbally until the President had given his promise to take no official notice. Aside from his usual unwillingness to incriminate others, Lee believed that mention of these men's errors and failings might be interpreted as an attempt to vindicate his own position.

The arrival of a fleet of Federal warships off Port Royal, South Carolina, on November 4 caused much anxiety in that area, and Davis, realizing the necessity for extending and strengthening the southeastern coastal defense, now organized it into a single military department. Foreseeing here another ideal assignment for Lee, he appointed him commander of the department. As George Cary Eggleston observed:

"When the two centres of strategic interest were at Winchester and Manassas, General Lee was kept in Western Virginia with a handful of raw troops, where he could not accomplish anything for the cause. . . . When there was no longer any excuse for keeping him there, he was disinterred, as it were, and reburied in the swamps of the South Carolina coast."

Lee knew that inefficiency and lack of organization plagued that quarter, too, and he was not eager to accept the assignment, anticipating, as he said, "another forlorn hope expedition" even worse than western Virginia.

The general public did not look favorably on Lee's appointment, and the Richmond *Examiner*, in reporting his departure to erect defenses, hurled a final taunt: "He is going where it is

31

hoped he will be far more successful with the spade than with the sword."

There were so many objections in other parts of the South that the President felt it necessary to write Governors Pickens of South Carolina and Brown of Georgia, "stating what manner of man had been sent" them.

But Lee had learned one invaluable lesson from his recent experience in West Virginia. As soon as he received his orders, he asked Davis to define his exact status. Davis told him that he was a full general in the regular army of the Confederacy, and senior officer in his department. Later, Davis wrote in apparent naïveté that he was certain from Lee's question and his manner of stating it that up to that moment, when he received his answer, he had not known his "relative position in the Confederate service."

Lee boarded the train for Charleston on the morning of November 6, taking with him the peerless Walter Taylor; his servants, Perry and Meredith; and his horse, Brown Roan, leaving Richmond to recuperate in Custis' care.

4

NEAR the end of this year, probably just before Lee left for Charleston, Mr. Schneider, the Washington blacksmith, was called on by a small boy who handed him two one-dollar gold pieces, and a note of apology. Shortly after Lee's return from Texas in March, he had taken the ironsmith the sketch of a coulter he had designed for breaking up heavy meadow sod, and asked him to make one. Schneider had set the price at two dollars, and when the tool was finished, the old marketman from Arlington had picked it up. But in the turmoil of those weeks when Lee was deciding his future, payment for the coulter was forgotten. Now it had been recalled, and Lee, with his usual attention to detail, had sent a young emissary.

Lee reached Charleston on November 7, during an engagement between the Federal fleet and the Confederate island forts of Beauregard and Walker, in Port Royal Sound, and took a special train to the nearest point, Coosawhatchie. That night, he received reports that the guns in both forts had been crippled, and the garrisons would have to be evacuated since they could be easily cut off. He did not hesitate, now that he knew the extent of his authority, but ordered immediate withdrawal from the forts, established his headquarters in an abandoned house in Coosawhatchie, and organized his staff.

"I have quite a Household when all my staff are present," he wrote Mary. "Capt. [Thornton] Washington, Adj. Genl., Major Long, Ordne. Offr., Capt. Taylor, Asst. Adj. Genl., Capts. Moffat & Walker aids de Camp & Mr. Menniger, clerk." Although not present each day, another staff member was Captain Stephen Elliott, "whose perfect knowledge of the coast enabled him to render valuable service."

Headquarters was again unpretentious. There were only two meals a day, breakfast at eight o'clock, and dinner at six. "The hungry ones have a lunch of what they can find, but I reserve myself for dinner," Lee wrote. "Our fare is plain but enough & we have appetites that make everything palatable. At nights we enjoy our camp beds & blankets. I endeavour to get in mine by 11 P.M. I am not always allowed to remain . . . till morg & last night was aroused twice."

Seated at the head of the table set with his tinware, he "always seasoned the meal with his good humor and pleasant jests, often at the expense of some member of the staff who seemed to miss the luxuries of the table more than himself," his ordnance officer recalled.

A young Virginian whose battery was stationed near headquarters also observed that Lee was surrounded with "none of the pomp and circumstance of war," that his dress bore no marks of rank, and that he was recognizable as a soldier only by his bearing.

It was Lee's habit to take walks alone in the late afternoon, most often through this battery encampment, where he always stopped by the stables to admire the horses. One evening he met a sergeant and a teamster walking together. The soldier recognized him and saluted, but the old driver, being deaf and therefore unaware that he spoke above a whisper, bellowed in his companion's ear:

"I say, Sergeant, who *is* that durned old fool? He's always a-pokin' round my hosses just as if he meant to steal one of 'em."

Taking advantage of the quiet that followed the Federal bombardment of the forts at Port Royal, Lee made an inspection of the coast defenses, going first to Savannah. With General Alexander R. Lawton and his staff, he visited Fort Pulaski, going down the river on the little steamer, *Ida.* They landed at the North Wharf and walked over to the fort, where Colonel Charles Ohlmstead, second in command, waited at the sally port to do the honors in the absence of the commander, General Hugh Mercer.

Ohlmstead was curious to meet Lee, for he had heard much about him from the Mackay and Stiles families. Afterward, he wrote in admiration:

He would have been recognized any where in the world as a man of mark, one upon whom Nature had set the stamp of greatness. Tall in stature, straight as an arrow, well knit and vigorous in frame yet graceful and easy in movement, a well shaped head just beginning to be touched with gray, and a face in which kindliness and sweetness of temper blended with firmness of purpose and a dignified and grave reserve.

Another man eager to see Lee was Francis J. Cercopoly, who had been coxswain of the barge that plied between Cockspur and Savannah when Lee was stationed at the island on his first assignment. Just as Lee was about to cross the outer bridge at the demilune, he stopped to look steadily at a man standing stiffly at attention, his hand drawn in salute. Then he walked forward "with both hands extended, a bright smile on his face, and the exclamation: 'Why Francis, is that you?'" After talking with the old captain for a few minutes, Lee introduced him to his party—"Just like I was one of his best friends," Cercopoly proudly told his cronies. This simple act of kindliness so impressed the group that several of them recorded it as evidence of Lee's greatness.

While touring the fort, Lee pointed to the nearest part of Tybee Island, some seventeen hundred yards away, and said to Ohlmstead:

"Colonel, they will make it very warm for you with shells from that point but they cannot breach at that distance."

With unerring strategic sense, Lee selected the exact spot where the Federals did place their cannon. What he could not anticipate in this prediction was the invention of the rifled Parrott gun (originated by his friend Robert Parker Parrott, a member of "the old set"), which was to breach those walls early the next year.

When Lee inspected St. Simon's Island, a private was impressed with his simplicity of attire: "We were visited the other day by Gens. Lee, Lawton, and Mercer, and a good many other little puffs," he wrote. "Gen. Lee was dressed very plainly while his inferiors were dressed 'within an inch of their lives.' "

When he returned to Savannah, Lee completed plans for the defense of Fort Pulaski and had materials for the work immediately sent on rafts to the site. Then he took the train for Charleston, arriving there on November 13.

Although Charleston's defenses were superior to any in other coastal cities, one man in the group that accompanied Lee on his tour noted that he did not seem "in particularly good humor concerning things here."

As Lee inspected Fort Sumter he was observed closely by the poet Paul Hamilton Hayne.

In the midst of the group, topping the tallest by half a head, was perhaps the most striking figure we had ever encountered [Hayne wrote], the figure of a man seemingly about 56 or 58 years of age, erect as a poplar, yet lithe and graceful, with broad shoulders, well thrown back, a fine justly-proportioned head posed in unconscious dignity, clear, deep, thoughtful eyes, and the quiet dauntless step of one every inch the gentleman and soldier. . . .

Inspection of the coast convinced Lee that conditions were even "worse than West Virginia," as he wrote, and he reached the major decision that it would be impossible to maintain all the small outlying batteries on islands and waterways. He would have to abandon them and use their guns and men to build up a concentrated, deep interior line to protect the most important areas. He began at Coosawhatchie, ordering there additional troops, and planning an extensive line of earthworks.

Among the reinforcements that came to Coosawhatchie was Captain Broun's command, and Lee once again saw the gray horse he had admired at Sewell Mountain. He asked Broun if he would consider selling Greenbrier, and, flattered, the soldier offered to give him the horse. Lee declined. The Captain then suggested that Lee had best ride him, since he had a peculiar gait, "a short, high trot" that some men found uncomfortable.

After Lee had tested the horse and found that it suited him perfectly, Broun wrote to his brother, the owner (absent from his command because of illness), and told him of Lee's offer. Thomas Broun replied that since Lee would not accept the horse as a gift, then the original purchase price, $175 in gold, would be satisfactory. Lee agreed and, to allow for depreciation in currency, gave Broun $200.

He began to use the gray at once, for Brown Roan was not bearing up well under hard service. The extensive line of defenses along the coast kept Lee almost constantly on the move— up to Charleston, down to Savannah, on to Fernandina, Florida, back to Coosawhatchie, and up to Charleston again, with sometimes no more than a day's interval between trips. He traveled the long distances by rail, but took his horse along to ride on his tours of the defenses.

Greenbrier's superb stamina led Lee to change its name to "Traveller," though he may also have been influenced by the fact that George Washington had a "Traveller" among his favorite horses.

On their daily rides through thickets of pine and palmetto, over sand and sedge, an extraordinary understanding and mutual affection grew between master and mount. Lee set aside his usual preference for mares, as Traveller, with his superior intelligence, became his favorite horse, and later, his most favored companion. The only photographs that Lee ever wanted taken, and the only ones in which he evinced much interest, were those where he was mounted on the gray, for then Traveller became the chief object of the viewer's attention.

From Charleston on November 15, Lee wrote to Mildred, away at boarding school, urging her to "labour" at her books in order to "gain knowledge & wisdom." In this letter, he made the first mention of the beard which became such a distinctive feature of his appearance. He described it as "a beautiful white one" that was "much admired. At least much remarked on."

He was not wholly accurate when he called it "white," for a year later, J. B. Jones, an observant War Office clerk, noted in his journal that Lee's "gray" beard had turned white, and had been allowed to grow "all over his face" so that he was "hardly recognizable." This first beard, then, was not only gray but trimmed and confined to the lower jaw.

Within three days he was back in Savannah, this time able to call at No. 75 Broughton Street, where the new beard was doubtless much admired and remarked on. "Good old Mrs. Mackay now 83" he found in the best of health; of her daughters, "the blessed creatures," only Mary Anne and Margaret were at home.

From Savannah, he went down to Amelia Island, where he found the defenses "poor indeed," and "laid off enough work to employ our people for a month. I hope the enemy will be polite enough to wait for us. It is difficult to get our people to realize their position."

In Savannah he had a joint letter from Annie and Agnes which turned his memory to boyhood. The girls, who were staying at Clydale, the summer home of their cousins the Richard Stuarts, had driven to Stratford, and wrote him of their visit. In his reply, he expressed his gratitude for their description of his birthplace:

It is endeared to me by many recollections & it has always been the great desire of my life to purchase it. Now that we have no other home, & the other one we loved has been so foully polluted, the desire is stronger with me than ever. The horse chestnut you mention was planted by my mother . . . You did not mention the spring, one of the objects of my earliest recollections.

By December 11, he was back in Charleston. As he walked up to the Mills House to dine with Walter Taylor he heard the fire alarm, but as fires were common occurrences in cities, he paid little attention. But while "partaking of our meal in a leisurely way, we became aware of great excitement prevailing outside . . . the rapid rush of people and the noise of passing engines and vehicles." Going to the front of the hotel, "we were amazed at the rapid progress of the fire." But as it was not yet of a size to cause uneasiness, they went into the parlor and passed the evening with Andrew Talcott, his wife and daughter, Mrs. Thornton Washington, and Major Armistead Long and his wife.

Around eleven o'clock when the rest of the party had gone to bed, Lee, Taylor, and Long went up to the hotel roof to look at the fire. From there "we had an unobstructed view of the grand and awfully sublime spectacle of a city in flames," Taylor wrote. Since the fire had now reached the opposite side of the street from the hotel, the men hurried down to the parlor, finding "everything in confusion" and all guests ready to leave.

Led by a guide with a lantern, Lee and his party hurried down a back stairway through the cellar, the only exit now open. An omnibus "providentially appeared" just as they came out of the door; they climbed in, and "amid a shower of sparks" drove to "the private residence of Mr. Charles Alston, on the Battery, out of the line of danger and kindly offered for General Lee's use."

By morning, the fire was under control, but the city stood in smoking ruins from the Ashley to the Cooper Rivers. The Mills House was undamaged, so later that day Lee and the others returned to their quarters there.

Robert was delighted to visit with the Talcotts again, and passed every evening in their rooms. Although he could report that "the Col. is one of the best men in the world," he found that the Beautiful Talcott, not unlike Mary, was "a little complaining at the world." Since the Confederate government was not inclined to make good use of Talcott's superior talents, he was planning to return to Mexico to continue his work on the Mexico and Pacific Railroad from Vera Cruz through Mexico City to the Pacific, which he had started in December, 1857.

Work on the defenses progressed much too slowly to suit Lee. He found that the greatest obstacle was the people themselves, who, though much exercised about their property and servants, were unable to comprehend that this was war and that there was necessity for exertion and haste. "In fact we all at the South have had so easy & comfortable a time, that it is difficult for us to practice self-denial & labour necessary for our protection. It will require misfortune & suffering I fear to induce us to do what we ought in this respect," he wrote.

Christmas Day at Coosawhatchie was observed with the usual inspection of the defenses in that area, though Lee exchanged gifts with his military family, who saw to it that the traditional roast turkey, baked ham, mince pies, and plum pudding replaced their usual frugal fare. The table with its garlands of pine, bowls of sweet oranges, and sparkling bottles of wine made even the famed tinware look less austere. In a mellow mood after the feast and the toasts, Lee spent the evening writing home. He exhibited a rare facetiousness at Mary's expense:

"So you do not like my invitation to Fayetteville? . . . Well it shews the perverseness of human nature. If you were to see this place, I think you would leave it too . . . [it] is too exposed to attack for the residence of a person as difficult to move as you are. You would be captured while you were 'waiting a moment.' "

To Daughter, he wrote:

Trifles even are hard to get these wartimes, & you must not therefore expect more. I have sent you what I thought would be most useful in your separation from me. . . . Though stigmatized as "vile dross," it has never been a drug with me. . . . To compensate for such "trash," I send you some sweet violets that I gathered this morning while covered with dense white frost, whose crystals glittered in the bright sun like diamonds, & formed a brooch of rare beauty & sweetness which could not be fabricated by the expenditure of a world of money.

In a letter to Charlotte, he joked about his third daughter: "Poor little Agnes! Somebody told me that a widower has been making eyes at her through his spectacles. Perhaps she is preparing for caps. But tell her not to distress herself. Her Papa is not going to give her up that way." He closed this letter

39

tenderly: "Kiss Fitzhugh for me & the baby, that is the sweetest Christmas-gift I can send them. I send you some sweet violets; I hope they may retain their fragrance till you receive them. . . . My heart with all its strength stretches toward you & those with you, & hushes in silence its yearnings. God bless you my dear daughter, your dear husband, & son. . . . Your devoted father, R E Lee"

Again Mary talked about returning to Arlington, and again Robert tried to reason with her:

As to our old home . . . with the number of troops encamped around it, the change of officers, &c., the want of fuel, shelter, &c., & all the dire necessities of war, it is vain to think of it being in a habitable condition. . . . It is better to make up our minds to a general loss. They cannot take away the remembrance of the spot. . . . I wish I could purchase Stratford. . . . I wonder if it is for sale & how much. Ask Fitzhugh to find out, when he gets to Fredericksburg.

Mary had also expressed hope that peace might result if the United States went to war with England, a possibility that arose over the Trent Affair, when the Union seized two Confederate commissioners from the British mail steamer *Trent*. "She will be very loath to do that, notwithstanding the bluster in the Northern papers," he told her. "Her rulers are not entirely mad, & if they find England is in earnest, & that war or restitution of their captives must be the consequence, they will adopt the latter. We must make up our minds to fight our battles & win our independence alone. No one will help us."

In January, he returned to Fernandina and on the way up the coast stopped at Cumberland Island. With Major Long, he walked up the alley of live oaks and magnolias to Dungeness, following the path Light-Horse Harry Lee had taken when he came here to die. The present owner, Mr. Nightingale, had gone with his family to the Georgia interior, but the caretaker invited them in to see the house, which Lee found had never been finished. In the spacious hall, they admired the carvings and the spiral stairway which wound past strangely contrasting walls of unfinished shell and mortar. In the dining room and parlor, they looked at the pictures. Lee remarked with some asperity upon the portraits of Mrs. Nightingale's father and uncle, both "rabid abolitionists," as he said. He also saw what he considered "a bad likeness" of General Greene, and "a handsome print of Florence Nightingale."

But the overgrown garden with its hedge of wild olive and its lemon and orange trees particularly pleased him. As they walked along the paths he stopped frequently to admire "the roses and beautiful vines," and to marvel at a tomato plant in "full bearing, with ripe fruit on it" in January.

When they reached the neglected cemetery, Lee told Long that he was going to visit his father's grave, and his aide waited for him outside the gate. He recalled that after a few moments Lee "plucked a flower and slowly retraced his steps. . . . We returned in silence to the steamer, and no allusion was ever made to this act of filial devotion." His only written reference to it was in a letter to Mary: "I had the gratification at length of visiting my father's grave. He died there, you may recollect, on his way from the West Indies, & was interred in one corner of the family cemetery. The spot is marked with a plain marble slab, with his name, age & date of birth. Mrs. Greene is also buried there, & her daughter Mrs. Shaw, & husband." When he wrote to Custis of his visit to Dungeness, he spoke only of the beauty of the garden "filled with roses."

When he got back to headquarters on January 23, he found an urgent message for him to come to Charleston. A fleet of some twenty-one enemy ships had appeared off the bar; due to a storm, their intent was unknown. The rain had stopped and the clouds were drifting away by the time Lee arrived, and he counted seventeen ships, five of them men-of-war, and noticed that twelve old merchantmen were being stripped in preparation for sinking in the channel. But as he said: "They cannot wall up the waters of the sea. . . . They will do but little harm to the channel, I think, but may deter vessels from running out at night for fear of getting on them."

Custis forwarded to his father the decree the Court of Appeals had finally handed down regarding Mr. Custis' will. Lee was powerless to act upon it now: "What more I can do in the execution of the will I do not know, nor how I can expedite its completion during the continuance of the war I cannot see. I must leave it to you & Fitzhugh to see to matters & to do justice to all parties."

At Savannah, there were signs of a Federal movement against the city. "Unless I have better news I must go there today. There are so many points of attack, & so little means to meet them on the water, that there is but little rest," he told Mary on January 29. He left that afternoon for Savannah.

The necessity for constant supervision of Savannah's defenses, which he found had "lagged terribly & . . . ought to to have been finished," caused him to move his headquarters there. Mrs. Mackay offered him his old room, and though he was there at times during the day and passed each evening with the family, he did not sleep in the house for fear of reprisal in case the city was captured.

Enemy gunboats, which drew only seven feet of water, had found a way to by-pass Fort Pulaski by coming up the creeks at high water (the tide rose seven feet) and, by means of dredges, to cross the marshes. Lee was powerless to stop them, for he did not have enough men and arms to protect the city, and was having to break up coastal batteries to provide for a strong interior line which the Federals would have to force before reaching Savannah. "It is on this line we are working, slowly to my anxious mind, but as fast as I can drive them," he wrote. When completed, this defense proved so effective that it held off the encircling enemy forces until the coming of Sherman on his famous march, late in 1864.

But there were times when Lee became greatly discouraged:

I have more here than I can do, & more, I fear, than I can well accomplish. I have been doing all I can with our small means & slow workmen to defend the cities & coast here. Against ordinary numbers we are pretty strong, but against the hosts our enemies seem able to bring everywhere there is no calculating. But if our men will stand to their work, we shall give them trouble & damage yet.

Here, as everywhere, he found indifference and a lack of cooperation he could not understand: "The people do not seem to realize there is a war. Our people have not been earnest enough, have thought too much of themselves & their ease, & instead of turning out to a man, have been content to nurse themselves & their dimes, & leave the protection of themselves & families to others." He had observed too that they did not hesitate to carp: "To satisfy their consciences, they have been clamourous in criticising what others have done, & endeavoured to prove that they ought to do nothing."

The greatest hindrance to his progress was the soldiers' aversion to manual labor. "The Vols: dislike work," he wrote tersely. Born to command, each scion of South Carolina and Georgia gentry who volunteered expected to be made an officer at once, and saw no reason to dig trenches and erect earthworks. As Jeb Stuart was to observe:

"They are pretty good officers now, and after a while they will make excellent soldiers, too. They only need *reducing to the ranks.*"

Confederate reverses in North Carolina and Tennessee prompted Lee to write: "It calls for renewed energies & redoubled strength on our part, & I hope will produce it. I fear our soldiers have not realized the necessity for the endurance & labour they are called upon to undergo."

Camp life proved the great leveler, yeoman and gentry alike sharing the plagues of measles, fevers, and dysentery; the lack of tents and blankets; and the shortage and poor quality of the rations. Officers frequently messed with their men, and in many cases, if they were more skilled, did the cooking. They were, therefore, without reverence for either uniform or rank. Lee's old friend, General Hugh Mercer, complained about the Georgia yeomanry who with total lack of ceremony dropped in to see him on any matter, or no matter at all, and referred to him as "that 'ar man."

While he was inspecting the defenses near Brunswick, Lee's train stopped near an encampment of Georgia State troops who, curious to see him, flocked around his car and called for a speech. When this course failed, they climbed on the train and filed through his car for a close look, expressing their opinions in nothing lower than stage whispers. One Cracker, after a long unabashed stare, turned to make his way to the door, crying out:

"Give me room, boys. I's seed the monkey."

Eliza Stiles had returned from a visit to her grandchildren, and noticing that Robert's wardrobe was in need of repair, took it in hand over his protests to mend his shirts and make him three new ones. "Necessity" had compelled him to accept her offer, "which I am ashamed to do, both on account of the trouble to her, & the exhibition of my rags. . . . Her sisters & niece had offered before, but my pride objected."

Now that he was enjoying family life again, he became keenly aware of his longing for his daughters. He wrote Annie: "It has been a long time since I have written to you, but you have been constantly in my thoughts. I think of you all, separately & collectively, in the busy hours of the day & the silent hours of the night, & the recollections of each & every one whiles away the long night, in which my anxious thoughts drive away sleep."

He told "Precious Life" that he had begun to feel the strain of the "anxious days & nights," and "have grown so old & become so changed that you would not know me. But I love you as much as ever, & you know how great a love that is."

But his anxiety did not keep him from having some fun at Mildred's expense. She had written him paradoxically that she was "well but in a starving condition, yet fattening." He hoped, he said, that she was not as bad as she sounded; and told her that she must not be concerned about gaining weight, for "it is not necessary for young ladies to become ethereal to grow wise." She was also concerned over her cat, Tom, left at Arlington in Uncle George's care. She was certain "his precious heart would break" if he did not see her soon.

"I shall have to get Gen¹ Johnston to send in a flag of truce & make inquiries," he teased.

As had so often happened with Lee's assignments, before he could finish, his orders took him away. On March 2, a telegram from the President summoned him to Richmond. Sensing the urgency of the brief message, he wired that he would be ready to leave on the morning of the fourth. He completed his final work so rapidly—even to the detailed instructions to General Lawton about finishing the defenses—that he was able to leave a day in advance.

He said his good-bys to the Mackay family on the evening of the second, and the next morning he and Walter Taylor took the train for Charleston, changing cars there for Richmond.

5

"NOW that they have got into trouble, they send for him to help them out, & yet he never gets any credit for what he has done," Mary complained to Eliza Stiles on March 11, 1862, when telling her about Robert's sudden recall to Richmond.

Trouble indeed! Not even the Congress knew that the arsenals were nearly bare, so that unless munitions could be brought through the blockade—which was but a faint hope— the army would soon lack even the means to fight its losing battle.

Congress, reflecting the administration's attitude, had looked to some means of deliverance other than by arms, placing its heaviest reliance on the delusion that once cotton was withheld, the powers in need of it would stop the war. It was believed that by February 1 the pinch for cotton would be so desperate that foreign intervention would come.

But with the arrival of February, there came instead the loss of Kentucky with the fall of Forts Donelson and Henry and the evacuation of Fort Columbus by Lee's old friend, General Albert Sidney Johnston. Roanoke Island was seized, the entire coast of North Carolina threatened, and it seemed that far-off New Orleans would soon fall. Still worse, General Joe Johnston was making a retrograde from Manassas Junction, pulling his lines in closer to Richmond, which he did not believe he could hold.

Only then did the President see the necessity to call on the governors for troops. Previously, he had made no effort to supply the army with any men except volunteers. This policy of

45

half-hearted warfare not only resulted in serious losses at the time but permanently impaired the Confederacy's ability to maintain the contest.

To add to the chaos, Beauregard and Joe Johnston were both in disfavor with Jefferson Davis, while Congress was at odds with the President and his War Secretary, Judah P. Benjamin. Ever since his appointment in the Confederate service, Johnston had been feuding over his rank. He claimed he was entitled to be "first general in the armies," since he was the only one of the five officers created full generals who had held the rank of brigadier in the old army. Davis argued that Johnston's appointment as quartermaster general, U.S.A., had been a staff appointment without command of troops, so that his rank as a line officer was lower than the others. But Joe continued to accuse Davis of having "degraded" him and tarnished his "fair name."

Beauregard, the debonair Creole whose looks, Gallic mannerisms, and temperament were strongly reminiscent of Napoleon, had captured popular fancy, and was often spoken of as a possible successor to Jefferson Davis. This doomed him at once, and it was not long until he was banished to the army of the West. One wise Virginian wrote at this time:

"I dare not speculate on public affairs. Nothing can exceed the imbecility of President Davis. His obstinacy and self will are dreadful. He will not have about him men of talent and force. . . . If our struggle be in vain and our cause lost, it will not be owing to the people, but to the men they placed at the head of affairs."

Congress was convinced that Jefferson Davis was not competent to direct the armies, and with its eye on Lee, passed an act stating that if the post of Secretary of War were to be held by a general, he would not have to forfeit his rank. When Davis approved this legislation it was assumed that he would name Lee; but when he did not, and asked that the post of commanding general be created, enabling the appointee to act as technical or military head of the War Department, Congress, certain that he had Lee in mind this time, obliged by creating the office of general in chief. The President vetoed this "for trenching on the executive prerogative," as those close to him put it, though he objected that it was unconstitutional since it clothed this post with the power of commander in chief, which was his under the constitution. It was said that Davis "defended his constitutional rights with no less zeal and with more success than he defended the country."

To appease Congress and retain his popularity, Davis re-organized his Cabinet, adroitly appointing Benjamin (who was held responsible for the loss of Roanoke Island, and therefore unpopular) Secretary of State, and George W. Randolph, a popular Virginian and descendant of Thomas Jefferson, War Secretary. To Lee he assigned "the conduct of the military operations in the armies of the Confederacy," which sounded as though he were at last conferring on him a post worthy of his talents, until one read the qualifying clause: "with duty at the seat of Government, under the direction of the President."

He wrote to Mary at once, explaining his position carefully so that she would have no mistaken notions of its importance: "I have been placed here to conduct operations under the direction of the President. It will give me great pleasure to do anything I can to relieve him & serve the country, but I do not see either advantage or pleasure in my duties."

Among Lee's responsibilities now was the counseling of the commanders of the smaller armies, though no movement, however insignificant, could he order without first submitting the plan to Davis for approval. Many and long were the conferences they held, time that Lee considered "lost in fruitless talk." Though Davis usually consulted him on major strategies and often accepted his advice, Lee was never allowed to put any of these plans into operation or see them through.

To add to his sense of frustration, "all papers relating to military matters of any sort . . . no matter how unimportant or purely personal" were now referred to Lee to be answered.

"Have I done something for the general interest? Well then, I have had my reward. Let this always be present to my mind," was a precept of Marcus Aurelius that Lee must have read often for consolation.

On Sunday, March 9, Robert found time to go down to the

White House to see Mary, who was staying with Charlotte and her little boy. This was his first meeting with Mary since he had left Arlington that April morning almost a year ago. It grieved him to find that she had to pass so much time in bed and in her chair, but he noticed that wherever she was her hands were always busy, and the pile of soldier socks she was knitting mounted steadily in the basket beside her.

During the afternoon, Robert and Charlotte walked out to look at the Arlington horses, brought there for safekeeping. Among them was Grace Darling, soon to foal, and her grown daughter, a handsome, solid bay with so many of her mother's good points that Lee decided to take her back to Richmond. As it happened, this was the last time he would stroke Grace's muzzle and talk to her as though she were one of them, for when General George B. McClellan left the headquarters he established at the White House later that year, the mare was taken and next seen, as Lee wrote, "bestrode by some yankee with her colt by her side."

Annie and Agnes were both visiting in Richmond, so Robert saw them occasionally; and Custis, now on the President's staff, he met almost daily. But since they no longer roomed together at the Spotswood, they did not pass many evenings together. During the winter, Custis had arranged with John Stewart of Brook Hill to use his town house at 707 East Franklin Street where, with several officer friends, he established a mess which his father named "The Smoking Club in Franklin Street," insisting that it was "so concealed in a cloud of its own raising" that even Cupid could not find entrance.

Rob had stayed on at the University of Virginia because he knew that his father wanted him to finish his schooling. But with two brothers in the army and most of his friends enlisting, he now wrote his father that he had decided to quit school and join the Rockbridge Artillery in Stonewall Jackson's command. Lee was agreeable, so Rob came to the Spotswood. He had seen little of his father during the last six years and stood somewhat in awe of him at first, but he soon found that he need not, for "he was just as sweet and loving to me as in the old days."

48

Lee took his son to buy his private's outfit, and have him measured for his uniform. As they walked down the street, he explained the exemption granted professors and university students, but as he wrote Mary: "Rob expressed no desire to take advantage of it."

Rob remembered that his father took pains in selecting his equipment, and complained some at not being able to find first quality. When Rob was ready to join his command in the Valley of Virginia, Lee went with him to the depot and sent him off with his blessing: "God grant that it may be for his good," he wrote.

He now planned to go down to the White House for another Sunday visit, but on Saturday morning, March 22, a telegram from the President, then at Fredericksburg, ordered him to go to North Carolina, for the Federals were now sweeping down the coast. He regretted this summons from both a professional and personal viewpoint, for, as he explained to Mary: "Our enemies are pressing us everywhere & our army is in the fermentation of reorganization. I am endeavouring by every means in my power to bring out troops & hasten them to their destination. This call away will retard the operations." He told her also that the shirts Eliza had started for him while he was in Savannah had just come. He had not had time to try them on, but they looked "very nice." He felt that "three new shirts are as many as a man requires these war times," so he sent a number of his old ones to Mary with instructions to replace the worn collars and cuffs. Since high collars were no longer stylish, he asked her to cut them down, though he cautioned her not to "let the points of the collars project too much." He was always hesitant to rely on her judgment: "I would only use those bodies for re-equipment that promise good service, otherwise they will soon be all collars & wristbands."

When he came back from North Carolina, he found the situation in the west so grave that he was led to write General Albert Sidney Johnston a tactful letter:

No one has sympathized with you in the troubles with which you are surrounded more sincerely than myself. I have watched every movement & know the difficulties with which you have to

49

contend. I hope your cares will be diminished if not removed when your junction with the other lines of your Army has been completed which must be accomplished by this time. My confidence in your judgment, skill & courage is so great that I do not apprehend a miscarriage where you are. I need not urge you when your Army is united, to deal a blow at the enemy in your front if possible, before his rear gets up from Nashville. You have him divided now, keep him so if you can. Wishing you my dear Gen1 every success & happiness with my earnest prayers for the safety of your whole Army—& that victory may attend your movements, I remain

Truly & sincerely your friend,

R E Lee

Shortly after this letter reached him, Johnston, a fearless fighter and an able general, was mortally wounded while leading a charge during the surprise attack he made on General Grant's army at Shiloh Church, which drove the Federals back to the cover of their gunboats at Pittsburg Landing. When news of his death reached Richmond, President Davis told Congress: "Without doing injustice to the living, it may be safely said that our loss is irreparable." Subsequent history of the war in the west justified this tribute.

When the Federals landed at Old Point Comfort in Virginia, Lee surmised that they would attempt to take Norfolk and Richmond—"for I cannot conceive what other use they can put their vast army to." He was concerned for the safety of his family at the White House, since one of the probable routes to the capital would be up the Pamunkey River where, fifty yards from the water's edge, stood Rooney's house—not white, incidentally, but "a sort of a pink color." As Robert wrote Mary, if the army should come there, it might prove "extremely annoying & embarrassing, as I believe hundreds would delight in persecuting you all for my & F.'s [Fitzhugh's] sake. I do not think their respectable officers would authorize such proceedings, but believe they would be unable to prevent them. I think . . . you should get out of the way."

But he might have spared his words, for bristling with defiance, Mary replied that she did not intend to move if the house were surrounded by the entire Union army. But when the Federals drew nearer, consideration for the young people (Agnes had by then joined her) led her to accept the offer of refuge with a neighbor, Mr. Gay, while Charlotte, Agnes, and the baby went off to the mineral springs in North Carolina. But she did not leave the house until she had written and posted on the door this notice:

"Northern soldiers who profess to reverence Washington, forbear to desecrate the home of his first married life, the property of his wife, now owned by her descendants.

A Grand Daughter of Mrs. Washington"

Robert was by no means at ease about her new location, hardly better than the White House, and wrote again urging her to consider a move to South Carolina or Georgia.

After she reached Mr. Gay's, two Federal officers from General Fitz John Porter's staff came to tell her that sentinels would be posted around the house. Seeing her face cloud, they hurriedly explained that the General only wanted her to have "proper care and protection with as little constraint to her wishes and movements" as possible, until she "had passed through the lines." This was an "indignity" to be under guard just like a prisoner, she told them, especially by the order of General Porter, who had often been a guest at Arlington. The only place she wanted to go was back to the White House "if not yet in ruins." They told her that she could go most anywhere within reason so long as she had a Federal escort.

"No," she said, "I will not stir under such conditions!"

When it was explained that this was also to protect her, she was somewhat mollified, and the visit ended "with more courtesy on her part than our reception promised," one of the officers wrote later.

Having had her verbal duel with the Yankees, she decided to go on to Malbourne, the home of Edmund Ruffin, who traditionally fired the first shot at Fort Sumter. But the enemy caught up with her again.

By this time, Mildred was with her, and with evident relish Mary wrote to Robert that the farm had been seized and the house surrounded by an entire troop of Federal cavalry. After this letter, there was silence, and Lee, who did not look on the adventure in the same light as his wife, decided it was time he took a hand. He made arrangements with General McClellan for his wife and daughter to pass through the lines, then rode out to Meadow Bridge to ask Captain W. Roy Mason for a favor.

"I have some property in the hands of the enemy, and General McClellan has informed me that he would deliver it to me any time I asked for it," he said. Growing serious, he told Mason the story, and asked him to take a courier with a flag of truce to Federal headquarters, where the ladies would come, and from there escort them to Mrs. Gooch's farm inside Confederate lines.

Soon after Joe Johnston crossed the Chickahominy with the greater part of his army, the President, wanting to learn his plans, rode with Lee to his headquarters. They were not certain what sort of reception they would get, since Johnston had recently written a long irate letter to Davis, among other complaints accusing Lee of ordering certain of his forces about. "My authority does not extend beyond the troops immediately around me," he said. "I request therefore to be relieved of a merely nominal geographical command."

Although the evening was passed peaceably, nothing was learned, for Johnston either had no definite plan or he was being secretive. The next day, Lee wrote and asked him to come to the capital to discuss the situation with the President but Joe did not reply. On May 21, Lee wrote again; and the following day, he and Davis rode out to see Johnston at Mechanicsville. Here they found a state of disorganization and lack of preparation that was frightening. That night, Davis wrote caustically to Johnston, saying among other things that if the Federals had chosen, they "might easily have advanced over the turnpike toward if not to Richmond."

On Thursday, May 29, Lee returned to Mechanicsville, for he had seen Johnston on the twenty-sixth and Joe had been less reticent; he told Lee that he planned to move against the enemy that "next Thursday." But Lee found no battle under way; the plans had been changed during the night, and Johnston was preparing to strike the Federals south of the Chickahominy.

Lee had recently attended a Cabinet meeting at which the possibility of Richmond being taken was discussed. Tears had filled his eyes at the prospect, and he had said:

"Richmond must not be given up! It shall not be given up!"

After his return to the capital on the twenty-ninth, he realized that there was a good chance that Richmond would be taken. It was impossible for him to restrain his warrior instincts any longer, and over his better judgment, for he knew how jealous of his powers Johnston was, he sent his aide, Colonel Long, to Mechanicsville to tell Joe that he had no desire to interfere but would like to offer his help in any capacity on the field where his services would be of the most value. Long reported afterward that Johnston had listened "politely" and "expressed gratification" at the offer, but said nothing about any service.

On May 31, it was announced by the newsboys in the streets that a battle would be fought that day, and "everybody was upon the tip-toe of expectation." Though it was obvious to Lee that Johnston did not want him on the field, he succumbed to the prevailing excitement and, strapping his overcoat on the saddle, for it threatened rain, mounted Traveller and trotted out three miles to Joe's headquarters on the Nine Mile Road. But Johnston had gone on to the New Bridge Road, so Lee rode off to find his friend in a house near the junction.

Here, the atmosphere was tense; couriers and officers were coming and going and there were obvious preparations under way for a big movement. But Johnston was not overly cordial, and told Lee nothing about his plans.

Around three o'clock that afternoon, Lee heard the unmistakable sound of musket fire in the direction of Seven Pines. He mentioned it to Johnston but Joe told him it was nothing more than an artillery duel. The President had just ridden onto the field and also heard the firing. He rode up to the house where he saw Traveller tied, but Johnston, seeing him approach, "sought to avoid a meeting by mounting quickly and riding rapidly to the extreme front."

Lee came out to meet Davis, who asked him what the musketry meant, and Lee answered his question by asking if he had heard it too. When Davis said yes, Lee told him that he was under that impression himself, but repeated what Johnston had said. It was obvious to both, as Davis wrote later, that "neither of us had been advised of a design to attack that day."

Together they rode down the road toward the sound of musketry, and soon found themselves in thick firing. Here, they encountered another appalling scene of mismanagement. Troops were halted without commanders, and commanders were waiting for troops and orders that never came. Crowds of stragglers were milling about, and there were groups of armed civilians who stayed so far from the danger that their shots fell thick among their own men.

Soon a courier rode up with word that General Johnston had been seriously wounded, perhaps fatally. On the heels of the messenger came litter bearers with Johnston just rousing to consciousness. The grievances of the moment before were forgotten as Davis took Johnston's hand, and inquired kindly into the nature of his wound. It was found that his injuries, though painful, were not mortal. A rifle ball had pierced his shoulder blade, and as he reeled in the saddle, a shell fragment struck him in the chest, breaking three ribs. Lee then came up, took his old friend's hand, and tenderly expressed his concern.

Since it was growing dark, the Federals were content to let matters rest, but they could be expected to resume battle at dawn. This put the Confederate army and Richmond in a precarious position, especially since the next in line for the command was the ailing Gustavus W. Smith, a former New York street commissioner, whom Lee and Davis found in a state of near collapse at the prospect of taking command. When Davis questioned him about his plans, he admitted that he had none. Leaving Smith to succumb completely to his nerves, Davis and Lee rode off on the road to Richmond.

It is probable that neither man talked much on the way, for each was occupied with his reflections on the terrible bungling he had seen that day. Davis was also having to consider a successor to Johnston. Although the obvious candidate rode beside him, Davis had so far avoided placing Lee in the logical position. But now there was little choice. He must select a man of ability or lose everything. In offering the command to Lee, it would not be necessary for Davis to relinquish any of his military powers. It could be a joint command in which he and Lee would consult on all major movements and direct them together.

Before reaching the city, Davis offered Lee the command and he accepted, though with customary modesty he told Davis that he wished "the mantle might fall on an abler man."

The next day when he wrote to Charlotte to say that Rooney was safe after the battle, he told her that he had taken to the field: "I wish . . . to drive the enemies back to their homes. I have no ambition & no desire but for the attainment of this object, & therefore only wish for its accomplishment by him that can do it most speedily & thoroughly."

McClellan's caution led him to wait until he received reinforcements to replace his losses, before he attacked. These were slow to reach him, for the rain had made quagmires of the roads, and floods had washed away several bridges he had built for a crossing of the Chickahominy. "The enemy cannot move his heavy guns except on the railroad," Lee wrote Davis. "You have seen nothing like the roads on the Chickahominy bottom."

On the afternoon of June 1, Lee took over the command from Gustavus Smith, who, broken in health, resigned from the service. Lee established his headquarters two miles from Richmond in the house of a widow "of the euphonius name" of Dabbs, as he said. She had given permission to use the house and left it, he wrote to Agnes, "delightfully clean, free of all the necessaries & comforts but her cat & kittens."

Lee brought his Richmond staff with him, with the addition of Colonel R. H. Chilton, his friend from San Antonio days, and Captain A. P. Mason, the only member of Johnston's staff who did not retire with his chief. As had always been his way, Lee and his household lived and messed together with a complete lack of restraint and formality.

In a few quarters, Lee's appointment was hailed as "the harbinger of bright fortune," but the average person, judging Robert from his record so far, felt that his reputation was greatly overrated. Though attempts were made to keep the news of Johnston's wounding and the change in commanders out of the newspapers, the Richmond *Examiner*, whose loyalty was suspect, announced scornfully: "Evacuating Lee, who has never risked a single battle with the invader, is commanding general."

McClellan soon learned of the change, and forming his opinion of Lee's mettle from the West Virginia campaign, declared that he preferred him as an opponent since he was "likely to be timid and irresolute in action." He shortly had reason to regret this hasty judgment.

But what concerned Lee more than the criticism and scorn was the threatened demoralization of the army. The lack of organization, discipline, and firmness of purpose had destroyed in the soldier all confidence in his leaders.

Lee's first act was to call a meeting of his division commanders at The Chimneys on the Nine Mile Road, to feel them out, to discuss the army's condition, and formulate a plan of defense. When Jefferson Davis walked in unexpectedly, the council was already in progress. He remembered that "the tone of the conversation was quite despondent," and that a number of officers, certain the army would not be able to maintain its position because the line was within shelling range of the enemy, were urging withdrawal nearer Richmond.

"If we leave this line because they can shell us, we shall leave the next for the same reason, and I don't see how we can stop this side of Richmond," Lee told them.

And when an officer began to figure with pencil and paper how McClellan could make his approach irresistible, Lee cried:

"Stop, if you go on ciphering, we are whipped beforehand!"

Lee resolved in spite of the opposition of his principal officers, whose confidence he still had to win, to maintain the army's present position. He made a personal reconnaissance over the entire line, and satisfied that it could be held, he issued orders for earthworks to be built across the front.

This act brought criticism from every quarter, and he was given still another derisive title—"The King of Spades." In the average opinion he was "merely an engineer," and fear was openly expressed that his troops would become more familiar with the spade than the musket.

56

Though the use of entrenchments for infantry was Lee's greatest contribution to military art, and marked the beginning of an epoch in military history, there were few who could appreciate its value; to most "this seemed little better than a confession of cowardice." The young artillery officer, E. P. Alexander, shared the belief that Lee would not be an aggressive fighter. One afternoon while riding along the lines with Colonel Joseph C. Ives—Lee's engineer in South Carolina and now on Davis' staff—Alexander said:

Ives, tell me this. We are here fortifying our lines, but apparently leaving the enemy all the time he needs to accumulate his superior forces, and then to move on us in the way he thinks best. Has General Lee the *audacity* that is going to be required for our inferior force to meet the enemy's superior force—to take the aggressive, and to run risks and stand chances?

Ives "reined up his horse, stopped in the road, and turning," said:

"Alexander, if there is one man above every other in *audacity*, it is General Lee! *His name might be Audacity.* He will take more desperate chances and take them quicker than any other general in this country, North or South; and you will live to see it, too."

But again progress was slow. "Our people are opposed to work," Lee complained to Davis.

Our troops, officers, community & press, all ridicule & resist it. It is the very means by which McClellan has & is advancing. Why should we leave to him the whole advantage of labour. Combined with fortitude & boldness, of which we have our fair proportion, it should lead us to success. What carried the Roman soldiers into all countries, but this happy combination? The evidences of their labour last to this day. There is nothing so military as labour, & nothing so important to an army as to save the lives of its soldiers.

He began to ride along the lines each day, encouraging the men, urging them to hurry, but most important, winning their confidence. By the second week in June, staff members noticed that the men already appeared in better spirits, and that the sullen silence with which they had begun the work was giving way to a normal amount of joking and laughter.

Discipline, which had been very lax under Johnston, was a major problem. Men unused to control of any sort were not disposed to obey "without good and sufficient reason given." One Virginia soldier aptly characterized his fellows when he wrote:

"These men were the people of the South, and the war was their own; wherefore they fought to win it of their own accord, and not at all because their officers commanded them to do so."

But the force of Lee's presence was soon felt. His efficiency and organization gave heart to an army where only favoritism, incompetence, indecision, and dissatisfaction had ruled. While a few Southerners had the vision to regard Johnston's wounding as their salvation, the majority of Northerners marked it as the turning of the tide against them, for discipline and excellent plans were immediately evident, and the troops, with growing faith in their commander, went into battle with shouts and fought "like infuriated tigers." By autumn, the men had begun to exhibit fully their implicit confidence in Lee's soldiership, certain, as one of them wrote, that "he was equal to any and every emergency."

The unexpected death of their only grandchild, the little boy whom Robert likened to a "sunbeam [who] lightens up the house so brightly & cheerfully," brought him deep sorrow, though when he thought about the child's "great gain by his merciful transition from earth to Heaven," he believed one should grieve only for those left behind. The boy had the congenital weakness of the Carters, and when he caught a cold at the North Carolina hot springs, it settled in his chest and developed into what the doctors called "gangrene of the lungs."

Rooney did not learn of his son's death for over a month, and when word finally reached him, he was not so easily reconciled to the loss as his father had been, admitting that the news was "overwhelming."

Lee now developed the first of his audacious plans; if it had been carried out with celerity and coordination of all commands, as he expected it to be, "the result would have been disastrous to the enemy." It has often been criticized as being too bold and

58

ambitious for the raw material he had to work with. Still, when the entire four years of the war are reviewed, not one of Lee's most daring ideas was ever executed with the rapidity, cooperation, or coordination he counted on when he devised it.

After thorough reconnaissance of the Federal position, Lee wanted to take the offensive by hurling his forces against the Union right wing, north of the Chickahominy. "I will then be on McClellan's tail," he told Davis when he submitted the plan for approval. Seeing that he could profit by Stonewall Jackson's victories in the Shenandoah Valley, which had so paralyzed the Federal administration that it had no other thought than for the safety of Washington, Lee decided to draw Jackson to his aid, swiftly and secretly. Orders were issued, and when Jackson reached Ashland, Lee left Generals Huger, Magruder, and Holmes with twenty-eight thousand men in the entrenchments around Richmond and moved the rest of his army to the north side of the river.

Unlike Johnston, who had guarded his strategy jealously from Lee and Davis but had taken so many others into his confidence that his intentions to fight on a certain day were announced in the papers, Lee told only the President and those commanders who would be engaged. Not until he was ready to move on June 26 did he send a message to the War Secretary, telling him where his headquarters were, in case anyone wanted to reach him. This was the first news the War Office had of the impending battle, and it was presumed by them that not even the Secretary knew of it before.

To make certain that spies would have no intelligence of his intentions, and that the field would not be overrun with stragglers, Lee gave orders that no one without express business with the army be allowed to pass the rear pickets in sight of the city, and even these could not enter the lines without a War Department pass.

Every day, great numbers of Richmond residents climbed the hill north of the Jewish Cemetery to listen for firing. To their minds, silence boded no good and subjected them to fits of gloom. On June 26, they had gathered there as usual but Lee's precautionary measures were so successful that only one man, a

War Department clerk, had any inkling of what was afoot (and he had only just learned).

Jefferson Davis rode out to the field that day and narrowly escaped death when he and his party, which included his staff, Cabinet, and an assortment of politicians, took shelter in a farmhouse. Lee sent a messenger to tell Davis that they must leave at once, because the Federals had one of their most powerful batteries trained on the house. Just as they galloped away, a storm of shot and shell riddled the house.

Not content with this one brush with death, Davis and company rode over the field to look for Lee, learning when they found him that he was not always deferential or amiable. Glaring at them, he asked:

"Who are all this army of people, and what are they doing here?"

No one spoke or moved, but all eyes turned toward the President, who squirmed in his saddle. After a painful pause, Davis replied deprecatingly in that "quick and rather pettish manner of his":

"It is not my army, General."

"It is certainly not *my* army, Mr. President," Lee said sharply, "and this is no place for it!"

"Well, General, if I withdraw, perhaps they will follow," Davis responded lamely, and lifting his hat, turned and rode slowly toward the bridge, seeing as he did so a man killed right in front of him, for the Yankees now had range of the road. But at this moment, nothing seemed as hazardous as Lee's wrath.

Toward dusk, Lee sat down to rest under a tree, and a surgeon bustled up and said:

"Old man, I have chosen this tree for my field hospital, and I want you to get out of the way."

"I will gladly give place when the wounded come, Doctor, but in the meantime there is plenty of room for both of us."

The surgeon was about to retort sharply when a staff officer rode up and addressed the "old man" as General Lee. To the apologies that followed Lee only repeated quietly:

"It's no matter, Doctor. There is plenty of room for both of us till your wounded are brought."

60

Around nine o'clock that night, the battle ended. The first part of Lee's plan to deal the enemy a fatal blow had failed chiefly because Jackson had not arrived for the opening of the fight. Up to now, Stonewall had been famed for celerity. Though aware of its present need, he had for some unaccountable reason taken his time, and the opportunity to cut off Fitz John Porter's corps at Beaver Dam—"the cream of the whole campaign"—was lost.

Due to a lack of coordination between commanders, all of the second day was squandered in partial attacks and small assaults, bloody but ineffectual. At seven o'clock that night, it was "anybody's fight" until Lee called for a general advance of every command on Porter's position.

The unearthly shrieking of the rebel yell could be heard above the din of artillery as the First Texas Brigade under the gallant John B. Hood penetrated the Federal works. In a few minutes, other regiments followed, the position was carried, and the plateau was covered with Yankees in flight. But as E. P. Alexander observed: "Had it been made hours earlier, the fruits of the victory would have been important. As it was they were so trifling as scarcely worth mention."

Nevertheless, Porter fell back, and McClellan wired Lincoln that night that his men "did all that men could do—all that soldiers could accomplish; they were overwhelmed by vastly superior numbers, even after I brought my last reserves into action. . . . I have lost this battle because my force was too small."

But this was not the kind of victory that brought Lee any comfort. He had expected to deal McClellan a staggering blow which he would follow with another and another, until the Federals would be driven "back to their homes," as he had told Charlotte.

The next day at dawn Lee, dressed in a brown-linen summer suit with a sack coat and brown thread gloves, ate his breakfast of bread and ham as he rode to the field. Since it was uncertain what the enemy would do next, General Richard S. Ewell, whose division had not yet been seriously engaged, was sent down the river to see if the Federals were inclined to cross and retreat by way of the Peninsula, while Jeb Stuart was ordered to swoop down on McClellan's headquarters at the White House in a swift cavalry raid. For the rest of the army the day was devoted to the care of the wounded and burial of their dead.

Finding the White House strongly defended, Stuart resorted to a ruse. Dismounting a large number of his men, he marched them in sight of the Federal lines to lead the Federals to think he had infantry. He ordered Major John Pelham's artillery to fire at long range into the yard, changing position from time to time to make it seem as though there were many cannon. Soon after nightfall, great clouds of smoke rolled across the Pamunkey and flames blazed high as McClellan fired his stores, preparatory to retreat.

By daylight he was gone, and Stuart with Rooney Lee's regiment as escort took possession of "Little Mac's" former headquarters, finding that many supplies had either been overlooked or failed to burn. Besides a pontoon train and a number of new cars and locomotives, there were "barrels of sugar, lemons by the million, cases of wine, beer and other liquor of every description, confectionery, canned meats, and fruits and vegetables, and great quantities of ice, all still in excellent condition," Stuart's engineer officer remembered vividly, for men who had been living for days on salt meat and crackers were in the proper mood to appreciate these delicacies and not likely to forget them. Seated on the grass beside the river, the men feasted on pickled oysters, canned beef, ham, French rolls, cakes, and candy, washed down with buckets of iced lemonade, and topped with Havana cigars.

Of Rooney's historic house only two chimneys remained. It was thought at the time that it had burned in the fire of the night before. Later, Rooney learned that the Federals had carefully guarded it out of deference to its associations with Washington, but that an incendiary had eluded the guards and set fire to it several days before.

This "act of vandalism," as Mary called it, served to embitter her further and she wrote bitingly about the "thievish villians," "these brave & Christian yankees who would woo us back to the Union. . . . Sooner than be reunited to such a people again, would I live under the despotic rule of Russia."

Sometime during the morning of the twenty-eighth, Lee had his folding iron cot and other camp equipment moved to Dr. Gaines' house, where General James Longstreet was staying, for as he told a son: "Gen. Longstreet is so slow I am compelled to encamp near his headquarters in order to hasten his movements," a practice he continued throughout the war. At noon when he came back to the house for dinner, a member of Longstreet's staff recalled that though couriers, generals, and other officers began arriving, Lee remained "as calm as a summer cloud," giving his orders "quietly, with precision, but always with courtesy, and anyone seeing him surrounded by a group of officers and not knowing the cause of his concentration, might well have assumed that they were merely guests invited to partake of the hospitality of this splendid and courteous host."

Before dawn the next morning, two engineer officers, Major Meade and Lieutenant Johnston, found while on reconnaissance that the chief Federal position at Golding's Farm, south of the Chickahominy, was deserted. When Lee received this news, he realized that for the present McClellan had abandoned plans to take Richmond. His relief was so great that he said "gaily" to the courier:

"Well, Major, you see what trouble that young man has given me!"

Though General John Magruder had orders to keep a vigilant eye on the position at Golding's and report any movement without delay, he was ignorant of its evacuation, and galloped up to Lee right after the courier had left.

"If you will permit me, sir, I will charge that hill with my whole force and carry it with the point of the bayonet!" he said, pointing toward Golding's Farm.

"No doubt you could *now* succeed," Lee replied, "but I have one serious objection to your making the attack at this time."

"May I ask what that objection is, sir?" asked the unwary Magruder.

"I am afraid, sir, that you will hurt my little friends Major Meade and Lieutenant Johnston. The enemy left about an hour ago, and they are over there with a reconnoitering party."

Now that Lee knew the Federals were retreating, he ordered

63

his army to commence a vigorous pursuit. His chance for destroying Porter's Corps was lost, but the enemy was encumbered by heavy trains as he traveled through swampy woods, and there might be a chance to bring him to a fight.

The plan was simple and obvious, yet the pursuit proved a failure, once again due chiefly to Jackson's strange reluctance to act with either speed or vigor. This was the Sabbath and he observed it strictly, though he knew that Lee was depending on him with the largest force to move swiftly by the most direct route to support Magruder.

When Lee rode to Savage Station the next morning, he found that Jackson had finally reached Magruder. Without a trace of rancor, Lee shook hands warmly and Jackson began to talk volubly in his jerky, impetuous way, with no apologies for the past but plans for the future. With the toe of his right boot he drew a diagram in the dust, and when he had finished "he raised his foot and stamped it down with emphasis saying 'We've got him,' and then signaled for his horse."

In view of Jackson's recent failures, this was an oversanguine remark, but Lee seemed satisfied that his "spell" had passed. Mounting Traveller, he rode off to give Magruder his orders in person and to supply him with a guide. Lee was taking no chances on the pursuit going astray. Then he trotted on to the Charles City road, where Huger was advancing, and finding everything to his satisfaction, went on down the Darbytown pike to join General A. P. Hill.

Later, on hearing the enemy's artillery from Huger's direction, he rode back to make a personal observation. Reassured by what he saw, he joined Longstreet at his field headquarters, set up so close to the rear of his battle line that men and horses among the couriers and staff were being hit by random shots. Here Lee was surprised to find the President, who, before Lee could say a word, began to rebuke him for unnecessarily exposing himself. Lee objected that he was only trying to learn something about the movements afoot and that he "could not understand things so well unless he saw them." He then asked Davis what he was doing there, and the President said evasively:

"Oh, I am here on the same mission as you are."

At this point, A. P. Hill rode up and ordered them both off the field, saying as he did so:

"One shot from that battery over yonder may presently deprive the Confederacy of its President and the Army of Northern Virginia of its commander!"

It was supposed that Jackson would make up for his inaction of the previous day, and now Lee, Longstreet, Hill, Alexander, and Davis waited impatiently in a field of small pines for the signal from either Jackson or Huger, preferably both.

For hours we stood there waiting—waiting for something which never happened. Every minute that we waited was priceless time thrown away. Twelve o'clock came and the precious day was half gone. One o'clock, two o'clock, three o'clock followed. Even four o'clock drew near, and now whatever was started, would be cut short by night. Our great opportunity was practically over, and we had not yet pulled a trigger [Alexander recalled].

Lee must have thought of those other wasted hours passed at Cheat Mountain, waiting for Rust's signal.

Though Jackson had made an early and promising start, he did not try to cross White Oak Swamp as others had done with comparative ease, but insisted that he needed a bridge. When this was finished and it was reported to him that the enemy was still unsuspecting, he got up from the fallen pine on which he was sitting, pulled his faded cap down over his eyes, and walked off, giving no orders for a movement across the swamp.

In the entire four years of the war with its crowded gallery of unfortunate days, this one would always be remembered as the most unfortunate. Never again would Lee find the enemy in full retreat across his front—and never again would the moral and physical effect of a victory have gained him so much.

6

LEE'S mood was grim that Tuesday morning following the unsuccessful pursuit. The Federals had escaped unpunished, united their army, and massed it on Malvern Hill. Lee made no comment on the report brought to him of the Hill's impregnability, which, because of "its commanding height, the difficulties of approach, its amphitheatrical form, and ample area, would enable McClellan to arrange his . . . field guns, tier above tier, and sweep the plain in every direction."

"If General McClellan is there in force, we had better let him alone," cautioned General D. H. Hill after he had given the report.

But Longstreet laughed and said: "Don't get scared, now that we have got him whipped."

Lee, who disliked overconfidence as much as timidity, said nothing, but he was too aggressive a fighter to lose the advantage of attacking McClellan's united army, and ordered the advance.

Again it turned out to be a battle fought by detachments against an enemy well posted and prepared.

"Yes!" Lee snapped at General Early when he said he feared McClellan would escape. "Yes! He will get away because I cannot have my orders carried out!"

The starless night mercifully ended the useless slaughter of Lee's men. A heavy rain beat out the torches of those who hunted for their wounded comrades among the fragments of bodies. To men already inured to sights on a battlefield, this one appeared to be a ghastly nightmare, "a gruesome picture of war in its most horrid shape," due to the ceaseless raking of McClellan's guns.

The morning dawned with a heavy fog and drizzle. As the Confederates cooked rations taken from the haversacks of their fallen foes and tried to dry out, their fires made bright rents in the white pall that covered the field and hid Malvern Hill from view. An informal truce prevailed as details of Federals and Confederates combed the bloody field for their dead, and brought in those wounded who had been overlooked in the dark. Out of the woods soldiers came singly and in groups, hunting for their commands, while officers rode about in search of their men.

In the dining room of Dr. Poindexter's house, Lee held a council of war to discuss the practicability of further pursuit, for by ten o'clock the fog had lifted, and it was found that the enemy was gone. Just as the meeting was starting, the President and his brother, Colonel Joseph Davis of his staff, walked in unexpectedly; they had been on a fruitless hunt for whiskey to issue to the wet and exhausted troops.

The early drizzle had soon turned into a heavy rain, and Lee had reports that the lowlands were again seas of mud. The weather and the army's condition made pursuit inadvisable although Jackson, when his opinion was sought, said quietly:

"They have not all got away if we go immediately after them."

These days, all that was aggressive about Stonewall were his words. But this time if his advice had been taken, and if Lee's orders could have been carried out quickly with unified action, McClellan would have been subject to heavy losses, for as a Federal general later testified, many of the troops were demoralized:

"It was like the retreat of a whipped army," he said, "and a few shots from the rebels would have panic-stricken the whole command."

When the council was over, Longstreet tried to console Lee by saying: "I think you hurt them as much as they hurt you." But Lee took no comfort in such words.

The dining-room doors were then opened, and the staff was free to join in the social conversation. Charles Marshall of Lee's staff brought in a silver flask of fine old whiskey, given to him by the recently captured Federal general, George McCall. Drawing off the cap, he handed it first to the President who took a sip and then offered it to Lee. But Lee said no, he would not deprive some younger officer who would appreciate the drink more than he would. Longstreet took "a good soldierly swig," while the abstemious Jackson passed it gravely by. Although Stuart also refused, he did so with a laugh and the remark that he knew General McCall would not be giving away good whiskey to Confederates unless he had drugged it "to poison someone"—a suggestion that failed to keep the staff from emptying the flask in short order.

Lee's army now moved back to the vicinity of Richmond,

where it would reinforce and rest, and Lee returned to his old quarters at the Dabbs house. From there he wrote to Mary of his profound gratitude for the "mercies extended by our Heavenly Father," although he admitted, "our success has not been as great or as complete as I could have desired, but God knows what is best for us." With this letter he sent a bundle of clothes to be washed, and asked for some thinner garments and his extra spectacles, as he had lost his other pair.

The press carped at his failure to win a more decisive victory, and complained that he had not "followed up" his advantage. This criticism moved him to remark that it was the gravest mistake to have allowed "all our worst generals to command armies, and all our best generals to edit the newspapers. . . . I am willing to serve in any capacity. . . . I have done the best I could in the field, and have not succeeded as I should wish. I am willing to yield my place to these best generals, and I will do my best for the cause by editing a newspaper." Many of Johnston's admirers protested that their man could have done better.

But the fickle public, which had a short time before been so scornful of Lee, now looked upon him as their champion, "the author of a great deliverance worked out for them" who had "turned the tide." Instead of derisive titles, they spoke of him as "The First Captain of the Confederacy" and "The Saviour of Richmond." Even one of his severest critics in South Carolina said with enthusiasm: "Now we are throwing up our caps for R. E. Lee."

There was reaction in the north, too. President Lincoln called General John Pope from the west, where he had some success, and placed him in command of the new "Army of Virginia," to become better known as "The Army of the Potomac."

Prior to the war, Pope had been chiefly notable for his years spent in fruitless search for artesian water in the wastelands of Texas, and his oversanguine reports on the prospects of success had given rise to a parody:

> Pope told a flattering tale,
>   Which proved to be bravado,
> About the streams which spout like ale
>   On the Llano Estacado.

He had not changed. When he came to reorganize the army, he kept his headquarters "in the saddle" and from this constricted center of authority issued an "address." He had come, he told his men, from an army which had seen only the backs of its enemies; "from an army whose business it has been to seek the adversary, and beat him when he was found; whose policy has been attack and not defence. . . . I desire you to dismiss from your minds certain phrases I am sorry to find much in vogue amongst you; I hear constantly of . . . 'lines of retreat'. . . . Let us study the probable lines of retreat of our opponents. . . ."

This bombast impressed his own people unfavorably and elicited ridicule from his foes. Stonewall Jackson is supposed, in a rare moment of levity, to have expressed his contempt for a commander who did not know "his headquarters from his hindquarters."

Lee soon had his opinion formed. It was obviously not a high one, since he took risks with Pope that he took with no other Union commander.

On July 12 it was reported that Pope had advanced, and was occupying Culpeper Court House. The next day there was a lunch and council of war at President Davis' house on East Clay Street in Richmond. Knowing the Northerner's inordinate fear for the safety of Washington, Lee proposed that the Confederate army seriously threaten the capital, thereby removing the theater of war from the James River. He suggested sending Jackson to Gordonsville at once, and if this move had the desired effect, he would then follow with the bulk of the army.

The President approved and after the meeting stood with Lee and Jackson on the top step outside the front door, making what seemed to one soldier "a very distinguished trio." An officer who saw Lee then for the first time wrote to his wife that he was "elegantly dressed in full uniform, sword and sash, spotless boots, beautiful spurs . . . by far the most magnificent man I ever saw."

But he did not appear impressive in his own eyes. Charlotte had asked him about his uniform, and he sent an unflattering description:

My habiliments are not so comfortable as yours, nor so suited to this hot weather. . . . My coat is of gray, of the regulation style & pattern, & my pants of a dark blue, as is also prescribed, partly hid by my long boots. I have the same handsome hat which surmounts my gray head (the latter is *not* prescribed in the regulations) & shields my ugly face, which is masked by a white beard which is as stiff & wiry as the teeth of a card. In fact, an uglier person you have never seen, & so unattractive is it to our enemies that they shoot at it whenever visible to them.

Plans for the coming campaign kept him so close to the Dabbs house that he was unable to get to Richmond to see his three daughters who were visiting there. He had time only for a few brief letters to the rest of his scattered family—Mary and Charlotte, staying with the Wickhams at Hickory Hill, a Carter property twenty miles north of Richmond; and Daughter and Custis at Carter Lee's home, Windsor, where Custis was recuperating from an illness. Nor was he in the mood to write to Eliza Stiles, whose letters he forwarded to Mary asking her to answer them and "say everything that is kind for me."

After Pope's bombastic orders came more serious ones directed against Southern civilians. The Federals under McClellan had established a hospital at Shirley, and Mrs. Hill Carter had charitably nursed their sick and wounded. In compliance with Pope's "pillage order," twelve thousand Union soldiers now came to Shirley and

took every living article of stock on the place, more than a hundred of hogs & sheep, all that they could not consume, they shot, colts, horses, mules, oxen, & then took their axes (which it seems they always carry about for such soldierly purposes), cut up all the wheat cradles, a large crop being ready for harvest. Cut all the spokes in the wagons, & cart wheels thus depriving a large plantation of women & children of the means of getting even bread. In all the annals of civilized warfare such conduct is unknown [Mary wrote bitterly to Eliza].

It has been said that Lee always referred to the enemy as "those people," "General ——'s people" (naming his opponent), or "our friends across the river." But Pope's orders prompted him to term the Federals "barbarians" who vio-

70

lated all rules of war: "I believe them capable of any enormity that meanness, pusilanimity & malice could invent." He spoke of that "miscreant Pope," and said that he could forgive his nephew, Louis Marshall, for "fighting against us, but not his joining Pope." He also revealed his intolerance of Northern convictions by referring bitingly to his brother-in-law Marshall's "B. [Black] republican principles."

Near the middle of August, Lee's wisdom in sending Jackson to Gordonsville was demonstrated when McClellan pulled out of his entrenchments along the James River. Lee then left two brigades under General Gustavus Smith (now recovered and back in the service) to guard Richmond against possible cavalry raids, and ordered the rest of the army to Gordonsville. He arrived there himself on August 15.

Before he left, he had expected to stop at "The Mess," as Custis' Franklin Street quarters were now called, to say good-by, for his son was back "at his castle with his bachelors looking quite well but reporting weak," and Daughter was with him, coaxing him back to health. But there was time only for a hasty note which accompanied a straw hat he asked Custis to "please give house room to."

On August 30, Lee's army met the Federals on the old field at Manassas and "achieved a signal victory" over the combined forces of Pope and McClellan, causing them to give serious thought to their own lines of retreat and making Pope's career remarkable for its brevity.

But this was not the fatal blow Lee had hoped for, and he must have wondered if he could ever count on his plans being carried out the way he expected them to be. He knew he always had to consider the human factor, so unpredictable and liable to err, and with the interposition of Providence in his favor or against him. But he had not thought that Longstreet would turn temperamental and display a recalcitrance which he was either unable or unwilling to combat.

"Old Pete," as Longstreet was known to his men, had come out Lee's most reliable commander after the Seven Days' fighting, and Robert had since then affectionately called him "my old war horse" and spoken of him as "a most brilliant soldier when once engaged." But three times during the recent fighting at Manassas, Lee had urged him to attack, and each time Longstreet had found reasons for not doing so. Later, Longstreet came to his own defense by saying that Lee "did not order him" to attack. "To one accustomed to his ways," Walter Taylor wrote of Lee, "it is easy to understand why he did not order an attack in view of General Longstreet's reluctance to make one." He had such implicit faith in his corps commanders, he always "accorded them great liberty in the exercise of their discretion as to the manner of the execution of his orders; having made clear his general plans, he left to them the details of carrying them out."

Lee has also explained the principles which guided his conduct: "I strive to make my plans as good as my human skill allows, but on the day of battle, I lay the fate of my army in the hands of God; it is my generals' turn to perform their duty." And again he said: "My interference in battle would do more harm than good. I have to rely on my brigade and division commanders."

However sound this reasoning may have been in abstract, it did not always work in practice; and Longstreet, establishing the precedent of imposing his will on Lee this once, was to do it again at a crisis when delay betokened defeat.

During this fighting at Manassas, Lee was performing one of the most exacting tests of military genius, one liable to cause the most experienced general to lose poise—the successful convergence of two armies (Jackson and Longstreet) on a battlefield. When minutes passed and Longstreet still did not come to Jackson's support, it seemed impossible for Stonewall's lines to last much longer. Some officers around Lee were so excited they could hardly sit still on their horses, "others about him were a-quiver. Everybody's nerves were at the tensest—everybody's except General Lee's. His countenance did not show the least excitement or concern." When some teams and wagons passed, he looked at the mules "as though he were making an inspection to the rear," and said to an officer near him:

"I observe that some of those mules are without shoes. I wish you would see to it that all of the animals are shod at once."

More time passed, and it seemed that Jackson's lines would surely break, which might mean "defeat, disaster, the ruins of the army." Still "Lee did not blink an eye." When at last Longstreet saw the necessity for obeying, and his guns opened, the relief was so great that these officers slapped each other on the back, shook hands over and over, and could hardly keep from throwing their hats in the air.

General R. F. Hoke of North Carolina looked expressly at Lee to see if he exhibited these same emotions, but "could not see the twitching of a muscle or the slightest change of expression. Throughout the whole of that nerve-wracking scene, General Lee's face exhibited the same calm composure, neither shaken by the shadow of defeat, nor elated by the success of his plans." Not always was he able to remain so detached. There would be times when his officers could not keep him from trying to lead his troops in person.

During the fighting around Gordonsville, when Lee and Longstreet were bivouacing together near Orleans, Mrs. Marshall, a resident of the village, invited the two generals and their staff to supper. It was noticed that Lee enjoyed himself, for besides the hostess, there were also a number of charming lady refugees staying in the house. When he left that night he said a final good-by, since he would be moving on at dawn. But before that time came, a small messenger arrived at Lee's tent with a breakfast invitation from Mrs. Marshall.

By dawn Lee had said his adieus to the ladies and taken his place at the head of the advancing column. Traveller was stimulated by the brisk air and broke into his noted "buck-trot," keeping it up until Lee and his staff were far ahead of the column. When they approached Salem, a quartermaster who had been still farther in advance came galloping back, shouting:

"The Federal cavalry are upon you!" A few hundred yards behind him was the head of a squadron.

Lee had with him about a dozen men, including his couriers. These men now acted with remarkable presence of mind. They quickly formed a line across the road, and told Lee to get out of sight while they held off the advancing cavalry. When the Yankees saw the line of horsemen, they stopped. Concluding

73

that it was the head of a column, they wheeled about and rode off rapidly in the opposite direction.

Word of Lee's coming reached a lady who lived with a family of handsome daughters near Salem. They were all anxious to see the General, so the mother got out her carriage and drove down the main road. Before they had gone a quarter of a mile, they had the misfortune to meet up with the bluecoats who had just "escaped" from Lee's staff. When they saw her handsome pair of matched bays, they took them in spite of the pleas of the beautiful daughters. By the time Lee arrived, the Yankees were far off, and the ladies had taken refuge in a nearby house. Hearing of their plight, Lee stopped and tried to cheer them by joking about their adventure. Afterward, they admitted that without the mishap they would never have had the chance to talk with Lee, although the mother was not easily reconciled to the price she had paid for their chat.

On the field at Manassas, Lee met Rob. To see the enemy, he and his staff rode to the hilltop where the artillery was placed, and Lee reined Traveller not fifteen feet from his son, standing beside his number-one gun. But the accumulation of red dust after four days of marching, and the grime of black powder, made Rob unrecognizable. He admired his father for a few minutes, then walked up to Captain Mason of the staff and identified himself, much to Mason's surprise. After Lee had put down his field glasses, the Captain said:

"General, here is someone who wants to speak to you."

"Well, my man, what can I do for you?" Lee asked kindly.

"Why, General, don't you know me?"

Lee laughed at Rob's appearance, but was greatly relieved to find him safe and well.

While riding over the field the morning after the battle, Lee came on a barefoot soldier carrying a pair of shoes he had just taken from a dead Federal. Sharply Lee called to him:

"What are you doing here, sir, away from your command?"

The soldier did not recognize Lee: "That's none of your business, by God!" he retorted.

"You are a straggler, sir, and deserve the severest punishment."

"It's a damned lie, sir," the trooper shouted. "I left my regiment a few minutes ago to hunt me a pair of shoes. I went through the fight yesterday, and that's more than you can say; where were you when General Stuart wanted your damned cavalry to charge the Yankees after we put 'em to running? You were lying back in the pine thickets and couldn't be found; but today, when there's no danger, you come out and charge other men with straggling, damn you!"

Lee was secretly amused, and without another word, rode off. A staff officer then asked the man if he knew whom he had been talking to.

"Yes! To a cowardly Virginia cavalryman, that's who!"

When told of his mistake, he said: "Ho-o-what? General Lee, did you say? And his staff?"

"Yes."

"Scissors to grind, I'm a goner!" he muttered, and ran on down the road.

Later this day, Lee, Longstreet, and Jackson dismounted in the woods to discuss arrangements for pursuit. It was raining and Lee was wearing a rubber poncho and overalls. Traveller, with his reins on his neck, was standing quietly beside Lee. Suddenly the horse was startled and gave a jump. As Lee sprang to catch the bridle, he tripped on his overalls and pitched forward, breaking the fall with hands extended. He was instantly on his feet and reproaching himself for what he called his "awkwardness."

Both hands were badly injured, so a surgeon was sent for. Until he came, young Henry Kyd Douglas of Jackson's staff occupied nearly an hour pouring water gently over Lee's hands to relieve the pain. As he poured, he noticed "what beautiful hands and feet he had and what a perfect figure: all parts of the handsomest man I ever saw."

The doctor found several small bones broken in the right hand, and the left, badly twisted; both wrists were sprained. Each hand was put into a splint, and the right one into a sling, so that for weeks Lee was practically helpless, having to be dressed and fed, to dictate all his reports and letters (Custis, still on sick leave, was his amanuensis for some while), and to ride in his ambulance. This accident led to a widespread report that he had been wounded, and the Northern papers printed detailed accounts of the "serious character" of the wound and how it was sustained.

A month later, Custis was writing for him to Agnes and Annie:

> You are right in supposing the great inconvenience I suffer in being disabled in both hands. It has been a great affliction & hindrance to me. . . . I am recovering the use of my left hand, and am now able to mount my horse. The bones in my right hand have united, but it is still powerless. I wish you had been with me to assist me in my feebleness. Think of my being left to the graceful ministrations of Perry, who had to dress, feed, & array me; but I can help myself a little now.

Jeb Stuart, believing Lee needed a less nervous horse than Traveller, presented him at this time with a gentle mare named Lucy Long.

To draw the enemy north of the Potomac and so relieve Virginia, and to feed his men, Lee now decided to cross over into Maryland. He knew that his army was not "properly equipped for an invasion of an enemy's territory. It lacks much of the material of war, is feeble in transportation, the men are poorly provided with clothes, and in thousands of instances are destitute of shoes, still we cannot afford to be idle, and though weaker than our opponents in men and military equipments, must endeavour to harass, if not destroy them," he wrote. There was also a political aspect to be considered, for it was believed in the South that Maryland had strong Confederate sympathies; an invasion would afford her the opportunity "to throw off the oppression to which she is now subject."

Just before the army left, Rob came to his father's tent. He was barefoot, and dangling from his hand were the remnants of a pair of boots.

"I only wanted to ask, sir, if I might draw a new pair, as I can't march in these," he explained.

"Have the men in your company received permission to draw shoes yet?"

"No, sir; I believe not yet."

"Then go back to your battery, my boy, and wait till they have."

A boy sat on a rail fence to watch Lee's army cross over into Maryland. He recalled that they were "the dirtiest men I ever saw, a most ragged, lean, and hungry set of wolves. Yet there was a dash about them that the Northern men lacked. They rode like circus riders."

In crossing the Potomac at White's Ford, the troops marched in fours, shouting, laughing, and singing, while the band played (hopefully) "Maryland, My Maryland."

After passing through Frederick City, where Barbara Friet-chie—ninety-six, bed-ridden, and staunchly Southern in convictions, supposedly (according to the fancy of the poet Whittier) —flaunted the stars and stripes in Stonewall Jackson's face, Lee, Longstreet, Jackson, and for a time Jeb Stuart, set up headquarters next to each other in Best's Grove.

As soon as the tents were pitched, the townspeople, especially the ladies, came out to the Grove, hoping for a glimpse of Lee and the others, or even a word with them. But Lee and Jackson kept close to their tents and declined to see most callers, for Lee's hands were still painful and Jackson was suffering from a back injury sustained when his horse reared and fell over with him. Although Longstreet had a chafed heel and had to wear carpet slippers, he dropped his usual reserve and became very sociable, while Jeb was, as always, eager to see and talk with every pretty girl who came.

Lee now issued a proclamation to the people of Maryland:

. . . The people of the South have long wished to aid you in throwing off this foreign yoke, to enable you again to enjoy the inalienable rights of freemen and restore independence to your State. . . . It is for you to decide your destiny freely and without constraint. . . . This army will respect your choice, whatever it may be; and, while the Southern people will rejoice to welcome you to your natural position among them, they will only welcome you when you come by your own free will. . . .

Either there was a stronger Union sentiment than suspected, or else Marylanders were unwilling for their state to become a theater of war, for the invasion did not spark a rebellion.

While Lee and his staff were riding through Hagerstown

77

(a courier was leading Traveller, since Lee's hands were still useless), a teacher, followed by her class of young girls, rushed from the schoolhouse into the middle of the road, stopped in front of Lee, and sang "The Star-Spangled Banner." When they were through, he courteously touched his hat to the schoolmistress, complimented the girls on their pleasant voices, and rode on. The lady, having failed to make a scene, "retired rather discomfited," it was recalled.

Lee had issued positive orders against pillage, but one day while riding to the rear of the lines he came on a straggler from Jackson's command, carrying to quarters a pig he had stolen and killed. Here was an offender on two scores. The blood rushed to Lee's face when he saw him, and he ordered the man arrested, returned to Jackson, and shot as an example to stragglers and pillagers.

When the prisoner was brought to Stonewall, he took a liberty with Lee's orders. Since men were already so scarce, instead of shooting him, he sent him to the front lines at the most threatened spot. The soldier survived the fighting, and redeemed his reputation by gallant behavior.

At Sharpsburg, there was a hard-fought battle in which the Confederates were closely pressed by the overwhelming numbers of their opponents under McClellan. Lee's brigades were so depleted by straggling that they went into the fighting reduced to the size of regiments and sometimes even of companies.

After the battle, general after general, some on the point of being unnerved, rode up to Lee with the same tale of discouragement, and counseled retreat. Not even Jackson, once again the fierce and tenacious fighter, suggested anything but a withdrawal. Lee heard each one in silence, and when they had finished and were waiting for orders to begin the retreat, he suddenly rose in his stirrups and said:

"Gentlemen, we will not cross the Potomac tonight! You will go to your respective commands and strengthen your lines. . . . If McClellan wants to fight in the morning, I will give him battle again. Go!"

They went, and as one observer wrote: "Lee's glorious audacity was justified; for he proved to all the world that McClellan did not dare to renew the attack."

Although McClellan withdrew, the condition of Lee's army precluded all thought of pursuit, and he ordered it to cross over into Virginia. In spirit, the troops were unrecognizable from those who had crossed a short time before with banners flying and bands playing. If anyone, even in derision, struck the tune "Maryland, My Maryland," he was shouted down with: "Damn my Maryland!" And Walter Taylor wrote his sister:

"Don't let any of your friends sing 'My Maryland'—not 'my Western Maryland' anyhow."

During this campaign the task of selecting the site for headquarters had fallen to Colonel Long since Lee credited him with "a good eye for locality." As the General was easily satisfied, Long's problems were minimized. Only once, when they were near Winchester after the return from Maryland, did he recall any objections.

Since the troops would be staying in one place for some time to rest and refit, Long was careful to choose a good spot, picking out a farmhouse that was set in a large shady yard. The owners were pleased to have headquarters on their grounds and offered to let Lee occupy rooms in the house.

Long ordered up the wagons and began unloading. Just then Lee rode into the yard and flatly refused to occupy either the house or grounds. Long had not expected him to depart from his rule of declining quarters in a house, but did not think he would find fault with the yard.

Annoyed at having to repack and search further, Long chose the first field he came to just down the road. Though the boulders and smaller rocks were so numerous there was hardly room for the tents and wagons, Long ordered headquarters set up anyway. The only redeeming feature was a stream of pure water, on the bank of which he had Lee's tent pitched.

When Lee rode up, he looked all about with a smile of satisfaction, and said:

"This is better than the yard, Colonel. We will not disturb those good people."

To this camp came Lieutenant Colonel Garnet Wolseley,

79

later Field Marshal Lord Wolseley. He was impressed with the simplicity of headquarters, consisting, as he wrote, of "about seven or eight pole-tents, pitched with their backs to a stake-fence, upon a piece of ground so rocky that it was unpleasant to ride over it. . . . In front of the tents were some three or four army wagons, drawn up without regularity, and a number of horses turned loose in the field. The servants . . . and the mounted soldiers called couriers . . . were unprovided with tents, and slept in or under the wagons." He noticed that many of these wagons were marked "U. S."

He was also surprised to find neither sentries posted in front of the tents nor "crowds of aides-de-camp loitering about, making themselves agreeable to visitors." The large farmhouse up the road, would "in any other army have been the general's residence *pro tem*," he wrote. The staff was crowded two and three in a tent, and none was allowed to carry more baggage than one small box apiece; Lee's, he noted, was "very little larger." Everyone approached Lee with "marked respect," but Wolseley was pleased to see "none of that bowing and flourishing of forage-caps which occurs in the presence of European generals; and, while all honour him and place implicit faith in his courage and ability, those with whom he is most intimate feel for him the affection of sons to a father."

The Britisher painted an engaging picture of Lee's appearance and personality:

> He is a strongly built man, about five feet eleven in height, and apparently not more than fifty years of age. His hair and beard are nearly white; but his dark brown eyes still shine with the brightness of youth, and beam with a most pleasing expression. Indeed, his whole face is kindly and benevolent in the highest degree. . . . He is a person that, wherever seen, whether in a castle or a hovel, alone or in a crowd, must at once attract attention as being a splendid specimen of an English gentleman, with one of the most rarely handsome faces I ever saw.

Though Wolseley had met Von Moltke and Prince Bismarck, Lee seemed to him "the ablest general, and . . . the greatest man I ever conversed with . . . one of the few men who ever seriously impressed and awed me with their natural, their inherent greatness."

That Lee chose the plain life which so impressed strangers was not from any desire to parade simplicity. He knew that he must create in his army a discipline suited to the character of the men, and he elected to live as nearly as possible the life they led, deliberate in his aim to tie them to him with strong bonds of respect and affection.

Many townspeople from Winchester called at headquarters, and not one failed to speak of the rocky ground. This always afforded Lee an ideal opportunity to make a joke at Long's expense, for he knew why the Colonel had selected this field, and enjoyed accusing him of revenge.

Evenings at this camp were often made lively by the company of ladies and the fun-loving Jeb Stuart, who always brought with him his court minstrels—Sam Sweeny, the banjo-player; Taliaferro, the fiddler; Bob, a mulatto boy who worked the bones; a guitarist; and several staff members who, like Stuart, had excellent voices. If the mood were gay, such rollicking tunes as "O Lord, Ladies, Don't You Mind Stephen," and "If You Want a Good Time Jine the Cavalry," were favorites. For the sentimental humor, there would be "Lorena," "Sweet Evelina," or "The Bugles Sang Truce," a solo Jeb "did to perfection," according to a young woman admirer; there was never a dry eye when he finished.

One night during such a serenade, when there were no ladies present, Lee came out to join the company, noticing, as he stepped from his tent, a demijohn (containing "some fine old rye," one present testified), set up on a boulder.

"Gentlemen," Lee asked, "am I to thank General Stuart or the jug for this fine music?"

Though Lee was keenly disappointed that the Maryland campaign failed to achieve all the objectives he had hoped for, it had far-reaching results for him personally. His reputation had been uncertain when he took command in June, 1862; but by the end of 1863, he had "become one of the best-known personages in the South. . . . The Southern people, from Virginia to the utmost limits of the Gulf States, resolutely persisted in regarding Lee as one of the greatest soldiers of history, and retained their confidence in him unimpaired to the end." Quite unconsciously he was establishing for himself an identity with the cause, and engraving on the minds of his countrymen the image of the reincarnate chivalric hero. Later, this image would unfortunately become so idealized as to strip him of most of his human characteristics, making him into an austere demigod.

The army had come to know its leader for his candor, sincerity, and kindly feeling for them. Whenever he appeared the camps buzzed with cries of,

"Here comes Marse Robert!" and men ran out to see him pass, saluting him with the rebel yell, or greeting him with a profound silence "expressive of the well-nigh religious reverence" with which many of them regarded him.

By this time, he had won their unquestioning faith. "We knew very well that he was only a man, and very few of us would have disputed the abstract proposition that he was liable to err; but practically we believed nothing of this kind," a Virginia soldier wrote. "Our confidence in his skill and his invincibility was absolutely unbounded."

"We loved him much, but revered him more. We never criticized, never doubted him," an artilleryman recalled. "The proviso with which a ragged rebel accepted the doctrine that 'the rest of us may have descended from monkeys, but it took a God to make Marse Robert,' had more than mere humor in it. . . . We never compared him with any other men, friend or foe. He was in a superlative and absolute class by himself."

Lee accepted this adulation with characteristic humility:

"I tremble for my country when I hear of confidence expressed in me. I know too well my own weakness & that our only trust is in God."

7

ROBERT carefully folded Mary's letter and, as was his habit, wrote on the upper corner of the back the date (since she almost never included it) and a brief summary of its contents;

then he took up the enclosure she had sent. It was a delight to read Markie's bold, clear hand after struggling with Mary's often illegible writing.

My dearest Cousin Mary [he read], Day before yesterday I went over to Arlington to endeavor to get from there my pictures and all of your things that I could take away. I took the furniture wagon for the purpose, and Aunt Brit accompanied me in the hack. The visit had been for some time a subject of sad contemplation, and I had written a note to the wife of the officer in command to say that we were coming. She did not receive it however, and the general was absent, so that I could not take anything. I saw what was there, however, and made an inventory of the things as well as I could.

Oh! what a sad, sad visit it was—so changed, so changed and yet so like itself, is the dear place. Where once peace and love dwelt, now, all the insignia of war is arrayed. Mrs. Whipple occupies *your* room, down stairs, as the parlor—In it is all the parlor furniture. . . . It presents a strange appearance and yet the surroundings are so familiar. . . . The garden is inclosed with a white washed fence and the roses and white jasmine were blooming as they used to in the happy days gone bye—Poor old Ephraim who tells me he has had the "typer fever". . . escorted me around the garden with the flower scissors—I walked in with tearful eyes, and gathered a bouquet.

As Robert read on, his eyes grew misty:

Uncle Ephraim said in an unusually loud tone, "Miss Martha, when you write Miss Mary please give my best love to her and all the family and tell her we miss them all very much indeed—These people does the best they can for us, but it ain't like those we was raised with." I saw the sentinel smile and tears rolled down my cheeks as I bid the poor old man good bye—Give Cousin R and all much love,

Ever your attached
M——

This little leaf came from the garden at A——

By now Mary had given up hope of returning to her home, but it concerned him that she proposed to rent a house in the capital.

I do not like you establishing yourselves in Richmond [he dictated to Custis]. It is a bad place for six unprotected women. . . . In the first place it will not be healthy, & second you will always be in the whirl of agitation & excitement. . . . Mildred I think had better go to school, & I know of no better one than at Raleigh. You had better fix her there at once. After that you had better endeavour to fix yourselves in some place more permanently. . . .

Once again he proposed Georgia: "Perhaps Mrs. Stiles can find some place near her which is far from danger and a healthy retreat; her society & that of her sisters I know will be a great pleasure to you." Knowing that his daughters were disposed to prefer "the whirl of agitation," he added:

"I know our little girls will think themselves banished from the world, but tell them that people manage to live there I know, and live happily and usefully."

He felt that his daughters should set an example of useful employment in home manufacture, and he often reminded them of their duty. "I don't like the idea of you fixing yourselves in Richmond," he repeated to Annie and Agnes. "I see no good you can accomplish there. You ought to be working out some good result, sewing, weaving, knitting for the poor soldiers."

But they were strong-minded, and determined at any cost to live in Richmond. Arrangements were made for Mildred to attend St. Mary's school in Raleigh, North Carolina, and her mother, Annie, Agnes, and a cousin, Ella Carter, escorted her there.

After leaving Mildred in Raleigh, they went on to the Jones Springs in Warren County. They had been there just a short time when Annie took sick. Her fever remained unbroken for nearly two weeks in spite of every effort to reduce it.

On October 19, her father wrote: "I hope my dearest Annie will soon be better again, & am glad that she has everything so comfortable about her. God grant that she may be relieved."

But before this letter reached them, Ann Carter Lee, his gentle Annie, was dead at twenty-three, fulfilling the tragic destiny of that name.

On October 20, Mary wrote courageously to Mildred:

"Your sister Annie left us this morning at 7 o'clock for a better world where her dear grandmama will be ready to receive her."

On the morning of October 26, the mail was brought to headquarters in the rocky encampment near Winchester, and the private letters were distributed first, as was the custom.

At the usual hour, Lee called in Major Taylor to consult about the business of the day, and when he had looked over the papers and given his orders, Taylor left. For some reason, he had to return within a few minutes, and with standard lack of ceremony, walked into Lee's tent unannounced.

He was shocked to see Lee overcome with grief, an open letter in his hands. Taylor immediately withdrew. He realized that the personal mail of the morning had brought news of Annie's death, but that Lee had with almost unbelievable self-control suppressed his grief until that moment.

In spite of unquestioning trust in the wisdom of God's ways, he was not easily reconciled to Annie's death.

I cannot express my dear Mary the anguish I feel. . . . To know that I shall never see her again on earth, that her place in our circle, which I always had hoped one day to enjoy, is forever vacant, is agonizing in the extreme. . . . I wish I could give you any comfort, but beyond our hope in the great mercy of God, & the belief that He takes her at the time & place best for her to go, there is none. [Crushed by his sorrow, he concluded:] I can write no more. The rest is pent up in my troubled thoughts.

At the end of the year he was writing to Daughter: "The death of my dear Annie was, indeed to me a bitter pang. . . . In the quiet hours of the night, when there is nothing to lighten the full weight of my grief, I feel as if I should be overwhelmed." He found some consolation in the birth of his second grandchild, a little girl sent, he felt, to fill "the aching void."

In November, before joining his army at Culpeper Court House, where he had sent Longstreet and the greater part of the cavalry under Stuart to check the enemy, Lee went to Richmond. He had a short visit with Charlotte and the baby, and with Mary and Agnes, who were staying with the Caskie family in their home at Eleventh and Clay Streets. Mrs. Ellen Caskie was related to Mary through Nelly Custis Lewis, though it was not until 1861, when they met again at the hot springs, that they became well acquainted. Now that the Lees were homeless, the Caskies asked Mary and the girls to stay with them, and Mr. Caskie, a wealthy tobacconist, offered to help Robert with his personal business.

The couple's only surviving child, Norvell, was an engaging young woman of buoyant spirits and intelligence, and became a great favorite of Robert's. Her company after his recent sorrow was helpful and an apparent stimulus, for after he reached Culpeper he began a sprightly correspondence with her, and each letter to Mary contained some playful message. The first one talked about sending a kiss by proxy:

"Tell Miss N. that I have scanned Major T. & T.'s faces with anxiety but they will not answer for my purpose. I could find nothing kissable in them. Perhaps I did not look at them with proper eyes."

Several days later, he had more on the same topic: "Tell Miss N. she must not recommend the Majors any more to me. When I look at them & think of her, nature revolts!"

Although the animated youth who passed himself off as a single man in order to reap unhampered the favors bestowed by pretty girls was gone, his appreciation of attractive women was in no way dulled. What he had written Jack Mackay a quarter of a century before was no less true, for he still met them "in no place, in no garb, in no situation" that he did not feel his heart "open to them like a flower to the sun."

Nor had he lost any of his appeal, for whenever he appeared socially the girls, to the chargin of their young admirers, flocked to his side to hold his hands, listen rapt to every word, and laugh at his jokes and teasing. He was gay and gallant with them, and enjoyed exercising his paternal prerogative of kissing these "daughters," many of whom he had known since they were babies. Nowhere but in their company could he find that complete escape from his personal sorrows and the daily routine.

As to his prerogative of kissing these girls, there was one instance that was never forgotten by the young man involved.

One day as Lee rode down Franklin Street to The Mess, he passed the Triplett house, and noticed Mary, soon to become a noted belle, seated on the front steps. Beside her sat a love-sick youth whose advances she was studiously avoiding. Taking the situation in at a glance, Lee dismounted, and climbing the stairs, bent down and kissed Mary. Then he turned to the suitor and said gravely:

"Wouldn't you like to do that, sir?" and went on his way.

He relished the love affairs of these young friends, and often involved himself in the dangerous pursuit of match-making. Frequently he suggested half-jestingly to the most attractive ones that they give serious consideration to Custis and Rob, each of whom he would gladly "save" for them.

However, his interest in their matrimonial prospects was not limited to the girls of his acquaintance, but included members of his staff and other officers whom he saw frequently. Occasionally he would speak of their love affairs in front of them, much to their surprise, for they did not suspect his interest.

He once asked a young officer who had just come back from a brief stay in Richmond, first about the health of his parents. Then he inquired:

"Did you see Miss ——?"

"No, sir, I did not."

"Did you see Miss ——?" Lee tried again.

"No, sir, I did not." Lee regarded him a moment in silence, then said drily:

"How *exceedingly* busy you must have been!"

On November 7, McClellan was superceded by Ambrose E. Burnside. The appointment created no apprehension in Lee's mind, since it was known generally that Burnside did not possess the capacity for an independent command. Lee regretted losing McClellan because, as he said to Longstreet:

"We always understood each other so well. I fear they may continue to make these changes till they find someone whom I don't understand."

It was soon evident that Burnside intended to vary the

87

route to Richmond this time, and go by way of Fredericksburg; so Lee ordered his army to Fredericksburg, and went there himself on November 20.

He arrived in the midst of a heavy rain at the headquarters Colonel Long had set up midway on the road between Hamilton's Crossing and Fredericksburg. Long had chosen this site at the edge of a wood because of a vacant house nearby, but Lee, as usual, insisted on staying in his tent.

During the snowstorm that followed, a lady from Fredericksburg thoughtfully provided him with a mattress, some preserves, and catsup; and Norvell Caskie sent a cake of her baking. In thanking Norvell, he said playfully: "I prefer kisses to cake."

He wrote Mary that he was able to keep "quite warm," but this brought no satisfaction, for he was worried about those men who were barefoot and poorly clad. The number of the former was so great that, in thanking Mary for a bag of socks she had knitted and sent, he admitted that his problem was not to find men in need of socks, but men "with shoes to put over them."

The death of his infant granddaughter, "that child of so many hopes & so much affection, & in whose life so much of the future centered," brought him more sorrow. He wrote to Charlotte:

"I can say nothing to soften the anguish you must feel, & I know you are assured of my deep & affectionate sympathy. . . . My horse is waiting at my tent door, but I could not refrain from sending these few lines to recall to you the thought & love of your devoted father."

Just before the army moved to Fredericksburg, Rooney, who had recently been promoted to the command of a brigade of Virginia cavalry, offered Rob the post of aide. But Rob did not accept until he had consulted Lee and secured his approval. Then, when he received his discharge from Jackson, he came to see his father, who gave him one of his swords, Grace Darling's daughter, and money to buy his outfit.

After the army reached Fredericksburg, Rob was able to see his father often, for it was his duty to report conditions on the front and flank. When there was time for a short visit, they would sit by the stove in the tent and talk about the family, about Rob and his horse, or the people and country where the cavalry was stationed. He always assumed correctly that his son was hungry, and he would ask his newly acquired white mess steward and personal messenger, Bernard Lynch, or Bryan, to fix something for him to eat. Rob noticed that his father always seemed to "brighten up" on his arrival.

As the fog slowly lifted on the morning of December 13, it revealed the Army of the Potomac drawn up one hundred thousand strong.

"It was a grand and beautiful sight; rarely is one more glorious vouchsafed to mortal eye," wrote Walter Taylor.

When the command to advance was given the Federals, a solid and regular line of blue moved steadily forward. Suddenly came the deafening roar and thunder of artillery, trembling the earth and wreathing the heights in smoke.

Lee was watching the enemy's rapid advance from his field headquarters set up next to Longstreet, and soon saw to his relief that the spirited charge was being reversed, and that from the woods ran bluecoats by the thousands, closely pursued by Jackson's veterans in butternut. The younger spectators on the hill cheered and slapped each other on the back, but Lee, struck by the dramatic quality of what might have been a pageant staged especially for their benefit, turned to General William Pendleton and said:

"It is well war is so terrible, or we should get too fond of it!"

A few moments later, a large Confederate cannon above them burst, and a piece weighing close to a third of a ton fell just beyond Lee and scattered dirt over him. He calmly turned and looked at the mass for a moment, then, without a word of comment, directed his attention again to the action below.

For two days, the Confederates waited vainly for a renewal of the battle, but on the morning of December 16 they found that Burnside had retreated.

"They went as they came, in the night. They suffered heavily as far as the battle went, but it did not go far enough to suit me," Lee wrote. "The contest will have to be renewed, but on what field I cannot say." Of the battle itself, he said:

"I was holding back all that day, & husbanding our strength & ammunition for the great struggle for which I thought he was preparing. Had I divined that was to be his only effort, he would have had more of it."

Since Burnside had obviously given up, the Army of Northern Virginia went into winter quarters. Lee's camp again "consisted of four or five wall tents, and three or four common ones" with nothing to indicate headquarters but the flag Walter Taylor chose to hang in front of his tent.

Pine branches were cut and piled against the tent walls to insulate them against cold, and bough shelters were built for the horses. There was a limitless supply of firewood from the forest, so that Lee and his staff were able to keep comfortable in an austere way.

In spite of the specter of starvation, which Lee recognized as his most formidable foe, he managed to keep cheerful, particularly when he turned into jokes his staff's complaints about the quality and quantity of the food. One morning when an aide commented on the unusual toughness of the biscuit, Lee told him:

"You ought not to mind that. They will stick by you the longer."

For his own supper he was content with plain boiled vegetables or cold sweet potatoes, and buttermilk to drink. On those rare occasions when there happened to be a roast of beef, ham, or mutton (of which he was especially fond), he would always refuse a second helping with the remark:

"I should enjoy another piece, but I have had my allowance."

In a letter to Mary he included a message to Charlotte who was sick, and grieving over the loss of her baby. It was calculated to bring a smile, but it unwittingly presented a picture of the Spartan life at headquarters:

"I am glad dear Chass is out of Richmond. I hope she will recover now. Tell her she must be very prudent, & whenever she eats think of her Pa'a & his military family at sunrise & at

90

dusk in the evg, with their tin plates & their tin cups freezing to their fingers out of doors, enjoying their beef & tough biscuit, & restrain herself."

One time during these lean days when Lee expected company, he asked Bryan to have as a special treat some middling bacon served with the boiled cabbage. When the main dish was set on the table, the piece of bacon was so small that every guest politely refused it. The next day, Lee remembered that the bacon had not been eaten, and asked for it. Bryan had to admit there was none, since he had borrowed it in the first place and had already returned it to the owner.

Another time when Lee invited a corps commander and one of his aides to dinner, the main dish was greens with bacon. Reposing in grandeur on a china plate was one slice of roast beef, sent to Lee by a lady. When Lee asked the general what he would have, he said greens and bacon; but when he asked the aide, he replied:

"Beef, if you please, General." Lee transferred the entire slice to his plate, and without qualm, the young man ate it up.

More than a year later, this same corps commander invited Lee to dinner. On the table was a whole roast of beef, along with several simpler dishes. When the host asked him what he would have, Lee looked directly at the same young aide, and said without rancor:

"I will thank you for a piece of beef, if Captain Smith does not want *all* of it."

During this winter, he carried on his usual teasing and joking with his staff. One morning, they saw a demijohn arrive at his tent, and immediately began to speculate on its contents—some fine old brandy, whiskey, or wine, perhaps. About noon, Lee came up and said:

"Perhaps you gentlemen would like a glass of something?"

They all accepted eagerly, so he asked Bryan to take the jug to the mess tent. The cork was drawn, the tin cups were filled and passed, but each man's face fell as he saw that his cup contained neither liquor nor wine but Lee's favorite drink— buttermilk. It was recalled, a little bitterly, that he was watching their reaction with evident amusement.

91

It seemed to his staff that they appreciated the gifts of food sent to Lee more than he did; he was the least fastidious eater among them and often, to their disappointment, sent delicacies to the hospital.

A small flock of chickens was a welcome present during this winter, for, in addition to providing good eating, Bryan found among them a laying hen whose daily egg he used for the General's breakfast. She proved to be a "very discriminating hen" since she selected Lee's tent in which to lay. Each morning she walked up and down in front of the door until all was quiet, then she would slip under his cot, lay her egg, and "depart with a gratified cackle." He appreciated her partiality, and cooperated by leaving the flap open for her.

When camp was broken for spring operations, Bryan found a place for her in the baggage wagon. For more than a year she campaigned with Lee's army, even into Pennsylvania. After the battle of Gettysburg, she could not be found, and since everyone at headquarters took a kindly interest in her, they organized a search. She was about to be counted among the casualties when Lee discovered her roosting contentedly in her accustomed place in the wagon—somewhere no one had thought of looking first. During the winter of 1864, she met an ignominious end in the stewpot, for she had by then grown fat and lazy, and once when Lee was expecting company for dinner, Bryan, at his wit's end, sacrificed her "on the altar of hospitality."

After the snow melted, many visitors came to headquarters. Gray-haired men tramped out to offer their "prayers for his health and happiness as the great leader of the South," prayers of which he admitted his need. "Aged ladies" rode out in delapidated carriages to greet him "with faltering expressions full of deep feeling and pathetic earnestness." Pretty girls with flowers, and little children clutching baskets of eggs and apples, or jugs of buttermilk, "received him with their brightest smiles."

Lord Hartington, Colonel Leslie, and Colonel Fremantle, all observers from the British army, came to see Lee, as did Francis Lawley, correspondent for *The London Times*. From the Prussian army came Justus Scheibert, a captain of engineers. He arrived early in April when Lee was just recovering from a severe sickness. When he received Scheibert's credentials, he was staying at the Yerby house but graciously invited the Captain to consider the headquarters tent his own, and to stay long enough to view the army and allow Lee to meet him. Scheibert stayed nearly six months, although he was shortly attached to Stuart's staff as a noncombatant. Lee found him highly intelligent, and had many serious talks with him on a variety of topics.

Near Fredericksburg lived some of Lee's relatives: the W. P. Taylors of Hayfield, and the Richard Corbins of Corbin Hall, at Moss Neck. Both places were highly attractive to him because of the number of ladies and children present. Staying with Mrs. Taylor were Mrs. Gwathmey and her troop of lovely daughters—connections of Mary's and Ellen Caskie's. At Corbin Hall was Mrs. Jane Corbin, whose husband was a private in the Virginia cavalry, their daughter of five, Jane Welch, and Richard's sister, Miss Kate Corbin.

Whenever Robert could spare an hour, he would ride over to either home, taking along one of his generals or staff. One afternoon, when curly-headed Janie Corbin with "her perfect unspoiled ways" climbed into Lee's lap for her usual kiss, she whispered that she would also like to kiss General Jackson. When Lee told Stonewall of the child's wish, that fierce warrior was observed "to blush like a school-girl."

Another time when the little girl came running to greet Lee, he said laughingly that she should select a younger man for her cavalier.

"Who?" she asked. Pointing to a young officer in a corner of the room, Robert said:

"There is the handsome Major Pelham!" He was also seen to "blush with confusion."

Christmas Day was mild and clear. Lee spent the morning writing to his family, of whom he had recently said:

"I constantly think of them & love them with all my heart. But what a cruel thing is war to separate . . . & destroy families & friends & mar the purest joys & happiness God has

93

granted us in this world. To fill our hearts with hatred instead of love for our neighbours & to devastate the fair face of this beautiful world."

He told Mildred, still at Raleigh: "My heart aches for our reunion. . . . You must write to me sometimes you precious child, without waiting for me to reply. I have little time for writing to my children. But you must be sure that I am always thinking of you, always wishing to see you." He also expressed his relief that "Genl Burnside & his army will not eat their promised Xmas dinner in Richmond today. I trust they never will."

He was gay with Charlotte as he sent word of Rooney's safety, teasing her for having married a young soldier instead of "an old 'exempt' " like himself, who would have loved her just as much.

But in his letter to Mary he hinted at the eventual failure of the cause which he felt would result from overconfidence on the part of the administration and the people, and their inability to face reality. The President and his Cabinet refused to recognize the superior power of the enemy in men, food, and munitions, and looked for their independence to be miraculously gained with an ever-dwindling supply of soldiers, arms, and supplies. As Jefferson Davis said:

"I cultivate hope and patience, and trust to the blunders of our enemy and the gallantry of our troops for ultimate success."

Lee took his Christmas dinner with Stonewall Jackson, who had also asked Generals Pendleton and Stuart with their staffs to his quarters in the plantation office at Corbin Hall. The incongruity of the ascetic Jackson's surroundings amused Lee, and he teased him about them. The Corbins, like most Virginia planters, were keen sportsmen, and the walls of the office were hung with traps and fishing tackle, animal skins and deer antlers; with engravings of famed race horses, of dogs of fine breed, and pictures of "game-cocks in bloody conflict."

Jackson was wearing the new trousers given him by admirers in the Valley, and the new uniform coat resplendent "with gilt buttons and sheeny facings and gold lace," a present from Jeb Stuart.

When the guests sat down to the table supplied by Mrs. Corbin with roast turkey and ham, and Jackson's waiter appeared in a white apron, Lee rallied him a good deal on what he called his "style," and suggested that if he wanted to know how *real* soldiers lived, he must come and have dinner with him. There was more joking when Stuart found the imprint of a fighting cock on the butter, and bemoaned this further indication of Stonewall's "moral degeneracy."

Mary, with Agnes and Charlotte, spent the holidays at Hickory Hill, where Orton Williams joined them. He brought Agnes a riding whip and a pair of gauntlets, which were her most cherished presents. Sometime during his stay, he asked her to marry him. Although there was much to recommend him, Orton had still not learned self-command. He was unpredictable, inclined to reckless ways and a fondness for drink.

Shortly before the battle of Shiloh, it was said that he had killed a young private in a quarrel over some breach of military discipline, of which Orton held strict ideas. This affair had made him so unpopular with the men that, in spite of his gallantry at Shiloh (for which he was twice mentioned in general orders), he had to transfer to another command. When he joined General Bragg's staff after this affair, it was as Lawrence Williams Orton, having taken the given name of his elder brother serving in the Federal army. His only surviving allusion to the change is found in the closing words of a letter written on December 19, 1862, to his sister, Markie: " . . . Your affectionate brother (I have changed my name), Lawrence Williams Orton."

As each of Lee's daughters did with her suitors, Agnes compared Orton with her father. It was a comparison by which any man would suffer ordinarily, but more so since Lee appeared to his girls "the splendid Hero," and all other men, "merc pigmies." This was perhaps the main reason none of them married.

Orton was rejected, as many another young man came to

be, and he left Hickory Hill, deeply hurt and bitter. As men often do after such an experience, he immediately turned to another woman for solace, asked her to marry him, and was accepted. It developed, however, that she already had a husband, with whom she was living, and she was regarded by Orton's family as "deranged."

The few hours that Lee passed at Hayfield and Corbin Hall were exceptional. The rest of his time was spent in hard work and worry, struggling against economic attrition. The short rations for man and beast kept him "miserable," he admitted. "I am willing to starve myself, but cannot bear my men & horses to be pinched. I fear many of the latter will die."

During this winter, while he was laboring so selflessly and with such dedication to fill up his ranks and obtain food and clothing for his troops, many of his officers and men thought he strongly resembled the Washington of tradition. He must have often looked to Washington's example for the courage to carry on his vain attempts to prod the administration into an awareness of conditions.

A glimpse of Jefferson Davis' purblindness was revealed by a remark he was fond of repeating to his wife:

"If I could take one wing and Lee the other, I think we could between us wrest a victory from those people."

Early in January, Lee was writing forcefully to War Secretary James A. Seddon about his need for men:

The success with which our efforts have been crowned, under the blessings of God, should not betray our people into the dangerous delusion that the armies now in the field are sufficient to bring this war to a successful and speedy termination.

While the spirit of the soldiers is unabated, their ranks have been thinned by the casualties of battle and the diseases of the camp. . . . The great increase of the enemy's forces will augment the disparity of numbers to such a degree that victory, if attained, can only be achieved by a terrible expenditure of the most precious blood of the country.

This blood will be upon the hands of the thousands of able-bodied men who remain at home in safety & ease, while their fellow citizens are bravely confronting the enemy in the field. . . .

96

Justice to these brave men, as well as the most urgent consideration of public safety, imperatively demands that the ranks of our army be immediately filled.

By this time, the private soldier had been reduced to a minimum, consisting, as a wag observed, of "one man, one hat, one jacket, one pair of pants, one pair of drawers, one pair of shoes (if he were lucky) and one pair of socks," all in a delapidated if not unwearable condition. Again and again, Lee called to the attention of the commissary general, Colonel Lucius Northrup, the fact that the present ration of "18 ounces of flour, 4 ounces of bacon of indifferent quality, with occasional supplies of rice, sugar, or molasses," was not enough to keep the troops in health and vigor during this inactive period. What then, he asked, were they to do during the coming campaign? But his pleas for men, clothing, and food were ignored.

Northrup was described by one who knew him as "a crotchety doctor," and believed by many of his friends to be insane. "Aside from his suspected mental aberration . . . he knew nothing whatever of the business belonging to the department under his control," wrote George Cary Eggleston.

Wholly without experience to guide him, he was forced to evolve from his own badly balanced intellect whatever system he should adopt, and from the beginning of the war until the early part of 1865, the Confederate armies were forced to lean upon this broken reed in the all-important matter of a food supply. . . . It was nothing to him that in the midst of plenty the army was upon a short allowance of food.

Jefferson Davis must have foreseen the disaster that would result from Northrup's "system." Yet he stubbornly refused to replace this man, solely because of his unwillingness to admit that he was guilty of an error in judgment in selecting Northrup for his post. By this single act of selfishness, Davis precipitated the Confederacy's fall.

"As far as I can judge at this distance, the proper authorities in Richmond take the necessities of the army generally very easy," Lee wrote bitterly. "What has our Cong: done to meet the exigency, I may say *extremity* in which we are placed. As far as I know concocted bills to excuse a certain class of men from taking service, & to transfer another class in service, out of active service where they hope never to do service." He must have often recalled that precept of Marcus Aurelius:

"Protest until you burst! Men will go on all the same."

In addition to his heavy official correspondence, Lee wrote personal letters of condolence to each friend and kinsman who lost a relative in battle. To every individual who had sent him a turkey, a mattress, gauntlets, a hat, or a pair of socks—so fine, he wrote the donor, that he intended to wear them some day without his boots—there was a note of appreciation. By no means least pressing were his private affairs; the foremost in his thoughts at this time was the freeing of Mr. Custis' slaves by the terms of his will.

He asked Custis to have all the manumission papers prepared: "Those that are hired out can be settled. They can be furnished with their papers & hire themselves out. Those on farms I will issue their free papers to as soon as I can see that they get support. The men could no doubt find homes but what are the women & children to do? . . . I desire to do what is right & best for the people."

During the opening months of 1863, he was worried because a few of them still had not been found, and asked his son to do all he could to locate and "liberate Harrison, Reuben & Parks." The future of two others, Seanthe and Jim, he considered with his usual thoroughness, deciding that it would be to their interest to stay with the lady for whom they were then working, so as to continue to draw wages—but this was to be "only if they choose." Mr. Caskie was helping in this matter, and Lee gave him his power of attorney.

As late as August of that year, he was worrying about the disposition of the Negroes at Romancokc (the name was now spelled this way). "Under the circumstances I think the best course to be pursued is to let those who can support themselves go with their families," he wrote Custis. "The old people can remain if they choose, cultivate their gardens, fowls . . . & I hope make a living. I do not know what else to do for them. . . . The men could get work in Richmond or in the army & draw their own wages."

Lee's act of liberating slaves while he was commanding an army that, according to Lincoln's proclamation of January 1, 1863, was fighting solely to preserve slavery, was paradoxical, and the irony of his position must have occurred to him. Most of the Negroes to whom he was issuing manumission papers were already freed by the Emancipation Proclamation, but he was not content until he had discharged his personal obligation to each one. Then he could say:

"I wish to close the whole affair."

His practical concern over the future of each of these people is in marked contrast to the attitude of the Federal administration and the abolitionist, each of whom, while espousing idealistic and abstract concepts of freedom, gave no thought to the *means* by which the Negro in his new status was to secure his daily bread, his clothing, and shelter.

Though Lee, in the recollections of his staff, usually kept his outward aspect of cheerfulness during this dark and inactive period, there were times when a despondent note would creep into his letters to Mary. He was again conscious of his health, which he termed "indifferent."

"I may be unable in the approaching campaign to go through with the work before me. . . . Old age & sorrow is wearing me away, & constant labour, day & night, leave me but little repose. You & I will have to find some spot, if that is possible, from which we shall be required to make one more journey."

In spite of his frequent allusions to his "constant labour, day & night," Mary tended to camplain about the intervals between his letters. He became a little impatient: "You forget how much writing, talking & thinking I have to do. . . . You lose sight also of those letters which you receive," he told her. Again when she complained about the infrequency of his letters, he reminded her:

"I see you are relapsing into your old error, supposing that I have a superabundance of time & only my pleasure to attend to."

It is not surprising to learn that his patience was often

easily exhausted and that his temper would rise at any petty annoyance during these trying months. From long experience, Walter Taylor knew Lee's dislike of "reviewing army communications. . . . I would never present a paper for his action, unless it was of decided importance, and of a nature to demand his judgment and decision." Once when he had not had an audience for several days, it became necessary to see Lee. As soon as Taylor entered the tent he saw that Lee "was not in a very pleasant mood," and while they discussed some matters of irksome character, Lee's neck and head began to give a little nervous twitch or jerk, a certain sign of bad humor, and his manner became harsh.

Concluding that his efforts to save Lee annoyance were not appreciated, Taylor got angry himself, and petulantly throwing down the offending papers, started to walk off. At the tent door Lee stopped him:

"Major Taylor, if I, with all the burdens of the army on my shoulders, should forget myself, I hope you will not forget yourself."

Chagrined at his hastiness, Taylor returned to the table and the business was finished amicably.

While he was accessible at all times, and kept an orderly in front of his tent only when he was not to be disturbed, his aides knew there were two kinds of audience he would refuse. One was with relatives or friends of soldiers condemned by court-martial, for "he could not bear the pain and distress" of their applications for reprieve or remission of sentence. In his kindliness he was always tempted to grant them, but knew how damaging this would be to discipline if he revoked the decisions of the judge advocate.

When officers wrote him of some injustice done them, he always turned their letters over to an aide with the order: " 'Suage him, Colonel, 'suage him," meaning that a diplomatic reply should be drafted. But he refused to be bothered with these complaints in person.

One day, however, a division commander came with a grievance and would not leave without an interview. He went into Lee's tent and stayed some time. Right after he left, Lee,

100

his face flushed, came into the adjutant's tent to demand hotly:

"Why did you permit that man to come to my tent and make me show my temper?"

The men's faith in Lee did not waver during this hard winter and they did not blame him for their privations. By now, his belief that the private soldiers, the men who, as he said, "fought without stimulus of rank, emolument, or individual renown" were the most meritorious class, and most deserving of respect and consideration, was understood by all.

Often when taking his daily ride on Traveller, he would stop along the way to talk to some "private soldier, grey-haired like himself. At such moments . . . a kindly smile lit up the clear eyes, and moved the lips half-concealed by the grizzled mustache. The *bonhomie* of this smile was irresistible, and the . . . private soldier, in his poor tattered fighting-jacket, was made to feel by it that his commander-in-chief regarded him as a friend and comrade."

One day he saw a private come up to his tent.

"Come in, Captain, and take a seat," Lee told him.

"I'm no captain, General; I'm nothing but a private."

"Come in, sir. Come in and take a seat. You ought to be a captain."

Just before a battle, Lee rode down the lines. He said nothing, but removed his hat as though in the presence of something sacred. After he had passed, a soldier with misty eyes turned to his companion and said:

"*That* was the most eloquent address ever delivered!" And another, who loaded his musket as he ran forward at the command to charge, shouted through his tears:

"Any man who will not fight after what Marse Robert said, is a damned coward!"

This love and reverence which he inspired in his men produced an invincible spirit probably unmatched by any other army. As one undernourished private said as he shook a ragged, empty sleeve:

"I did it for Marse Robert, and by God, I'd do it again!"

Napoleon wrote: "It is not men who make armies, but a man."

8

LEE'S victories had given impetus to the movement for European recognition of the Confederacy, particularly in Great Britain. But with the coming of January 1, 1863, Lincoln's Emancipation Proclamation precluded formal acceptance of the Confederate States by any nation that had espoused the abolition of slavery as long as England had done. Lee was the only Southern leader who fully appreciated the far-reaching effects of Lincoln's clever act of statesmanship, for he knew that wars are not won on battlefields alone.

At the start of the war he had met Bishop Joseph P. B. Wilmer, who asked him if he believed that slavery would be the issue. Lee said "yes," and that if the slaves of the South were his, he "would surrender them all without a struggle to avert this war."

As far as I have been able to judge [he wrote], this war presents to the European world but two aspects. A contest in which one party is contending for abstract slavery & the other against it. The existence of vital rights involved does not seem to be understood or appreciated. As long as this lasts, we can expect neither sympathy or aid. Nor can we expect the policy of any Government towards us to be governed by any other consideration than that of self interest. Our safety depends upon ourselves alone.

Jefferson Davis was unable to see that he had been masterfully outwitted by a skillful political move, and as late as July, 1864, he was still counting heavily on European recognition and aid.

Lincoln was no abolitionist, for it will be remembered that the slaves were not freed in all states but only in those states and parts of states * which were "in rebellion against the United States," but he had the sagacity to see that the Emancipation Proclamation would prevent that much-feared foreign inter-

* In Virginia this meant that slaves were not freed in "the counties of Berkeley, Accomac, Northampton, Elizabeth City, York, Princess Ann, and Norfolk, including the cities of Norfolk and Portsmouth."—Lincoln

vention in behalf of the Confederacy, and at the same time give the war an issue that could be easily understood.

Though the morale of the Army of Northern Virginia had every reason to be low during this winter of privation and cold, Lee found that its spirits had never been so high since he had taken command. Toward the end of January when the snow was deepest, the troops waged a great snow fight. There were four or five thousand on a side, with generals in command, their staffs leading brigades, and colonels and majors leading regiments. When riding down the battle lines, several miles long, officers had to withstand the bombardment of frozen snow balls, often thrown with such force as to break an arm or leg, or draw blood.

One morning, General Law's brigade came three miles to make a surprise attack on General Jenkins. Jenkins's men had no ammunition prepared, so they "were right badly used up," a soldier wrote. But the next morning, Jenkins had his men up at daylight, and with their haversacks filled with frozen balls, they stole up on Law's brigade while it was cooking breakfast.

With the eerie "who-who-ey! who-who-ey! who-ey!" of the rebel yell, they drove Law's men out of camp, took over their huts, and ate up their breakfasts.

Part of the fight took place just outside Lee's tent. "He came out to see it, and found much difficulty in protecting himself from the balls, which made the air white. He was struck several times."

Lee did his part to keep up morale by maintaining his cheerfulness, and lost no opportunity to joke and tease his officers and staff. One day, General Hood came along when he and Colonel Chilton were discussing the difficulty of keeping soldiers from stealing pigs and burning fence rails. Hood seemed to feel called on to defend his troops against such charges. Lee listened in silence, then remarked drily:

"Ah, General Hood, when you Texans come about, the chickens have to roost mighty high."

On January 20, a bitterly cold day, Rooney's cavalry brigade held a review. Lee rode over to see it and was pleasantly surprised to find a number of ladies had come in spite of the weather. Mrs. Gwathmey and her pretty daughters had driven over in a four-mule wagon, and Robert gave each of the Misses Gwathmey "a kiss for their Aunt Ellen & Cousin Norvell."

During this winter, a great religious revival swept through Lee's army, and then spread to the other armies of the Confederacy. Many believed it was due directly to Lee's influence and example. It was noticed how many of the "openly sinful" grew more temperate in speech and "reverent in their regard for things religious"; that there was less swearing and profligacy, and that gambling at cards was greatly reduced. Most commands held regular worship services, and nightly before tattoo the woods resounded for miles with the "unscientific but earnest music" of Lee's veterans singing hymns and revival songs. Lee took a great interest in the spiritual awakening and gave it encouragement by attending prayer meetings and church whenever he could.

On January 19, 1863, scouts brought reports that Burnside was preparing to advance, so Lee made ready to meet him. But on the twentieth, a rain storm which lasted all night and the next two days turned the roads into mires that held up the passage of Federal troops, wagons, and artillery. One lad in blue remarked to his companion:

"This looks like a funeral procession stuck in the mud."

"I'm afraid we shall never get this *corps* along in season for the resurrection morning!" quipped the other.

> Genl Burnside's designs have apparently been frustrated either by the storm or other causes & he last Sunday took a special steamer to Washn to consult the military oracles at the Federal seat of Govt. Sunday I heard of his being closeted with President Lincoln, Sec. Stanton, & Gen. Halleck. I suppose we shall have a new program now next week [Lee wrote].

He felt that Burnside had played "a shabby trick, running off to Washn while we were waiting for him."

The new program included a new commander. Burnside was superceded by General Joseph ("Fighting Joe") Hooker, a good administrative officer though not considered capable of independent command. With bombast that echoed strongly of an unsuccessful predecessor, he told his troops that the "enemy must either ingloriously fly or come out from behind his defences and give battle on our ground, where certain destruction awaits him." He spoke confidently of the Confederate Army being "the legitimate property of the Army of the Potomac. They may as well pack up their haversacks and make for Richmond, and I shall be after them."

Lee was unable to predict what Hooker would do first, "for they keep very close & we cannot get within their lines to discover their movements." To Custis he wrote telegraphically:

We have mud up to our eyes. River very high. Enemy seems very strong in our front. Cannot as yet ascertain what he is going to do, unless it is to remain where he is, till better weather, then push his columns now at Newport News up the James River, thus cause us to fall back. . . . Seems to be his best plan. Must try & defeat it. To do this will require our regiments to be filled up. Can you devise any plan to get laggards out?

Meanwhile Hooker, as Lee told Agnes, was "playing the Chinese game. Trying what frightening will do. He runs out his guns, starts his weapons & troops up & down the river & creates an excitement generally. Our men look on in wonder, give a cheer & all again subsides 'in statu quo ante bellum.' "

Two weeks later, he was complaining: "I owe Mr. F. J. Hooker no thanks for keeping me here in this state of expectancy. He ought long ago to have made up his mind what to do." And while he waited, he admitted to being "so cross now I am not worth seeing anywhere."

By the year 1863, there were few veterans who did not have occasion to report home about the embarrassing condition of their trousers, and Lee was no exception. "I am in my last pair, & very sensitive, fearful of an accident," he wrote. As soon as he learned that some good cloth "to be applied to the necessities of this Army" had been received in Richmond, he asked Custis to have a pair of trousers made for him, and included his usual exact instructions:

"They have my measure at the clothing Bureau, or any one can measure you, increasing all the horizontal measures around, girth, hips, &c. I like the legs full, & so cut as to spring over

105

the boot. Please have them made at once & sent to me, with or without stripes on seams as circumstances may render convenient."

Although he was offered a new overcoat at this time, he refused it, for he was making his "old Blue" serve him "yet awhile."

He was deeply concerned about the scarcity of clothing for his men, but he did not take his daughters' complaints about their shortages in this line very seriously. When Mildred wrote him about her slim wardrobe, he asked Mary:

> What can be done for her? I have some socks & other garments with which I can supply her & can lend her a long pair of boots that cover up a great deal of space. She could hang over them some drapery which would make her comfortable. I think she will have to come up to the army where we are accustomed to short commons every way, & scant wardrobes are fashionable.

Someone brought him reproductions of portraits of Stonewall Jackson and himself by a foreign painter. He was amused at his picture, and sent both on to Mary with a spirited note:

> I send you Mrs. Lee a likeness of your husband that has come from beyond the big water. He is a hard favored man & has a very rickety position on his pins. I hope his beard will please you, for the artist seems to have laid himself out on that. We are poor judges of ourselves & I cannot therefore pronounce as to his success. But I can say that in his portrait of Gen. Jackson he has failed to give his fine candid & frank expression, so charming to see & so attractive to the beholder.

Near the middle of March, Lee was called to Richmond for a consultation with the President, and managed a visit with Mary and Agnes, still with the Caskies. He teased Norvell this time about her considering Rob as a suitor and kept up the banter by mail after his return to camp.

Shortly after he returned to his headquarters, he came down with what he termed a "violent cold." He was certain that he had caught it in Richmond from either "going in or coming out of a warm house, or perhaps both." The virus settled in his chest, was accompanied by fever and "an annoying cough," and subjected him to paroxysms of sharp pain in his back, chest, and arms.

The doctors advised immediate removal from the tent; although Perry had "entrenched" him, his quarters were still subject to floods, and the floor was, as he described it, in "a fluid" state. A room was found for him at the Yerby house, about a mile from camp. Here the doctors examined him thoroughly, tapping him all over "like an old steam boiler," he wrote. They pronounced him "tolerable sound" though threatened with some malady which he concluded must be "dreadful" if it remotely resembled the name—which he had forgotten. They found symptoms of "inflammation of the heart-sac," which suggests a cardiac disorder having its origin in what was probably a streptococcic infection.

In the Yerby house, whose owner reminded Lee of Sir Charles Grandison, the hero of the Richardson novel, he occupied the smallest bed in a large room that held three beds. He offered the two canopied four-posters with valances to Custis and Agnes, both of whom had written that they were coming to see him. When their visit was postponed because Agnes accepted a "pressing invitation" from friends, her father wrote in disappointment:

"You would have soon made me well, for you could have taken all my pills, &c. & so kept the Drs off me."

But when she did come, he warned, she must bring none of her friends: "You must leave your troops behind you. I am too weak to stand the knocks & bruises they occasion. My pins are remarkably unsteady at this time & the vigour & violent movements of young women might knock them from under me."

As soon as the days grew warmer, he was allowed to go out: "I am able to ride out every day, & now that the weather has become good, I hope I shall recover my strength. My pulse is still 90, the Drs say too quick for an old man, but I hope fresh air & exercise will reduce it some."

Word of his sickness soon spread, and every day some present of food was brought to his room—turkey, ham, tongue, butter, eggs, apples, sweet potatoes, tea, and sugar, were a few that he listed in letters to Mary. In addition, Mr. Yerby's

107

daughter regularly augmented his dinner with a bowl of nourishing soup, a custard, or some delicacy. He felt that it might
do to remain ill.

Mr. Caskie invited him to recuperate at his home, and
though he admitted that the thought of being waited on by
Norvell was most appealing, he believed he should not be so
far from his headquarters. He worked each day until midafternoon on official papers.

There were three refugee families from Fredericksburg
staying at the Yerby house, among them a number of pretty
girls who attracted many beaux, so the house was always full.
For years, Lee had shunned crowds of strangers or those with
whom he had nothing in common. His sickness gave him a good
excuse to keep to his room and have Perry serve his meals, for,
as he confessed to Agnes:

"You know how pleased I am at the presence of strangers,
what a cheerful mood their company produces. Imagine then
the expression of my face & the merry times I have."

He was soon suggesting to the doctors that he move back
to his tent, but they refused to allow him to go until the weather
settled. By April 16, the days had become milder and he returned that day to his camp. After his arrival, he wrote to Mary
that he felt "feeble & worthless & can do but little," and was "oppressed by what I have to undergo for the first time in my life."

Still, he could write with fine contempt of "Mr. F. J.
Hooker's" methods:

The enemy is making various demonstrations either to amuse
themselves or deceive us, but so far they have done little harm.
Last week they infested all the fords on the upper Rappak as far
as Warrenton Springs. Tuesday they abandoned them. Sent down
the river their Infy & Arty & with their Cavy swept around by
Warrenton toward the Blue Ridge as if intending to visit the
Valley. Day before yesterday they made their appearance on the
lower Rappak. Formed in line of battle, threw out skirmishers,
advanced with their Arty, brought up their wagons, built up large
fires, & after dark commenced chopping, cutting & sawing as if
working for life till midnight, when the noise ceased & at daylight
all had disappeared but 8 or 10 men keeping up the fires. I suppose

they thought we were frightened out of all propriety & required refreshment . . . Yesterday morn at daylight a party crossed at Port Royal in the Pontoon boats, stole from our citizens all they could get, & recrossed before we could get them. These expeditions will serve as texts for the writers of the Herald, Tribune, & Times for brilliant accounts of grand Union victories & great rejoicings of the saints of the party.

Mr. Cowell, a Richmond photographer, came into camp at this time. Lee agreed to have his picture taken if Jackson would, and sent Cowell up to the Yerby house, where Stonewall was then visiting with his wife and baby daughter, Julia. Mrs. Jackson persuaded her husband to have his picture taken, so the photographer then set a time for Lee. But Robert insisted that the notice of the appointment reached him too late: his horses were grazing on the hill, and by the time one was saddled, he would be unable to reach the Yerby house in time. "My portrait I think can give pleasure to no one & should it resemble the original would not be worth having. Get the portraits of the young, the happy, the gay," he wrote with a tinge of sadness.

On the morning of April 29, Hooker began to move in earnest and crossed the Rappahannock just below the mouth of Deep Run. With the prospect of action, Lee's spirits rose and to one of Jackson's aides who rushed up with the news that the enemy was crossing in heavy force on his front he said gaily:

"Well, I *heard* firing, and I was beginning to think it was time some of you lazy young fellows were coming to tell me what it was all about. Say to General Jackson that he knows just as well what to do with the enemy as I do."

Since both armies were maneuvering into position and throwing up defenses, the fighting that day and the next was limited to skirmishes.

On the morning of May 1, Lee and his staff rode over to a ridge close to Chancellorsville, a settlement that consisted only of the Chancellor mansion and its dependencies, and set up field headquarters. After studying the reports of his engineers and scouts, he decided against an attack from the front, for the enemy was well protected by the woods and covered with artillery. He sent Major Jed Hotchkiss, Jackson's topo-

109

graphical engineer, to see if there were a feasible route around Hooker's right flank. His report and map satisfied Lee that it was practicable, and he called in Jackson, for he had selected him to make this movement—a movement that was to establish for all time Stonewall's reputation as "the supremest flanker and rearer" in the world.

During the meeting, it was noticed that Lee displayed "buoyant confidence" in the plan and that both men seemed "never more ready for a fight." When the council ended, Jackson rode off to his camp and Lee stretched out on the ground at the foot of a pine tree and, using his saddle for a pillow, went to sleep. The night was clear and cold, and he had only his overcoat as a covering.

He had been sleeping just a short time when he was wakened by the coming of Captain James Powers Smith of Jackson's staff. Smith had just returned from a reconnaissance and was looking for Stonewall. Lee sat up and beckoned to him:

"Ah, Captain, you have returned, have you? Come here and tell me what you have learned on the right."

As the young man took a seat beside him, Lee passed an arm around Smith's shoulders and drew him near in what seemed to Smith "a fatherly way that told of his warm and kindly heart." After listening to his report, Lee thanked him and then began to joke with him.

When Smith left, Lee continued his banter with those officers lying near him, and even after the scout had ridden into the pine thicket toward his camp, he could hear the sound of Lee's "hearty laughter" that "again and again broke upon the stillness of the night."

When Smith reached his camp, he found Jackson sleeping without a blanket. He took off his cape and laid it over him. But Jackson wakened once in the night, and finding the cloak, removed it and covered Smith. When Stonewall rose at dawn, he had a chill. A cold resulted from his exposure, and doubtless predisposed his system for the fatal attack of pneumonia that followed his wounding on May 3.

Colonel Long brought the shivering Jackson a cup of steaming coffee and, while the two stood close to the campfire, talking, Stonewall's sword, which he had propped against a tree, suddenly fell clattering to the ground. Long picked it up and Jackson buckled it on; but the Colonel was deeply impressed by this ill omen and never forgot it.

On the night of May 2, the whippoorwills sang "so long and so loud" as to almost banish sleep in the pine thicket where Lee and his staff were bivouacing. When Captain Wilbourn of Jackson's staff rode into the camp around two-thirty A.M. to report that Stonewall was wounded, he saw Lee rolled up in his blankets on the ground. Wilbourn gave the report to Walter Taylor but their voices wakened Lee. He listened quietly as Wilbourn told about the Confederate victory, but when the captain began to relate how their own men had fired on Jackson, believing that he and his party were Federals, Lee moaned aloud, and Wilbourn saw tears fill his eyes.

"Ah, Captain," he interrupted, "any victory is dearly bought which deprives us of General Jackson even for a short time."

When Wilbourn, into whose arms Jackson fell as he reeled from his saddle, began to give details, Lee stopped him:

"Don't talk about it—thank God it is no worse!"

After the interview, Lee got up and put on his boots. He wanted to ride over and talk with Jeb Stuart, who had taken temporary command of Jackson's Second Corps. As he buttoned up his coat, he told Wilbourn, who had been through the day's fighting and had spent all night in the saddle, to help himself to a basket of food sent him by a lady; when Wilbourn hesitated, Lee opened the hamper and set it out for him. After he had eaten, Lee told him he must get some sleep.

Just as Lee was going to mount Traveller, a messenger came with another report. He listened with interest until the courier started to tell him the story of Jackson's wounding.

"I know all about it, and do not wish to hear any more," he interrupted, "it is too painful a subject."

When he reached Stuart's position, he rode to an eminence from which he could watch the battle. At the crisis, when the balance could swing either way, Captain Scheibert of the Prussian Army joined him and noticed that Lee was within range of enemy fire. His complete calmness astounded the German, and when Lee turned to him and began to discuss in that "sententious" way "which made all his utterances peculiarly forceful" the subject of popular education of the future, he was further astonished at his ability to ignore his surroundings.

Later in the day when Lee rode over to Hazel Grove, Major Heros von Borcke, another German on Stuart's staff, was also impressed with Lee's composure:

"I found him with our twenty-gun battery, looking as calm and dignified as ever, perfectly regardless of the shells bursting round him and the solid shot ploughing up the ground in all directions."

This apparent insensibility to danger did not arise from the temperamental indifference or disregard of its existence that some stolid persons are known to possess. Lee was highly sensitive. At all times, he must have been keenly aware of the perils and the confusion. This faculty of keeping apart from the distractions of his environment was not new, but it was none the less remarkable. In a conversation with a nephew right after the war, Lee said:

Necessary noise never troubles me. In the midst of battle, for instance, with the roar of artillery and musketry around me; midst the screaming and bursting of shell and whistling bullets, and amid all the noise and hub-bub of such an occasion, I could sit on my horse, attend to my duties and write a despatch or other papers, undisturbed by what was going on. . . .

He also talked of his daily rides on Traveller:

When I got on my horse . . . no matter what battle or movement was impending, and no matter what my cares and troubles were, I put all such things out of my mind and thought only of my ride, of the scenes around me, or of pleasant things, and so returned to my work refreshed and relieved and in a better and stronger condition. If it had not been for this power, I do not see how I could ever have stood what I had to go through with.

During the morning of May 3, Lee learned that the Confederates had taken Chancellorsville. When he reached there about noon, he saw the tangled wilderness in which the fierce battle had been fought enveloped in flame, and the victorious yelling soldiers in gray driving before them the superior forces of the enemy. As Lee "with full staff, galloped to the front," he was recognized by his men. At the sight of him "the troops were transported with the wildest excitement." They waved their hats and greeted him with "tumultuous shoutings."

Lee was moved by this ovation, and "lifted his hat, taking it by the crown with his right hand and holding it suspended above his majestic head." Then his men shouted:

"What a head, what a head! See that glorious head! God bless it, God bless it!"

As Charles Marshall looked at him "in the complete fruition of the success which his genius, courage, and confidence in his army had won, I thought that it must have been from some such scene that men in ancient days ascended to the dignity of gods."

Someone who witnessed this scene imagined the pride and sense of triumph Lee must be experiencing.

"Does it not make the General proud to see how these men love him?" an observer asked one of Lee's staff.

With an insight into his commander's soul, he answered: "Not proud. It awes him."

When the fighting was over, Lee's first concern was to have the wounded of both armies removed from the danger of fire. A courier found him in the midst of the confusion and handed him a note from Jackson. He was unable to open it with his gloved hands, and gave it to Charles Marshall, asking him to read it aloud.

It had been found necessary to amputate Jackson's left arm, Marshall read. Stonewall minimized his operation, and congratulated Lee on the important Confederate victory.

"I shall never forget the look of pain and anguish that passed over his face as he listened," Marshall recalled. "With a voice broken with emotion he bade me say to General Jackson that the victory was his, and that the congratulations were due him."

While Marshall wrote this message, giving "expression to the thoughts of his exalted mind," he "forgot the genius that won the day" in his "reverence for the generosity that refused its glory."

On May 5, Lee gathered his forces at Chancellorsville, to deal Hooker the *coup de grâce*, but as was the way with Federal generals who had had enough, he had left. Under cover of a dark and stormy night, Hooker had withdrawn across the Rappahannock, so when General Pender's skirmishers advanced that morning they found the woods empty.

When it was reported to him that the enemy had escaped without further punishment, Lee was angry:

"That is the way you young men always do. You allow those people to get away. I tell you what to do, but you don't do it!" he told Pender.

With considerable warmth of manner he commanded:

"Go after them and damage them all you can!"

Lee's concern for Jackson, for whom "he held a great affection," was deep. It was noticed that he seemed on a closer footing, and to unbend more with Stonewall than with other generals, and that their councils were more like meetings between loving brothers. Jackson, in turn, considered Lee a "phenomenon. He is the only man whom I would follow blindfold!"

Lee looked forward with customary optimism to Jackson's recovery. When Beverley T. Lacy, Jackson's chaplain, brought the news on May 7 that Stonewall had developed pneumonia, Lee was unwilling to believe that this portended the worst. He sent Jackson his "affectionate regards," and said to Lacy:

"Tell him to make haste and get well, and come back to me as soon as he can. He has lost his left arm, but I have lost my right arm."

On May 10, a beautiful day, the Reverend Lacy held worship under the trees at Hill's headquarters. The text of the sermon, "We know all things work together for good to them that fear God," was an appropriately hopeful one. Though it was reported that Jackson was delirious and, in his mind, wandering over the battlefields, Lee still refused to give up hope. He said to Mr. Lacy after the service:

"When you return I trust you will find him better. When a suitable occasion offers, give him my love, and tell him that I wrestled in prayer for him last night, as I never prayed, I believe, for myself."

The Virginianism "give him my love" was used only when

114

two men were "closely and firmly bound by long association and friendship."

That night, a courier came with word that Jackson was dead. A sob shook Lee when he heard. He had not believed it possible for "God in His wisdom and mercy to take him at such a time."

"It is a terrible loss. I do not know how to replace him," he wrote Custis the next morning.

On Monday, Captain Douglas of Jackson's staff was sent to Lee by officers of the Stonewall Brigade to ask if he would permit the Brigade, or part of it, to escort Jackson's body to Richmond.

He received me kindly [Douglas wrote], listened patiently, and then in a voice gentle and sad replied: "I am sure no one can feel the loss of General Jackson more deeply than I do, for no one has the same reason. I can appreciate the feelings of his old brigade; they have reason to mourn for him, for he was proud of them. I should be glad to grant any request they might make to show their regard for him. . . . But it cannot be. Those people over the river are again showing signs of movement and I cannot leave my headquarters long enough to ride to the depot to pay my dear friend the poor tribute of seeing his body placed upon the cars. . . . He never neglected a duty while living and he would not rest easier in his grave if his old brigade had left the presence of the enemy to see him buried.

Then his eyes filled with tears, and he went on in a low voice:

"Tell them, Captain, how I sympathize. Tell them that deeply as we all lament the death of their General, yet if his spirit remains behind to inspire his corps and the whole army, perhaps in the end his death may be as great a gain to us as it is to himself."

9

LEE'S spirits were resilient. When it was rumored that Major von Borcke, the great German whose warmth and gaiety had won so many hearts in Richmond, had been killed at Chancellorsville, Governor Letcher asked Lee to have the body sent to the capital to lie in state. Lee was amused, for von Borcke was in the best of health, and replied laconically:

"Can't spare it! It's in pursuit of Stoneman!"

His mood was still gay after his return to the camp at Hamilton's Crossing, and he teased Norvell about her navy beaux whom Smith Lee had sent to sea. He pretended to envy his brother because he was an "*Iron clad*, safe in his position & able to get about & enjoy himself," for Smith was now an admiral, and chief adviser to Confederate Naval Secretary Stephen Mallory. And he wrote brightly about the "delights of camp":

"I had a nice basket of strawberries sent me last evg. & this evg. I am invited to eat ice cream. See what enjoyments we have."

He sent messages of love to all his favorites, and the promise of a lock of hair to one girl provided she would not laugh at the gray in it. And he even found amusement in the attempts of the Northern press to twist the Federal defeat into a great victory:

"It will be incomprehensible news to those engaged in the battle," he observed drily.

There was little time to indulge his high spirits, for as soon as the army returned to its old camp near Fredericksburg, he had to reorganize and plan for the coming campaign. His most perplexing problem was the replacement of Jackson. As he said to General Hood:

"I agree with you in believing that our army would be invincible if it could be properly organized and officered. There were never such men in an army before. They will go anywhere if properly led. But there is the difficulty—proper commanders. Where can they be obtained?"

Although Richmond had become untenable almost as soon as the Federals had seized the York and James Rivers, the administration insisted that its defense be of prime consideration. This attitude caused Lee to say many a time that "Rich-

mond was the millstone that was dragging down the army."
Once again, the safety of the Confederate capital would have
to be the nucleus of his plans.

To divert the enemy, to draw him off as he had done in
the Maryland campaign, suggested itself as the most logical
way to relieve the capital and provide rations and forage for
his army.

"I considered the problem in every possible phase, & to
my mind, it resolved itself into a choice of one or two things—
either to retire to Richmond & stand a seige, which must
ultimately have ended in surrender, or to invade Pennsylvania,
penetrating the State in the direction of Chambersburg, York,
or Gettysburg," he wrote later.

He would be forced to assume the offensive, and by bold
maneuvering, pry the Federals from the Rappahannock, thus
"relieving the Valley of the presence of the enemy & drawing his
army north of the Potomac," and enabling the Army of Northern Virginia to enter the rich farming centers in enemy
territory.

While he was working out the details of the plan, he was
called to Richmond for a conference with the President. At a
Cabinet meeting, Lee presented his plan for an invasion of the
North, and it was approved by everyone but the postmaster
general.

He stayed three days in the capital, and visited Mary, still
with the Caskies. It grieved him to find her in "so helpless &
suffering a state" (she would soon be confined to a "rolling
chair"). At her request, he put on his full-dress uniform, called
at Mr. Minnis' studio, and submitted to what he termed the
"ordeal" of having his picture taken. The result was a little
austere, for as Rob once said:

"My father could never bear to have his picture taken, and
there are no likenesses of him that really give his sweet expression."

After his return to camp, he was still distressed by thoughts
of Mary's condition and wrote Agnes that she and her sisters
must take good care of themselves: "You girls have no time to

117

be sick. You have a sacred charge, the care of your poor mother." He urged Mary to try the mineral springs in the summer but could do no more than pray for her relief.

The plan for invasion was now fully matured, the details worked out with the corps commanders. Lee's only opposition came from Longstreet, who was convinced that his own scheme —to reinforce General Bragg in Tennessee with troops detached from Lee's army and then to defeat Rosecrans—was superior. He clung to his idea and argued with Lee as though Lee were the subordinate. Since he had imposed his will on Lee at Second Manassas, he expected to do so again. When he found Robert firm, he acquiesced, although he seemed determined to make Lee see the weakness of his plan for invasion by contributing to its failure.

The army was ready by June 1, and to one observer it appeared "the best disciplined, the most highly spirited, and enthusiastic army on the continent." On the second, Ewell's corps, preceded by Stuart and the cavalry, left for Culpeper Court House; and on the seventh, Lee arrived there.

The next day, a cavalry review was held in his honor. He was in high spirits, and declared afterward that it had been "a splendid sight. The men & horses looked well. They had recuperated since last Fall. Stuart was in all his glory."

The young women of Culpeper had put a garland of flowers around the neck of Jeb's charger, and when he rode up beside Lee, Robert teased:

"Take care, General Stuart! That is the way General Pope's horse was adorned when he went to battle at Manassas!" Then with a laugh, he touched the spurs to Traveller's flanks and the generals were off at a gallop past the front line of cavalrymen. Without a pause at the end of the three-mile line, they turned and raced back again.

At the blast of a bugle, the cavalrymen then passed the reviewing stand; first at a walk, then at a trot, and finally, a full gallop. Many of Hood's men were present, looking on with the infantryman's usual contempt for the mounted soldier:

"Wouldn't we clean 'em out if old Hood would let us loose on 'em?"

118

During the dash past the stand, the hats and caps of the charging column would often blow off, and before the owners could retrieve them, the Texans bore them off in triumph.

An ambulance in which a number of girls were seated was drawn up near Lee. Several times he had looked toward it, as if to say something, but turned away again. But when the horse artillery came up, he asked an officer next to him to go and "tell that young lady with the blue ribbon in her hat" that a certain battery was coming. When the message was delivered, the girl blushed, and "there was a universal shout, while the General looked on with a merry twinkle in his eye."

He was pleased to see Rooney "on his black charger & Rob by his side," and to find that both sons were "well & flourishing." He was amused that his nephew Fitz Lee was not in the saddle, "but sitting by some pretty girls in a carriage." He was supposed to be suffering from rheumatism in the knee, his uncle reported.

On this ground the next day, just such charges would be made in earnest, following a crossing by Federal cavalry at Beverly's Ford. The battle lasted until after dark, when Stuart, with the assistance of Rodes' division, drove the enemy back over the Rappahannock.

During the fighting, Rooney was wounded in the leg and his father came on him as he was being carried from the front. After the battle, Lee went to see his son and could report that he was "comfortable & cheerful." He was relieved to learn that neither the bone nor the artery was injured. "He is young & healthy & I trust will soon be up again," he wrote.

The next day, Rooney was moved to Hickory Hill, where Charlotte had converted the plantation office into a sickroom. Rob, as his aide, was to stay with him until his wound was healed; and his mother and sisters, Agnes and Mildred, came up from Richmond to help nurse him.

I am so grieved, my dear daughter, to send you Fitzhugh wounded [Lee wrote tenderly to Charlotte]. But I am so grateful that his wound is of a character to give us hope of a speedy recovery. . . . As some good is always mixed with the evil in this world, you will now have him with you for a time, & I shall look

119

to you to cure him very soon & send him back to me, for though I saw him seldom, I knew he was near. . . . I want all husbands in the field, & their wives at home encouraging them, loving them, & praying for them.

The Army of Northern Virginia moved at noon on Monday, June 16, and by three o'clock on the morning of the twenty-fifth was ready to cross the Potomac at Williamsport. Awaiting Lee's arrival on the Maryland shore was a committee of ladies, all smiles and flowers, though the spokeswoman had been inopportunely chosen, if one accepts the verdict of an officer who claimed that she had "a face like a door-knocker." As Lee rode up the bank, she presented him with a wreath for his mare's neck (he was riding Lucy Long, as he usually did on extended marches), and introduced the committee. He received them graciously, but refused to have his horse adorned with flowers. Since the ladies were crestfallen, he asked a courier to carry the wreath, and "smiles then returned to all faces."

The crossing of the river by our troops was very picturesque [a witness wrote]. General Lee was on the bank on the Maryland side surrounded by the ladies who came down to see the sight and to admire him. The soldiers waded into the water without stopping to roll up their pantaloons and came over in good order as if on review, cheering at every step.

"Well, boys, I've been seceding for two years and now I've got back into the Union again!" said one soldier as he stepped on Maryland soil.

But there were not only smiles and flowers awaiting the troops. From those who were loyal to the Union, there were the same hard, sullen looks as there had been the year before, although this time the women failed to curse the Confederates.

Leighton Parks, a boy of eight or nine, had watched the troops pass by the previous autumn. Now he climbed up to his perch on top of a rail fence to see them again. This time, he marveled at their numbers, hosts of them, it seemed, as day after day an unbroken line passed due north. At night, the rumble of their wagons kept him awake. He noticed that the men were better clad than they had been when on their way

120

to Sharpsburg, and in even better spirits, for they had about them the air of men accustomed to conquering. Flags were flying, and the bands were playing "Dixie," "Maryland, My Maryland," "The Bonnie Blue Flag," and "The Girl I Left Behind Me." He recalled that the Yankees liked to march to the latter song, too.

Soon after the troops came into town, Dr. Doyle, the father of a friend of Leighton's, was asked to meet with General Lee and allowed his son to invite Leighton to go with them. The doctor was a huge man who completely filled the gig, so the boys had to sit behind on the springs.

Along the Williamsport pike, they came up with Lee. He was dressed, Leighton noticed, in blue trousers of summer cloth, worn tucked into his Wellington boots, a checked shirt, a gray jacket with three stars on the collar, and a high felt hat. He was standing beside Lucy Long, whom a courier held, and had an open map in his hand.

The doctor drove right up and announced himself, and Lee walked over to the gig; leaning on the shaft, he put his head under the hood. He thanked Dr. Doyle for having come so promptly, and then questioned him about the roads and the countryside.

Did the Cavetown pike cross the mountain? What sort of crossing was it? Could cannon be easily brought over it? His right flank then, was protected by the Blue Ridge until he reached Gettysburg? Were there good roads running to the river west of the one on which he now stood? Could artillery be moved over them? Was the valley well wooded and watered all the way to Gettysburg?

Suddenly he became aware of the two boys looking at him attentively through the back curtain of the gig.

"Doctor, are these boys yours?"

"One of them is. The other is the son of Dr. Parks. You must have known his father in the old army."

Both youngsters were then called up and introduced, and Lee, pointing to Lucy Long, asked them:

"Would you boys like to get on that horse?"

121

Leighton was an especially observant lad and, when it was his turn to ride the mare, noticed that Lee kept his pistol in the holster on the left of his saddle, and the bullets in the right one.

In the excitement of riding General Lee's horse, the boys' attention was diverted from the conversation they had overheard, which had been Lee's purpose in making the suggestion.

The next forenoon, Master Parks rode a borrowed horse out to Lee's headquarters in a hickory grove, three miles above Williamsport. In one hand, he carefully carried a basket of raspberries, a present from his mother to Walter Taylor, whom she had known since childhood. Soon after his arrival, Lee came riding in with Longstreet, Ewell, and A. P. Hill.

After Lee had dismounted, Taylor led Leighton up to him, saying:

"General, this gentleman has brought me some raspberries, and I have asked him to take a snack with us."

Lee smiled pleasantly, and said: "I have had the pleasure of meeting your friend before," and leaned over to kiss him.

When Lee removed his hat, the boy saw that his hair was almost entirely white and he recalled then that he had heard his family say that Lee had aged considerably since they had seen him last.

After lunch, the company went to sit in Lee's tent, and Robert took Leighton on his lap, talking with him in that winning way he had with young people, until he was interrupted by business. Then as the boy slipped from his knees, General Hill beckoned him to come to his lap. In a few minutes, Longstreet grumbled:

"Come, Hill, you've had him long enough; pass him over."

But the pleasant interlude ended when Lee came up and said: "Well, gentlemen."

Then Taylor whispered to Leighton that the visit was over. He stood up, gave his thanks, bowed, and said good-by, and Hill called to a servant:

"Bring the Captain's horse!"

This presented a problem, for Leighton was accustomed to mount with the help of a fence. But he was determined to keep up appearances, and while an orderly held the bridle, Master

Parks stretched his leg, touched the stirrup with his toe, then slipped and sat down hard on the ground. Staunchly, he rose and was about to try again when he felt himself lifted lightly into the saddle. He turned and saw that it was Lee, who smiled at him and said:

"Give him time, he'll do for the cavalry yet."

Lee left this camp in a torrential rain the next morning, and when he rode into Hagerstown, where the greater part of the people were Union in sympathy, he was surprised to find a delegation of ladies out to meet him. A cavalry officer who watched them greet Lee and present him with flowers thought that they "seemed overcome with their emotion." One young woman took the courage to ask him for a lock of hair. He refused with the excuse he normally gave—that she would laugh at his gray hairs—and suggested that she apply to one of the younger officers, indicating Pickett and Longstreet.

Other women had defied the storm to display their hostility. One girl, who stood on her front terrace waving a miniature stars and stripes, drew attention to herself because of her comeliness. The soldiers looked at her in admiration, but refrained from audible comment, "offering no insult to the flushed beauty as she flaunted her flag in their faces," one officer wrote. But when General Lee rode by, "his noble face and quiet, reproving look met her eye, and the waving flag was lowered. For a moment she looked at him, and then, throwing down the miniature banner, exclaimed audibly, as she clasped her white hands together,

" 'Oh, what a magnificent man! I wish he was ours!' "

Once again Lee issued strict orders against straggling, maltreatment of citizens, and pillage. Private property was respected to such an extent that no man was "allowed even to go into a yard to get water without permission of the owner." All supplies were to be procured by the quartermaster and commissary, and paid for in Confederate specie. The British observer, Colonel Fremantle, testified as to the strict observance of the orders:

"I saw no straggling into the houses, nor were any of the inhabitants disturbed or annoyed by the soldiers. . . . To one

123

who has seen, as I have, the ravages of the Northern troops in Southern towns, this forbearance seems most commendable and surprising."

It was impossible to control every man, and there were a few cases of individual pillaging that prompted Lee to issue a message in which he congratulated the troops on their deportment but reminded them of their duty and reputation. He was unable to excuse his foe for waging war on noncombatants and was outspoken in his condemnation:

The commanding general [he told his soldiers] considers that no greater disgrace could befall an army, and through it our whole people, than the perpetration of the barbarous outrages upon the innocent and defenseless, and the wanton destruction of private property that have marked the course of the enemy in our country. . . . It must be remembered that we make war only on armed men, and that we cannot take vengeance for the wrongs our people have suffered without lowering ourselves in the eyes of all whose abhorrence has been excited by the atrocities of our enemy, and offending against Him to whom vengeance belongeth, without whose favour and support our efforts must all prove in vain.

The people of Chambersburg were loyal to the "old flag," which they displayed everywhere. The windows and porches of their houses were filled with women and children "covered with flags," while others waved the stars and stripes over the troops as they passed, or under their very noses, often accompanying these demonstrations with caustic comment.

The soldiers generally exercised forbearance, but occasionally one would respond with some equally sharp retort, or a bit of sarcastic humor. To one citizen who said of Lee:

"What a big neck he has!" a passing Confederate replied loyally:

"Yes, it takes a damn big neck to hold his head."

A Virginia infantryman was overheard telling a bold-looking girl who had a large flag draped over her shoulders and bosom:

"Look here, Miss, you'd better take that flag off!"

"Why should I?"

124

"Because, Miss, these old rebs are hell on breastworks."

Lee camped for five days in a grove along the Gettysburg pike. One afternoon, Mrs. Ellen McLellan, a Chambersburg woman, came to ask him for the release of flour, since all mills and stores were in Confederate hands. When she told him that some families would starve unless they got bread and flour, he explained that the only reason he had turned the supplies of food over to his men was to keep them from ravaging homes. In order to know how much wheat to release, he asked her to send a miller to see him.

Mrs. McLellan was impressed with Lee's courtliness and his magnanimity, and "the strength and sadness of the man." As she left, she asked for his autograph.

"Do you want the autograph of a rebel?"

"General Lee, I am a true Union woman, and yet I ask for bread and your autograph."

"It is to your interest to be for the Union, and I hope you may be as firm in your principles as I am in mine," he told her.

He said it might be dangerous to possess his autograph, but he finally gave her one and then quickly changed the subject to the cruelty of war and his desire to be able to return home and eat his own bread in peace.

Lee now learned of the change in Federal commanders. "Fighting Joe" Hooker had been replaced by General George Gordon Meade. Lee expressed surprise that a change would be made at this critical time, but believed it would prove advantageous to the Union cause. When an aide asked for his opinion of his new opponent, he said:

"General Meade will commit no blunder in my front, and if I make one he will make haste to take advantage of it." If he felt any misgivings, he kept them to himself.

His chief concern was the absence of intelligence concerning the enemy's movements. Stuart had been ordered to make the cavalry's movements correspond with those of the Federal army, and to report all important information. But instead of maintaining his proper position between the two armies, Jeb had, in his anxiety to gain more glory by some further bold raid

(Stuart was now famed for his raids), carried his men beyond their range of usefulness by gaining the enemy's right flank and severing his communications with Lee.

As a result of Stuart's action, two Confederate armies invaded Pennsylvania. "One of those armies had little cavalry, the other had nothing but cavalry. One was commanded by General Lee, the other by General Stuart." There were many officers and men who felt that Stuart was this time "overdoing the sensational."

Lee expressed some concern at Stuart's prolonged absence, and a good deal of annoyance at his silence, complaining that he had been "kept in the dark ever since crossing the Potomac." His information was so scant that when he reached Chambersburg he was under the impression that the Federals had not yet crossed the Potomac. Not until the night of June 28, when one of Hood's scouts reported to him, did Lee know that Meade had reached Frederick.

This knowledge necessitated a rapid concentration of the army, and before dawn the next morning orders were issued for an immediate junction. On the thirtieth, the united Confederate forces and the Army of the Potomac were both moving toward Gettysburg.

That night Lee and Longstreet camped at an abandoned sawmill near the western base of South Mountain, and the next morning, July 1, as they were climbing the slope, they heard firing from the east. Lee was very uneasy, for he was ignorant of the enemy's position as well as conditions on his own front. He at last became so disturbed that he left Longstreet and galloped on to Cashtown.

Here he met A. P. Hill, who told him that Heth's division was in advance, and he suspected that they had met the enemy; he volunteered to investigate. Within a short time, Lee received an urgent message from Hill asking for reinforcements, for he was engaged with two Federal corps.

Anderson's division had by then reached Cashtown, and Lee sent for Anderson, hoping he might have some information.

I cannot think what has become of Stuart. I ought to have heard from him long before now [Lee told Anderson]. He may have met with disaster, but I trust not. In the absence of reports from him, I am in ignorance as to what we have in front of us here. It may be the whole Federal army, it may be only a detachment. If it is the whole Federal force, we must fight a battle here.

But Anderson could tell him nothing, so Lee ordered him on to relieve Hill and then galloped off toward Gettysburg. He reached the field near the close of the fighting, and was relieved to find the Union forces being driven off after a heavy loss.

Had Lee not been moving blindly, he would never have continued along a route that was going to lead him headlong into Meade's entire army, for it was his stated intention upon reaching Pennsylvania to maneuver, to alarm the enemy, threaten his cities, and hit him any swift blows he could deliver without risking a general battle. Toward autumn, he intended to return to his former base.

But battles are frequently the offspring of chance and accident, and unforeseen circumstances often combine to force a fight or change its course, and set at naught all plans and calculations. The battle of Gettysburg, above all others, is a prime example of those elements of luck and error, and the moods and caprices of men, which dictate the result. Stuart's failure to keep Lee informed forced the battle, and Longstreet's unwillingness to obey orders and arrive at the appointed time contributed materially to its loss. Many men and officers believed that Longstreet was solely responsible for Lee's failure to win the battle. As one observer commented:

Gettysburg was not lost by Lee's defective strategy or any errors in tactics, but only because he suffered his second in command to *argue* instead of march.

Longstreet was so certain he had the superior plan for the battle that he attempted on two consecutive days to force it on Lee. When it was not accepted, he sulked, and deliberately delayed his attack, hoping that by being slow he could compel Lee to change his mind.

After the war, Lee told Governor John Lee Carroll of Maryland that "the battle would have been gained if General Longstreet had obeyed the order given to him and attacked early instead of late."

127

Later, Lee ascribed its loss to "a combination of circumstances. It was commenced in the absence of correct intelligence. It was continued in the effort to overcome the difficulties by which we were surrounded, & it would have been gained, could one determined & united blow have been delivered by our whole line. As it was, victory trembled in the balance for three days."

Lee was certain who could have delivered that determined and united blow—Stonewall Jackson. Not long before Lee died, he was discussing the war with his cousin Cassius and told him that if Jackson had been at Gettysburg, they would have gained a great victory, "for Jackson would have held the heights which Ewell took on the first day."

When Stuart finally reached Gettysburg on July 2, Lee greeted him coldly:

"Well, General Stuart, you are here at *last!*"

But for Longstreet's disobedience there was no rebuke at all, though there is ample evidence that Lee was irritated by the delay.

"What *can* detain Longstreet! He ought to have been in position now," he said impatiently to Colonel Long on the morning of the second.

He felt that if he could find Longstreet, he could hasten him, and asked Colonel Walker, Hill's artillery chief, to guide him.

"As we rode together," Walker wrote, "General Lee manifested more impatience than I ever saw him exhibit upon any other occasion; seemed very much disappointed and worried that the attack had not opened earlier, and very anxious for Longstreet to attack at the very earliest possible moment."

Many general officers saw Lee pacing up and down at his positions of observation, noted that his forehead was flushed and his temple veins swollen, those certain signs of bad humor. Even the imperturbable Longstreet admitted:

"The General is a little nervous this morning. He wishes me to attack; I do not wish to do so without Pickett. I never like to go into battle with one boot off."

There are two reliable references to the possibility that

128

Lee was suffering from camp diarrhea at Gettysburg. It may have been that he did not feel well enough to discipline Longstreet. Yet Lee seemed singularly inept at all times to cope with Old Pete's fits of sullenness and obdurateness. One who knew Lee well wrote that he "had a reluctance to oppose the wishes of others, or to order them to do anything that would be disagreeable and to which they would not consent"—admirable for a country gentleman in his relations with his friends and neighbors, but not compatible with the character of a revolutionary leader.

Because of Lee's excessive consideration for the feelings of his subordinate commanders, his reluctance to impose his will over theirs, and his solicitude for their reputations, his claim to perfection as a military leader has to suffer. There were countless times when he was known to "sit down pretty hard" on offenders, and speak so frankly and even harshly that his words were withering. But this inability to deal forcefully *at all times* with refractory and overbearing officers, allowing them to impose their will on his, must be acknowledged a weakness. But inconsistency is only human.

On the morning of July 2, General Hood watched Lee walk up and down in the shade of some large trees. His coat was "buttoned to the throat, sabre belt buckled round the waist, and field glasses pending at his side." Every now and then Lee would halt, raise his glasses, and look at the enemy. "He seemed full of hope, yet at times buried in thought."

That afternoon, an aide was impressed by his composure as he looked at Lee sitting quietly on a tree stump on Seminary Ridge. Occasionally, he would get up and say a few words to his staff, then sit down again and turn his field glasses toward the wooded heights opposite. He admired the defiant spirit of a Confederate band playing waltzes and polkas in the midst of the most furious cannonading, but was at most times "thoughtful."

But to Captain Scheibert, who had also been observing Lee closely, he did not appear collected. The "quiet self-possessed calmness" that had so impressed him at Chancellors-

129

ville was missing. Lee "was not at his ease," he wrote, "but riding to and fro, frequently changing his position, making anxious inquiries here and there, and looking careworn."

On July 3, when Lee saw that Pickett's attack was failing, he rode Traveller forward unaccompanied—which he could have done only at express orders—to join E. P. Alexander with the artillery. It was Alexander's impression that Lee believed the enemy might pursue, and that he had purposely left his staff and couriers behind so that he could, without interference, rally the stragglers about the guns, and personally lead "a desperate defense."

"No soldier could have looked on Pickett's charge and not burned to be in it," Alexander wrote. "To have a personal part in a close and desperate fight at the moment would, I believe, have been at heart a great pleasure to General Lee." He thought that Lee seemed "calm and self-possessed."

But what turmoil of thought and emotion must have seethed beneath that calm exterior as he realized the extent of the disaster and watched the men pass in complete disorder. He knew then that this was the turning of the tide, knew that never again could he muster so powerful an army, knew that he could only delay but not avert the coming ruin.

When Colonel Fremantle saw him a few minutes later, he found him "perfectly sublime," and noted that his face was as usual "placid and cheerful" and that he exhibited not the slightest sign of "disappointment, care or annoyance." The Englishman also observed with what remarkable detachment Lee turned his attention to Lieutenant Colston of Alexander's staff, reproving him for what seemed a needless cruelty to a frightened and balky horse:

"Oh, don't whip him, Captain, don't whip him. I've got just such another foolish horse myself, and whipping does no good."

Lee then rode on down the slope, stopping frequently along the way to talk to the soldiers in that "grave, kindly voice," assuring them:

"All this will come out right in the end. We'll talk it over afterward."

He spoke sympathetically to the badly wounded, many of

whom "removed their hats and cheered him," while to those who could make their own way to the rear, he said:

"Come, bind up your hurts and take a musket, my son."

Only the most demoralized failed to answer his appeal. Their confidence in him was unshaken. Fremantle overheard many saying to one another:

"This day's work will do him no harm," and "Uncle Robert will get us to Washington yet, you bet he will."

The scene recalled to some the tales of the battle of Monmouth when George Washington, mounted on his white charger, had rallied his broken troops, "cheering them by his voice and example." That day Lafayette had written: "Never had I beheld so superb a man." This day another foreign officer said of Lee:

"He was perfectly sublime."

But when Lee urged Fremantle to take cover from the Federal fire, he revealed a glimpse of those troubled thoughts masked by composure.

"This has been a sad day for us, Colonel, a sad day," he said. Then recollecting himself, he added more cheerfully:

"But we can't always expect to gain victories."

Gettysburg was the supreme test for all the years of practice in self-mastery, and Lee emerged victorious. When Pickett, overcome by the disaster to his men, sobbed: "I have no division left!" Lee laid his hand on his shoulder and said gently:

"General, they did nobly; it is all my fault."

When General Wilcox, who was "almost crying," as Fremantle noticed, attempted to describe the condition of his brigade, Lee took his hand and said quietly:

"Never mind, General, all this has been *my* fault. It is *I* who have lost this fight, and you must help me out of it the best way you can."

When Lee rode by a wounded Federal prisoner lying on the ground not far from Cemetery Ridge, the soldier recognized him and shouted:

"Hurrah for the Union!"

Lee heard him, and dismounting, walked over to the boy, who stated afterward he was sure the General intended to kill him. Lee looked down at him sadly, extended his hand, and grasping the other's, said:

"My son, I hope you will soon be well."

In Lee's mind there was no choice now but retreat. He wrote Mary from Bunker Hill:

The army has returned to Va. . . . Its return is rather sooner than I had originally contemplated, but having accomplished what I proposed in leaving the Rappak viz: relieving the valley of the presence of the enemy & drawing his army north of the Potomac, I determined to recross the latter river. The enemy after concentrating his forces on the front, began to fortify himself in his position, bring up his local troops, militia &c.—& all those around Washington & Alexa. This gave him enormous odds. It also circumscribed our limits for procuring subsistence for men & animals which with the uncertain stage of the river, rendered it too hazardous for us to continue on the north side.

The night of July 3, Lee called on A. P. Hill, whose Third Corps he had selected to lead the retreating column, and they held a long council over a map. It was past midnight and bright moonlight when Lee rode Traveller back to his camp. General John Imboden had been ordered to wait for him and was the only witness to the agony of spirit that had finally mastered him.

When Lee reached the encampment, Imboden noticed that he was so exhausted he had trouble dismounting, and that when he reached the ground he leaned heavily against his horse, threw one arm across the saddle, and with his head bent slightly and eyes fixed on the ground, stood in silence. "The moon shown full upon his massive features, and revealed an expression of sadness that I had never before seen upon his face," Imboden wrote.

He walked up to Lee and said sympathetically:

"This has been a sad day for you, General." Lee looked up startled, as though aware of Imboden for the first time, and replied mournfully:

"Yes, it has been a sad, sad day for us."

Then he relapsed into his reflective mood and attitude. Imboden was reluctant to intrude, so kept silent, busy with his own thoughts on the course of the day. He was therefore startled when after a minute or two, Lee straightened up to his full height, and with "an unusual excitement of manner" said in "a voice tremulous with emotion":

General, I never saw troops behave more magnificently than Pickett's division of Virginians did today on that grand charge upon the enemy. And if they had been supported as they were to have been—but for some reason not explained to me, were not—we would have held the position they so gloriously won at such a fearful loss of noble lives, and the day would have been ours.

There was another lapse into silence while Lee relived his moment of exultation as he watched his Virginians make that heroic assault through a deadly hail of shot and shell and, with a fierce yell, leap the enemy's breastworks and plant their standards on the captured guns. He saw the enemy close in on every side when Pickett's reinforcements failed to come, and concentrate all his guns on that gallant band. And he saw those Virginians, unable to withstand the withering fire, break, and fall back, and then stream by him in confusion. He recalled all the fury, the tears, and the savage irony of those moments.

Suddenly the stillness was rent with Lee's cry of anguish as he addressed not Imboden, certainly, nor any man, for the agony of his soul carried him into the infinite:

"Too bad! *Too bad!* OH! TOO BAD!"

10

THAT night when the men went into camp, many unashamedly "shed tears at the way in which our dreams of liberty had ended," and when the dead were buried the next day, it was with more care and reverence than usual.

On July 4, Lee's army concentrated on the hills west of Gettysburg and offered battle, but the Federals fired only a few random shots, indicating, as a cavalryman wrote to his wife, "that we had so punished the enemy . . . they were incapable of an advance."

During the day, Lee issued an address to his troops. It

was described by one soldier as "beautiful" and in marked contrast with the "apologetic bombast the yankee generals pour out to their own troops after a repulse. He does not claim a victory, takes all the blame on himself." With warmth and sincerity he thanked the men for their gallantry, which he knew would assure their success in the future.

Details for the retreat were completed this day, and written orders were issued to prevent errors. At nightfall, the withdrawal began. The ordinary difficulties were increased by a heavy rain which commenced shortly after noon. But as one cavalryman wrote:

"The army did not feel at all like a beaten one. There was no rout or confusion; not even a pursuit to remind us that our invasion had come to an end."

Another soldier told his wife: "There is not the least resemblance of a retreat except that we are counter-marching . . . and Lee's orders about depredation are as well obeyed, as when we were advancing."

Lee was quick to suppress any talk that might undermine morale. When he overheard an officer say that he hoped the other corps were in as good condition for work as his was, Lee asked him coldly:

"What reason have you, young man, to suppose they are not?"

On July 6, the army reached the north bank of the Potomac. The heavy rains had swollen the river, and Lee sent his aide, Charles Venable, to investigate the crossing at Williamsport. Venable found the river too high for fording, and the pontoons all swept away. It seemed to him that the army was trapped.

He reported this to Lee, talking loudly in his excitement. Lee reprimanded him sternly for speaking of such important matters in a voice that any passing soldier could overhear. Venable was offended and stalked off angrily.

When Lee's anger had cooled, he invited Venable to drink a glass of buttermilk with him. Although Venable came, Lee sensed that he was still hurt. When the crossing was made a week later, Venable, who had been without sleep for forty-eight hours, threw himself on the wet ground to snatch a little rest.

Near dawn, Lee found him lying uncovered in the rain. Lee dismounted, and taking off his rubber poncho, laid it gently over his aide. When Venable awoke and realized what Lee had done, his resentment vanished. All his life he cherished this act of thoughtfulness.

Lee's willingness to assume all the blame did much to bolster morale. "It's all my fault, I thought my men were invincible," he told Longstreet. And later he wrote that he had "expected impossibilities" of them.

It took four days to build a pontoon bridge at Williamsport. One soldier described it as "a crazy affair" while another termed it "first-rate." It was improvised from pieces of old warehouses and damaged pontoons swept away in the flood, and covered with brush to muffle the tramp of feet and rumble of wheels.

Just before dawn on July 14, Lee, who had been personally supervising the crossing, rode over to the southern shore to help clear the bridge. As he watched the bulk of the rear guard pass over safely, he "uttered a sigh of relief, and a great weight seemed taken from his shoulders. Seeing his fatigue and exhaustion, General Stuart gave him some coffee; he drank it with avidity, and declared as he handed back the cup, that nothing had ever refreshed him so much," wrote John Esten Cooke of Stuart's staff.

Just the knowledge that they were once again on Southern soil—"home in dear old Virginia"—gave wings to the army's spirits, and they could better bear the ceaseless rain and the mud. Lee was able to report: "Our noble men are cheerful & confident."

In order to relieve them, he sent back into Maryland for shoes and clothing, and for horseshoes for the cavalry mounts, since almost half were unserviceable on this account.

The press and the stay-at-homes were displeased with the results of the invasion, and eager to find fault with the way it had been conducted. To find a scapegoat for the loss of the battle, general after general was accused and put on the rack.

Lee loyally defended each one, and publically assumed all responsibility for the failure. He even refused, in his official report, to mention Stuart's disappearance or Longstreet's delay, as this would seem to lay blame on others.

Charles Marshall, who wrote out the first draft of Lee's reports, tried to convince him that certain statements, no matter how damaging, were essential to the accuracy of a report. But Lee told him that he "disliked in such a communication to say aught to the prejudice of others, unless the truth of such statements had been established by an investigation in which those affected by them had been afforded an opportunity to defend or justify their actions."

"He often struck out observations of mine on subjects that aroused my liveliest interest and excited my feelings," Marshall wrote, "saying in a playful way, 'Colonel, if you speak so strongly of this you will have nothing left to say of something better.'"

The official report of Gettysburg was accurate as far as it went, but in Marshall's opinion it did not go far enough, for Lee insisted on eliminating "many statements which he thought might affect others injuriously, his sense of justice frequently leading him to what many considered too great a degree of leniency . . . he assumed the entire responsibility of the issue of the battle of Gettysburg, and thus covered the errors and omissions of all his officers."

It was noticed by those close to Lee that he was more than usually cordial with Longstreet, in order to make it clear that he held no resentment and had no sympathy with the mounting wave of blame directed at Old Pete. With Marcus Aurelius he reasoned:

"Another's error—let it lie. If a man mistakes, reason with him kindly. If you cannot prevail, blame yourself or no one."

It is possible that Lee may have written at this time his observations on the responsible use of power. While in Texas, he had started writing down his philosophic concepts; many of these notes were found in his army satchel after his death.

The forbearing use of power [he wrote] does not only form a touchstone, but the manner in which an individual enjoys certain advantages over others is a test of the *true gentleman*. The power which the strong have over the weak, the magistrate over the citizen, the employer over the employed, the educated over the unlettered, the experienced over the confiding, even the clever over the silly—the forbearing or inoffensive use of all this power or authority, or total abstinence from it when the case admits it, will show the gentleman in a plain light. The gentleman does not needlessly & unnecessarily remind an offender of a wrong he may have committed against him. He can not only forgive, he can forget; and he strives for that nobleness of self & mildness of character which impart sufficient strength to let the past be but the past. A true man of honour feels humbled himself when he cannot help humbling others.

Before he left Pennsylvania, he received a letter from Mary and one from Eliza Stiles. Mary's contained the disquieting news that Rooney had been snatched from his sickbed by a body of Federal cavalry and taken to the prison hospital at Fort Monroe. Bitterly, Mary wrote how the Yankees had searched the house and office for important papers, had turned out the contents of every drawer, cabinet, and closet, from attic to cellar. But far worse was their mistreatment of Charlotte's grandfather. As Robert read this, his own words, "We make war only on armed men!" must have returned to him forcefully.

By the time he replied, his anger had cooled and he could view it all objectively:

We must expect to endure every injury that our enemies can inflict upon us & be resigned to it. Their conduct is not dictated by kindness or love, & therefore we should not expect them to behave otherwise than they do. But I do not think we should follow their example. The consequences of war is horrid enough at best, sur-rounded by all the amelioration of civilization & Christianity. Why should we aggravate them? I am sorry for the injuries done the family at Hickory Hill & particularly that our dear old Uncle Williams in his 80th year should be subjected to such treatment. But we cannot help it & must endure it.

From Eliza's letter he learned of the death of her daughter, the beautiful Mary Cowper Low, who had not survived the ordeal of premature childbirth. On July 25 from his camp set up near Culpeper, he wrote Eliza a tender note:

My thoughts have been with you ever since I left Penna. I grieve, deeply grieve, over your irreparable loss. But your loss is mine too, for your sweet child was as dear to me as my own daughter. I know your anguish & know how to sympathize with you. . . . May He give you strength & support in your great affliction. . . . With sincere love to all your family, I remain

Truly & affy yours,

R E Lee

At dusk on the "hot, murky night" of June 8, two superbly mounted Federal officers rode up to the tent of Colonel John P. Baird, U.S.A., at Fort Granger, near Franklin, Tennessee. The elder and taller of the two introduced himself as Colonel Lawrence Auton (or Orton, Baird was not sure) of the Army of the Potomac, and his companion and assistant, Major Dunlop. They were on an inspection tour of Western troops, and had just come from General Rosecrans in Murfreesboro. Since they had to push on to Nashville that night, Auton asked Baird to have their passes made out.

While they waited, Auton told how near Eaglesville they had been attacked by rebels who had taken their servants and money. Could Baird lend something for their immediate expenses?

Baird did not have enough money, so applied to Colonel Carter van Vleck, who had been smoking outside his tent and looking on in incredulous silence. He told Baird he did not think the men were what they claimed to be. Although Baird scoffed at the suggestion, when he gave Auton fifty dollars he asked to see their papers. They were in order; their instructions were directly from War Secretary Stanton. Baird then wished them well, and saw them on their way regretfully, for he had taken a fancy to Auton and was disappointed that he could not accept his invitation to stay overnight.

After they were gone, Baird thought for the first time about forgery and sent Colonel Louis Watkins to bring them back on any pretense for questioning. He also sent a telegram to Murfreesboro, asking for identification of the two officers.

"There are no such men as Insp. Gen. Lawrence Orton (or Auton), Colonel U. S. Army, and assistant Major Dunlop, in

138

this army, nor in any army, so far as we know. Why do you ask?" James A. Garfield, Chief of Staff, replied.

When Auton was shown this telegram, he readily admitted that he was Colonel Lawrence Orton, C.S.A., originally Williams, at one time an aide on General Scott's staff. His assistant was his cousin, Lieutenant Walter Peter. This news was then sent on to Garfield, who replied:

"The two men are no doubt spies. Call a drumhead court-martial tonight and if they are found to be spies, hang them before morning, without fail. No such men have been accredited from these headquarters."

The officers assembled quickly in the headquarters tent for the midnight drumhead court-martial, the swiftest and most terrible of law courts. The prisoners were brought in, and there began one of the strangest trials on record: the trial of men accused of being spies, though they had made no attempt to gain any information, had asked no questions, had not looked at the works; men who had on them no plans of fortifications or other incriminating evidence; men who had nothing to condemn them but an intent that would never be known.

Orton and his cousin insisted they were not spies, and many members of the court, including Baird, were convinced they were "not spies in the ordinary sense." They told the court they were on a mission to Canada and Europe. What its nature was Orton alone knew but refused to reveal.

The trial lasted barely an hour, and both men were condemned to hang.

Baird was most sympathetic and made a last-minute effort to save them. He and Orton wrote an appeal for clemency to General Rosecrans, who had known Orton's father well. But no answer was ever received.

Both prisoners asked permission to write letters, and when paper and pens were brought, Orton said to Markie:

"Do not believe that I am a spy; with my dying breath I deny the charge. Do not grieve too much for me. . . . Altho I die a horrid death I will meet my death with the fortitude becoming to the son of a man whose last words to his children were, 'Tell them I died at the head of my column! . . . "

139

The final letter was to the woman he was planning to marry:

"When this reaches you I will be no more. Had I succeeded I would have been able to marry you in Europe in a month. The fate of war has decided against us. I have been condemned as a spy—You know I am not. . . ."

What Orton's mission was will probably never be known. It was presumed by most Southerners that it was undertaken on his own account since no one possessed or admitted knowledge of it. It is more likely that he was working under direct orders from Judah P. Benjamin, to whom he was known as a private and confidential agent of the government. Three weeks after his death, secret orders (discovered thirty-four years later) were given by Benjamin to a Lieutenant Capston, who was instructed to go to Ireland and discourage the Irish from emigrating to the United States at the instance of Federal agents whose object was to recruit soldiers for the Union Army.

This may have been Orton's mission, or it may have been some other. Often these expeditions were suggested by the men embarked on them, and were known only to themselves and the Confederate official who gave them their authority and orders, never in the usual form, but in a personal letter.

Lee first learned of Orton's death from the newspapers. "It is in such accordance with the spirit of our enemies," he wrote Mary. "If he did go into Franklin as is stated, his life was forfeited under the laws of war, & yet even under those circumstances I see no necessity for his death except to gratify the evil passions of those whom he offended by leaving Gen¹ Scott." Three years later, he admitted that his grief was "as poignant" as on the day he first learned of the tragedy, and "my blood boils at the thought of the atrocious outrage against every manly & Christian sentiment which the Great God alone is able to forgive. I cannot trust my pen or tongue to utter my feelings."

It was a sorrow from which neither Agnes nor Markie ever recovered. Over the years they found comfort in talking and writing to each other about Orton. After the war, Markie admitted to Agnes: "I have never been to Georgetown or Washington since my great grief. I feel as though I could never go again. Every place there is associated with him. . . . Sometimes I wish I could go to Europe & live where I'd never see anything to remind me of bygone days."

When Agnes confided to Markie what she could not reveal to her family, Markie replied:

Yes, I can easily imagine the interest you feel in all connected with him. You were children together. In my mind's eye I can see you now—you & our darling Annie & he sitting around the nursery fender telling fairy tales. And when you had grown up, it was always—"Where are Agnes & Orton?" Those forest shades could tell. And your rides on horseback! . . .

Whether Agnes blamed herself for rejecting Orton, thereby assuming responsibility for his tragic end, will remain her secret unless her letters to Markie should be discovered.

When Rooney was first taken to prison at Fort Monroe, he was well treated, but on July 15 he was put into a casemate and ordered held as a hostage for the safety of two Federal officers sentenced to die in retaliation for the execution of two Confederate officers.

"If it is right to shoot those men, this should make no difference in their execution," Lee wrote Custis, "but I have not thought it right to shoot them, & differ in my ideas from most people on the subject of retaliation. Sometimes I know it to be necessary, but it should be rarely resorted to at all times, & in our case policy dictates it should be avoided whenever possible." Though he believed the Federals capable of any "meanness or malice," he did not think "even they could perpetrate such an act" as to put Rooney to death.

The Federals were not executed and Rooney was released from his cell but the period of suspense took its toll from the delicate Charlotte. Since the death of her two children, Rooney was her sole interest in life, and during this period of uncertainty she began literally to pine away.

My darling daughter [Robert wrote her], you must not be sick while F—— is away, or he will be more restless under his

141

separation. Get strong & healthy by his return, that he may the more rejoice at the sight of you. You give such an account of yourself as I can scarcely recognize you. . . . I can appreciate your distress at F——'s situation; I deeply sympathize with it, & in the lone hours of the night I groan in sorrow at his captivity & separation from you. . . . I can see no harm that will result . . . except his detention. I feel assured he will be well attended to. He will be in the hands of old army officers & surgeons, most of whom are men of principle & humanity. . . . You may think of F——, & love him as much as you please, but do not grieve over him or grow sad. That will not be right, you precious child.

Later he asked Mary to tell Charlotte that his sympathy for her "was not the less because expression is restrained. I am accustomed to bear my sorrow in silence."

At the end of July when Mildred returned to school at Raleigh, Mary decided that a change would be good for them all, and with Charlotte and Agnes, and Rob as an escort, went to the Hot Springs in Alleghany County. But after a month of enduring the wretched food, they moved on to Bedford County where, at the foot of the Peaks of Otter, they stayed at the farm of an old acquaintance, Captain Buford, who took in paying guests.

Toward the end of October, Mary and the girls returned to Richmond. Custis had found for his mother part of a house on Leigh Street at Third, but it was too small to accommodate Charlotte, who had to find a room somewhere else. This arrangement did not suit Robert, who complained to Mary:

"It takes from me half the pleasure of your accommodation, as I wish to think of you all together, & in her feeble condition & separation from her Fitzhugh, no one can sympathize or attend to her as yourself & her sisters."

During the summer, a Federal general in Libby Prison asked Lee to effect a special exchange between himself and Rooney. But Lee refused to ask any favor for his son that could not be asked for a private. Early in August, Lincoln applied for the special exchange of the captured General Graham, and Rooney's name was submitted as a candidate for exchange. Lee hoped it would work out but did nothing to expedite it.

At the end of July, Lee moved from Culpeper to a new camp near Orange Court House. Since the enemy was still quiet, he had leisure to evaluate the results of the Pennsylvania campaign. When he thought about the number of untrained officers on whom he had to rely, he marveled that he ever won any battles, and had to feel content that he had at least frustrated the Federal campaign for the season. As he told A. P. Hill when Hill wanted to hold a court of inquiry to investigate General Wright's blunders:

These men are not an army, they are citizens defending their country. General Wright is not a soldier, he is a lawyer. I cannot do many things that I could do with a trained army. The soldiers know their duties better than the general officers do. . . . Sometimes I would like to mask troops and then deploy them, but if I were to give the proper order, the general officers would not understand it, so I have to make the best of what I have and lose much time making dispositions.

By this time, dissatisfaction with the battle of Gettysburg had culminated in a general explosion of unfavorable comment in the press. The denunciations of Longstreet and Stuart were withering, and the editors pointed out all the errors of the campaign. This prompted Lee to write:

Even as poor a soldier as I am can generally discover mistakes *after it is all over*. But if I could only induce these wise gentlemen, who see them so clearly *beforehand*, to communicate with me in advance, instead of waiting until the evil had come upon us, to let me know what they *knew all the time*—it would be better for my reputation and, what is of more consequence, far better for the cause.

There was some criticism of Lee but this was restrained, for faith in his character and ability were not easily shaken. Personal criticism never bothered him when he knew that he held the confidence of his superiors, and he now told the President: " . . . as far as I am concerned, the remarks fall harmless." But he was worried about the effect on the army, and the people at home.

On July 27, Davis forwarded him a highly caustic editorial from the *Charleston Mercury*, and wrote him the next day:

Misfortune often develops secret foes and oftener makes men complain. It is comfortable to hold some one responsible for one's discontent, and threats of alienation are said to exist, with preparation for organized opposition. There are others who, faithful but dissatisfied, find an appropriate remedy in the removal of officers who have not succeeded. . . . If a victim would secure the success of the cause, I would freely offer myself.

To a man of Lee's sensibilities, this letter dictated his future course by subtle suggestion. Was Davis not hinting that Lee should offer himself as the victim? This is how it appeared to him, and if Davis did not have this in mind, it was utterly tactless to mention such a subject to a man in Lee's position.

It was consistent with Davis' temperament and his attitude toward Lee to want him to offer his resignation—not because he really desired to replace him, for he was wise enough to know this was impossible—but so that he could grant him clemency.

Lee deliberated on his letter of resignation for over a week. In considering all aspects, he found much to recommend release from his responsibility. Physically, he was still suffering from his illness of the spring; he admitted that his vitality was often low, and that he sometimes wondered how he could find strength to carry on. Once again he probably thought of that peaceful retreat where in the little time he believed was left him he could at last enjoy the company of his children. He had been hearing that siren call for thirty years; now was perhaps the time to heed it.

On August 8, he wrote Jefferson Davis a long letter:

. . . I know how prone we are to censure & how ready to blame others for the nonfulfillment of our expectations. This is unbecoming in a generous people, & I grieve to see its expression. The general remedy for the want of success in a military commander is his removal. . . . I have seen & heard of expression of discontent in the public journals at the result of the expedition. I do not know how far this feeling extends in the army. My brother officers have been too kind to report it, & so far the troops have been too generous to exhibit it. It is fair, however, to suppose that it does exist. . . . I therefore, in all sincerity, request Your Excy

144

to take measures to supply my place. I do this with the more earnestness because no one is more aware than myself of my inability for the duties of my position. I cannot even accomplish what I myself desire. How can I fulfill the expectations of others? . . .

". . . Where am I to find that new commander who is to possess the greater ability which you believe to be required?" Davis replied. "To ask me to substitute you by some one in my judgment more fit to command, or who would possess more of the confidence of the army, or of the reflecting men of the country, is to demand an impossibility. . . ."

If Davis believed that his refusal of Lee's resignation would restore his popularity, silence the batteries that accused him of having failed to give Lee the proper support during the invasion, and turn the criticism into praise, he was wrong. Lee became the object of the people's pride, and he was extolled for his "selfless and noble act" in offering to resign. The latest stories of his magnanimity and kindliness were told.

On the march into Pennsylvania, he and Longstreet had made a short midday halt in a little rising grove beside the road. It was the hottest of July days and the troops were moving listlessly, suffering greatly from the dust and heat. Suddenly a soldier, perspiring at every pore, left the ranks and walked toward Lee. Someone tried to stop him, but Lee encouraged him by saying kindly:

"Well, my man, what can I do for you?"

"Please, General, I don't want much, but it is powerful wet marching this weather. I can't see for the water in my eyes. I came aside to this old hill to get a rag or *something* to wipe the sweat out of my eyes."

"Will this do?" Lee asked as he took out one of his last five handkerchiefs.

"Yes, *my Lordy*, that indeed!"

"Well, then, take it with you, and back quick to the ranks; no straggling this march, you know, my man."

Mopping his face, the trooper hurried back to the road, vowing to a comrade that he would follow Lee to hell if necessary.

Another popular story concerned the time when Lee had spoken highly of a certain officer's merits, and said that such worth deserved promotion. Several of his staff expressed surprise, and reminded him that this officer had often talked disparagingly of him.

"I cannot help that, he is a good soldier and would be useful in a higher position," he told them.

Nothing remained for Lee but to go on. Realizing that he must prepare for "heavier blows & harder work," he placed his trust "in Him who favours the weak & relieves the oppressed," and set to work.

Two months of comparative quiet followed. Camp, set up near the home of the Erasmus Taylors, was comfortable, and Mrs. Taylor insisted, over Lee's protests, on supplying his table daily with buttermilk, bread, fruit, ice, and vegetables. Bryan would scour the countryside, appealing in his brogue for nourishing food for the "Gineral," so there was always enough to eat. After a meal, Lee would often lean back in his chair, and resting both hands on the table, say to some member of his staff:

"Well, Colonel, we are just as well off as if we had feasted on the best in the land; our hunger is appeased, and I am satisfied."

During the last week in August, Rob stopped by to see his father. He wrote to his mother that "Pa" was unchanged in appearance and manner, and "was very well & in good spirits & does not seem at all demoralized." He offered his son "all kinds of nice fruits, a hat, a pair of boots & a pair of gloves all of which I declined. He took a great fancy to those homespun shirts, two of which you have, so you had better have them sent down to him."

Lee enjoyed hearing from Rob the latest news of his family and friends, and learned among other things that Custis' love affair with Sally Warwick was progressing satisfactorily, though Rob did not think they would be married that year. "So Mrs. Lee you have no immediate prospect of acquiring any new daughters, & you must take good care of your old ones," he wrote brightly.

During the last days in August, he went to Richmond for

a conference, and while there, took another heavy cold which he described in unpunctuated form as having been caught in "the hot & badly ventilated rooms of the various depts which resulted in an attack of rheumatism in my back, which has given me great pain & anxiety for if I do not get relief I do not see what is to become of me."

For the rheumatism, which was probably a recurrence of his cardiac trouble, the doctor gave him a bottle of lotion, "which I applied faithfully a week to the almost excoriation of the back & without apparent benefit. . . . I wish I had Daughter's back to apply it to, it might do some service." (She also had rheumatism).

He found the motion of his horse so uncomfortable he took to riding in a spring wagon, but the bad roads made this motion almost as painful as the horse.

Another consultation called him to Richmond early in September. "I slept in Custis' room—Breakfasted at the neighbours & dined with the Pres:—" he wrote in haste, though he was not too busy for a visit with Norvell Caskie and with his handsome Stuart cousins, Margaret and Caroline, both of whom he persuaded to accompany him back to the army.

When they reached camp, he placed the girls in Mrs. Ewell's care, but as she could find no rooms closer than Mr. Hiden's house in Orange Court House, two miles away, he despaired of seeing them often.

As soon as they were settled, he wrote a note addressed to "My dear daughters" and signed "your fond father" asking about their comfort, and offering them a wagon for transportation, or two horses if they could ride without saddles. If they did not like it where they were, he would find them another room—or better still, pitch a tent next to his own. "You would make an ungainly camp very bright & cheerful & we would hail your presence as the advent of angels," he wrote gallantly.

Two days after his return to camp, he ordered a review of the Second Corps; and two days after that, one of the Third, though he did so with "fear & trembling" for he was still unable to ride his horse.

These reviews, unlike Jeb Stuart's, were not just for the

sake of entertainment. The men needed to have their confidence restored and the people wanted reassurance of the army's might.

At both reviews, officers and men from all parts of the army came to watch, among these Rob and his cousin, Daingerfield Lewis. From all parts of the country, even from Richmond, civilians came in trains, on horseback, on foot, and in every kind of vehicle.

The evening before the first review, Lee sent the Stuart girls an invitation. Their note of acceptance came so late the next day, he was afraid that the wagon sent to fetch them would not get back in time for the opening. With the driver went a note, rallying them on their tardiness:

Your numerous beaux, the "Stonewall band," I fear kept you up too late last night. Ask Mr. Hiden to close his doors at ten o'clock. That is the proper time for you to retire your bright eyes from the soldiers' gaze. I hope you have a pleasant visit this morning, & an agreeable ride this evg. with the Major & the Major Genl. Poor Custis & Rob.

He enjoyed facetious matchmaking between these girls and his sons.

For the review Lee was in full uniform, and as he rode up on Traveller, he presented "a perfect picture of grace and power." No one would have suspected that he had mounted by sheer will power, though once in the saddle he was agreeably surprised to find that he suffered no discomfort.

At a signal, General Hill and his staff joined him, and together they galloped around the front and rear of each of the three divisions standing motionless on the plain, their muskets glistening in the sun, their battle flags waving in the breeze. Traveller had started out with a long lope, a gait he kept up along the entire line, so that finally Lee was riding alone as the less enduring horses were left behind.

Flushed with the exertion of his nine-mile gallop, Lee drew up under the fluttering banners at the reviewing stand, removed his hat, and saluted. From every throat burst a spontaneous shout of applause and admiration, and many a hardened veteran felt tears on his leathery cheek.

148

At a quickstep, the corps then passed at review. A newspaper reporter noticed how many of the thousands of men who passed by Lee looked eagerly to the right to see him. "Though a person may have seen him a hundred times, yet he never tires looking at him," the correspondent wrote.

When it was over, Lee rode up to the line of carriages and wagons to greet his friends. He brought up his generals one by one to meet the Stuart girls, introducing them each time as "my daughters." The reporter who was trailing him wrote for his paper that two of General Lee's daughters attended the review. They "have exceedingly pleasant and intelligent faces, both having dark and piercing eyes, and both bearing some resemblance to their father," he told his readers.

When Rob, Daingerfield Lewis, and several other young officers came up to see the Stuarts, Lee began to tease them about each other, but wrote later in mock disappointment that the beautiful Carrie did not look "at Robertus *once*."

Sally Warwick had also come to the review. On Lee's last visit to Richmond, he had noticed that Dr. Shirley was a frequent caller at Miss Warwick's, but whether on professional visits, acting as intermediary for Custis, or in the role of suitor, he could not decide—nor would Sally tell. But as he watched her flirting with all the officers at the review, he decided that she had not "the least notion in the world of marrying Custis." He regretted that she had not considered his son seriously, but he liked her none the less and described her now as being "as sweet as ever."

Margaret and Carrie's company brought him, as he wrote their mother, "the only sunshine, save for the occasional glimpse I have had of my own family, that has shown on my path during the war." He had hoped to see more of them, but they had been always surrounded with "Genls. Cols. & Majors."

"I commiserate you deeply," he told Mrs. Stuart. "I see that you will loose them all. . . . They will not last till the end of the war."

A report that Meade was being reinforced with troops from Grant's army in the west was brought to Lee over a hundred miles by a young cavalryman who had been ordered to ride at full speed, and impress relays of horses as fast as his broke down. He reached headquarters about midnight, after Lee was asleep, but wakened him to deliver the message. After Lee had read it, he asked the young man for particulars of his ride and, seeing his exhaustion, insisted that he sleep in his bed; Robert dressed and sat in his chair until morning.

Lee had tried to keep secret the news that Longstreet's corps had been sent to Tennessee, but in spite of his precautions, it was printed in the papers. When Lee learned that Meade was going to take advantage of Longstreet's absence and press on to Richmond, he crossed the Rapidan River on October 9 and advanced to the neighborhood of Madison Court House.

For almost two months, Lee and Meade engaged in a series of movements not unlike a game of chess, for wits were of more advantage than bullets as each commander maneuvered to take the other at a disadvantage but failed because of the alertness and skill of his opponent. The cavalry was constantly in use, to the delight of Stuart, who enjoyed the challenge.

When Jeb came on the enemy's rear guard at Culpeper and it withdrew, he pursued and forced a fight on the old ground at Brandy Station. It was not much of a battle, for, as one of Stuart's staff wrote: "The Federals just up and left." But Stuart's spirits were high and he kept sending messages to Lee. During the early afternoon he said to an aide:

"Ride back to General Lee, and tell him we are forcing the enemy back on the Rappahannock."

The messenger found Lee on the Griffinsburg highroad, talking with General Ewell. He turned aside to listen to the report. With a bow, "and that grace and courtesy he exhibited alike toward the highest and lowest soldier in his army," he said:

"Thank you. Tell General Stuart to continue to press them back toward the river. But tell him, too, to spare his horses—spare his horses. It is not necessary to send so many messages."

Pointing to this officer and to another who had arrived just ahead of him, Lee said to Ewell:

"I think these two gentlemen make eight messengers sent me by General Stuart!"

150

That night the enemy retired across the Rappahannock, blowing up the railroad bridge behind him, and Lee hurried to reach the Orange & Alexandria Railroad in time to intercept him. But lack of provisions caused Lee to stop over a day at Culpeper to collect supplies.

During this halt, the townspeople flocked out to see him. One woman, though, came with a complaint. She was alarmed at the friendly relations established between the young ladies of the town and the officers of Federal General Sedgwick's headquarters. These foolish girls, she told Lee, were in the habit of going to hear Sedgwick's band concerts; but what was worse, they were talking, and who knew, perhaps even flirting, with his staff.

The girls were troubled, for Lee looked grave. When the woman finished, he said:

"I know General Sedgwick very well. It is just like him to be so kindly and considerate, and to have his band there to entertain them. So, young ladies, if the music is good, go and hear it as often as you can, and enjoy yourselves. You will find that General Sedgwick will have none but agreeable gentlemen about him."

The next day the Army of Northern Virginia set out along a route nearly parallel to that on which Meade was retiring. Stuart was expected to harry him as much as possible, and this time to keep Lee fully informed. He harassed the Federal as far north as the Bull Run, where on October 19 he inflicted a final blow that was referred to facetiously ever after among Confederates as the "Buckland Races."

Stuart surprised the enemy cavalry on the Warrenton-Buckland road, attacking his front and flank. But "they did not wait for us to get halfway to them before they broke, and then it was a race like a fox chase for five miles," a participant wrote. The Yankees were well mounted and the country was open. After them tore the Rebels with yips and halloos, right up to their infantry supports.

"The most exciting sport I ever had," Jeb's engineer officer wrote.

By this date, Lee had come back to camp in "a nice pine

151

thicket," where Perry built a chimney of pine wattling in front of his tent.

To Mary he now wrote of Meade:

I could have thrown him farther back, but saw no chance of bringing him to battle, & it would only have served to fatigue our troops by advancing farther. I should certainly have endeavoured to throw them north of the Potomac; but thousands were bare-footed, thousands with fragments of shoes, & all without overcoats, blankets, or warm clothing. I could not bear to expose them to certain suffering & an uncertain issue.

He knew Meade would come on again as soon as he had re-paired the railroad. "If I could only get some shoes & clothing for the men, I would save him the trouble."

On November 1, he was called on by a soldier's wife who had come from South Carolina to visit her husband, whom she had not seen in over two years. He had written her for clothes, so she had decided to bring him the suit for which she had spun the yarn and woven the cloth.

"She had been here a week & must return tomorrow, & thought she could not go back without seeing me," Robert wrote Mary. "Her husband accompanied her to my tent, in his nice gray suit. . . . Ask Misses Agnes & Sally Warwick what they think of that. They need not ask me for permission to marry until they can do likewise."

On November 26, "with ten days' rations and in light marching order," Meade crossed the Rapidan and moved right up to Lee's position. But as a cavalry officer wrote in disgust:

When said adversary appeared what did he do? Instead of *attacking* he went to *entrenching*—was there ever anything so absurd? There was Richmond nearer to him than to us, he having assumed the offensive; and yet as soon as he found the enemy he sought, sits down to digging dirt. . . . For four mortal days did Meade remain digging dirt for dear life . . . and keeping up a spiteful skirmish fire within our lines.

Each day, Meade's attack was expected and at dawn Lee and Stuart would ride along the whole line of entrenchments. Often Lee would direct some important change or rectify "mistakes readily detected by his educated eye." He tried to impress on the officers in charge the importance of these works in the impending engagement, and presented them "an example of untiring energy and zeal."

About three o'clock on the morning of December 1, one of Stuart's scouts, who had passed the night riding about in Meade's army, returned with the report that as far as he could judge, the enemy was moving his whole army backward. The scout had made his way through the Federal lines by holding up an official envelope and calling out in an authoritative voice: "Make way!"

Stuart's engineer officer, William W. Blackford, had been called in to hear the report, and was asked to take the information to Lee at once.

The weather had been so bitter, with a heavy fall of snow on November 11, that Lee had moved his cot, small camp writing desk, a chair, and several stools into a vacant frame house beside the road, a few hundred yards from Stuart's headquarters; he had admitted to Mary that he felt the cold as he had never done before, and worried about what he would do when winter really set in.

Though it was long before daylight when Blackford went into Lee's quarters, he found him already up and partially dressed:

He was walking backwards and forwards in his shirt sleeves before a bright wood fire, brushing his hair and beard. He spoke to me cordially and listened attentively to my report; then, as he had a way of doing with young officers with whom he came in contact, he began asking me questions, and every word he said impressed itself so firmly on my memory that I can give them now just as he said them.

"*Well, Captain,*" said he, "*what do you think they are going to do?*," pausing in his walk before me, and holding his hair brush in his hand: I told him I thought they would turn our right flank.

"*Why do you think so?*" said he. I told him I thought the ground on that flank was the only part of our line where they could possibly hope for any success, as it was leveler and more favorable in every way. He then resumed his walk and the brushing of his hair for a while and then faced me again and said,

153

"Captain, if they don't attack us today we must attack them!" slapping the palm of his left hand with the back of the brush, *"We must attack them, sir!"* slapping his hand with the back of the brush more sharply, and stamping with his foot, while his eyes flashed with excitement.

"And you young men must exert yourself! You must exert your-selves, sir!" slapping with his brush again. I assured him I would do all I could, and then took my leave, much impressed by the personal magnetism of our great commander.

When Blackford stepped out of the house, he found the road filled with a column of marching troops, troops that were ordered to make the attack which Lee had planned before the young engineer officer ever saw him.

11

"I AM too old to command this army. We should never have permitted those people to get away!" Lee said to the officer who reported that instead of maneuvering for an attack, Meade had retreated.

Although Lee ordered immediate pursuit, the Federal had taken advantage of the dense forests through which his roads of retreat lay, and had quietly begun his withdrawal the previous afternoon; his light marching equipment enabled him to out-strip his pursuers.

You will have probably seen that Gen! Meade has retired to his old position on the Rappak without giving us battle [Robert wrote to Mary on December 4]. I had expected from his move-ments & all that I had heard, that it was his intention to do so, & after the first day, when I thought it necessary to skirmish pretty sharply with him on both flanks to ascertain his news, I waited patiently his attack. Tuesday, however, I thought he had changed his mind, & that night made preparations to move around his left next morg. & attack him. But when day dawned he was nowhere to be seen. . . . We pursued to the Rapidan but he was over. Ow-ing to the nature of the ground it was to our advantage to receive rather than to make the attack, & as he about doubled us in

154

numbers, I wished to have the advantage. I am greatly disappointed at his getting off with so little damage.

When he saw the wanton destruction of civilian property, he was even more bitterly disappointed that Meade had escaped unpunished:

"Houses were torn down or rendered uninhabitable, furniture and farming implements broken or destroyed, and many families, most of them in humble circumstances, stripped of all they possessed and left without shelter and food," he reported to General Cooper, the Adjutant and Inspector General. "I have never witnessed on any previous occasion such entire disregard of the usages of civilized warfare and the dictates of humanity."

After returning to his headquarters at Orange Court House, he learned the disquieting news of disaster in Georgia and Tennessee.

"Gloom and unspoken despondency hangs like a pall everywhere," a Richmond diarist wrote.

On December 3, Lee warned the President that there was a good chance of the enemy penetrating Georgia and seizing important manufactories and depots of supplies. He tactfully suggested that Beauregard be sent to replace the unsuccessful Bragg, who had resigned.

Davis replied by telegram, asking Lee if he would go to Dalton, Georgia, and take command.

There were a number of serious drawbacks which Lee called to the President's attention: Unless this were a permanent command, he could not see that any good would result; recalling his experience in West Virginia, he was afraid he would not receive "cordial cooperation." Since General Ewell's health was feeble, it would be necessary to find another commander for the Army of Northern Virginia. And finally, there was a question of his own health:

"I have not that confidence either in my strength or ability as would lead me of my own option to undertake the command in question."

On December 9, he was called to Richmond; believing that Davis intended to send him to Georgia, he made preparations.

155

He wrote a final note of instruction to Jeb Stuart, asking him to look out for good forage for the cavalry but, aware of Jeb's disposition to wander, warned: "Be not too far away from the field of operations."

As if in hail and farewell, he expressed much in a few words when he told Stuart: "My heart and thought will always be with this army."

When he reached Richmond he was given a hero's welcome, hailed by many as "the very first man in the world." He assumed the role easily and graciously, and only his intimates knew how much he disliked the crowds of strangers and the fanfare.

On Sunday the thirteenth, he was observed by a Richmond diarist as he walked down the aisle in St. Paul's Church "bowing royally right and left," acknowledging a silent ovation, and smiling to his friends and acquaintances. His only pleasure lay in the acclaim of the ladies. A kinswoman said to a friend at this time:

"If it pleased God to take poor Cousin Mary Lee—she suffers so—wouldn't these Richmond women campaign for Cousin Robert?"

Not until December 15 was it finally settled that Lee would not be sent to Georgia. Since the President refused to appoint Beauregard to head the Army of the West, Lee tactfully suggested Davis' other enemy, Joe Johnston. In Davis' mind, the problem resolved itself to a selection of the lesser of two evils and he took Johnston. One who knew the President well said:

"Certainly Jeff Davis did hate to put Joe Johnston at the head of what is left of it [the army]."

It may have been during this stay in Richmond that Lee met Senator Benjamin H. Hill, who asked his opinion about the propriety of moving the Confederate capital farther south.

"That is a political question, Mr. Hill, and you politicians must determine it. I shall endeavor to take care of the army, and you must make the laws and control the government."

"Oh, General," protested the Senator, "but you will have to change that rule, and form and express political opinions, for if we establish our independence the people will make you Mr. Davis' successor."

"Never, sir, that I will never permit. Whatever talents I may possess (and they are but limited), are military talents. My education and training are military. I think military and civil talents are distinct if not different, and full duty in either sphere is about as much as one man can qualify himself to perform. I shall not do the people the injustice to accept high civil office."

"Well, but General," Hill argued, "history does not sustain your view. Caesar and Frederick of Prussia and Bonaparte were great statesmen as well as great generals."

"And great tyrants. I speak of the proper rule in republics, where, I think, we should have neither military statesmen nor political generals."

"But Washington was both, and yet not a tyrant," Hill responded in triumph. With a beautiful smile, Lee replied:

"Washington was an exception to all rule, and there was none like him."

During Lee's absence, his staff began to speculate whether or not he would stay in Richmond to spend Christmas with his family—for the first time since 1859.

On December 20, Walter Taylor wrote Elizabeth Saunders, his fiancée, that it would be more in accord with Lee's character if he returned to his headquarters, since he was apt "to suppress or deny personal desire when it conflicts with the performance of his duty." The next day, Lee arrived at camp.

Taylor's analysis was in part correct, but beyond Lee's desire to set an example, there was something deeper: the burden of his personal sorrows. Mary's constant suffering, Rooney's imprisonment, and above all, Charlotte's illness, he found at times overwhelming. He differed emotionally from those who can find comfort in mingling their tears and commiserating with one another. Many times he had said that he preferred to be alone with his sorrow.

When he parted with Charlotte, he felt "oppressed with sorrowful forebodings" for "she seemed stricken with a prostration I could not understand." He was gay with her, and as he kissed her good-by, he made her promise to be better next morning; before leaving Richmond he wrote her "in a cheerful & hopeful mood" he was far from feeling. But he was of a sanguine dispo-

157

sition, and still clutched at slender threads of hope for her recovery.

On Christmas Eve, a messenger brought a letter from Mary telling him that Charlotte's end was near. In his reply, he said:

. . . That you may know my sorrow in all its breadth & depth, as far as I know my own heart, I feel for her all the love I bear Fitzhugh. That is very great. I pray she may be spared us. Yet God's will be done! The blow so grievous to us is intended I believe in mercy to her. She was so devoted to F——, seemed so bound up in him, that apparently she thought of & cared for nothing else. They seemed so united that I loved them as one person. I would go down tomorrow, but from your letter have no hope of finding her alive, or of being able to do anything for her. I feel that all will be done for her that human power can do, & oh I pray that our Merciful Father will yet spare her, or gently take her to Himself! Telegraph me if I can reach there in time.

When news that Charlotte was dying reached Rooney, he immediately applied for a forty-eight hour leave, Custis having formally volunteered in writing to take his brother's place as a hostage until Rooney's return. His application was "curtly and peremptorily refused," and man's incredible inhumanity to man denied the devoted Charlotte the presence of the one person who would have brought the most comfort in her final moments.

On the night of December 26, a telegram from Custis brought word of her death. With a poetic beauty born of his anguish, Robert wrote:

Thus dear Mary is link by link the strong chain broken that binds us to earth, & smooths our passage to another world. . . . I grieve for our lost darling as a father can only grieve for a daughter. I loved her with a father's love, & my sorrow is heightened by the thought of the anguish her death will cause our dear son, & the poignancy it will give to the bars of his prison.

Though he consoled himself with the "glorious thought" of Charlotte joining "her little cherubs & our angel Annie in Heaven," it was months before he could speak her name without breaking into tears.

At the beginning of the new year, he prepared for the coming campaign by applying to the quartermaster general for leather for shoes, to the President for reorganization of certain commands, and to Northrup for increased rations for his army.

That Northrup consistently ignored the needs of the Army of Northern Virginia while sending adequate supplies to other armies, and reduced rations only for Lee's soldiers, seemed to Robert more design than accident. He was indifferent to his personal needs. He had recently asked Mary not to send him food: "I want less and less every day." But to appease the hunger of his men and give them strength to endure hardships, he took vigorous action.

I have been mortified to find that when any scarcity existed this was the only army in which it was found necessary to reduce rations [he wrote Northrup]. I have never heard of any reduction in the meat ration issued to troops in and about Richmond, Petersburg, Wilmington, Charleston, Savannah, Mobile, or in the Southwest. Many of these troops are in a measure stationary, less exposed to the inclemency of the weather, and undergoing less hardship and danger than the troops of this army. Many of them could with propriety . . . be placed on a lighter diet than the troops in the field. . . . I am always glad to hear of troops receiving abundance of provisions at any point, but think all ought to fare alike, if possible. It stops complaint and produces more contentment.

Northrup ignored his appeal and by January 22, Lee feared that unless he got food the army would be dissolved. This time he wrote to the Secretary of War, James Seddon. He wasted no words:

A regular supply of provisions to the troops in this army is a matter of great importance. Short rations are having a bad effect on the men, both morally and physically. Desertions to the enemy are becoming more frequent, and the men cannot continue healthy and vigorous if confined to this sparse diet for any length of time. Unless there is a change, I fear the army cannot be kept together.

A private wrote Lee that if there were a necessity for such short rations, he and his comrades would bear it. But he wondered if the General knew how little his men were getting to eat.

159

Lee knew that thousands of other men were wondering this same thing. Rather than reply to the one soldier, he issued a general order assuring the troops that the reduction in rations was caused by circumstances beyond his control. The army's welfare, he told them, was an object of his "constant and earnest solicitude, and no effort has been spared to provide its wants."

In spite of a half-filled stomach, laughter came easily to these men who made any odd or common occurrence the butt of their levity. If the bass drummer walked by, toting his oversize instrument, he was hailed with all manner of uncomplimentary remarks and facetious requests for him to "pick a tune on that 'ar thing."

If a bumpkin in an uncommonly big hat passed, he was startled by countless shouts:

"Come down out o' that hat! Come down! 'Tain't no use to say you ain't there. I see your legs hangin' out!"

A cavalryman who had lavished his full forty dollars' pay on a pair of boots would be similarly accosted:

"Come up out o' them boots!—come out! Too soon to go into winter quarters!"

To while away their time, the men held debates, tableaux, and theatricals in which a few of the young women of the neighborhood took part.

The interest in religion, which had started the previous winter, continued to grow and Lee again made every effort to encourage it.

The cold he had taken in August revived the severe back and chest pains and "general stiffness."

"I fear I will never be better & must be content," he wrote Mary that December. But believing that exercise was beneficial to most illness, he took long daily rides on Traveller. These often took him as far as the banks of the Rapidan where Jeb Stuart had his headquarters. He always stopped for some light-hearted talk and banter with his cavalry chief, and "on these occasions he had good-humored speech for all, not overlooking the youngest officer," an aide recalled.

At his doctor's orders he was still diligently, though unwillingly, applying the lotion to the painful areas, with no relief,

160

and also carrying on a detailed correspondence with Mary about the making of flannel drawers for daytime wear, and jackets to sleep in. The doctor prescribed flannel in preference to knitted material for warmth and reduction of pain.

"Please have the flannel well shrunk before being made up," he asked. To ensure their usefulness after Perry had washed them, he suggested that she "get any pattern to fit a big old man & cut them large," or "measure Custis & give an extra size or two."

His need for warm underclothes was soon known among his relatives and friends, and his cousin Carrie Stuart sent him a pair of flannel drawers, for which he thanked her with charming gallantry:

"Your handiwork will impart to them I am sure an additional warmth. I examined them anxiously to see if I could discover any impression of your sweet self, but could not. I fear you did not look at them during your work."

Kitty Stiles of Savannah sent two knitted jackets which he described as "very elastic & nice," though he was afraid they would not be as warm as the prescribed flannel. Her package also contained "peach leather," and preserved quinces and cherries.

Eliza also sent a package of dried peaches, accompanied by a letter. The fruit he found "excellent," and he was pleased to hear about her and her family. But the most happiness was derived from the knowledge that she had thought of him. In thanking her for having remembered him, he assured her:

"I never forget you."

Although he still declined all offers of a comfortable room— "I of course cannot go to a house & be alone, as a crowd is always around me," he wrote—the people were determined that he should have plenty to eat, and brought in person or sent by servants baskets of eggs, bread, cabbage, and apples; crocks of butter, jugs of buttermilk, and cake. His officers sent presents of ham, turkey, buckwheat, and three barrels of sweet potatoes. He was distressed that he had no way of returning the generosity, or of sharing the plenty with Mary and his daughters, all of whom were sick.

161

Not all of his presents were edible. An anonymous admirer in Alexandria sent him a handsome pair of gilt spurs, and Judge Field sent a saber. And there were socks, gloves, a new hat, and a beautifully carved pipe, made in camp by a Mississippian who had used only his penknife. When he received the pipe, he wrote to ask if "Robertus" would "recommend my taking up the inspiration at this late day." When Rob did not advise him, he decided to send the pipe to Richmond for safekeeping:

"I infer that Bertus does not recommend my indoctrination into the odourous art, as he has withheld his desired advice. I fear it is rather late for me to learn anything good."

The United States Congress passed a law that levied taxes on all property in the "insurrectionary districts within the United States," and appointed commissioners to assess and collect the taxes. Robert's Alexandria cousin, Philip R. Fendall, whose ancestor had married the Divine Matilda's widowed mother, acted on his behalf, and tendered the amount due on Arlington. The commissioners refused the money, as there was a ruling that payment must be made by the owner in person.

The Richmond city council was aware of "the humble proportions" of the house Mary and her daughters occupied on Leigh Street, and had considered buying a house and presenting the title to Lee. As soon as they learned that Arlington would be forfeited for delinquent taxes, they acted. Hearing of their proposal, Lee refused graciously:

. . . The house is not necessary for the use of my family, & my own duties will prevent my residence in Richmond. I should therefore be compelled to decline the generous offer, & I trust that whatever means the City Council may have for this purpose may be devoted to the relief of families of our soldiers in the field, who are more in want of assistance, & more deserving of it, than myself.

To Mary he wrote: "The kindness exhibited towards you as well as myself by our people in addition to exciting my gratitude causes me to reflect on how little I have done to merit it, & humbles me in my own eyes to a painful degree."

He was concerned again about some of the Negroes at Romancoke who had still not received their manumission papers.

"I do not see why they cannot be freed & hire themselves out as others do," he wrote Custis. "I am afraid there is some desire on the part of the community to continue them in slavery, which I must resist."

When Mildred came to Richmond at Christmas, she decided that she would rather stay with her mother than return to school at Raleigh. Custis was unable to find them a larger house, so he and his brother officers offered them a haven at The Mess. They moved in around the first of January. Robert was disappointed that they had not selected a "more retired location."

"In my own case," he wrote Mary, "I would rather be in a hut with my family than in a palace with others. The gentlemen too, I suspect feel the encroachment & it will end in their going to Church Hill or some other eminence."

But his womenkind were delighted to be in the midst of things, a fact Lee was never able to understand, and the location of The Mess, in the center of a fashionable neighborhood and just two blocks from Capitol Square and St. Paul's Church, was exactly to their taste.

Mary took a back room on the main floor. This room soon became the most popular one in the house, a gathering place for relatives and friends. Mary allowed no one to sit idly and chat, but set each one to scraping lint, rolling bandage, or knitting socks and gloves. On nice days she would have her rolling chair pushed onto the porch which overlooked the little back garden planted all to white—white roses, white periwinkle, white crêpe myrtle, and jasmine.

Knitting for the soldiers was now Mary's chief interest. Yarn was supplied by what she called her "yarn scouts" who worked all over the country, and knitting needles, which she wore out rapidly, the ordnance department furnished by the gross.

In nearly every letter from then until summer, Robert mentioned the receipt of a bag of socks and gloves which he distributed to the most needy soldiers. The count Mary made and included almost never agreed with Robert's count on the bag's arrival, and he suggested that she had better "get one of the girls to count them accurately & set down the number." When at last one count agreed with his, he remarked drily:

"The number of pairs stated by you was correct—30 pairs good & true. I am glad to find there is arithmetic enough in my family to count 30."

Contrary to his prediction, Custis, Major Coxe, Robert Shirley Carter, and Chapman Leigh did not "feel the encroachment" and move out. Instead, they seemed to enjoy the ladies' presence. Mildred took on the duties of housekeeper, chief sockknitter, and official counter. Her father was gratified:

"I shall expect great numbers now. I have given out that my daughter just from a celebrated school is at work & the expectations of the soldiers are raised."

A few days later he sent a message: "Tell Life my reliance is on her. I think I hear her needles rattle as they fly through the meshes."

Mary Boykin Chesnut and several friends called on Mary in February. That night, Mrs. Chesnut wrote in her diary: "Her room was like an industrial school, with everybody so busy. Her daughters were all there, plying their needles, and also several other ladies. . . . When we came out, I said: 'Did you see how the Lees spend their time? What a rebuke to the taffy parties!'"

During the visit, Mary showed the ladies the beautiful sword sent to Robert on February 13 by S. F. Cameron in behalf of "a son of Maryland" who had designed it especially "for your use in the camp and field, bearing your name on the one side of the blade and the motto, *Aide toi, et Dieu t'aidera.*"

Since he wore a sword only on dress occasions and had another in his camp chest, he brought this one with him when he came to Richmond to confer with the President in mid-February. His family did not know he was coming, and the house was so crowded with guests the night he arrived that he had to sleep in Custis' bed, while his son rolled up in a blanket on the floor.

The next morning, he had breakfast at the President's house. While they ate, Senator Phelan of Alabama planned the coming campaign for him. Another guest wrote later that Lee "smiled blandly the while, though he did permit himself a mild sneer at the wise civilians in Congress who refrained from trying the battlefield in person, but from afar detailed the movement of armies."

One evening, Lee overheard his daughters talking about a local Titian-haired beauty who had obtained, through the blockade, sixty yards of tulle for her wedding dress and veil. When other girls were being married in calico and homespun, or at best their mothers' and grandmothers' gowns, this extravagance set tongues wagging. Robert listened for a while in silence, then said wistfully:

"Oh, if she would only give it to me to make my soldiers some breeches!"

Rare was the animal that did not find favor with Lee, from mouse to rattlesnake. But Mildred's pet squirrel, Custis Morgan, named for her brother and the famed Confederate cavalryman, John Hunt Morgan, aroused his immediate dislike. After his return to camp he wrote of Mildred's ability to give the family a treat: "Squirrel soup thickened with pea nuts. Custis Morgan in such an exit from the stage would cover himself with glory."

When a few weeks later the squirrel had the indiscretion to bite Mary's new doctor, Robert asked: "Did he have recourse to the homeopathic application to his finger, for the bite of Custis Morgan, & insist on another grip? I should have recommended squirrel soup for your disease immediately."

When the squirrel ran away, he wrote: "I was much pleased . . . to hear . . . that Custis Morgan was still among the missing. I think the farther he gets from you the better you will be."

After Mary moved into The Mess, the little girls of the neighborhood made a habit of running in and out, and were especially numerous when Robert was there. One won the privilege of riding his horse from the stable to the door, and when she was lifted down she would dash up to his room to claim a kiss and a jog on his knee. To this young favorite he gave a prize he had denied many an older one—a lock of his hair. When she asked, he handed her the scissors, kneeled down, and put his

165

head in her lap. She carefully snipped off a curl just above his neck—a memento she preserved and handed down to her children.

At one house where he always called were two little girls who were noted for their good behavior. But no sooner was the parlor door shut after Lee's departure than they would begin to push and pull each other, and bite and pinch, until at last one of them managed to slip into the chair Robert had occupied. She was then declared the victor, and peace was re-established.

Mary suggested that Lee assign Rob to his staff. He admitted that Rob's company would be a great comfort and that he would be very useful,

but I am opposed to officers surrounding themselves with their sons & relatives. It is wrong in principle, & in that case the selection of officers would be made from private & social relations, rather than for the public good. . . . There is the same objection to him going to Fitz Lee. He has Lees & relatives enough around him. I would prefer Rob's being in the line in an independent position where he could rise by his own merit & not through the recommendations of his relatives.

Rooney was now exchanged, and returned brokenhearted. Tears filled his father's eyes when he told an acquaintance:

"Poor boy, he is sadly cut up about the death of that sweet little wife of his."

Though he wished to talk with his son to help him recover his spirit, he found his own heart "too full" at these first meetings.

On February 29, Lee's stay at the capital was cut short by a Federal cavalry raid led against Richmond by General Judson Kilpatrick and Colonel Ulric Dahlgren. Lee left at once for Madison Court House, taking with him a bag of sixty-seven pairs of socks, and narrowly missing capture when the raiders reached the railroad right after his train had passed.

When Dahlgren was killed, there was found on his body orders for his men to release all Union prisoners in Richmond, to burn the city and its bridges, and execute President Davis and his Cabinet. The Southern people were aroused, and demanded retaliation. Though Lee was also enraged at "the char-

166

acter of the war our enemies wage against is, & the unchristian & atrocious acts they plot & perpetrate," he was unable to recommend execution for those prisoners taken during the raid. His reply to the Secretary of War, who had written for his opinion of the army's attitude, was that of a man whose reasoning and sense of justice had remained in balance in the midst of hysteria. Referring to the orders found on Dahlgren, he wrote:

> These papers can only be considered as evidence of his intentions. It does not appear how far his men were cognizant of them, or that his course was sanctioned by his Government. . . . I do not think it right therefore to visit upon the captives the guilt of his intentions. I do not pretend to speak the sentiments of the army, which you seem to desire. I presume that the blood boils with indignation in the veins of every officer & man as they read the account of the barbarous & inhuman plot, & under the impulse of the moment, many would counsel extreme measures. But I do not think that reason & reflection would justify such a course. I think it better to do right, even if we suffer in so doing, than to incur the reproach of our consciences & posterity.

12

AFTER Lee returned to his headquarters camp on the southern slope of Clarke's Mountain, on March 17 he received from Rooney a letter in which his son talked only of his hopeless grief. Tenderly, Lee replied:

> God knows how I loved your dear, dear wife, how sweet her memory is to me, & how I mourn her loss. My grief could not have been greater had you been taken from me. My heart is too full to speak on this subject, nor can I write. . . . But we cannot indulge in grief, however mournfully pleasing. Our country demands all our strength, all our energies. To resist the powerful combination now forming against us will require every man at his place . . . & you had better join your brigade. This week will in all probability bring us active work, & we must strike fast & strong.

Rooney took his father's advice and went back to his command, finding that the active life soon restored his spirits.

In March, General Grant, who had been promoted to lieutenant general and put in command of all the Union armies, attached himself personally to the Army of the Potomac. He had none of the bombast of his predecessors. In an awareness of what lay before him, he decided on a new system of operations. In his own words, he was not planning a campaign of skillful strategy and tactics but one which would *"hammer continuously* against the armed force of the enemy and his resources, until by *mere attrition*, if nothing else, there would be nothing left for him but an equal submission with the loyal section of our common country to the Constitution and the laws."

From what information Lee could gather, he concluded "that the great effort of the enemy will be made in Virginia. . . . All the information that reaches me goes to strengthen the belief that Gen[l] Grant is preparing to move against Richmond." With unerring instinct, he selected the area near Petersburg as subject to attack by troops sent up the James.

The next step was to make "every preparation to meet the storm which will apparently burst on Virginia," and to do so, Lee asked for the return of all troops belonging to his army, and that any men not needed in the Carolinas be placed under Beauregard and sent to Petersburg. He called on the war secretary to collect, at "suitable and safe places," "adequate supplies of provisions and forage." He urged that the railroads be devoted exclusively to this purpose, and that all private travel on them be suspended for the present.

Robert had long ago despaired of getting cooperation from Northrup, so he made his appeal for increased rations (the meat allowance had been cut one-half in February) and enlarged supplies directly to Davis. On April 12, he wrote:

I cannot see how we can operate with our present supplies. Any derangement in their arrival or disaster to the railroad would render it impossible to keep the army together, & might force a retreat into North Carolina. . . . We have rations for the troops today & tomorrow. . . . Every exertion should be made to supply the depots at Richmond & at other points.

Jefferson Davis had his own ideas about how to conduct the campaign, so he kept Beauregard in North Carolina and sent no troops to Petersburg. The only men he returned to Lee (and only after repeated appeals on Lee's part) were Longstreet's corps. As late as May 4, after the Federal army had begun to move, Lee was literally begging Davis for the return of his troops.

During the reorganization of the cavalry, Stuart assigned one of General Wade Hampton's brigades to Fitz Lee. Hampton was angry and complained in person to Robert. The meeting was stormy, and Lee told him:

"I would not care if you went back to South Carolina with your whole division!" Afterward, Hampton told a friend that Lee's manner made this speech "immensely mortifying."

When Longstreet, then in Greeneville, Tennessee, received orders on April 11 to "move without delay to General Lee," he admitted to Major Moxley Sorrel "that while it was more honorable, possibly, to have a separate command, he preferred to be under Lee, as it relieved him of responsibility and gave him assured confidence." Old Pete had had his fill of an independent command.

By April 29, Longstreet's corps had reached Mechanicsville, six miles below Gordonsville, and since the enemy was still quiet, Lee went there to review the returned troops.

He was wearing a new hat, "a thing to be remembered for his old one had served him long." When he reined up in front of the long double lines, the clarion notes of a bugle sounded, the guns thundered a salute, and the bands struck up "Dixie" and "The Bonnie Blue Flag." Then he bared his "good gray head" and looked at his men.

"We give him the 'rebel yell' and shout and cry and wave our flags and look at him once more," wrote a private. "General Lee must have felt good in getting the welcome extended to him by those who had been lost to him so long." After the review, "the men hung around him and seemed satisfied to lay their hands on his gray horse or to touch his bridle, or the stirrup, or the old general's leg—anything that Lee had was sacred to us fellows who had just come back. And the General—he could not help breaking down . . . tears traced down his cheeks, and he felt that we were again to do his bidding."

169

Lee wore no other insignia of rank than three stars on his collar, which every Confederate colonel was entitled to wear. This caused many people to mistake him. When asked why he did not wear shoulder straps and gold lace, he said:

"Oh, I do not care for display. And the truth is, that the rank of colonel is about as high as I ought ever to have gotten."

One day, a farmer rode up to him as he sat outside of his tent, and addressing him as "Colonel," began to chat about crops and weather. After a few minutes he told the colonel that he had come out to the camp in hopes of seeing General Lee. Did he think he could? Lee then identified himself, and set the man at ease by thanking him for his trouble, and telling him as he shook his hand:

"I am most happy to have met you."

Custis had been anxious to get into the field for some time. But when he was offered the command of the Department of Richmond, as successor to General Elzey, he hesitated, for he had never led troops in battle. He wrote his father for advice, and Lee told him to accept:

The time is coming, indeed has come, when everyone must put out their strength. They cannot consult their feelings or individual opinions where to serve, but must take positions where it would be reasonably evident they will be of most value. . . . Grant is now with the Army of the Potomac. . . . Everything at this time is suggestive of another attempt on Richmond. . . . The troops around Richmond may have an important part to play. They should be well prepared & well commanded. I would rather have you there than any one I could now select. . . . You refuse command because you have no experience in the field. . . . But until you come into the field you will never gain experience.

Feeling that he should gain his field experience in some less responsible position, Custis suggested to his father that he apply for the post of his chief of staff. Lee objected that such an appointment would be open to charges of nepotism, and would afford Custis less opportunity to shine in his own right, though it would be "very agreeable" to have him there, and he needed all the help he could get. "I feel a marked change in my strength since my attack last spring at Fredericksburg, & am less competent for my duty than ever."

But the prospect of battle always cheered him, and he said to Walter Taylor one morning:

"Colonel, we have got to whip them, we must whip them, and it has already made me better to think of it!"

In March, Lee ordered all women to the rear. Since the enemy showed no sign of moving, a number of officers' wives stayed on. Toward the end of April, one of those wives decided to leave, and her husband, a cavalryman, was escorting her home. They had just taken seats in the train when Lee entered the car. He appeared to them "larger and more imposing than ever." When he came to where they were sitting, he stopped and asked the Captain to introduce his lady. Mrs. Ranson jumped up, and with a quaver in her voice, said:

"Oh, General Lee, I disregarded your order. It was my doing and not my husband's, and I beg you to forgive us both."

Pray do not disturb yourself. My order was not intended for you at all. It was intended only for your husband. I expect to get a great deal of work out of him this summer, and he cannot work unless his horses are in condition.

Every evening for some weeks, about nightfall, I have observed that he mounted his horse and galloped off towards Orange Court House . . . and every morning he came galloping back about sunrise. Now you know this is not good for the horses. By the time I should need his services they would be worn out,—and I was obliged to put a stop to it.

Then he smiled, sat down beside her, and "talked . . . so pleasantly that her fears were relieved and her love and veneration were greatly increased."

Captain Ranson admitted that he had been taught what others had already learned from experience: that it was no use trying to throw dust in Marse Robert's eyes.

On May 4, the Army of the Potomac made an uncontested crossing of the Rapidan. That morning, Lee invited his principal commanders to breakfast, a better meal than usual as there was real coffee. After saying grace, he announced cheerfully that Grant had crossed the river. "In fact, he is crossing now. We might even have him in to breakfast."

When A. P. Hill's corps started to move that morning along the Plank Road toward Chancellorsville, Lee accompanied it.

171

Ewell had been ordered to advance along the Orange turnpike, while Longstreet, who had one division at Mechanicsville and another a little north of Gordonsville, had orders to move to Todd's Tavern and form the Confederate right.

Fitzhugh Lee has stated that Lee sent an engineer officer to show Longstreet the way, but that Old Pete, with customary perverseness, dismissed the guide, promptly took the wrong road, and lost twenty-four hours in reaching the field. Longstreet later denied the accusation, insisting that time was consumed in resting his troops and readying them for the fight. Whatever caused the delay, the fact remains that he did not come at the appointed time, and failed Lee again.

On the night of May 4, Lee camped at New Verdiersville. From there, he wrote the President that the long-threatened effort to take the capital had begun; he regretted that there was to be still further delay in concentrating troops at vulnerable positions. He appreciated the advantages of capturing New Berne, North Carolina, but these would not compensate for a disaster in Virginia. He stressed his inferior numbers, and asked once again for the immediate return of those troops belonging to his army, and suggested that Beauregard be brought without delay to Richmond.

By morning, it was evident that Grant, like Hooker, proposed to plunge into the Wilderness, that "wild, tangled forest of stunted trees" and "impassable undergrowth," and Lee took care not to hinder such a desirable end. His staff noticed that he was "in the best of spirits" and during the conversation at breakfast even put aside his usual reluctance to discuss coming operations by speaking confidently of the result and expressing surprise that Grant had not profited by Hooker's experience.

That day, a strong attack was made first on Ewell's corps and then on Hill, but Lee was able to report to Seddon that, by the blessing of God, they had maintained their position against every effort until night ended the contest.

At five o'clock the next morning, the Federal fire opened at a point where Confederate resistance was weak, and General Cadmus Wilcox's line was soon forced to give ground.

Down the road, Wilcox's men began to pour past the field

172

of small scattered pines where Lee sat on Traveller. This could mean disaster, and he sent Walter Taylor on the gallop to Parker's Store to prepare the wagon trains for immediate retreat in case of a rout. He sent another aide to hurry Longstreet, while he rode into the road to help rally the troops. He found himself in the midst of McGowan's South Carolinians bound for the rear.

Several officers noticed that Lee's face was flushed and his eyes were flashing.

"My God! General McGowan, is this splendid brigade of yours running like a flock of geese?"

"General, these men are not whipped. They only want a place to form, and they will fight as well as they ever did."

Just then, Lee saw men coming on the double-quick. Riding up to General Gregg, he asked:

"What brigade is this?"

"The Texas brigade," Gregg said.

"I am glad to see it." This meant Longstreet had come up. "When you go in there," Lee told Gregg, "I wish you would give those men the cold steel—they will stand and fire all day, and never move unless you charge them."

"Attention, Texas Brigade!" Gregg shouted, "the eyes of General Lee are upon you. Forward march!"

Lee raised himself in his stirrups, removed his hat, and waving it above his head, shouted "above the din and confusion of the hour":

"Hurrah for Texas! Texans always move them!"

"I would charge hell itself for that old man!" one veteran said through his tears, then added his voice to the chorus of the rebel yell, as the Texans rushed toward the tangled undergrowth.

Suddenly they were aware that Lee, with the regimental flag in his hand, had spurred Traveller through an opening and was following close. When they saw that it was his intention to lead them in this charge, they shouted:

"Go back, General Lee! Go back!"

Then, slowing down, they said: "We won't go on unless you go back!"

All eyes were on Lee as the brigade halted. Several of his staff came up and tried to reason with him; and they took hold of his arms and grabbed the reins. But like a man in a trance, he shook them off and moved ahead, his eyes still flashing.

Then a soldier stepped from the ranks, seized the bridle rein, and stopped him. Obstinately, he told Lee he would not budge an inch unless he went back.

Walter Taylor came up and took the battle flag from his hand. But it was not until Colonel Venable directed his attention to Longstreet on a nearby knoll, and suggested that he might want to talk with him, that Lee turned Traveller around and reluctantly accompanied Venable.

The Texans then went on and as they passed Lee, every man turned to look at him. Several remembered that his face "was flushed and full of animation," and that he was evidently under "great excitement." He was indifferent, they noticed, to the Minié balls and volleys of musket fire coming from two directions, for his attention was fixed on the fight taking place south of the Plank Road.

He turned in his saddle and called to an aide "in a most vigorous tone, while pointing with his finger across the road":

" 'Send an active young officer down there!' "

"I thought him at the moment the grandest specimen of manhood that I ever beheld. He looked as though he ought to have been and was monarch of the world."

When he saw more soldiers on their way to fill up the gap, he asked:

"What troops are these?"

"Law's Alabama brigade!" a private shouted.

"God bless the Alabamians!" Lee cried.

The men responded with a resounding cheer; then taking up the rebel yell, rushed into the fight.

By the time he had reached Longstreet, Lee had regained his composure, and when a courier rode up on a foaming mount, he rebuked him sternly:

"Young man, you should have some feeling for your horse; dismount and rest him!"

Then, taking from his saddlebag half a buttered biscuit,

174

Lee fed it to the exhausted animal, speaking gently to it all the while.

As Lee stood talking with Longstreet, a sudden enemy charge came close to capturing him. This was the second time in twenty-four hours that the grandest prize of all had slipped from Federal fingers.

Around three o'clock the previous afternoon, he was with Stuart and Hill on a little shaded knoll, waiting for the head of Hill's column to come up. Suddenly a party of Federal skirmishers came out of the cover of low pines just beyond them. Lee and Stuart both got up quickly from the grass and hurried off, Lee shouting orders to Walter Taylor to have the enemy driven back. But the Yankees were so alarmed at finding themselves inside the Rebel lines that they hurried off without firing a shot.

The fresh troops soon sent the Federals reeling back to the Brock Road, which was Lee's objective, since he wanted to bottle Grant up in the Wilderness. But the wounding of Longstreet by his own men temporarily halted the Confederate advance.

Believing, as Old Pete said afterwards, that he "had another Bull Run on them," and would soon drive the Federals back across the Rapidan, Longstreet rode jubilantly toward the front with a party of mounted officers and staff. Just as had happened with Stonewall Jackson, his own flanking column mistook his party for enemy cavalry and fired on it, killing General Micah Jenkins, Captain Foley, and several orderlies. Longstreet was wounded in the shoulder so close to the throat that he was nearly strangled with blood.

When Lee was brought the report of Longstreet's wounding, he must have been impressed by the coincidence of his two corps commanders having been shot down in a time of crisis under the same circumstances in the same tangled wilderness.

Around four o'clock that afternoon, the battle was renewed with Lee standing by to help General Charles Field, the temporary commander of Longstreet's corps. But the enemy had not been idle and had used the intervening hours to strengthen his position and bring up reinforcements.

As had happened in the battle of Chancellorsville, the musket volleys set the Wilderness afire, and soon the whole valley

175

was wrapped in smoke and flame. In this somber thicket of low-limbed pine and scrub oak and chinquapin, two hundred thousand men in blue and gray prowled through the tangled undergrowth like beasts of prey. At the rustle of a bush, the snap of a twig, they sprang and grappled as in "blind wrestle at midnight, and fell and writhed and died unseen, their bodies lost in the bushes, their death-groans drowned in the steady, continuous, never-ceasing crash."

"I never saw a man so agitated in my life," Charles Francis Adams wrote of General Grant that night.

Another officer recalled that Grant went into his tent, "and throwing himself face down on his cot, gave way to the greatest emotion." There was good reason: at the end of that day he found himself on the defensive, with losses nearing 17,666 men as opposed to Lee's 7,600.

The next morning, May 7, the expected Federal attack did not materialize and the day was passed with only an exchange of picket fire. What Grant intended to do next was a debatable question.

Would he also retreat, as Hooker had done? Lee did not think so, and that night he said to John B. Gordon:

"General, you will prepare to move tonight to Spotsylvania Court House."

"Did your scouts not report that Grant has suffered heavy losses, and is preparing to retreat, sir?"

"Yes," Lee said, "my scouts have brought me such reports; but General Grant will not retreat, sir; he will move to Spotsylvania. That is his best manoeuvre and he will do what is best."

Lee's prediction was fulfilled when Grant's troops reached Spotsylvania almost simultaneously with the head of the Confederate column. It had been a race for the position, and Lee had won. Grant had not fathomed his adversary with such unerring judgment as Lee had done. He had expected Lee to retreat, as any ordinary general would have done under the circumstances.

Grant had yet to learn that Lee was a rule unto himself, responding instantly to the demands of the occasion, and that he had his greatest success when he departed farthest from established principles. Lee once said to D. H. Hill:

"If you can accomplish the object, any risk would be justifiable."

At such times, as was said of Napoleon, Lee broke loose from the world of men into the world of Titans.

By this masterly stroke in which he defied all precedents, Lee completely outgeneraled his opponent, passing unsuspected entirely around the Army of the Potomac, and placing his army (supposed by Grant to be fifteen miles in the rear) squarely across his line of advance to Richmond. Grant was momentarily off guard, and retired in some confusion. But he soon determined to extricate himself by desperate fighting.

At two-thirty on May 8, Lee wired the Secretary of War that the Federals had been repulsed "with heavy slaughter," and that Spotsylvania Court House was in Confederate hands.

On the ninth, the action was limited to skirmishes; but on the following morning, a little after ten o'clock, the shelling began and several assaults were made, concentration being near the junction of Ewell's and Longstreet's corps.

As the Federals marched around the Confederate left flank, the Southern soldiers fully appreciated the danger, but displayed no fear for the outcome. Two infantrymen were watching the steady progression of fire, and at a sudden increase in the volleys, one of them took his pipe from his mouth, spat deliberately on the ground, and said:

"Look here, Tom, if those fellows get much farther around there, we would be in a bad fix here; we'd have to get out of this."

"Law, John!" his comrade responded, "Marse Robert'll take care of those fellows. He knows just what to do."

Toward sunset, an assault broke through the line held by General George Dole's brigade, the exultant Federals streamed through the breach, and disaster seemed imminent.

Lee then spurred Traveller to that sector to rally the brigade, and as they quickly reformed, he rode to the head of the column, prepared to lead the countercharge. Once again, his

177

staff remonstrated and the men refused to move until he retired. With great reluctance and not a little annoyance, he yielded, saying to his officers:

"Then you must see that the ground is covered!"

In an instant, Walter Taylor rode into the midst of the troops, dismounted and, seizing a battle flag, led a furious counterattack which pushed the enemy back.

As if to give themselves heart, the Federal bands began to play around eleven o'clock that night, and kept on, hour after hour, until nearly dawn.

On the morning of May 13, Lee rose at three o'clock as was his habit during this campaign, and after a hurried breakfast, mounted Traveller and rode through the fog-shrouded woods toward General Edward Johnson's lines, from which he had earlier heard heavy firing. He soon came on men running to the rear. He took off his hat, and waving it about, called to them in his deep voice:

"Hold on! We are going to form a new line!"

A few recognized him and stopped, but most ran past in panic.

"Shame on you men, shame on you! Go back to your regiments; go back to your regiments!" he said angrily.

Just then, one of Johnson's staff officers rode up to report that the line was broken at the salient.

Lee rode off to find Gordon, who had orders to move his division to the most threatened point. The messenger went with Lee, giving him the details as they rode along. During the night, the enemy had massed troops so near the front of the angle that with one quick rush his column had gone over the breastworks at dawn, capturing Generals Johnson and George Steuart and a large number of their men. This meant that Lee's army was cut in two and nothing could save it but an impetuous countermovement.

Lee reached the angle just as Gordon was moving in for the crucial charge. With perfect composure, Lee rode majestically to the front of Gordon's battle line. His head was bared and he appeared to Gordon "a very god of war."

"Calmly and grandly, he rode to the point near the center of my line and turned his horse's head to the front, evidently resolved to lead in person the desperate charge and drive Hancock back or perish in the effort," Gordon wrote.

Gordon hastily spurred his horse across Traveller's front, and seizing the right cheek of the bit, stopped him.

"General Lee, you shall not lead my men in a charge. No man can do that, sir. Another is here for that purpose. These men behind you are Georgians, Virginians, and Carolinians. They have never failed you on any field. They will not fail you here. Will you, boys?"

Like a mighty anthem came the response:

"No, no, no; we'll not fail him!"

"General Lee to the rear!" Gordon shouted, and the men took up the cry as they gathered around Lee and turned Traveller in the opposite direction, determined, if necessary, to push him by force to a place of safety. The men's concern moved him and he yielded, riding off amidst a chorus of:

"Lee, Lee, Lee to the rear! Lee to the rear!"

"Remember your promise to General Lee!" Gordon said. "His eyes are upon you!—Forward!"

With the rebel yell, the troops "with the fury of a cyclone," rushed on Hancock's column and hurled it back. Before the Federal lines could be reformed, Gordon's officers rode among the troops, chanting in unison:

"Forward men, forward! Forward men, forward!"

Gordon recalled that this additional encouragement was unnecessary. His men were under a spell—the spell of Marse Robert.

When the wounded began to file to the rear, a young Georgian with a badly shattered right arm passed close to Lee. Noticing him, Lee said:

"I grieve for you, my poor fellow. Can I do anything for you?"

"Yes, sir! You can shake hands with me, General, if you will consent to take my left hand."

Lee was on fire this day with the ardor of battle. He was "very sensitive about his lines being broken. It made him more than ever personally pugnacious," a cavalryman recalled. Later,

179

when Lee rode in the rain to the courthouse to order reinforcements to General Ramseur, he came on Harris' Mississippians
resting beside the road. He ordered Harris forward, and went
with the advancing column.

Shortly, they came into the range of Federal artillery, and
Traveller, usually calm under fire, began to rear as shells burst
near him and tree limbs severed by musket shots crashed to the
ground all around him. There seemed to be the hand of destiny
in Traveller's action, for after Lee had quieted him, he reared
just once more. As he did so, a round shot passed directly under
his girth, barely missing the stirrup. If Traveller had been on
the ground, Lee probably could not have escaped death.

"This habit of exposing himself to fire, as they sometimes
thought unnecessarily, was the only point in which his soldiers
felt that Lee ever did wrong," wrote an artillery officer, and the
men now came up and placed themselves between him and the
enemy barrage, shouting to him:

"Go back, General, go back! For God's sake, go back!" and
they tried to turn Traveller to the rear.

Although he was again touched by their devotion, he was
unwilling to relinquish the opportunity to lead the column, and
complained sharply:

"I wish I knew where my place is on the battlefield: wherever
I go someone tells me that is not the place for me to be!"

During the late afternoon when Lee was talking to Colonel
Pegram, Captain McCabe, and several other officers, a courier
galloped up with a dispatch from Richmond: Jeb Stuart was
dying! He had been shot through the body by a dismounted
Federal during an encounter with General Phil Sheridan the
previous afternoon at Yellow Tavern.

The words were staggering. Stuart, "the eyes and ears of
the army," dying! He could be ill spared at any time, and least
of all now.

Jackson gone, Longstreet disabled, and now Stuart. Inscru-
table indeed were the ways of the all-wise Providence.

"Gentlemen," said Lee as he folded the telegram, "we have
very bad news. General Stuart has been mortally wounded: a
most valuable and able officer."

180

He was silent for a minute, and then as if to himself, he said in a voice "vibrant with emotion":

"He never brought me a piece of false information."

That night, word came that Stuart was dead. Lee excused himself and went into his tent. When a member of Stuart's staff came to see him later, he found him in a mood of "deep melancholy" and when the young man spoke of Stuart, Lee said in a voice he "had difficulty controlling":

"I can scarcely think of him without weeping."

It was probably at this time that he wrote on a slip of paper which he filed in his satchel:

"The warmest instincts of every man's soul declare the glory of the soldier's death. . . . There is a true glory & a true honour: the glory of duty done—the honour of the integrity of the principle."

13

THE Federals remained quiet for almost ten days. During this time, Lee's army gained some much-needed rest, but for its commander, no such word existed.

"Does he never, never sleep?" wondered Major Robert Stiles as he withdrew from Lee's tent late one night. Every other officer he had wanted to see had already gone to bed. Even the indefatigable Walter Taylor was on his knees, with his prayer book open.

But there was a light in the headquarters' tent, and Stiles found Lee "wide-awake, poring over a map stretched upon a temporary table of rough plank, with a tallow candle stuck in a bottle for a light."

Lee continued to rise at three o'clock each morning, and to ride along the lines during the day, causing his military family to wonder how he could "remain in the saddle all day and at his desk half the night."

On one of these rides, a six-gun Federal battery opened on Lee and the officers with him. A shell struck the ground beside them and ricocheted right over their heads.

"Our horses soon became excited and quickened their pace

until it became a gallop," one officer recalled. "This did not suit General Lee. Traveller was curbed and punished into a walk, when the General remarked that he did not wish to have the appearance of being nervous under fire in the presence of the men."

On May 12, Lee telegraphed Jefferson Davis, suggesting that troops be withdrawn from the Carolinas, Georgia, and Florida, since Grant had recalled most of his soldiers from those states. The next day, he wired again, telling Davis that he was greatly outnumbered and that constant labor was impairing the efficiency of his men; he would at least like the return of Hoke's brigade.

On the eighteenth, he sent two telegrams asking that men from Richmond be sent to him at once. In his second dispatch, he said that if he did not get the requested reinforcements, he would have to fall back.

Davis carefully pointed out the necessity for keeping troops concentrated at the capital.

Lee replied that he was "fully alive to the importance of concentration and being near base," but that this consideration might force him to withdraw.

Davis then suggested that Lee call in reinforcements from the Shenandoah Valley. Lee replied that this was too hazardous.

On the twenty-first, Lee told the Secretary of War that Grant was changing base, and begged again for troops.

Grant was moving, so Robert wrote Mary, because he had grown "tired of forcing his passage through us." But one of Lee's engineers maintained bluntly that the "intolerable" stench of his unburied dead on his front caused the Federal to leave.

As soon as Lee learned of Grant's movement, he put his men on the march, and with that faculty "of discovering as if by intuition, the intention and purpose of his opponent," he headed them for Hanover Junction. They reached there a day before Grant, enabling them to take up a strong position, so that when the Army of the Potomac arrived, it found itself intercepted once again, and faced by a frowning line of entrenchments.

"Still I begrudge every step he makes toward Richmond," Lee wrote.

During the advance to Hanover, Lee drew off the road one day to watch the Stonewall Brigade pass. No matter how many times these men had seen him, they were always eager to see him again, and every glance was directed his way.

Suddenly, an old gray private, unable to suppress his desire for personal contact with Marse Robert, broke from the ranks and walked up to him. "They shook hands warmly, and at once engaged in animated conversation." As the lines moved on, one of his comrades looked back to see the soldier, his musket in one hand, the other on Traveller's neck, still chatting amiably with Lee.

When the Federal artillery opened fire on May 23 to effect a crossing of the North Anna River, Lee was watching the enemy from the garden of the Fox house on the riverbank. Mr. Fox stepped out and invited Lee to take a glass of something just as the batteries opened. Lee thanked him and declined, explaining that he would have to move on directly. But it was not every day that one had the chance to play host to General Lee, and Mr. Fox was insistent. Lee agreed to take a glass of buttermilk.

Mr. Fox brought out the glass of buttermilk and a slice of bread, which was stale; he apologized, but it was all he had. Just as Lee started to drink the milk, a round shot from a Federal cannon imbedded itself in the doorframe, missing him narrowly. Some keen-eyed Yankee had spied the figure on the porch, though it is doubtful if he recognized it as a Confederate soldier, for Lee was wearing his blue trousers of summer cloth, a checked shirt, and a brown linen sack coat.

Lee finished the milk with a composure that astonished Mr. Fox, and thanking him, hurried off before his presence caused the house to be destroyed.

It was unfortunate that Lee had not been more firm in his refusal of Mr. Fox's hospitality, for the buttermilk was tainted, and during the night he was taken sick with a severe intestinal disorder. On the twenty-fifth, he was described as "quite unwell," and had to stay in bed. He "could attend to nothing except what was absolutely necessary for him to know and act upon," Walter Taylor wrote in his journal. He was very ill, much more seriously than was generally suspected, and "those near him were very apprehensive lest he should be compelled to give up."

Lying there in misery and helplessness, he was sure that the opportunity for delivering Grant the decisive blow was escaping him, and he was overheard to cry out in frustration:

"We must strike them a blow! We must never let them pass us again! We must strike them a blow!"

To Dr. Gwathmey he said:

"If I can get one more pull at him, I will defeat him."

He was so upset by the thought of Grant's escape that his disposition suffered. He and Charles Venable, also quick to anger, got into an argument and both men soon lost their tempers. A good many hot words were exchanged before Venable bolted from Lee's tent "in a state of flurry and excitement, full to bursting," and shouted:

"I have just told the Old Man that he is not fit to command this army, and that he had better send for Beauregard!"

News of Lee's sickness and its nature soon spread, and a gentleman from the neighboorhood sent him a bottle of brandy, which brought Robert some relief. Others sent port wine, custards, and white bread, and from Richmond came a hamper of comestibles from Mrs. Stannard, Mrs. Tucker, and Mrs. Randolph. Mary was holding a bottle of whiskey in reserve if he should need it.

By the morning of the twenty-seventh, he was up, and when his scouts reported that the enemy was moving again, he ordered his army to Ashland. Colonel Taylor knew that only his "indomitable will" kept him going that day, for he was still weak, in pain, and unable to ride his horse. But he insisted on accompanying Ewell's corps, and was driven in a small carriage as far as the Jenkins house on the road to Atlee's, where he spent the night. The next day, he rode on to Atlee's and accepted a room in the Clarke house.

On the morning of the twenty-ninth, he telegraphed Beauregard, who had finally been recalled from Carolina and put in command at Richmond, to come up and confer about the transfer of several of his brigades to Lee's depleted ranks.

184

Beauregard came but insisted that he could spare no men, since he had only twelve thousand infantry.

The next day, Lee wrote Davis asking for reinforcements from Richmond.

The war in Virginia was now reduced to the attack and defense of Richmond. With the enemy so close, Davis and the other terrified guardians refused to part with any more local troops, their excessive fear blinding them to Lee's reasoning:

"If this army is unable to resist Grant, the troops under Genl Beauregard and in the city will be unable to defend it."

But Grant did not choose to fight on this ground, and began to move slowly toward the Chickahominy River.

"How General Lee finds out Grant's intentions I cannot imagine," an officer wrote his wife, "but as soon as Grant commenced to move Lee commenced also, though in some instances as much as twenty miles apart. Yet when Grant formed his new line, there was Lee in front of him as surely as they had moved by concerted action."

On May 31, Lee's desperation was such that he ordered every available man brought into the ranks. "Gather in all stragglers and men absent without proper authority. Send to the field hospitals and have every man capable of performing the duties of a soldier returned to this command. . . . Let every man fit for duty be present."

Grant now believed that he could deal one final, decisive blow that would crumple Lee's army. On the morning of June 3, he began his attack on the ground at Cold Harbor. This has been described as one of the

most desperate contested and murderous engagements of the war. Along the whole Federal line a simultaneous assault was made on the Confederate works, and at every point with the same disastrous result. Rank after rank was swept away until the column of assault was almost annihilated. Attack after attack was made, and men fell in myriads before the murderous fire from the Confederate lines.

In less than an hour, the battle was over, and thirteen thousand dead and wounded Federals lay in front of their lines. "The sight on our front was sickening, heartrending to the

185

stoutest soldier. Nothing like it was seen during the war," Colonel Sorrel wrote.

A few hours later, orders to renew the attack were received by the Federal division and brigade commanders, and there occurred a sight seldom seen on a battlefield and one that was never forgotten:

"The officers with drawn swords pointed the way, but the men stood motionless in their ranks, a silent, effective protest against further 'attrition.' "

A Union officer wrote bitterly to his sister:

"I am disgusted with the generalship displayed. Our men have, in many instances, been foolishly and wantonly sacrificed. Assault after assault has been ordered upon the enemy's entrenchments, when they knew nothing about the strength or position of the enemy. Thousands of lives might have been spared by the exercise of a little skill; but, as it is, the courage of the poor men is expected to obviate all difficulties. I must confess that, so long as I see such incompetency, there is no grade in the army to which I do not aspire."

And a Northern private spoke for many of his comrades when he wrote: ". . . may I inquire, without criticism, if the advantages gained justified these disproportionate losses? If not, was not General Grant balked and outgeneraled up to this time? It was evident to the private soldiers of the army that the principle of 'continuous hammering' had proved more damaging to the Union hammer than the Confederate anvil."

On June 4, Lee wrote to Mary from his headquarters at Gaines' Mill that he was "getting so well" he did not think it necessary for Mrs. Randolph to send him a bottle of blackberry wine, for he still had a bottle of port. He was pleased to hear that Mary and the girls planned to visit Fluvanna, and suggested that she go as soon as possible, for "it is evident that great danger is impending over us; & therefore those not required to meet it, or who might be overwhelmed by it should it fall upon us, should get out of harm's way in time."

He was interested in Mary's account of Mildred's recent visit at Shirley. A guard of four Federal cavalry officers was stationed about his mother's old home, and one day the eldest approached Mrs. Carter, saying that he had heard that one of General Lee's daughters was at the house. He had served with Lee in the Mexican War and in Texas, he explained, and admired him greatly.

"I'd be so proud if his daughter would come out and speak to me."

Hill Carter was indignant at such a suggestion, but Mildred was game, and went out to talk with the officer. He was delighted, and was soon talking about old army days. At recollections of her father, tears filled his eyes.

Robert was amused at Mildred's independence but was glad to hear that she had returned to The Mess. "You had better all keep together & go somewhere where you can get peace & quiet & not return to Richmond."

While he was inspecting a battery below Richmond, the soldiers gathered around to see him in such a large group it shortly attracted enemy fire.

"Men," Lee said quietly, "you had better go farther to the rear; you are exposing yourselves to unnecessary danger."

They obeyed, but Lee, seemingly unconscious of any personal danger, walked through the rain of bullets to pick up some small object from the ground and place it on a tree limb above his head. Later, it was learned that he had removed from danger an unfledged sparrow that had fallen from its nest.

For a short time, Lee was unsure of Grant's next move, for the Federal, having learned the futility of direct assault, had abandoned these tactics. Walter Taylor wrote jubilantly that "old U. S. Grant" seemed "pretty tired" of it all, while Lee's army was still in fine fettle, and just waiting for the signal to renew the fight.

On the morning of June 9, Grant made a surprise attack on Petersburg. It was repulsed valorously by the home guard, the militia, troops under General Wise, and reinforcements under Beauregard. Major Archer, a hero of the Mexican War, commanded the reserves. His old body servant, on his own initiative, dragged a small cannon from the public square to the waterworks, keeping up a constant fire to give the impression of a fort. Another Negro, a musician, gathered his little band, and

187

hurried up to Braggs Hill to play "Dixie" and "The Girl I Left Behind Me," hoping that the Yankees would think reinforcements were coming.

By June 18, Lee knew that Grant's whole force had crossed the James and, suspecting that he planned another attack on Petersburg, ordered his army there, leaving Richmond's outer defenses in charge of Custis, who had finally taken to the field.

When the Confederates reached Petersburg, they built formidable entrenchments, giving Grant pause. The extreme heat temporarily suspended all military operations.

Lee had come out of this recent, bloody campaign more endeared to his men than ever—"they idolize him now," an officer wrote. Tales of his personal bravery, his repeated attempts to lead assaults in person, and his countless acts of sympathy and kindness toward the private soldier were known to his men. His daily rides along the lines and his presence in the thick of fighting had given more soldiers the chance to have some personal contact with him. With no other pretext than the desire to shake his hand and say a few words, the "lowliest private" did not hesitate to approach, knowing that he would be met with kindness and candor.

It seemed to one officer that "what remained of the army were now more like comrades than mere private soldiers under his orders." With the exception of a few simple-minded fellows who would greet Lee with a "Howdy do, Dad" (to which he always returned an unaffected "Howdy do, my man"), they were comrades who regarded him with reverence.

One day when riding through the woods, he came on a private standing to one side. His head was bared and his face wore a look of rapture.

"Good-day, my man," Lee said.

"Good-day, General."

After Lee had passed, the soldier said:

"God bless Marse Robert! I wish he was emperor of the country and I was his carriage-driver!"

The men's faith in him was limitless. A sick soldier, making his way back to his regiment at Petersburg in the belief that a

188

battle would cure him, asked an officer he met for news from there. The officer, also going to Petersburg, could tell him only that Beauregard was there.

"General Beauregard is a pretty good general," the private said.

The officer then thought to add:

"General Lee has gone there also."

At this news, the veteran's face lighted up, and turning to some sick and wounded in an ambulance, he said:

"You hear that, boys? It's all right now in Petersburg. General Lee's gone over there. I ain't goin' to make myself miserable about the thing any more!"

Lee's consideration for his soldiers was manifested in many ways. On a train, a young private with one arm in a sling was struggling to get his overcoat on, for the morning was icy. He was using his teeth as well as his good arm in his efforts. None of the other passengers paid any attention, but Lee came up and gently drew the coat over the wounded arm and then buttoned it up comfortably. After saying a few pleasant words, he quietly went back to his seat. The soldier recognized Lee and never forgot his small act of kindness.

During the nine months of seige which marked Grant's attempt to take Petersburg, Lee was forced continually to extend his lines of entrenchments to meet Grant's threats; they finally reached the Southside Railroad, thirty-five miles distant. This extensive line was defended by some thirty thousand men, whom Northrup placed on half rations. This number was constantly decreasing because of desertion, disease, and casualties.

The enemy had a numerical superiority of at least two to one and had easy access, by means of the James River, to unlimited reinforcements, munitions, and food. Lee knew that it was only a matter of time until his line, stretched so thin, would break.

That it did not break until the following year was due entirely to Lee's courage, example, and personal magnetism, which were able to hold together a ragged, vermin-invested, starving army until he—not they—gave in to overwhelming odds.

189

"It is doubtful if, in any other struggle in history, the hopes of a people were more entirely wrapped up in a single individual," wrote a soldier. He noted that during the winter of 1864–65, to Lee "alone all men looked as the deus ex machina to extricate them from the danger surrounding them. . . . It was seen in the faces and the very tones of voice of all."

Old people came to his tent to beg him "with faltering voices not to expose himself, for, if he were killed, all would be lost. . . . All classes of people thus regarded the fate of the Confederacy as resting, not partially, but solely, upon the shoulders of Lee."

During communion one Sunday morning, as an officer's wife stood behind Lee at the chancel, she gently took hold of a button on his coat. After service, her husband asked why she had done it, and she said:

"I only wished to say when I went home that I had touched the hem of his garment."

These good people undertook to feed and clothe him and provide him with all necessities. Mrs. Randolph sent the blackberry wine, which he found "delicious," in spite of his playful protests that sight of her would do him more good. Kitty Stiles sent him socks, a lady from Petersburg also gave him blackberry wine, while from another came a "sett of sheets." Still others gave him bread, rolls, cheese, tea, soap, and material for shirts. Some men in Richmond sent a new suit of clothes.

"They are so much admired, I fear I shall have many applications for their loan from the beaux," he wrote.

Whenever possible, he shared the food with Mary or sent it to the hospitals. He was most appreciative of the ladies remembering him; this he insisted he enjoyed more than their presents, for he feared they were depriving themselves "of what is not necessary to me & may be to them."

It grew so "dreadfully hot" that he asked Mary to send from his trunk two brown linen vests, and two "gauze undershirts."

Headquarters tents were set up on the lawns at Violet Bank, the country home of Mrs. Shippen. It was a pleasant house in a grove of shade trees, and the mistress proved most attentive, supplying Lee daily with rolls, milk, vegetables, and occasional delicacies.

Mrs. Shippen interested him because she had had arthritis in every joint for three years. The previous winter, while recovering from pneumonia, her arthritis had been cured and she was able to walk again. This gave him hope that Mary might experience similar relief in some manner; as she had been very sick early in June, he wrote her the encouraging details of Mrs. Shippen's case. He chose June 30 on which to write, and tried to cheer her further by mention of their wedding anniversary:

"Do you recall what a happy day thirty-three years ago this was? How many hopes & pleasures it gave birth to?"

For the first time since the winter passed at Fredericksburg, he was able to visit local homes and find relaxation in the company of women and children. He had many friends in Petersburg, among them the Banisters and the Bollings, whose daughter, Mary Tabb, he greatly admired.

Every Sunday, he took dinner with Mrs. William A. Banister, whose husband had been killed during the defense of Petersburg. There was a bond here, for Light-Horse Harry Lee had been an intimate friend of William's grandfather, Colonel John Banister, and they had fought together in Lee's Legion. In this home, there were several daughters who brought Robert pleasure, although thirteen-year-old Anne was his favorite.

The menu for Sunday dinner at the Banister home never varied. There were always Irish potatoes, one slice of bacon apiece, dried apricots sweetened with sorghum, and sweet-potato coffee. Anne recalled that Lee never seemed to tire of it, and always complimented Mrs. Banister on her meal. "He was the kindest, dearest friend to my mother and to us all and as loving to me as a father," Anne wrote.

It distressed Lee that Anne had little chance to play out of doors in the besieged city, and one Sunday he suggested that she come out to Violet Bank, where there was no danger from shells. He asked her to invite all her friends, and promised to send a wagon for them the next day. After that, the trip to Violet Bank was almost a daily event.

191

Lee enjoyed visiting the charming wife of General A. P. Hill, whose little girl was also dear to him. One day when she met him at the door, she was holding a puppy in her arms.

"Oh, General Lee, here is 'Bobby Lee'; do kiss him!"

Robert, to her delight, leaned down and pretended to kiss the puppy affectionately.

One day, a number of small girls were rolling their hoops along the sidewalk in town when word was passed from one to another that General Lee was coming up the street. They stopped their play to watch him. To their surprise, he dismounted, and walking up to the group, gave each one a kiss; then with a wave and a smile, he rode on.

Another day when he went to see a special little friend, he was told by the servant that she was sick. He asked to be taken to her room, and when her mother returned from the neighbor's, she found Lee entertaining her daughter with games and stories, and the child sitting up and obviously better.

Lee's old love of banter revived as soon as he regained his health. One day, General Hampton, restored to good graces, happened to be at headquarters when it was time for dinner, and Lee asked him to stay. A small tureen of soup and some cornbread and bacon was all that Bryan could offer. Lee divided the soup with Hampton and, looking around the table, said gravely:

"I am creditably informed that the young men of my staff never eat soup."

When an old favorite returned to Richmond, he wrote spiritedly:

"I am glad to hear of Miss Carrie Mason again. I feared the Philistines had her. It is a little singular that she & Col. Jenifer should visit Richmond always at the same time. I fear it is ominous. Has she any superstition on the subject? Tell her to put away her idols. She must devote herself to her country. If she wants to do a good thing, tell her to come & see me. I hope she is as fair as ever."

In another letter, he asked Mary to tell "Miss Bettie Brandon that Col. Marshall is busy having his photograph taken. I do not see what she wants with the original & copy too."

Of a belle visiting Petersburg and "agitating the thoughts of the soldiers" by her presence, he wrote:

"I see her bright face occasionally as she flashes it on her beaux, but in pity she turns it away from me, for it is almost dazzling."

When writing of his nephew, Fitz Lee, who had been wounded, he reverted to the colorful imagery of his earlier years:

"How is my wounded nephew? . . . No wonder he covers his breast with his beard, which he hopes like the shield of Achilles will turn aside the darts of such fair archers. Cupid is always busy when Mars is quiet & our young heroes think it necessary to be killed in some way. It matters little to them which."

When Custis came to visit his father, Lee wrote that he felt "flattered" until he learned that "Miss Jenny Fairfax & a bevy of young damsels" had come down in the same train to attend a festival at the artillery camp. "That is the way children humbug their fathers," he said in mock disapproval.

He sent Mildred the notice of a meeting of the Cliosophic Society, which he had been invited to attend. "The only benefit that I could be to the oratory of the fair members would be to exhort them to practice saying 'yes,' so as to be prepared for an emergency."

He had recently seen Rob and wrote: "He has equipped himself with a new uniform from top to toe, & a new & handsome horse, is cultivating a marvelous beard & preparing for conquest."

One day, a number of his staff were seated around a table, discussing a mathematical problem; on the table was a jug and two cups. Lee came in to ask some question, then gave a solution to their problem, and walked out. The next morning, one of the aides was recounting in detail a strange dream he had had that night. Lee was listening with apparent interest, and when the story was finished, he remarked quietly:

"Well, that is not at all remarkable. When young gentlemen discuss at midnight mathematical problems, the unknown quan-

193

tities of which are a stone jug and two tin cups, they may expect to have strange dreams."

With the untrained officers who made up so great a part of his army, with those armed citizens who had rallied to their country's defense, and with the privates themselves, he often found opportunities to teach them or set an example.

One day as he rode along the lines with General Gordon, he remarked deprecatingly that certain works were "very badly located." Noticing that some young officers were closer than he had realized and had doubtless overheard, he added:

"But these works were located by skilful engineers who probably know their business better than we do."

Another time when inspecting the lines with General Henry Heth, Lee asked him if a certain fort he had ordered was completed yet. Hesitantly, Heth replied that he thought it was almost finished, so Lee suggested that they ride over and see it.

Lee found that no work had been done since his last visit. Turning to Heth, he said:

"General, you say this fort is about finished?"

"I have misunderstood my engineers, sir."

"But you did not speak of your engineers. You spoke of the fort as nearly completed."

Anticipating a severe reprimand, Heth grew nervous, and his agitation was sensed by his high-spirited horse. The animal began to prance and curvette, and Heth had trouble controlling him. Lee knew that the horse had been given to Mrs. Heth. Assuming his blandest manner, he asked:

"General, doesn't Mrs. Heth ride this horse occasionally?"

"Yes, sir."

"Well, General, you know I am very much interested in Mrs. Heth's safety. I fear that horse is too nervous for her to ride without danger, and I suggest that in order to make him more quiet, you ride him at least once a day to this fort."

One of Lee's generals on the lines near Richmond was often conspicuous for his absence, especially at times when there was heavy fighting. It was not known that Lee was aware of this until they met one day.

"Good morning, General," Lee said witheringly, "are you not

194

afraid to trust yourself so far from the city, and come to where all this firing and danger is?"

"Oh, General, I am somewhere upon the lines every day."

"Indeed? I am very glad to learn it, sir. Good morning!" And he rode off.

Another day when he came on a working party extending the trenches to keep up with Grant, he said to the officer in charge:

"Good morning, my young friend. I feel sorry for you."

"Why so, General?"

"Because you have so much to do."

From these few tactful words, the officer knew that Lee expected a great deal of work from him.

Members of his staff were frequently treated to lessons, even to the proper method of buttering hot bread. Captain A. R. H. Ranson, assigned to headquarters duty the previous winter, was with Lee the morning he reached Petersburg. Temporary headquarters were set up in a public building, and the ladies of the town sent in a breakfast of coffee, loaves of fresh bread, and sweet butter.

Lee noticed that Ranson was crumbling his hot bread as he buttered it. Taking up a loaf, Lee spread butter on the end, cut off the slice, and handed it to his aide, saying:

"Now, that is the way to cut bread and butter. Look what a mess you have made by cutting off your slice first and then trying to butter it afterward."

When he came to Richmond for conferences with Davis, his friends noticed that he looked "vigorous and cheerful." While in the capital, he took the time to call on all his favorite young women, but complained that they were so surrounded with beaux he could only get a "glimpse." But even a glimpse of an especially pretty one was heartening, he admitted, and helped carry him through.

The truth was that when Lee was in a room the young men soon had reason to complain, since the girls immediately flocked to his side, and stayed there until he left.

A number of these belles were in doubt whether he would approve of the occasional dancing parties they gave, and one day called on him for an opinion.

"Why, of course, my dear child," he told the spokeswoman, "my boys need to be heartened up when they get their furloughs. Go on, look your prettiest, and be just as nice to them as ever you can be."

At this time he accused Custis of "ruining" his character with the young ladies and causing the family's fidelity to be suspected, for several girls, "wishing I suppose to see how they would like me for a father-in-law, have requested my photograph, which I have promised, & have relied on those you were to have sent me. Not one has ever reached me & I am taxed with breach of promise. See what a strait you have placed me in."

Early in November, when the grove at Violet Bank lost its leaves and exposed the encampment to the range of Federal batteries, headquarters had to be moved. Colonel Long had some time ago been promoted to General of artillery, so it fell to Walter Taylor to find a suitable place. The Beasley house on High Street was vacant, so Taylor moved in, had Lee's room prepared with a cheerful fire, and "everything made as cozy as possible." But, as Taylor wrote, "it was entirely too pleasant for him, for he is never so uncomfortable as when comfortable." A day or two later, Lee told him that he wanted to visit the cavalry.

So we packed up bag and baggage, books and records, and moved to a point about eight miles distant, pitched our tents, and concluded we were fixed for some days [Taylor wrote]. The next morning, however, the general concluded that we had better return. So back I came to Petersburg, and, as I could find no better place—nor a *worse* one that was suitable—I returned to the house we had just vacated.

The stay at the Beasley house was cut short when the newly married couple who had rented it wanted to move in. Taylor knew that Lee would prefer his tent, but he also knew that both Mary and Rooney had been urging him to consider his health. Recently, Lee had written Mary:

I am as sensible as you & Fitzhugh can be of my failing strength & approaching infirmities, & am careful to shield myself from exciting causes as I can be. But what can a man give to himself in time of war? It is from no desire of exposure or hazard that I live in a tent, but from necessity. I must be where I can speedily & at all times attend to the duties of my position & be near or accessible to the officers with whom I have to act. What house can I get to hold all the staff. Our citizens are very kind in offering me a room or rooms in their houses where I could be sheltered, but it would separate me from the staff officers & delay the transactions of business & turn the residence of my landlords into barracks where officers, couriers, distressed women, &c. would be entering night & day.

If Colonels Marshall and Venable had not been sick, it is unlikely that Lee would have consented to accept Mr. Turnbull's invitation to occupy Edge Hill about two miles from town. They could use almost the entire house, for Mr. Turnbull had sent his family away "for fear of Genl. Grant & his missles."

Taylor took advantage of Lee's absence in Richmond to make the move. After selecting suitable rooms for Lee and his fellow staff members, Taylor found that all that was left for him was "one of the miserable little back rooms." But Mr. Turnbull offered him the parlor, and delightedly Taylor described his quarters:

"I am finely fixed . . . with piano, sofas, rocking-chairs, and pictures—capital surroundings for a winter campaign."

When Lee returned, he seemed pleased with his room, but on coming into Taylor's, he said:

"Ah, you are finely fixed. Couldn't you find any other room?"

"No," Taylor told him, "*but this will do;* I can make myself tolerably comfortable here."

"He was struck dumb with amazement at my impudence, and soon vanished," Taylor wrote.

But Lee found the house "dreadfully cold" and longed for "a good wood to encamp in, where I could pitch my tent." His door refused to shut entirely, and he complained: "I have a goodly company of cats & puppies around my hearth."

One sunny afternoon, he was delighted to have three little girls call on him. Each carried a basket. The eldest, Fanny, who was not over eight, brought eggs laid by her hens; the second girl had pickles made by her mother, and the youngest had popcorn she had grown in her garden.

197

They were the daughters of a Mrs. Nottingham who was a refugee from the neighborhood of Arlington. They were further endeared to Lee when they told him that Fanny spun thread for their mother to weave the cloth of their brothers' clothes.

"I have not had so pleasant a visit in a long time," Robert wrote. "I fortunately was able to fill their baskets with apples, which distressed poor Bryan, & I begged them to bring me nothing but kisses & to keep the eggs, corn, &c. for themselves."

The girls became regular callers, always bringing something besides kisses, and often a present to be sent on to Mary, who started a correspondence with them.

In spite of the generosity of the townspeople and the tireless efforts of Bryan, headquarters fare was often meager. General Ewell told about once when he was unable to stay for the evening meal, Lee insisted that he take two cold sweet potatoes reserved for his own lunch.

After the Hon. Thomas Connally, Irish M.P. from Donegal, had visited Lee at Edge Hill, he told his hostess, Mrs. Roger Pryor, that she was better provided for than the General.

"You should have seen 'Uncle Robert's' dinner to-day, Madam! He had two biscuits, and he gave me one."

Another day he told Mrs. Pryor:

"We had a glorious dinner to-day! Somebody sent 'Uncle Robert' a box of sardines."

When the partisan ranger, Colonel John S. Mosby, stopped at Edge Hill in February, he found Lee "not only kind but affectionate." He insisted that the Colonel take dinner with him, though he warned him that it was apt to be meager. When a leg of mutton was served, Lee good-humoredly accused his staff of having stolen it.

At Christmas, the people contributed the soldiers' dinner, sending to Richmond great quantities of ham, mutton, beef, chicken, turkey, duck, geese, vegetables, and dried fruit. These were prepared at the Ballard House, placed in barrels, and shipped to the fronts. A special barrel containing a dozen fine turkeys was delivered to Edge Hill.

Lee's staff opened the barrel in the yard, and laid the turkeys

198

on a board in the snow, putting the largest one, tagged for the General, in the middle. When Lee came up, he said:

"This then, is my turkey. I don't know, gentlemen, what you are going to do with your turkeys, but I wish mine sent to the hospital in Petersburg so that some of the convalescents may have a good Christmas dinner."

As he walked off, the young men looked at each other in silence, then, without a word, replaced the turkeys in the barrel, and sent it to the hospital. There was no need for regret, for all the staff received dinner invitations for Christmas Day. In his foragings, Bryan was given a plump turkey which he roasted for dinner.

Christmas morning, Robert attended church to "offer my feeble praise to our Merciful Father for the precious gift of his Holy Son." After service, he invited Colonel Talcott to have dinner with him.

He and the Beautiful Talcott's son had "nice turkey & potatoes" all to themselves, for, as he told Mary, "my young family had gone to more pleasant feasts." But he enjoyed the quiet day. When Mary wrote of the large gathering she had assembled, he replied:

"I am unable to have any enjoyment of that kind now."

14

LATE in November, Longstreet's adjutant reported to Lee that "over 100 of Gen. Pickett's men are in the guard-house, charged with desertion. He explains this state of things by the fact that every man sentenced to be shot for desertion in this division for the past two months has been reprieved."

Lee endorsed this with the notation: "Desertion is increasing in the army, notwithstanding all my efforts to stop it. I think rigid execution of the law is mercy in the end. The great want in our army is firm discipline," and sent it to the Secretary of War, who in turn gave it to the President, "for his information."

199

On November 29, Davis returned the report to Lee with this biting endorsement: "When deserters are arrested they should be tried, and if the sentences are reviewed and remitted, that is not a proper subject for the criticism of a military commander."

Lee knew that virtual starvation was the chief factor in desertion. Often the daily quota consisted of one-third pound of rancid Nassau bacon (which the soldiers insisted the blockading fleet had allowed to slip through, to poison them) and a little corn meal. Frequently, there was nothing at all, and the men would then gather the spilled corn from under the horses's feet, and parch and eat it to keep alive.

But even in this extremity, they retained their spirits and could laugh at their plight. If one of them grew sick from such a supper, the next morning he might greet his commanding officer:

"Hello, General; I'm all right now. I ate a lot of corn last night, and if you'll just have the commissary issue me a good mess of hay for breakfast, I'll be ready for the next fight."

By January, 1865, Lee's thin gray line had become yet thinner, and he wrote forcefully to the Secretary of War, in his candor treading heavily on official toes. He told Seddon about the "alarming frequency" of desertions, and forwarded him papers to prove it. He ascribed the dissatisfaction to "insufficiency of food and non-payment of troops."

I know there are great difficulties in procuring supplies, but I cannot help thinking that with proper energy, intelligence, & experience on the part of the Commissary Department a great deal more could be accomplished. There is enough in the country . . . if it was properly sought for. I do not see why supplies that are collected from day to day, could not by intelligent effort, be collected in such a manner as to have more on hand at a given time. The fact that they are collected at all is proof that they exist, and it must be possible to gather more in a given time than is now done. It will not answer to reduce ration in order to make up for deficiencies in the Subsistence Department. The proper remedy is increased effort . . . and intelligent management.

Lee's emphasis of the word *intelligent* did not find favor with Jefferson Davis.

Hopes for the success of the cause waned with the loss of Savannah, the reverses in the Valley, and Sherman's devastating march through South Carolina. Popular discontent with the President, his Cabinet, and Congress was so marked that when the *Richmond Examiner* suggested a counterrevolution as the only solution, it seemed so reasonable no one was even startled. On January 19, the *Examiner*'s editor wrote:

There is but one known way to us of curing this evil; it is by Congress making a law investing General Lee with absolute military power to make all appointments and direct campaigns. It may, indeed, be said that in this new position General Lee would have to relieve generals and appoint others and order movements which perhaps might not satisfy the strategic acumen of the general public; and how, it might be asked, could he satisfy everybody any more than Mr. Davis? The difference is simply that every Confederate would repose implicit confidence in General Lee, both in his military skill and in his patriotic determination to employ the ablest men, whether he liked them or not.

The *Examiner* had come a long way from the days when it had pointed a taunting finger at "Evacuating Lee."

The popular movement that would force Davis to resign and let Lee take his place, vesting him with dictatorial powers, gained widespread support. If it had been offered to him, Lee would have refused the office, for he had expressed his views strongly on the subject of military heads of state. But the association of his name with the movement was enough to cause strained relations, inaugurated by Davis, between Lee and the President.

When Lee advised that General W. H. C. Whiting be sent south, Davis pettishly endorsed the letter: "Let General Lee order General Whiting to report here, and it may then be decided whether he will be sent south or not."

When Sherman was marching unhindered, Lee wrote realistically to Davis: "I fear it may be necessary to abandon our cities, and preparation should be made for that contingency." Davis branded this suggestion as "pernicious."

When Lee advised the destruction of tobacco in Richmond warehouses to prevent it from falling into enemy hands, Davis regarded the intimation that the Federals would ever reach the capital as "treasonable."

Davis, in his message to Congress, stated that the Confederacy had no vulnerable points, and that operations in the field that year had resulted in no disadvantages to the cause. He promised the people great victories after the destined reverses had run out, provided they refrained from despondency and filled the ranks of the army.

He now telegraphed Lee: "Rumors, assumed to be based on your views, have affected the public, and, it is reported, obstructed needful legislation. A little further progress will produce panic."

He asked Lee to come to Richmond and discuss certain measures with him. Lee was unable to leave the army, and replied:

"Send me your measures and I will send you my views."

Davis wrote a long and angry letter, which he concluded witheringly:

"Rest assured I will not ask your views in answer to measures. Your counsels are no longer wanted in this matter."

After Lee read the letter, he took the next train to Richmond to " 'suage" the President.

Davis' petulance became general knowledge and prompted one shrewd observer to write:

"Never before did such small men rule such a great people."

To quiet some of the agitation, Davis proposed to enlarge Lee's powers by assigning him command of the armies in the South Atlantic states. This would shift to Lee's shoulders responsibility for the reverses there, which nothing could now prevent.

But Lee had more than he could do to provide and plan for his own army and the department of North Carolina, and he declined the offer. But dissatisfaction with the conduct of the war was so strong that on January 17, Congress addressed an appeal to the President to make Lee commander in chief of the Confederate Armies.

It seemed that this time Davis would be forced to appoint him, but while he was deliberating, he heard a rumor that

Lee had decided to accept command of the South Atlantic states. If true, it might not be necessary to create the new post. He wrote Lee for confirmation.

I do not know how such a report originated, nor am I aware of having said anything to authorize it [Lee replied]. If I had the ability I would not have the time. The arrangement of the details of this army extended as it is, providing for its necessities & directing operations engrosses all my time & still I am unable to accomplish what I desire & see to be necessary. I could not therefore propose to undertake more.

No reply could have pleased Davis better. He showed it to members of Congress as proof of Lee's unwillingness to take on more responsibility, which would of course include the office of commander in chief, if it should be created.

But Davis had hedged on this issue too long. In response to "the clamorous demands of the people," he signed the bill creating a general in chief and on February 1, appointed Lee—"at least two years too late," was the general reaction.

On February 2, General Gordon reviewed General John Pegram's troops. Regardless of the wintry weather, it was decided to hold the inspection in honor of Mrs. Pegram, a bride of less than a month. She was Hetty Cary of Baltimore, and described as "the handsomest woman in the Southland." Invitations were sent to all generals in the area, and to many ladies in Richmond and Petersburg.

This day as the troops filed by they did not have eyes only for Marse Robert, but also for the radiant figure beside him. When she rode off the field after the review, her horse knocked down "an excited 'Tar Heel,'" who jumped up and as she began to apologize, "broke in as he seized his old hat from his head:

" 'Never mind, Miss. You might have rid all over me, indeed you might!' "

Three days later, while Lee was in church in Petersburg, a courier brought the message that the enemy in strong force had come up to Hatcher's Run, and part of his infantry, with Gregg's cavalry in support, had crossed the brook.

He left after he had taken communion, and rode rapidly to

the right, where he found his troops already engaged. There were some recruits among them who were frightened by their first encounter with the enemy, and were making for the rear. When Lee tried to rally them, one terrified man shouted as he streaked by:

"Great God, old man; get out of the way! You don't know nothing!"

Toward night the Federals retired, but the next morning there was a hard-fought and bloody encounter in which General Pegram was mortally wounded. In the confusion that followed, his division fell back; but when General William Mahone's troops were brought up, the enemy was driven to his defenses.

The men suffered intensely from the cold as they stayed in battle line for three days, without shoes, blankets, or warm clothing, and no meat ration. They were subjected alternately to hail, sleet, and four inches of snow. As Lee rode down the lines, some haggard shivering soldier would appeal to him as to a father:

"See, General; I have no shoes." Or, "I have had nothing to eat."

This needless suffering angered him. On February 8, he wrote the Secretary of War the most forceful letter yet:

If some change is not made and the Commissary Department reorganized, I apprehend dire results. The physical strength of the men, if their courage survives, must fail under this treatment. Our cavalry has to be dispersed for want of forage. . . . I had to bring William H. F. Lee's division forty miles Sunday night to get him into position. Taking these facts in connection with the paucity of our numbers, you must not be surprised if calamity befalls us. . . .

Yielding to pressure, Davis relieved Northrup, replacing him with the energetic Isaac M. St. John, who had successfully headed the mining and niter bureau. He was a man in whom Lee had faith.

Davis did not part willingly with his favorite. He was still unable to see, or was unwilling to admit, Northrup's failings, and wrote to his friend, Dr. John Craven, expressing surprise that even Lee, "otherwise so moderate and conservative, was

finally induced to join the injurious clamor" against his commissary general.

On February 9, Lee issued General Order No. 1, announcing his acceptance of the command: "Deeply impressed with
the difficulties and responsibility of the position, and humbly
invoking the guidance of Almighty God, I rely for success upon
the courage and fortitude of the army, sustained by the patriotism and firmness of the people. . . . The headquarters
of the army . . . will be, for the present, with the Army of
Northern Virginia. . . ."

The people, and his friends and relatives, continued to
shower him with presents. From "kind Kitty Stiles" came two
more knitted jackets, some catsup, pickles, preserved cherries,
and a letter filled with family news. His cousin Carrie Stuart
had, during a momentary lapse, made him a pair of drawers
so small, he doubted "whether sweet Carrie could squeeze her
sweet self into them, much less a man of my ample dimensions."
He sent them on to Mary with the suggestion that she put "a
broad strip down the back." A Richmond admirer thoughtlessly
gave him a dog:

"He would be very much out of place following me in a
campaign. He would be exposed to danger, hunger, & thirst,
& I think he would be equally miserable cooped up in Richmond." He suggested if it were agreeable to all concerned,
that the dog be given to Dr. Charles Cocke, who lived at
Bremo: "He could roam the country & sport in the James."

But with Sherman and Schofield both advancing virtually
unopposed, there was little time to consider the fate of the dog
or to acknowledge his more practical gifts.

"I shall endeavour to do my duty & fight to the last," he
wrote Mary. "Should it be necessary to abandon our position
to prevent being surrounded, what will you do? . . . You
must consider the question & make up your mind. . . . It is a
fearful condition."

At 2 A.M. on March 3, General Gordon was asked to report
to Lee's quarters at Edge Hill.

As I entered [Gordon wrote], General Lee, who was entirely alone,
was standing at the fireplace, his arm on the mantel and his head

resting on his arm as he gazed into the coal fire burning in the grate. He had evidently been up all the previous night. For the first time in my intercourse with him, I saw a look of depression on his face. . . . The hour had come . . . when he could no longer carry alone the burden or conceal his forebodings of impending disaster.

He appeared to Gordon to be suffering from physical illness, but in answer to questions about his health, Lee said that he was well enough. He had sent for Gordon to discuss the prospects. Lee motioned him to a chair at a table covered with recent reports from every portion of the army, and sat down opposite. Together they went over them.

Though Gordon knew that the army was in desperate straits, he learned that the situation was far worse than he had imagined.

"The revelation was startling," he admitted.

When they finished the reports, Lee began to give his estimate of the situation, talking of the numbers of men he had to throw against Grant, and the disporportionate numbers of the enemy.

Lee's vein of humor often exhibited itself when least expected, and while talking about Grant's superiority of men and resources, he lightened the mood by saying:

"By the way, I received a verbal message from General Grant today."

"What was it?" Gordon asked.

"General Grant sent under a flag of truce a request to cease fire long enough for him to bury his dead between the picket-lines."

When the officer reached Lee's tent, he explained his mission, and then said:

"General, as I left General Grant's tent this morning he gave me these instructions: 'Give General Lee my personal compliments, and say to him that I keep such close touch with him that I know what he eats for breakfast every morning.'"

I told that officer [Lee said] to tell General Grant that I thought there must be some mistake about the latter message, for unless he had fallen from grace since I last saw him, he would not permit me to eat such a breakfast as mine without dividing his with me. I also requested that officer to present my compliments to General Grant, and say to him that I knew perhaps as much about his dinners as he knew about my breakfasts.

Lee got up, and resting one hand on the reports, stood silently contemplating them for a moment. Then he began to walk "to and fro across the room, leaving me to my thoughts," Gordon recalled. "He again took his seat facing me at the table, and asked me to state frankly what I thought under these circumstances it was best to do . . . Looking at me intently, he awaited my answer." Gordon told him:

"First, make terms with the enemy, the best we can get. Second, abandon Petersburg and Richmond, unite with Johnston in North Carolina and strike Sherman before Grant can join him.

"Lastly, fight, and without delay!"

Though Lee did not say so directly, he led Gordon to believe that he thought immediate steps should be taken to make peace. Gordon then urged him to see the President at once but Lee was reluctant, as a soldier, to interfere in political matters. But he at last said to Gordon:

"I will go."

"It was near sunrise when I left him," Gordon wrote. "Although he had not slept during the night, he took the first train to Richmond."

Lee did not tell Gordon that he had written Grant the previous day to propose a meeting between them.

This letter to Grant had been suggested by Longstreet, who, during a flag-of-truce meeting with Federal General Edward Ord, was led to believe that Grant would willingly hold an interview with Lee to discuss "the possibility of arriving at a satisfactory adjustment of the present unhappy difficulties by means of a military convention."

Jefferson Davis had said again and again that reunion with the North was "unthinkable," and he refused to discuss peace unless the Confederacy were recognized and treated as an independent nation. Lee condemned his attitude as "shortsighted in the extreme."

Davis was therefore not responsive to any suggestions from anyone to treat for peace. But no man is ever entirely consistent, and as jealous as Davis was of his powers, and as opposed to peace on any terms but his own, he did consent to Lee's proposal to meet Grant.

But such a meeting was not to be, for when Grant sent Lee's letter to Secretary of War Stanton, and asked for orders, he was told:

The President directs me to say that he wishes you to have no conference with General Lee, unless it be for the capitulation of General Lee's army or some minor or purely military matter. He instructs me to say that you are not to decide, discuss, or confer on any political question. Such questions the President holds in his own hands, and will submit them to no military conferences or conventions. Meantime you are to press to the utmost your military advantages.

This was followed by a second message that disclosed Stanton's pettiness:

". . . I will add that General Ord's conduct in holding inter-course with General Longstreet upon political questions not committed to his charge is not approved. . . . You will please in the future instruct officers appointed to meet with rebel officers to confine themselves to the matters specially committed to them."

While in Richmond, Lee went before Congress to urge immediate action in behalf of the army. But his strong, simple words which told of the thinning lines, the lack of clothing, and the near-starvation of men and animals, fell on deaf ears.

That night, he went to the house on Franklin Street and after dinner, when the girls had gone to their mother's room, the men went to sit in the parlor. Custis lighted a cigar and, seating himself on one side of the fire, prepared to read the newspaper. His cousin, George Taylor Lee, Carter's son and a private in the cadet corps called in to help with local defense, took a chair opposite.

Lee was too much engrossed with his thoughts to be still, and paced the room, up and down, up and down, his face grave,

Robert E. Lee in 1862

This picture is believed to have been taken by the Richmond photographer, Minnis, of Minnis and Cowell. In the Cook collection.

Walter Herron Taylor

Lee's indefatigable and indispensable Assistant Adjutant-General, who joined the staff when Lee was in command of Virginia's forces and stayed with him four years.

William Henry Fitzhugh ("Rooney") Lee

Robert E. Lee's second son in his Confederate uniform; he was a major-general of cavalry. He went to Harvard, pulled stroke oar on the crew, and served in the United States Army until April, 1861. In the Cook collection.

COURTESY THE VALENTINE
MUSEUM, RICHMOND, VA.

Eleanor Agnes Lee

She was always called Agnes. When still a baby her father unerringly predicted that this third daughter would be "the prettiest of the flock."

COURTESY THE CONFEDERATE
MUSEUM, RICHMOND, VA.

Lee's Camp Chest

On top is the tinware to which his fastidious staff members objected strenuously.

COURTESY THE CONFEDERATE
MUSEUM, RICHMOND, VA.

Robert E. Lee in 1863

On June 11, Lee wrote his wife that he had asked their son
Custis to pay Mr. Minnis for some photographs, a dozen of
which he had asked be sent to her. "I want none myself," he
added. This is doubtless the picture to which he was referring.

Robert E. Lee in 1864

That year, the young Richmond sculptor, Edward V. Valentine, then studying in Berlin, offered to make a statuette of Lee to be sold at a bazaar in Liverpool, England, for the benefit of disabled Confederate veterans. Since a worthy cause was involved, Lee probably posed more willingly than usual for the Richmond photographer, J. Vannerson. He heartily disliked being photographed or painted. His youngest son wrote that, because his father "could never bear to have his picture taken, there are no likenesses of him that really give his sweet expression." In the Cook collection.

COURTESY THE VALENTINE MUSEUM, RICHMOND, VA.

The First Picture of Lee on Traveller

This picture of Lee on his favorite horse was probably taken in the autumn of 1864, when the Army of Northern Virginia was at Petersburg, Va.

COURTESY WASHINGTON AND LEE UNIVERSITY

Robert E. Lee in April, 1865

The photographer Mathew Brady asked Lee to sit for a picture "the day but one" after his return from Appomattox. Lee's first reaction was negative. He was eventually persuaded by Mrs. Lee. He is seated on the back verandah opening on the garden of the Franklin Street house. At Lee's right stands his eldest son, Custis, and at his left the peerless Walter H. Taylor.

"The Mess"
707 East Franklin Street
Richmond

Robert E. Lee returned to this house after the surrender at Appomattox. The house served first as bachelor quarters for Custis Lee and several brother officers stationed in Richmond. Early in 1864 Mrs. R. E. Lee and her daughters joined the household.

COURTESY THE VIRGINIA STATE CHAMBER OF COMMERCE

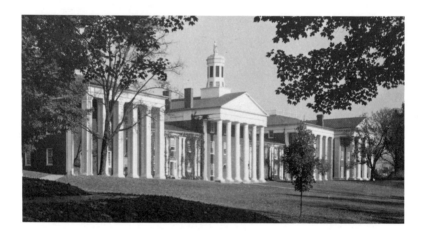

View of Washington and Lee University Campus

Robert E. Lee was President of this school, known then as Washington College, from October, 1865, until his death in October, 1870.

COURTESY WASHINGTON AND LEE UNIVERSITY

The Chapel on the Campus

Custis Lee selected the plan and his father supervised the chapel's construction.

The New "President's House" on the Campus

Over Lee's protests that the money should be spent for the benefit of the College, the Trustees voted in 1868 to build a larger and more comfortable house for the President. It was finished early the next year.

Robert E. Lee in April, 1869

While in Washington at the end of April, Lee called on President Grant. He also had his picture taken by Alexander Gardner in Mathew Brady's Washington studio. Lee already shows signs of his illness.

COURTESY WASHINGTON AND LEE UNIVERSITY

Mrs. Robert E. Lee

This portrait is attributed to L. M. D. Guillaume, and was probably painted around 1867, a time when she had a maid, Milly Howard, who "took great pride in dressing her up, so far as she was allowed, in becoming caps, etc. to receive her numerous visitors." Mrs. Lee had no interest in clothes or fashion. Portrait in the collection of Mrs. George Bolling Lee.

The Last Photograph

This is doubtless the last time Lee (on right) posed for a photographer. While in Savannah in April, 1870, on a tour for his
health, he visited his West Point classmate, Joseph E. Johnston,
opposite whom he is seated in this picture. The two old warriors, probably at Mrs. Johnston's suggestion, were photographed together in several poses. Lee appears to be much
older than his sixty-three years. Six months later he was dead.

his eyes fixed on the floor, and his hands clasped behind his back. Suddenly he stopped beside his son, and said:

"Well, Mr. Custis, I have been up to see the Congress and they do not seem to be able to do anything except to eat peanuts and chew tobacco while my army is starving. I told them the condition the men were in, and that something must be done at once, but I can't get them to do anything—or they are unable to do anything."

Custis did not respond, and his father continued his promenade. After a few more turns to the end of the room and back, he stopped in front of his son again.

"Mr. Custis, when this war began, I was opposed to it, bitterly opposed to it, and I told these people that, unless every man should do his whole duty, they would repent it. And now— they will repent it!"

When he returned to Edge Hill, he called Gordon in to tell him that nothing could be done in Richmond, "for Congress was unable to appreciate the situation." Although he spoke only in the highest terms of Davis' devotion to the cause, he did say this:

"You know that the President is very pertinacious in opinion and purpose."

He did not tell Gordon how many times Davis had ignored his suggestions that the government make preparations to move.

One afternoon shortly after his return to Petersburg, he rode out three miles to Cottage Farm, to call on Mrs. Roger Pryor. He took her small daughter in his lap, and as he caressed the child, talked to the mother on a variety of subjects. Presently he asked her why she had never come to see him during the winter, and she said that she had not wanted to bother him, had not wanted to join what she called the "buttermilk persecution"—the procession of children and servants who came with pails of buttermilk and other presents.

"Persecution! Such things keep me alive!" he told her. "Last night when I reached my headquarters, I found a card on my table with a hyacinth pinned to it, and these words: 'For General Lee, with a kiss.' "

Tapping his breast he added:

"Now I have my hyacinth and my card—and I mean to find my kiss!"

When he was ready to go, he walked over to the window and looked out at the barren fields.

"You only, General, can tell me if it is worth my while to put the ploughshare into those fields," Mrs. Pryor said.

"Plant your seeds, Madam. The doing it will be some reward."

There was no alternative but to fight on. Lee made a flank attack on March 31, boldly taking the initiative by falling on the enemy while he was entangled in a swampy forest. The first results were encouraging, but on meeting the main body of Federals, the Confederates were forced back.

The next day, the enemy broke through Lee's lines, forcing them from their position.

General A. P. Hill—"chivalrous, dashing, distinguished on many hot fields"—was killed in this engagement. It was whispered that, in his despair, he had purposely ridden far beyond his lines into the enemy fire.

Tears filled Lee's eyes when he received the report. "He is at rest now, and we who are left are the ones to suffer," he said quietly.

To the young man delegated to tell the lovely Mrs. Hill, Lee said:

"Colonel, break the news to her as gently as possible."

It was noticed that Lee was more than usually heedless of Federal fire these days. A staff officer who was bringing him a report saw him mounted on Traveller on the top of a hill in view and range of the enemy. When the officer rode up the exposed side of the hill, Lee rebuked him for taking unnecessary chances. The young man said he was ashamed to seek shelter when his commander was so exposed.

"It is my duty to be here," Lee said sharply. "I must see. Go back the way I told you to, sir!"

On April 2, Lee wired the Secretary of War:

"I see no prospect of doing more than holding our position here till night. I am not certain that I can do that. . . . I advise that all preparations be made for leaving Richmond tonight. I will advise later, according to circumstances."

This telegram was received at the capital at 10:40 A.M., and a messenger was sent at once to St. Paul's Church, where Jefferson Davis was attending service.

"The President, without any show of excitement, got up and walked out. I soon followed him as did many others, feeling there was important news," an officer wrote his wife.

Later that day, Lee telegraphed both the President and the Secretary of War: "It is absolutely necessary that we should abandon our position tonight" or run the risk of being cut off. He gave the War Secretary his destination as Amelia Court House. At three o'clock that afternoon, he wrote a letter to the President, notifying him that the troops would all be directed to Amelia Court House.

Jefferson Davis was now faced with the grim reality of evacuating the capital. Since it was a subject he had consistently refused to consider, he was entirely unprepared, and sent Lee a telegram, telling him that to leave that night would "involve the loss of many valuables both for the want of time to pack, and of transportation." By this time, Lee was completely out of patience with him. On receiving the message, he tore it into bits.

"I'm sure I gave him sufficient notice!" he said angrily, recalling his repeated efforts over the last months to make Davis recognize the necessity for evacuation and prepare for it.

This same day, Walter Taylor telegraphed his brother, Robinson, on duty near Richmond, that he wanted to get married that afternoon and for him to make all necessary preparations. A message to the same effect was delivered to the young lady in question, Elizabeth Saunders, while she was in church.

After Taylor finished his work at headquarters, he asked Lee for permission to go to Richmond and say good-by to his mother and sisters—and marry Miss Saunders—before the army set out to join Joe Johnston. Lee was surprised and at first reluctant but, ever-sympathetic with the course of true love, he consented.

Dr. Minnegerode, the rector of St. Paul's, performed the ceremony in the Crenshaw home, where Miss Saunders was

211

staying. As Taylor wrote afterward: "As will be readily understood, the occasion was not one of great hilarity, though I was very happy."

Around four o'clock that morning, he kissed his wife goodby, sprang on his horse, and galloped back to rejoin Lee in retreat.

Self-contained and serene, he acted as one who is conscious of having accomplished all that was possible in the line of duty, and was undisturbed by the adverse conditions in which he found himself [a staff officer wrote of Lee]. There was no apparent excitement and no sign of apprehension as he issued his orders for the retreat of his sadly reduced army.

He had few comments to make and these were always brief.

"This is a bad business, Colonel," he said to one staff member; while to another he remarked with a trace of sadness, that young man thought:

"Well, Colonel, it has happened just as I told them it would at Richmond. The line has been stretched until it has broken."

Early the next morning, Anne Banister stood on her front porch watching the troops file quietly by.

"Not one soldier in five had any shoes," she remembered. "Their clothes were in rags but their heads were held proudly up as they marched by."

She saw two soldiers carrying a cumbersome chair that had on one side a table that swung to the front, while the other arm was in the form of a small writing desk and drawer. It was being returned with a note of appreciation to her neighbor, Dr. Pryor, who had loaned it to Lee.

"So with pangs and sorrows and memories of all kinds, we all marched away," a romantic cavalryman wrote in his diary, as with the coming of daylight he found in his buttonhole a faded red rose which he felt was symbolic of their drooping spirits. The flower was a souvenir from a serenade given to Agnes Lee who had selected this inopportune time to visit her father—the first wartime visit from any of his daughters.

She had written on March 26 of her intention to come, and he had told her:

"I fear you have put off your visit too late. Gen. Grant is

evidently preparing for something & is marshalling & preparing his troops for some movement which is not yet disclosed. . . . It would be very dreadful if you should get caught in a battle. . . ."

Agnes did not take her father's warnings seriously, and arrived in Petersburg on the twenty-ninth, to stay with a family friend, Mrs. Meade. Lee was so busy that by April 1 he still had not seen her, and wrote her a note:

"I am obliged to go to the right today & will be compelled to visit Richmond the first moment I can. I do not know when I shall see you. You must therefore make your arrangements to return irrespective of me. . . ." The withdrawal from Petersburg abruptly ended her stay.

Dawn was breaking over the budding April countryside when the retreating troops stopped to rest near Chesterfield Court House. There was a headiness to the sweet air that was stimulating after nine months passed in stinking filthy trenches. The promise of a full meal from the rations to be left at Amelia Court House appeased the cravings of the inner man, while the prospect of joining Johnston gave hope for the future.

That noon, Lee and Longstreet, with their staffs, stopped to rest at Summit, near Winterpock Creek. Judge James H. Cox of nearby Clover Hill sent an invitation for them to have dinner with him. His house was already crowded with guests, and Lee and Longstreet were soon surrounded with admirers. When the mint juleps were served, Kate Cox, the Judge's daughter, recalled:

General Lee took his glass and according to the universal custom, asked me to taste it. He scarcely touched it himself, but took a goblet of ice water, saying as he looked around at the men who were enjoying their juleps:

"Do you know that this glass of cold water is, I believe, far more refreshing than the drinks they are enjoying so much?"

When dinner was announced, Lee insisted on Kate's going with him, "although I protested and told him that we had decided . . . that every morsel prepared that day should be eaten by his men."

When coffee was served, Kate noticed that Lee poured cream in his cup.

"General Lee, do you take cream in your after-dinner coffee?" she asked.

"I have not taken coffee for so long I would not dare take it in its original strength."

Kate learned later that he had been sending all his gifts of coffee to the hospitals and to his wife.

As soon as Grant became aware of Lee's line of retreat, he pushed forward his whole available force, and Lee pressed on as quickly as possible to reach Amelia Court House and the expected rations, ahead of the Federal cavalry. But when Lee's army reached Amelia, there were no food supplies waiting for the ravenous men.

I shall never forget the broken-hearted expression his face wore or the still sadder tones of his voice [recalled an officer who came up to him for orders]. No one who looked upon him then, as he stood there in full view of the disastrous end, can ever forget the intense agony written upon his features. And yet he was calm, self-possessed, and deliberate.

After the war Jefferson Davis felt it necessary to defend himself against accusations of having deserted Lee and his starving army in their moment of supreme need. He stated that Lee's only message giving his destination as Amelia Court House was the telegram sent to the Secretary of War on April 2, but that it was delayed in transmission and not received until seven o'clock that night.

Walter Taylor has stated that Lee also notified his chief commissary and chief quartermaster of his destination, and gave them orders for the disposition of supplies. While it cannot be proved that these men, in turn, communicated with the heads of their departments in Richmond, in view of their previous record of efficiency and intelligence, Taylor was certain that they had done so.

In the confusion, each of these messages may have been delayed, or lost, or simply ignored. By seven o'clock, the first time—so Davis said—that any one in the government learned Lee's destination, all trains had been impressed to carry the

President, his Cabinet, the Confederate bullion, and the archives out of Richmond.

Though the facts seem to exculpate Davis and his fleeing bureauracy, they cannot escape censure. From Lee's first telegram received at 10:40 A.M., both Davis and John Breckinridge, the new Secretary of War, knew that he was withdrawing from Petersburg. With 350,000 rations of meat and bread in Richmond awaiting transportation to Lee's army, it seems strange that of the eight trains impressed to transport the government, not one was held in reserve to carry supplies to Lee as soon as his destination was known.

To many men who had been sustaining themselves on hope and a handful of parched corn, this was the final blow and they began to drift off in search of food or, as one disillusioned cavalryman wrote, they "followed the example of the government, and fled." However, a singularly large portion of these loyal men chose to stay and starve to the end.

But now

. . . the best disciplinarians in the army relaxed their reins. The best troops became disorganized, and hardly any command marched in a body. Companies were mixed together, parts of each being separated by detachments of others. . . . Many commands marched heedlessly on without orders, and seemingly without thought of whither they were going. Others mistook the meaning of their orders, and still others had instructions which it was impossible to obey in any case.

It is little wonder then that when, on April 5, Lee met infantrymen without guns, and teamsters without wagons, fleeing in a disordered mass before the Federal cavalry, he straightened in the saddle and exclaimed:

"My God! has the army been dissolved?"

But to his men and officers he had never before "appeared more grandly heroic."

Failure and the sufferings of his men grieved him sadly, but they could not daunt him, and his moral greatness was never more manifest. [All eyes were now turned to him] for deliverance which no human power seemed able to give. He alone was expected to

215

provide food for the starving army and rescue it from a powerful and eager enemy. Under the accumulation of difficulties his courage seemed to expand.

"Keep your command together & in good spirits, General; don't let it think of surrender. I will get you out of this," he wrote to Rooney.

When he sent Mahone's troops in to reinforce Gordon at Sayler's Creek (Ewell's corps had been surrounded and forced to surrender), Lee took up a scarlet battle flag and, spurring Traveller ahead, rode up amongst the disordered troops to rally them. As soon as he was recognized, a tumult arose: men let loose with the rebel yell, then "with hands clinched violently and raised aloft they called on him to lead them."

"It's General Lee!" they shouted. " 'Uncle Robert'! Where's the man who won't follow 'Uncle Robert'?"

If General Mahone had not galloped up and seized Traveller's bridle, and taken the colors from Lee's hand, he would have swept on down that green hill, past the dark woods, and into the very thick of the fighting.

15

BEFORE dawn on April 7, the remnant of "that grand old Army," as Walter Taylor affectionately called it, began to straggle into Farmville, where a halt was called to await the arrival of wagon trains on their way with two days' rations.

Lee stopped at the house of Patrick Jackson and asked if he might rest there a while, and Mrs. Jackson offered to cook his breakfast. He declined, with the excuse that he was not hungry, but admitted that he had been longing for a cup of tea. It happened that she had some, so she brewed a cup which he drank with relish. When he left, she insisted that he take with him a leg of fried chicken and some fresh bread.

When Richmond was evacuated, the cadet corps was disbanded. Lee's nephew George Taylor Lee, a member of the corps, went home, picked up a horse, and without even waiting to eat, set out in search of the army. He found it at Farmville, and though he was looking for his commander and cousin, Custis Lee, he saw his Uncle Robert first. Lee was still carrying the chicken wrapped in a slice of bread. George thought he looked "very grave and tired." Without any salutation, Lee "said in a tone of distress":

"My son, why did you come here?"

"I thought it was my duty to come, sir."

"You ought not to have come. You can't do any good here."

"But if I stayed at home, I would be made a prisoner."

"No, I don't think they would do that," Lee said kindly.

When George asked about Custis, Lee said:

"I fear he has been captured." He did not tell him what was rumored: that Custis had been killed in the fighting at Sayler's Creek.

Just then a group of officers came up, and Lee asked George: "Have you had any breakfast?"

"No, sir."

Lee handed him the untouched chicken and bread and told him to go off somewhere and eat it, for he would now have to talk with these men.

The hopelessness of extricating the army from its surrounding difficulties caused a number of its principal officers to decide that—in order to lighten Lee's responsibility and soften the pain of defeat—it was time to tell him that, in their opinion, further resistence was useless and negotiations for peace should be opened.

The Reverend General Pendleton was their spokesman. He found Lee resting on the ground and alone. Lee listened in silence, and when Pendleton finished, he sat up, and said with some "harshness of manner," for he did not like such unsolicited suggestions from his officers:

Oh, I trust it has not come to that, General. We have yet too many bold men to think of laying down our arms. They fight with great spirit, whereas the enemy does not. Besides, if I were to say to the Federal commander that I would listen to terms, he would regard it as such a confession of weakness as to make it the condition of demanding unconditional surrender—a proposal to which I will never listen.

He recognized the validity of Pendleton's arguments, but to admit their truth at this point would only serve further to undermine discipline. Lee wanted to maintain morale to the end.

It became necessary, before all rations could be issued, to move the wagon trains to keep the enemy from capturing them, and the starving, weary men were ordered on to Appomattox Court House. While Lee and Longstreet stood talking about the disposition of troops, a colonel rode up to report that all his men—hungry and discouraged—had deserted. His attitude alarmed Lee, and after he had gone, Lee said to Longstreet:

"This is very bad. That man is whipped. It is very bad!"

He fell silent, then after a moment exclaimed defiantly:

"General Longstreet, I will strike that man a blow in the morning!" He meant Grant.

Around nine o'clock that night, a letter from Grant was brought Lee at his camp near Cumberland Church. He opened it and read:

April 7, 1865—5 P.M.

General R. E. Lee, Commanding C.S.Army,
General,—

The result of the last week must convince you of the hopelessness of further resistance on the part of the Army of Northern Virginia in this struggle. I feel that it is so, and regard it as my duty to shift from myself the responsibility of any further effusion of blood by asking of you the surrender of that portion of the Confederate States Army known as the Army of Northern Virginia.

Very respectfully, your obedient servant,
U. S. Grant, Lieutenant-General

Without comment, he handed it to Longstreet, who was sitting near him. Longstreet read it and, handing it back, shook his head and said:

"Not yet."

There was a difference of opinion among the officers present as to the kind of answer Lee should send, for a few (among them Old Pete) believed it was still possible to save the remnant of the army for a junction with Johnston. Under Lee's direction, Charles Marshall wrote:

218

I have received your note of this date. Though not entertaining the opinion you express of the hopelessness of further resistance on the part of the Army of N. Va., I reciprocate your desire to avoid the useless effusion of blood, and therefore before considering your proposition, ask the terms you will offer on condition of its surrender.

About dark the following evening, as Lee was resting beside the road near Appomattox Court House, a courier brought him another message from Grant. Colonel Venable fetched a small wax candle which he lighted and held for Lee to read by.

Peace being his sole desire, Grant wrote, the one consideration upon which he would insist was that the men and officers surrendered would be disqualified from carrying arms until properly exchanged. With consideration for Lee's feelings, he proposed that if he did not wish to meet with him, he would designate officers to meet any officers Lee should name, to arrange the surrender.

After Lee had read the letter, he handed it to Venable, and when he had finished with it, Lee asked:

"Colonel, how would you answer that?"

"I would answer no such letter."

"Ah, but it has to be answered," and he called Marshall to draft a reply. He told him to tell General Grant that in his previous letter he had not intended to propose surrender, but merely wanted to learn "the terms of your proposition."

"I do not think the emergency has arisen to call for a surrender of this Army," he dictated. He could not admit either to his officers or the Federal commander that he no longer had hope.

"Tell General Grant I will be pleased to meet him at 10 A.M. tomorrow on the Old Stage Road to Richmond, between the picket lines of the two armies," he said to Marshall.

They now left the road and turned into a dense oak grove to make camp. Lee decided to hold a council, and summoned Gordon, Fitz Lee, Wade Hampton, and Pendleton. There were no camp chairs left, so the men sat on saddles and blankets close to the fire, for the night was cold. Lee explained the situation, told of his correspondence with Grant, and asked their advice.

"If all that was said and felt at that meeting could be given,

219

it would make a volume of measureless pathos," Gordon wrote. "In no hour of the great war did General Lee's masterful characteristics appear to me so conspicuous as they did in that last council."

Though there was little chance for success, his officers advised "Fight on!"—words Lee liked to hear.

Longstreet would bring up the rear; Gordon, supported by Fitz Lee, would try to cut through Grant's line at daybreak.

When the council was over, the officers went off to their camps, leaving Lee and Longstreet to snatch a few hours rest. Lee had just put his saddle down for a pillow and rolled himself up in his blanket when one of Gordon's staff officers came back and said:

"Please, sir, the General neglected to ask where he was to halt and make camp tomorrow night. Are there any directions, sir?"

Lee was amused:

"Yes," he said, "tell General Gordon I should be glad for him to halt just beyond the Tennessee line"—a distance of some 176 miles.

Gordon inferred from this answer that Lee knew there was little hope for the escape, but that if they should succeed, he expected him to press toward the mountains.

Shortly after 1 A.M., the camp was wakened by the sound of infantry marching down the road. A staff officer sat up and listened for clues. Was it "Fed" or "Cornfed," as the Rebels now facetiously termed the enemy and themselves? He heard someone chanting the Texas doggerel:

> The race is not to them that's got
> The longest legs to run,
> Nor the battle to that people
> That shoots the biggest gun!

He relaxed, for this was Hood's old Texas Brigade. Soon, all the staff was astir.

We made our simple toilet, consisting of putting on our caps and saddling our horses [wrote Charles Marshall]. We then proceeded to look for something to satisfy our ravenous appetites. Somebody had a little cornmeal, and somebody else a tin can, such as is used to hold hot water for shaving. A fire was kindled, and each man in turn, according to rank and seniority, made a can of cornmeal gruel and was allowed to keep the can until the gruel became cool enough to drink. General Lee . . . did not, as far as I remember, have even such refreshment as I have described.

Lee dressed with special care that morning. He took from his baggage his new gray suit, a silken sash, gilt spurs, and the handsome dress sword with the motto *Aide toi, et Dieu t'aidera* etched on the blade; with forethought, he had brought this sword with him from his last visit to Richmond.

By 3 A.M. he was in the saddle, and rode with his staff toward Appomattox Court House. They soon heard heavy firing, announcing that Gordon had begun to open the way; Lee sent Venable ahead to learn what he could.

Venable found Gordon on the front lines, conferring with Fitz Lee. It was not possible to advance farther, for having forced his way through the cavalry, Gordon found himself blocked by overwhelming numbers of Federal infantry. He said to Venable:

"Tell General Lee I have fought my corps to a frazzle, and I fear I can do nothing unless I am heavily supported by Longstreet's corps!"

Venable knew that this was impossible, for two of Longstreet's depleted divisions were then holding off Meade in the rear. That morning only eight thousand Confederates had stood to arms: the rest of the valiant Army of Northern Virginia was captured, scattered, demoralized, and destroyed.

When Venable delivered Gordon's message, Lee said miserably:

"Then there is nothing left me but to go and see General Grant, and I would rather die a thousand deaths."

"Oh, General, what will history say of the surrender of the army in the field?" an aide blurted through his tears.

"Yes, I know they will say hard things of us," Lee told him sadly. "They will not understand how we were overwhelmed by numbers. But that is not the question, Colonel: the question is, is it right to surrender this army. If it is right, then *I* will take *all* the responsibility."

However calmly he may have talked, he appeared, to several officers who were observing him, close to being unnerved. It seemed to one that his deep voice was "filled with hopeless sadness" when he said to an officer beside him:

"How easily I could be rid of all this and be at rest! I have only to ride along the line and all will be over!"

Then sighing heavily, as though removing a great weight from his heart, he added:

"But it is our duty to live. What will become of the women and children of the South if we are not here to protect them?"

General Pendleton now rode up. He expressed his surprise at seeing Lee in full dress.

"I have probably to be General Grant's prisoner, and I thought I must make my best appearance," Lee explained.

When Lee saw General Alexander, he called to him and together they walked over to a fallen tree from which Lee first carefully peeled the bark before sitting down. He then took from his breast pocket a well-worn map, unfolded it, and pointing to the place where they now were, said:

"Well, we have come to this junction, and they seem to be here ahead of us. What have we got to do today?"

Alexander assured him that his men were in fighting trim, only waiting for his orders. Then Lee said:

"I have only two divisions . . . sufficiently organized to be relied upon. All the rest have been broken and routed and can do little good. Those divisions are scarcely four thousand apiece, and that is far too little to meet the force in our front."

Alexander then suggested that, to spare him the humiliation of unconditional surrender and to preserve the army's "unblemished record," it could break up into squads, which could return to their respective states and let the governors make more honorable terms.

This would not do [Lee told him]. They would become mere bands of marauders, and the enemy's cavalry would pursue them and overrun many sections they may never have occasion to visit.

We would bring on a state of affairs it would take the country years to recover from. And, as for myself, you young fellows might go to bushwhacking, but the only dignified course for me would be to go to General Grant and surrender myself and take the consequences of my acts.

He paused a moment, and then said:

"But I can tell you one thing for your comfort. Grant will not demand an unconditional surrender. He will give us as good terms as this army has the right to demand, and I am going to meet him in the rear at 10 A.M. and surrender the army on the condition of not having to fight again until exchanged."

At this moment, Colonel Taylor rode up. He had spent the whole night parking the wagon trains safely, and now came to report.

"Well, Colonel, what are we to do?" Lee asked him.

Taylor was afraid they would have to abandon the trains, but hoped that once relieved of them the army might make good its escape.

"Yes," said Lee, "perhaps it could; but I have had a conference with these gentlemen around me, and they agree the time has come for capitulation."

"Well, sir, I can only speak for myself," Taylor replied, "but to me any other fate is preferable."

"Such is my individual way of thinking," Lee said.

"But," Taylor went on, "of course, General, it is different with you. You have to think of these brave men and decide not only for yourself but for them."

"Yes, it would be useless and therefore cruel to provoke further effusion of blood, and I have arranged to meet General Grant with a view to surrender, and wish you to accompany me."

A courier now rode up with a message from General Seth Williams of Grant's staff. He had been adjutant at West Point when Lee was superintendent, and they had been good friends. Williams wanted to relieve Lee's mind by letting him known that Custis, though captured, was safe and unhurt.

Although Lee had received no reply from Grant, he rode with Taylor and Marshall for the meeting on the Old Stage

Road. Riding ahead with a flag of truce was A. P. Hill's courier, Sergeant G. W. Tucker, who was remembered for having asked during the Wilderness campaign to be allowed to go to the skirmish line and kill a Federal cavalryman, so as to replace his own dead horse.

The troops "cheered General Lee to the echo," but he waved his hand to suppress them, afraid this might attract enemy fire. When they came to the Union skirmish line, Tucker was halted and Lee asked Marshall to find the Federal commanding officer. Marshall took off his shabby sword and his pistol, and holding a white handkerchief, walked on. He soon met Colonel Charles Whittier with a letter from Grant. Marshall took the letter back to Lee, who asked him to read it.

Grant wrote that since he had no authority to treat on the subject of peace, the proposed meeting for that morning would lead to no good.

I will state however, General, that I am equally anxious for peace with yourself, and the whole North entertains the same feeling. The terms upon which peace can be had are well understood. By the South laying down their arms they will hasten that most desirable event, save thousands of human lives and hundreds of millions of property not yet destroyed. . . . [He hoped that all difficulties would be settled] without the loss of another life.

After thinking for a few minutes, Lee said to Marshall:

"Well, write a letter to General Grant and ask him to meet me to deal with the question of the surrender of my army."

He also asked for a suspension of hostilities until this message could reach Grant, then with Sheridan on the Appomattox front.

While Marshall was writing, Colonel John Haskell of Longstreet's artillery came by "riding like the wind." When he saw Lee, he tried to pull up, but having only one arm, could not stop until he had gone nearly a hundred yards beyond. Lee went out to meet him, exclaiming:

"What is it? What is it? Oh, why did you do it? You have killed your beautiful horse!"

But Haskell had news that warranted the speed: Fitz Lee had learned of a road over which the army could escape.

So far as Lee was concerned, it was too late for such considerations now, and he told Marshall to go on with the letter. Later, it was found that no such road existed.

When Marshall finished, he gave the letter to Lee to sign and then returned to the skirmish line and delivered it to Whittier.

Soon after Lee had returned to his field headquarters, he was brought a message from General Meade, telling him that hostilities had been suspended as he had requested. Almost simultaneously came the sound of guns along the Confederate front. Lee galloped off to Appomattox Court House, reaching there just as Fitz Lee came in triumphantly with some two hundred prisoners. He told his nephew of the temporary truce and then rode down the slope to an apple orchard where he reined and dismounted.

To the foot of an apple tree on whose branches a few new leaves were appearing, Colonel Talcott dragged some rails and spread them with blankets. On this improvised couch, Lee lay down and went to sleep.

About an hour later, a Federal officer with a flag of truce was seen coming from the direction of the Court House. Marshall reported his approach to Lee, who told him to meet the officer. It was Colonel Babcock from Grant's staff, with a message from the General explaining the delay in answering Lee's note of the morning, and asking him to appoint the place of meeting for the surrender—in either the Confederate or Federal lines, whichever was most convenient.

Lee then asked Walter Taylor to get ready to go with him, but his young adjutant knew that he was too upset to be able to witness the surrender calmly and excused himself on the pretext that he had ridden through the lines twice that morning.

Lee did not press him but asked Marshall if he would go. "I was in a very dilapidated state," Marshall remembered, but he managed to borrow a dress sword, a pair of gauntlets, and a clean shirt collar.

When he was ready, they rode up the hill toward the village. At the stream, Traveller stopped to drink and Lee waited patiently until the animal had its fill. He then asked Marshall to ride ahead and find a suitable place to meet General Grant.

Marshall and Sergeant Tucker spurred ahead. The first person they met as they came into town was Wilmer McLean, who had ironically left his former house on the battlefield of Manassas and come to Appomattox to escape the war.

Marshall explained his mission, and McLean took him first of all to a tumble-down vacant house. Marshall told him that would not do.

"Maybe then my house will do," McLean suggested, and led them to a comfortable brick house surrounded with lawn and shaded with locust trees. Marshall then sent Tucker to escort Lee and Babcock and, at Mr. McLean's invitation, went to sit in the parlor.

Presently Lee and Babcock came in, and they began to talk in "the most friendly and affable way."

In about half an hour, they heard horses come into the yard and then Grant, accompanied by Generals Sheridan, Ord, and Porter, and Colonels Parker and Badeau, entered the room.

Grant was dressed in his "rough traveling suit, the uniform of a private with the straps of a lieutenant-general." The blouse of dark blue flannel was unbottoned in front, showing the waistcoat beneath. His trousers were tucked into ordinary military top boots which were spattered with red mud; he was without either spurs or sword, and wore dark yellow thread gloves. He appeared to Marshall to have had "a pretty hard time," for his clothes were "somewhat dusty and a little soiled."

When Lee heard the horses come into the yard, he rose and was standing at the end of the room opposite the door when Grant came in. The Federal greeted him in "a most cordial manner." After shaking hands, Grant began to talk about "the weather and other things in a very friendly way." Then he brought up his officers and introduced them. When Lee shook hands with Ely Parker, Grant's Indian military secretary, Lee looked hard at him a moment, and then said:

"I am glad to see one real American here."

"We are all Americans," Parker replied.

Lee then asked for Seth Williams, to thank him for having sent word of Custis' safety, and Grant sent someone out to get him.

226

The two commanders then took chairs, and as Grant wrote: "We soon fell into conversation about old army times." He was surprised that Lee remembered him "very well from the old army." He recalled Lee perfectly, but as he said, "from the difference in our rank and years . . . I had thought very likely that I had not attracted his attention sufficiently to be remembered by him after such a long interval."

He did not know that Lee never forgot a face and rarely a name. The only recorded instance of such a lapse occurred not long after the surrender, when he was taking a visiting clergyman to the chapel on Washington College campus. At the door, he met the officiating minister, Dr. Jones, and introduced his guest as simply, "the Reverend Doctor." All during service, he was trying to recall the man's name and afterward asked Jones to find out for him. He was vexed at his forgetfulness, and spoke of it the next day:

I really was very ashamed at not knowing that gentleman yesterday; I ought to have remembered him at once, for he spent at least an hour in my quarters in the City of Mexico just after its occupation by the American army, and although I have never seen him since, he made a very agreeable impression upon me, and I ought not to have forgotten his name!

In the McLean house, Grant remembered: "Our conversation grew so pleasant, that I almost forgot the object of our meeting." Lee, who was understandably anxious to get down to business, had to recall Grant from this amiable reminiscence by reminding him that he had asked for the interview to learn what terms he proposed for the surrender of the Army of Northern Virginia.

Grant told him that he "meant merely that his army should lay down their arms, not to take them up again during the continuance of the war unless duly and properly exchanged."

But Grant was obviously not anxious to come to the point, and allowed the talk to wander again on foreign matters.

"This continued for some time, when General Lee again interrupted the course of the conversation by suggesting that the terms I proposed to give his army be written out. I called for Colonel Parker . . . for writing materials."

Parker brought a small table from the corner for Grant to write on. But when he came to put his pencil to the manifold field notebook, he admitted that he did not know how to begin:

I only knew what was in my mind, and I wished to express it clearly, so that there would be no mistaking it. As I wrote on, the thought occurred to me that the officers had their own private horses and effects, which were important to them, but of no value to us; also that it would be unnecessary humiliation to call upon them to deliver their side arms.

After Grant had finished writing, he walked across the room to hand the book to Lee, who rose and, meeting him, took it and went back to his seat.

Lee then took his spectacles from their case, and after wiping them carefully with a handkerchief, put them on and began to read. When he reached the bottom of the first page, he looked up and said:

"After the words 'until properly' the word 'exchanged' seems to be omitted. You doubtless intended to use that word."

"Why, yes," Grant replied. "I thought I had put it in."

"With your permission I will mark where it should be inserted."

"Certainly."

Lee felt for a pencil, but found none, so Horace Porter stepped over and handed him his. Lee thanked him, placed the carat, and went on reading. When he reached the part of the terms which allowed the officers to retain their side arms, horses, and private baggage, he remarked:

"That will have a very happy effect." When he finished, he told Grant that Confederate cavalrymen and artillerists also furnished their own horses, and already looking toward peace he said: "And these men will want to plough ground and plant corn."

Grant pointed out that the terms as written allowed only officers to take their private property, but that he would instruct his officers to let all men who claimed a horse or mule take the animals home with them "to work their little farms."

"That will have a very happy effect," Lee said again.

Lee looked over the letter once more, and being satisfied, asked Marshall to write the reply. Grant then called on Colonel Parker to copy his draft in ink.

Parker took the little table back to the corner, but found the ink in Mr. McLean's inkstand as thick as pitch. Marshall then loaned him his pen and screw-boxwood inkstand which he always carried in a little satchel. When Parker finished, he returned Marshall's equipment, and Marshall then wrote the reply.

Meanwhile, Grant was introducing Lee to the large group of Federal officers who had at the beginning of the interview slipped in and ranged themselves "quietly about the sides of the room, very much as people enter a sick chamber when they expect to find the patient dangerously ill," Horace Porter thought.

Lee then told Grant that he had about fifteen hundred Federal prisoners for whom he had no rations, and Grant called to his cavalry chief:

"Sheridan, how many rations have you?"

"How many do you want, General?"

"General Lee has about a thousand or fifteen hundred of our people prisoners, and they are faring the same as his men, but he tells me they haven't anything. Can you send them some rations?"

Sheridan said he could send twenty-five thousand rations.

"Is that enough, General?" Grant asked.

"Plenty; plenty; an abundance," Lee told him.

"Order your commissary to send to the Confederate Commissary twenty-five thousand rations for our men and his men," Grant said to Sheridan.

By now, Marshall had finished the letter, but when Lee read it over, he said:

"Don't say 'I have the honor to acknowledge the receipt of your letter of such a date'; he is here; just say, 'I accept these terms.'"

Marshall sat down and rewrote the letter. Grant then signed his letter, and Lee put his signature on his, the two secretaries exchanged the papers, and the surrender was accomplished. It was then about 3:45 P.M.

What General Lee's feelings were I do not know; as he was a man of much dignity, with an impassable face, it was impossible to say whether he felt inwardly glad that the end had finally come, or felt sad over the result, and was too manly to show it [Grant wrote]. Whatever his feelings, they were entirely concealed from my observation; but my own feelings . . . were sad and depressed. I felt like anything rather than rejoicing at the downfall of a foe who had fought so long and valiantly, and had suffered so much for a cause. . . .

Beneath the surface of Lee's calm dignity, who could tell "what a storm of feeling was beating within his soul!"

A general conversation of "a most agreeable character" now took place. For the first time since entering the room, Grant was aware of the splendor of the man to whom he was talking. He admired the new uniform, and the sword with its ornate gold and leather scabbard, and the gold-embroidered Russia-leather sword belt.

"In my rough traveling suit . . . I must have contrasted strangely with a man so handsomely dressed, six feet high and of faultless form." He apologized for his appearance. When Lee's last letter had reached him, he was four miles from the wagon that held his uniform and side arms, he explained, but he felt that Lee would rather receive him as he was than have to wait longer while he sent back for his baggage.

"I am very much obliged to you. I am glad you did not send back," Lee told him.

Lee now took up his hat and gauntlets, ready to go. He shook hands with Grant—"Lee and I separated as cordially as we had met"—bowed to the officers, who were all standing, and walked to the door. He paused for a second before going onto the porch, and Federal General George Forsyth, who saw him then for the first time, wrote in the notebook he had ready:

. . . a clear ruddy complexion—just then suffused by a deep crimson flush, that rising from his neck overspread his face and even tinged his broad forehead, which, bronzed where it had been

230

exposed to the weather, was clear and beautifully white where it had been shielded by his hat. [He noted the] deep brown eyes, a firm but well-shaped Roman nose . . . in his right hand he carried a broad-brimmed soft gray felt hat, encircled by a golden cord, while in his left hand he held a pair of buckskin gauntlets. Booted and spurred, still vigorous and erect, he stood bareheaded, looking out of the open doorway, sad-faced and weary.

Stepping out, Lee put on his hat, and those Federal officers who had crowded up on the porch to wait for the end of the meeting, stood up and saluted. Lee responded "mechanically but courteously."

At the top of the stairs, Lee paused again, this time to draw on his gauntlets. As he looked off into the distance, he abstractedly smote his gloved hands together several times, then suddenly recalling his thoughts, glanced right and left, and not seeing Traveller, called in a voice that was hoarse and half-choked:

"Orderly! Orderly!"

Sergeant Tucker answered from around the corner of the house where he was holding the rein as the gray browsed hungrily on the lawn.

Lee walked down the steps and waited while Tucker replaced the bridle. As he was buckling up the throat latch, Lee reached up and drew the forelock from under the browband, parted and smoothed it, and absently patted Traveller's forehead.

As Tucker stepped back, Lee

caught up the bridle reins in his left hand, and seizing the pommel of the saddle with the same hand, he caught up the slack of the reins in his right, and swung himself slowly and wearily, but nevertheless firmly, into the saddle . . . as he did so there broke unguardedly from his lips a long, low deep sigh, almost a groan in its intensity, while the flush on his neck seemed if possible, to take on a still deeper hue.

Just then, General Grant came down the stairs and started across the grass to where his horse, Cincinnati, was waiting. Suddenly, he stopped and removed his hat, and those who were watching did the same. Lee raised his hat in acknowledgment of the silent tribute, then without a word rode off into the lengthening golden shadows of that April afternoon.

16

WORD that Marse Robert had gone to meet with General Grant spread like wildfire among the men, and their suspense was insufferable.

Then they saw him, erect, head held high, come riding down the sunny slope toward his lines. He appeared to them grander than ever, and they started to cheer him. But as he came near, they saw that he stared straight ahead like a man in a dream, his face flushed and set. Their cries froze in their throats, and those nearest him called hoarsely:

"General, are we surrendered?"

They saw the look of agony come into his face, and they knew the worst. Like loving children, they ran up to comfort him and to receive comfort, weeping and sobbing as they stretched out their hands to take hold of him, gently touching his coat, his legs, his feet, even his horse's bridle. Through their brimming eyes, they saw the tears coursing down his cheeks.

He took off his hat and spoke to them in a voice so low and choked with emotion that it could not he heard twenty yards away.

"You will be paroled and go to your homes until exchanged," he said.

But when he tried to say good-by, his voice failed him.

Overwhelmed by their own feelings, the men drew aside and let him pass. They were downcast, but they were not whipped.

"General, we'll fight 'em yet. Say the word and we'll go in and fight 'em yet!" they called after him.

When he had gone, many men, no longer able to control their feelings, threw themselves on the grass and wept unrestrainedly. One general sat down on a stump and cried as loudly

232

and bitterly as a child. A private flung down his musket and shouted:

"Blow, Gabriel, blow! My God, let him blow, I am ready to die!"

Slowly, Lee rode on to the apple orchard, around which he now ordered sentinels posted to keep out intruders, for as soon as the surrender became generally known, "quite a number of enterprising Yankee soldiers came wandering over among our camps seeking relics and gossiping generally."

Lee's temporary headquarters in this orchard gave rise to the story that the surrender took place under an apple tree, and energetic souvenir hunters pared away the entire tree under which he supposedly met Grant. Right after the war, someone asked Lee:

"You met under an apple tree, did you not, General?"

"No, sir, we did not. We met in Mr. McLean's parlor. If there was an apple tree there I did not see it!"

There were many details of the surrender still to be attended to, the most important being the transfer of rations for the starving army, so Federal officers were in and out of Confederate lines for the rest of the afternoon. Lee's staff sat in the shade of an apple tree near the road. Colonels Talcott, Taylor, and Venable took care of the business, while Lee retired to a tree far removed from the bustle.

Robert was suffering from exhaustion and lack of food. Since three o'clock that morning, he had been under heavy strain. He was now experiencing the reaction. As is often the case with emotional people, this took the form of anger. William Blackford noticed that he "paced backwards and forwards . . . looking like a caged lion. . . . General Lee seemed to be in one of his savage moods and when these moods were on him it was safer to keep out of his way; so his staff kept to their tree except when it was necessary to introduce visitors."

Quite a number came. Some were of high rank. "It was evident that some came from curiosity, or to see General Lee as friends in the old army. But General Lee shook hands with none of them."

Whenever he saw Walter Taylor coming with a party, "he would halt in his pacing and stand at 'attention' and glare at them with a look which few men but he could assume. They would remove their hats . . . and stand bareheaded during the interview while General Lee sometimes gave a scant touch to his hat in return and sometimes did not even do that."

Grant's commissary wagons began to arrive and the most pressing business was finished for that day. The sun was sinking and clouds were gathering in the west when Lee started for his headquarters a mile to the rear. The road skirted the hill on which the army was encamped.

When the soldiers saw the well-known figure of Lee on Traveller,

there was a general rush from each side of the road to greet him as he passed, and two solid walls of men were formed along the whole distance. Their officers followed and behind the lines of men were groups of them, mounted and dismounted, awaiting his coming. . . . As soon as he entered the avenue of soldiers, the flower of his army . . . wild heartfelt cheers arose which so touched General Lee that tears filled his eyes and trickled down his cheeks as he rode his splendid charger, hat in hand, bowing his acknowledgments.

The sight of his tears changed the cheers to "choking sobs as with streaming eyes and many cries of affection they waved their hats as he passed. Each group began in the same way with cheers and ended in the same way with sobs, all the way to his quarters."

As they had done earlier that day, "grim bearded men threw themselves on the ground, covered their faces with their hands and wept like children. Officers of all ranks made no attempt to conceal their feelings, but sat on their horses and cried aloud. . . ." Among them was Rooney Lee.

Only for Traveller was it like a splendid review. He had always taken as much pleasure in applause as a human being and acknowledged the tributes by tossing his head. Now the men cheered him in his last appearance, and he answered back, "his head tossing a return to the salutes all along the line, which greatly added to the effect," Blackford thought.

When Lee dismounted at his tent, the men crowded around to shake hands and say good-by. For them there were no stern looks or rebuffs, but tears and his blessing.

As man after man came up to press his hand, and in husky voices murmur: "Good-by, General; God bless you!" or tell him of their readiness to fight on if he would give the order, Lee made no attempt to hide his feelings: his heart was full, his cheeks were wet, and his voice was as choked as theirs. He took their outstretched hands, returned the blessings and, looking down the road to reunion, told them to go home and plant their crops.

The gloom was made more poignant by a chilly rain the next day. It was only natural for the men to review the last four years and ask themselves:

"And what for?"

Four years passed away, in most cases four years of their prime, and what was there to look forward to?

But youth is always resilient, and after a day or two the pall was lifted and the future suddenly brightened with the parting of the clouds. Just being alive brought satisfaction to most.

It was noticed that on the morning of the tenth Lee went about his work with characteristic composure. This was, however, a forced calm hiding the tumult of heart, for many observed that he seemed abstracted at times.

The previous evening he had sat with his staff around a fire in front of his tent, pitched in the shelter of a large white oak. They had talked about the events of the day and the army. Lee had expressed his affection for his men in the strongest terms, and Charles Marshall had been deeply moved by his words. Before retiring, Lee had asked Marshall to write a final order for the troops, and Marshall had promised to do it the first thing in the morning.

But there had been many people coming and going to and from headquarters on the tenth, and Marshall had been out on business. He had dropped his spectacles and, being helpless without them, lost his way in the heavy rain. A courier had found him wandering about and led him back to camp.

235

When Lee learned around ten o'clock that the final order had still not been drafted, he told Marshall to take paper and pencil and get into the ambulance. To keep him from being interrupted, Lee stationed an orderly in front.

It took Marshall but a "few minutes" to write that deeply moving address, known officially as General Order No. 9 but to become famous as Lee's Farewell Address. He took it to Lee, who struck out one paragraph he felt would tend to keep alive sectional enmity, and made a few other changes; otherwise, it stood as Marshall wrote it.

General Grant now decided to go back to Washington, but before leaving, he wanted to suggest that Lee accompany him and meet President Lincoln.

When Lee received Grant's message to meet him, he put on his old blue overcoat to protect the new uniform from the rain, and galloped off. He came on Grant in an open field close to the Lynchburg Road. Here, as they sat on their horses, they talked for over half an hour. Peace for the entire country was the topic.

Lee said that the South was a big country, and that the Federal army might have to march over it three or four times before it could be subdued. He did not doubt that they could do it, but hoped this would not be necessary, for it would cause more suffering and loss of life.

Grant felt this was the proper time to ask Lee if he would go with him to Washington and talk with Mr. Lincoln.

I want you to meet him. Whatever you and he agree upon will be satisfactory to the reasonable people of the North and South. If you and Mr. Lincoln will agree upon terms, your influence in the South will make the Southern people accept what you accept, and Mr. Lincoln's influence in the North will make the reasonable people of the North accept what he accepts. And all my influence will be added to Mr. Lincoln's.

Then Grant said:

"General, there is not a man in the entire Confederacy whose influence with the soldiery and the whole people is as great as yours. If you will now advise the surrender of all the armies, I

236

have no doubt your counsel will be followed with willingness and alacrity."

Lee said that he would be delighted to do anything in the world that would restore peace.

"But, General Grant, you know that I am a soldier of the Confederate Army, and I cannot meet Mr. Lincoln. I do not know what Mr. Davis is going to do, and I cannot undertake to make any terms of that kind. Nor can I urge the other armies to surrender without first consulting the President."

Grant was disappointed, but he understood Lee's position and knew, as he wrote later, that "there was no use to urge him to do anything against his ideas of what was right."

They then shook hands and parted cordially.

Several officers who were among Grant's escort now asked permission to return with Lee to look up some of their old army friends. Lee was willing, so Generals Seth Williams, Rufus Ingalls, and the jaunty Phil Sheridan rode back with him. After finding their friends, they obtained Lee's permission to escort them into the Federal lines and held an informal reunion at the McLean house.

As Grant listened to their animated talk and laughter, he thought that it seemed more like a meeting of old friends "separated for a long time while fighting under the same flag. For the time it looked very much as if all thought of war had escaped their minds."

As Lee was riding back from this interview with Grant, he met General Meade, who had been over to see him but finding him gone was returning to his own lines.

"Good morning, General!" Meade called cheerily.

For a second, Lee stared hard at the heavily bearded man with the turn-down slouch hat, but as Meade uncovered, Lee recognized him and greeted him warmly.

"But General, what are you doing with all that gray in your beard?" Lee asked. "The years are telling on you!"

"Ah, General Lee, it is not the work of years. You have to answer for most of it!"

Meade then introduced his aides—his son, Captain George

Meade, and Colonel Theodore Lyman. As Lyman shook Lee's hand, he thought he detected "an extreme depression, which gave him the air of a man who kept his pride to the last, but who was entirely overwhelmed."

Lee invited Meade to return to his tent and as they rode in sight of the lines, Lee's soldiers began to cheer.

"Unfurl that flag!" Meade ordered his color-bearer.

As the stars and stripes fluttered free, a private in tattered homespun shouted:

"Damn your old rag! We're cheering General Lee!"

That day, General Henry J. Hunt, who had been with Lee at Fort Hamilton and in the Mexican War, came into the lines to see him. He found Lee "weary and careworn, but in this supreme hour the same self-possessed, dignified gentleman that I had always known him."

Though by the tenth all business that demanded Lee's attention had been completed, and he could have gone on to Richmond, it was consistent with his character that he chose to stay until after the formal surrender—the stacking of arms and furling of battle flags—which took place on the twelfth. Although he did not ride out to see the ceremony, which was held in an open field near Appomattox Court House, he was not far off and his men knew this.

Magnanimity had characterized Grant's meeting with Lee at the McLean house and this same feeling was present at the formal surrender. When the Confederates, under General Gordon, approached the field, General Joshua Chamberlain, commanding the Maine brigade that faced the grounds, ordered his men to present arms. Gordon immediately saluted and ordered his troops to do the same.

When the last Confederate brigade marched to its place, "someone in the blue line broke the silence and called for three cheers for the last brigade to surrender. It was taken up all about him by those who knew what it meant. But for us this soldierly generosity was more than we could bear. Many grizzled veterans wept like women, and my own eyes were as blind as my voice was dumb," wrote a cavalryman.

Lee had spent that morning with Charles Marshall going

over a long letter to Jefferson Davis advising him of the surrender. Lee did not spare him. He stated candidly that the reason for his surrender was the failure of rations to be sent to Amelia Court House as he had ordered:

. . . Nearly twenty-four hours were lost in endeavoring to collect in the country subsistence for men and horses. This delay was fatal, and could not be retrieved. The troops, wearied by continued fighting and marching for several days and nights, obtained neither rest nor refreshment. . . . If we could have forced our way one day longer it would have been at a great sacrifice of life; at its end, I did not see how a surrender could have been avoided. We had no subsistence for man or horse, and it could not be gathered in the country. . . . The men deprived of food and sleep for many days, were worn out and exhausted. . . .

These were bitter words for Davis. After reading the letter, he handed it without comment to an aide, then turned away, and wept silently.

Lee was ready to break camp. Colonels Taylor, Marshall, Venable, Major Giles B. Cooke, who was sick and rode in an ambulance loaned by the Federals, and Lee's young courier, Will McCaw, were going with him. Just as they were ready to leave, twenty-five handsomely mounted and caparisoned Federal cavalrymen rode up. They had been sent to escort General Lee all the way to Richmond. He politely declined the offer, but found the dragoons so disappointed that he agreed to let them ride with him part way.

That afternoon, they came on a squad of Confederates resting beside the road. Lee stopped to talk with them. He learned that they were from the Stonewall Brigade, and were now on their way home to the lower end of the Valley of Virginia, some two hundred and fifty miles away. He then took from his pocket the well-worn map, unfolded it, and carefully directed them by the shortest and best roads. When he said good-by, he urged them to look to the future, and "be as faithful citizens as they had been soldiers."

Then he turned to the officer in command of the escort and said:

"Captain, you see I am in my own country and among friends

239

and do not need an escort. I am giving you unnecessary trouble, and now request you to withdraw your men and rejoin your command."

For some hours, Lee rode ahead of his party, obviously wanting to be alone. But word of his coming somehow raced ahead of him, and at every house and cabin, women and children were waiting to wave their handkerchiefs and to smile and weep. In spite of their poverty, many had prepared food for him; and little girls ran out to hand him tightly clutched bouquets of hyacinths and daffodils. These simple exhibitions of love moved him deeply, and he said to one of his staff:

"Colonel, these people are kind—too kind. Their hearts are as full as when we began our campaigns in 1861. They do too much—more than they are able to do—for us."

Charles Venable was the first to leave them, turning off on the road that led to his family home in Prince Edward County. The parting with Lee was solemn. He clasped Venable's hand firmly and looked straight into his eyes. When the grasp relaxed, Venable withdrew his hand and turned away. Not a word was spoken. Both hearts were too full.

Camp was made before dark in a wood near Buckingham Court House. Though Mrs. Martha Shepherd, the owner of the grove, invited Lee to take dinner and pass the night at her house, he courteously refused, preferring to stay in his tent with his mess served by the faithful Bryan.

Walter Taylor remembered that all during the trip the conversation was free and of a general character, and that to everyone he met along the road he gave the same counsel:

"Go home and take up any work that offers. Accept conditions as you find them. Consider only the present and the future. Do not cherish bitterness."

It was not Lee's nature to repine. "Human virtue should be equal to human calamity," he said.

Late in the afternoon of the fourteenth, Lee came on a young soldier limping along, barefoot. The boy drew up and saluted, and Lee stopped to question him.

Yes, he was on his way to his distant home.

Yes, he had claimed a mule with his parole, but it had run off and was lost.

"My boy," Lee said, "you are too badly off for the long journey ahead of you; you have no shoes. I am going to spend the night at the home of my brother, Charles Carter Lee, who lives five miles ahead at Five Creek Mills. I will find you a pair of shoes, and you must stop there to get them."

When the veteran stopped at Carter's house, the shoes were waiting for him. He also received a godspeed from his old commander.

At bedtime that night, Robert refused to crowd Carter's family with three extra people (by now Giles Cooke had turned off to his home). He also declined the invitation of neighbors, Mr. and Mrs. Gilliam, asking them instead to take in a sick officer and his wife who had stopped along the road and were preparing to camp out. So as not to hurt the Gilliams' feelings, he agreed to have breakfast with them.

So the tent was pitched for the last time and Lee went into camp, to the disappointment of Walter Taylor, who wrote that though he appreciated Lee's desire to have his men know that he had shared their privations to the last, he, personally, could have easily done without this final bit of self-denial.

The presence of ten-year-old Polly Gilliam made breakfast additionally pleasing for Robert, who took her on his knee afterward and talked to her in that engaging way he had with children. When it came time to go, he kissed her and whispered:

"Polly, come with me to Richmond, and I will give you a beau."

It was warm and overcast that morning, with more rain threatening. Along the River Road, they came up with Rooney and his cousin, John Lee, with their wagons and equipment. Once again, word of Robert's coming sped on ahead and all along the way people were watching for him.

At noon, they stopped at a roadside house to ask for refreshment, to the horror of two soldiers who were sitting on the front piazza listening in rapture to the rattle of the flour sifter and bacon sizzling in the skillet. When Lee's party came, the troopers executed, as one of them wrote, "a rather rapid and undignified flank movement to gain the right and rear of the house.

"The lady of the house . . . pushed her head through a crack of the kitchen door, and, as she tossed a lump of dough from hand to hand . . . addressed the soldiers:

" 'Ain't that old General Lee?' "

" 'Yes; General Lee and his son and other officers come to dine with you,' they replied.

" 'Well,' she said, 'he ain't no better than the men that fought for him, and I don't reckon he is as hungry; so you just come in here. I am going to give you yours first, and then I'll get something for him!' "

When they reached Manchester, across the river from Richmond, the rain began to fall heavily, and as Lee turned Traveller down Hull Street, the Reverend William Hatcher stepped out on his porch to see him pass. He noticed that the mud-splattered gray hung his head in weariness, but that "the horseman himself sat his horse like a master; his face was ridged with self-respecting grief; his garments were worn in the service and stained with travel; his hat was slouched and spattered with mud."

Dr. Hatcher was deeply moved: "Even in the fleeting moment of his passing my gate, his rectitude and his sorrow, were so wrought and blended into his visage and so beautiful and impressive to my eyes that I fell into a violent weeping."

Richmond was waiting for Lee, too. As soon as he was recognized, small boys raced home to shout:

"General Lee's coming!" And then raced out so as to miss nothing. As word of his arrival sped from house to house, the people flocked into the streets.

He rode up Fourteenth Street to Main where, at the corner, a number of Federal soldiers stood in the crowd. As Lee's party drew near, one Richmondite spoke up:

"Here comes General Lee. *I* am going to take off my hat to him!"

"Damned if I don't, too!" said the Yankee soldier next to him.

242

When Lee passed, every Northerner in the group uncovered, and though the General looked straight ahead, he lifted his hat in acknowledgment.

To many, Lee in his "old gray coat, dingy from long, hard usage," his staff, "gaunt and pallid in ragged uniforms, on bony, weary old horses," the dilapidated ambulance and the headquarters wagon covered with an old quilt in lieu of canvas seemed to symbolize the lost cause. Overwhelmed by this realization, their cheers gave way to sobs and tears.

Before going to The Mess, Lee took his courier, Will McCaw, to his father's house. Dr. McCaw came out to meet them, and Lee said:

"Here, Doctor, is your boy. I've brought him home to you."

Will had by this time dismounted and was standing next to Traveller. He had one arm tightly clasped around Lee's leg. Suddenly he burst into tears, "crying as if his heart would break." Robert put his hand on the boy's head, and said gently:

"No more fighting—that's all over. You've been a good fighter, Will. Now I want to see you work for your country's welfare in peace. Be a good boy. I expect a fine Christian manhood of you.—Goodbye!"

When Lee stopped in front of the red brick house at 707 East Franklin Street, the people were waiting for him there, too. Weeping and sobbing, they surrounded him, kissed his hands, clung to his coat, and threw their arms around old Traveller's neck.

Once again, Lee made no effort to suppress his feelings. Tears flowed down his cheeks and choked his voice as he held the outstretched hands and sought to speak heartening words. He was so overcome with emotion, he had trouble dismounting.

Giving Traveller to his driver, he walked through the crowd and up the granite stairs. At the top, he turned and bowed, then walked into the house and closed the door.

II

A Private Citizen

*April 15, 1865 * October 2, 1865*

II. A Private Citizen

ALL THE family was there to greet him except Rob, who, in the belief that the struggle was not over, had gone with his command to Greensboro, North Carolina.

Lee tried to keep the talk from himself by encouraging Mary and the girls to relate their experiences during the evacuation.

Agnes told him how friend after friend had hurried in that hectic day when the Sabbath calm was turned suddenly into panic and near riot, to urge Mary to leave the city; and how, with leonine courage, she had stubbornly refused to stir. She had not become frightened even when the blaze had spread unexpectedly from the tobacco and government warehouses and arsenals (purposely fired) to the flour mills, and then, out of control, had roared up Main Street as far as Eighth, destroying seven hundred houses. Not even when the next-door house caught fire and sparks ignited her own front door would Mary consider leaving. Instead, she asked Daughter to stand on the top step with a bucket of water ready to put out the flames "while she sat in her chair, calmly knitting away on her soldier sock."

Mildred told how, on the morning of the third, Emily Mason, "the Florence Nightingale of the Confederacy," and Mrs. Rhett met General Weitzel, commanding occupation troops, to tell him that Mrs. Lee was an invalid, unable to walk, and that her house was endangered by fire.

"What! Mrs. Lee in danger? General Fitz Lee's mother who nursed me so tenderly when I was sick at West Point? What can I do for her? Command me!"

"No, General, Mrs. Robert E. Lee. We want ambulances to move Mrs. Lee and other invalids and children to places of safety."

Using his knee as a desk, Weitzel wrote out an order for

five ambulances. But when the ambulance stopped at her door, Mary Lee refused to use it.

General Weitzel established martial law immediately, so that those who had predicted lawlessness and disorder at the hands of the Federals were pleasantly surprised—or disappointed, depending on their viewpoint. The only disturbances in the city were committed by their own people.

To protect Mrs. Lee and her family, a guard was stationed in front of the house and General Weitzel ordered rations issued to her at once. She greatly appreciated these courtesies.

"It is impossible to describe the kind attention of the Union soldiers to me," she told Robert.

She had reciprocated as best she could by sending the sentinel his breakfast on a tray each morning—a practice that was branded by some die-hards as "uncalled for."

Even when Abraham Lincoln had come to the city, "no bells rang, no guns boomed in salute. He held no levee. There was no formal jubilee." To those Southern men who came out to meet him he said kindly:

"You people will all come back now, and we shall have old Virginia home again."

To his children, Lee appeared well physically, though he looked older, grayer, seemed more quiet and remote, and was unwilling to discuss the war or anything pertaining to it. His silence arose from physical and mental exhaustion, and his reluctance to talk about the war arose chiefly from his resolve to look ahead.

From the moment he had turned his back on the village of Appomattox, his mind had been concerned with the future— Virginia's future being foremost, since her fate was so closely bound to his own. He said to a young officer who asked him for advice about taking the oath of allegiance:

"I would advise you to take it."

When the boy protested that it was an unnecessary indignity since his parole took care of it, and threatened to go to another country where he could preserve his self-respect, Lee counseled:

248

"Do not leave Virginia. Our country needs her young men now."

As it had been to his father, Virginia was Lee's country. But this attitude did not warp his perspective of the entire South's future, and he said to another young man:

"Now, more than any other time, Virginia and every other state in the South needs us. We must try and, with as little delay as possible, go to work to build up their prosperity."

He gave this same advice to his sons. Rooney took it to heart and, with his cousin, John Lee, went to the White House plantation. Together, they built a shanty, and putting their cavalry horses to the plow, broke up the ground and planted corn.

When Rob came back, his father suggested that he return to the University and prepare himself for some profession. But if he preferred to work Romancoke, Lee was agreeable. Until he could decide, Rob joined Rooney and John, to see how he would like farming.

Lee now wrote to Markie to thank her for her messages of sympathy, revealing his philosophic resignation to the inevitable:

"I know how you sorrow for us, but you must not be too distressed. We must be resigned to necessity & commit ourselves in adversity to the will of a merciful God as cheerfully as in prosperity."

Lincoln's assassination on April 14 was a mad deed that "set the whole country crazy. The South was aghast, natural recoil intensified by apprehension. The North, convulsed with anguish, was newly aflamed. . . ."

Lee, like all other reflecting Southerners, deplored Booth's act. Because he hoped to allay this revived feeling against the South, he consented to talk with the *New York Herald*'s reporter when he called at the house on April 29. The correspondent urged Lee to make a statement, as it might have a good effect.

The South has for a long time been anxious for peace [Lee said]. In my earnest belief, peace was practicable two years ago, and has been since that time whenever the general government should see fit to give any reasonable chance for the country to escape the consequences which the exasperated North seemed ready to visit upon it. They have been looking for some word or expression of compromise and reconciliation from the North upon which they might base a return to the Union, their own views being considered. The question of slavery did not lie in the way at all. The best men of the South have long desired to do away with the institution and were quite willing to see it abolished. But with them in relation to this subject, the question has ever been:

"What will you do with the freed people?"

That is a serious question today. Unless some humane course based upon wisdom and Christian principles is adopted, you do them a great injustice in setting them free.

Moderation towards the South is the part of wisdom as well as mercy [he went on]. Oppression would keep the spirit of resistance alive.

Throughout the interview, the journalist noted, "he spoke of the North and South as 'we,' and expressed his own willingness to contribute in every way in his power to the establishment of the communal peace and prosperity."

For many days after he came home, Lee passed long hours in sleep, and took no other exercise than pacing the back verandah. But it was not possible to remain quietly apart and recover his health. Dozens of people he knew taxed his strength by calling at the house to cheer him and offer help. Dozens more (many of them strangers) wrote him, and he insisted on answering each letter. He worked on getting the release of Confederate soldiers in Libby Prison. One of his men in the prison had written to ask if he could not get them freed. "But if you can't, just ride by Libby, and let us see you and give you a cheer. We will all feel better after it."

Lee wrote at once to General Grant, suggesting that all men and officers of the Army of Northern Virginia captured or surrendered since April 2 be granted "the same terms as given those surrendered by me on the 9th. I see no benefit that will result by retaining them in prison; but on the contrary think good can be accomplished by returning them to their homes.

250

Indeed, if all now held as prisoners of war were liberated in the same manner, I think it would be advantageous. . . ."

On April 27, he wrote Grant again, this time to protest that his soldiers should not be forced to take the oath before being allowed to go home: "Officers & men on parole are bound on their honour to conform to the obligations they have assumed. This obligation can not be strengthened by any additional form or oath, nor is it customary to exact them."

Aside from those persons who offered their help, there were hundreds of others, most of them strangers, who called: officers and soldiers from both armies; politicans, journalists, photographers, ministers, mothers and wives of missing sons and husbands, and Northern tourists who had come to Richmond to stare curiously at everyone and everything in the Rebel capital.

The noted photographer, Mathew Brady, came to the door "the day but one" after Lee's return. "It was supposed that after his defeat it would be preposterous to ask him to sit," Brady said afterward, "but I thought that to be the time for the historical picture."

Lee's first reaction was negative:

"It is utterly impossible, Mr. Brady. How can I sit for a photograph with the eyes of the world upon me as they are today?"

But Brady called on Mrs. Lee, whom he had also known before the war, and it was Mary who finally persuaded Robert to pose. Brady said subsequently:

"He allowed me to come to his house and photograph him on his back porch, several sittings. Of course I had known him since the Mexican War when he was on General Scott's staff and my request was not as from an intruder."

For the "ordeal," Lee put on his new gray uniform and asked Custis and Walter Taylor to pose with him, though Brady did take several of him alone, seated and standing.

It soon became impossible for him to go out of the house until after dark, when, with Mildred, he could safely take his exercise without being thronged by admirers or the idle curious. Occasionally he would call on friends.

251

One evening, he stopped at General Chilton's house. Channing Smith, Chilton's nephew, was there. He was one of Colonel Mosby's as yet unsurrendered Rangers, who had come secretly to Richmond. Channing had a question from his chief:

"What are the Rangers to do—fight on, or surrender?"

Lee explained that since he was under parole he could give no advice.

"But, General, what must *I* do?"

"Channing, go home, all you boys who fought with me, and help build up the shattered fortunes of our old State."

To protect Lee from being overwhelmed by his callers, a male member of the family was stationed at the door at all times to carefully screen the visitors. One afternoon, a Federal soldier, an Irishman, rang the bell; with him was a Negro boy carrying a large willow basket which contained a ham, some cheese, canned fruit, vegetables, and many delicacies. When the "guard," this day Rob and his cousin Dan Lee, questioned the soldier, he said that he had heard that the Lee family was suffering for want of food:

"I served with the Colonel when he commanded the Second Cavalry in Texas, and as long as I have a cent, my old colonel shall not suffer!"

Lee overheard from the next room and came into the hall. As soon as the Irishman saw him, he threw his arms around him, and with tears streaming down his face, said:

"Sure, sir, you are a grand soldier, and it's I that know it. I've been fighting against you all these years and many a hard knock we've had. And now they tell me you are poor and in want."

He wiped his eyes and then went on:

"I've brought this basket and beg you to take it from a soldier."

Lee was touched, and thanked him, but explained that he was not in need. He suggested that the soldier send the food to some of his wounded comrades. But this would not do. To keep from offending him, Lee agreed to accept the present.

"God bless you!" the soldier said and started off before Lee could change his mind. At the door he turned back, and lowering his voice, said:

"If I could ha' got over in time, Colonel, I would ha' been with you!"

The next day the basket was sent to a Federal hospital.

Another day, an equally warm-hearted Irishman, a Confederate, came to the door. Lee was answering letters and had asked that no one interrupt him. The young man who opened the door explained this.

"I know he is busy, but I will detain him no more than one moment. I only want to take him by the hand."

Again Lee overheard and came out.

"I have come all the way from Baltimore to take your hand. I have three sons born during the war—Beauregard, Fitz-Lee, and Robert Lee. My wife would never forgive me if I should go home without seeing you. God bless you!" And he was gone.

It was impossible to keep these loyal men away. Another afternoon when Custis answered the bell, there was a tall ragged soldier in gray, his left arm in a sling, at the door. He asked to see the General.

"I am sorry, he can see no one today," and Custis explained how his father had said he would receive no callers until he had caught up with his correspondence.

A shadow crossed the veteran's face. He said that he had served with Hood for four years, that he was starting off now to walk to his home in Texas, and he had hoped before going to take his old commander by the hand and say good-by. But he was philosophical—if he couldn't, he couldn't—and turned to go.

But Custis knew how his father would feel, and asked the soldier to step into the parlor—possibly the General might make an exception; he would see.

Presently Lee's "stately step" was heard coming downstairs. With his hand extended in greeting, he came into the room. The Texan grasped the outstretched hand, looked Lee in the eye, and tried to say something but he could not utter a sound. Silently he wrung Lee's hand, then dropping it, burst

253

into tears and, burying his face in his arm, turned and walked slowly out of the house.

A witness to the scene recalled: "General Lee gazed after him for a few moments motionless, his fine, deep, dark eyes suffused and darkened with emotion, and then . . . he left the room and returned upstairs. Not a single word was spoken during the meeting. . . ."

Such encounters were deeply gratifying to Lee but took their toll emotionally.

This was not the time for useless repining such as Mary often indulged in. For her sake and for his own, Robert decided to look for a refuge far from the bustle and the constant reminders of war, where she could have the needed diversion and he, the peace.

"I am looking for some little quiet house in the woods, where I can procure shelter & my daily bread if permitted by the victor," he wrote General Long. "I wish to get Mrs. Lee out of the city as soon as practicable."

To other friends he spoke of his desire to buy a small farm (he was not destitute, for some of his investments had weathered the storm), where he would be away from the throngs who, in their attentiveness, were overtaxing his strength.

Reports from Rooney did not encourage him to settle in that devastated area, which he had considered, so he decided to look on his own.

One morning early in June, he rode out of the city and along the road that led to Pampatike, the home of his cousin, Colonel Thomas Hill Carter, on the Pamunkey River between Piping Tree and New Castle Ferries, twenty-five miles from Richmond.

At three o'clock, just as the family was sitting down to dinner, he rode up to the door. After he had received permission to turn Traveller loose on the lawn—"for grass, and his liberty are what he needs most"—he joined the family at the table.

These few days he spent with the Carters were the happiest he had had for a long time. He followed the two little girls, aged three and five, about in their play, talking baby-talk to

254

them and coaxing them to talk to him. At his request, they came to his bed each morning to play games or listen to his stories.

In these peaceful surroundings, his spirits began to revive, and he was no longer silent. He talked to his cousins about a variety of subjects, including Mexico, its people, climate, and scenic beauty; and learned from them the latest Carter family news. "But he said very little about the recent war, and only in answer to some direct questions."

While at Pampatike, Lee read President Johnson's amnesty proclamation, and after thinking about it and perhaps discussing it with his cousin, decided to apply for individual pardon. Though he would never have admitted the truth of Grant's statement that there was not another man in the Confederacy whose influence was as great as his, his modesty was not false. He knew that thousands of those men who had looked to him in time of war were looking for his example now. It was his duty "to reconcile his people to the consequences of defeat, to inspire them with hope, to lead them to accept freely and frankly the government that had been established by the result of the war, and thus relieve them from military rule." This, then, was the first step.

"True patriotism sometimes requires of men to act exactly contrary, at one period, to that which it does at another, and the motive which impels them—the desire to do right—is exactly the same," Lee wrote Beauregard, who was considering leaving the country and had asked him for advice.

The circumstances which govern their actions change; and their conduct must conform to the new order of things. History is full of illustrations of this. Washington himself is an example. At one time he fought against the French under Braddock, in the service of the King of Great Britain; at another, he fought with the French at Yorktown, under the orders of the Continental Congress of America, against him. He has not been branded by the world with reproach for this; but his course has been applauded.

When Lee reached home, he learned that the Federal government was planning to indict him for treason. He was not

255

concerned but he was surprised, for he thought he was protected under the terms of his parole.

"Well, it matters little what they may do to me; I am old,
and have but a short time to live anyway," he told a friend.

But he was deeply anxious for the sake of thousands of
other men whose paroles he wanted to see respected, and on
June 13, wrote to General Grant:

Upon reading the President's proclamation of the 29th ult., I
came to Richmond to ascertain what was proper or required of me
to do, when I learned that, with others, I was to be indicted for
treason by the grand jury at Norfolk. I had supposed that officers
and men of the Army of Northern Virginia were, by the terms of
their surrender, protected by the United States Government from
molestation so long as they conformed to its conditions. I am ready
to meet any charges that may be preferred against me, and do not
wish to avoid trial; but, if I am correct as to the protection granted
by my parole, and am not to be prosecuted, I desire to comply with
the provisions of the President's proclamation, and, therefore in-
close the required application, which I request, in that event, may
be acted on.

To President Johnson he wrote: "Being excluded from the
provisions of the amnesty and pardon contained in the proclamation of the 29th ult., I hereby apply for the benefits and full
restoration of all rights and privileges extended to those included in its terms. . . ."

When he handed Custis the rough draft to copy in ink, he
said "it was but right for him to set an example of making a
formal submission to the civil authorities, and that he thought,
by so doing, he might possibly be in a better position to be of
use to the Confederates who were not protected by military
paroles, especially Mr. Davis."

Word of his indictment brought offers of legal aid from all
over the North and South, and many offers of haven, here and
abroad. Both Senator Reverdy Johnson of Maryland, a Union
supporter during the war, and the Count Joannes of New
York immediately asked to defend him. And a British noble-
man wrote to say that Lee could have a mansion and estate

"commensurate with his individual merits and the greatness of an historic family." To this Lee replied:

"I am deeply grateful; I cannot desert my native State in the hour of her adversity. I must abide her fortunes, and share her fate. . . ."

To a cousin who suggested a refuge in Europe, he wrote:

"But there is much to detain me here, & at present it is my duty to remain. I shall avoid no prosecution the Gov^t thinks proper to institute. I am aware of having done nothing wrong & cannot flee."

One day, two ragged underfed Confederates rang the bell. They were spokesmen, they explained, for "sixty other fellows around the corner," too shabby to make an appearance. They wanted the General to come to Botetourt County, where among them they owned a good house and several hundred acres which they would stock and work for him.

"We hear that Underwood [the federal judge who had asked for the indictments] intends having you indicted for treason and rebellion. But there is a defile near the farm we offer, and there the whole Federal army can be defied!"

Tears were in Lee's eyes when he told them:

"But you would not have your general run away and hide. He must stay and meet his fate."

They must not worry, he said, for he was protected under the terms of his surrender; he had faith in Grant's word. He then sent Daughter to his room to get some spare clothing for them. When he handed them the clothes, they kissed them reverently, then hurried off to join their comrades.

Still another day, a soldier in tattered homespun came to the house. As he held Lee's hand, he said:

"General Lee, I followed you four years and done the best I knowed how. Me and my wife live on a little farm away up on the Blue Ridge. We heard the Yankees wasn't treating you right, and I come down to see 'bout it. If you will come up thar, we will take care of you the best we know how as long as we live."

By this time, the veteran was holding both of Lee's hands

257

and tears were in Lee's eyes, too. But he managed to free one hand and took up a box of clothing that had been sent him.

"My friend, I don't need a thing. My friends all over the country have been too kind and have sent me more clothes than I can possibly use. I want to thank you for coming, and I want you to take this suit."

The soldier dropped Lee's hand, and crossing his arms, straightened up and said firmly:

"I can't take nothin' offen you!"

After a moment he relaxed, put one hand on the box, and said:

"Yes, I will, General. I will carry them back home, put them away, and when I die the boys can put them on me."

General Grant had told his wife that he knew the suffering in the South would be "beyond conception." Those "who speak of further retaliation and punishment do not conceive of the suffering endured already, or they are heartless and unfeeling." He answered Lee's letter at once, assuring him that Southern officers and men were fully protected by their paroles. He also said that he would ask that Judge Underwood "be ordered to quash all indictments found against paroled prisoners of war, and to desist from further prosecution of them." He enclosed a copy of his recommendation, sent to the President, that Lee's application for pardon be accepted.

Mrs. Elizabeth Randolph Cocke now wrote to the Lees, offering the use of Derwent, a four-room cottage on her estate, Oakland, in Cumberland County about six miles from Cartersville on the James River and Kanawha Canal. Although Robert told Markie that he would have preferred a retreat in Orange County, he accepted because Mary was able to travel only by water without undue suffering.

It was a pleasure for him to correspond regularly with Markie again: "There is nothing my dear Markie that I want, except to see you, & nothing that you can do for me, except to think of & love me."

But Markie's devotion had to be partly manifested by deeds, so she made and monogrammed a number of handerchiefs which she sent to Robert, including in the parcel several pens and some laudatory newspaper articles.

In his reply, written just before leaving for Derwent, he told her he was tempted to scold, for in giving him new handkerchiefs she had forced him

to give my four old friends, that have continued with me in heat & cold, care & danger, to wounded *rebels*, & replace them by new ones. It gives me acute pain to part with old friends, though as in this case I may be the gainer. The marking is beautiful. . . . So splendidly have you succeeded, that Mildred proposes your appellation be changed from Mark *ie* to Mark *er*. You see how bright is the wit of the establishment.

He read the newspaper clippings with interest, but could not agree with the writers: "I feel much humbled by the commendations attempted to be bestowed. Praise I never deserve, & the censure of others is so much lighter than what I inflict upon myself, that it fails in its object."

When it was known that the Lees were going to leave Richmond, The Mess was thronged with visitors. The most numerous were the girls who came in "flocks," either with pictures they wanted autographed or to ask for a photograph, a button from his coat, or some other souvenir. He responded to these appeals with "ineffable sweetness."

On the day of departure, many old friends came to say good-by, among them a number of girls who were visiting Agnes and Mildred in their mother's room. Lee was leisurely packing his trunk, but every so often he would come into Mary's room with some memento he thought would be of interest—his Mexican bit, an ornate saddle blanket, a handsome sword. Presently he came in with "a wide-brimmed hat of drab, gray-brown felt."

"Miss Josie, has your father a good hat?" he said to Josephine Stiles, an old favorite to whom he had already given a "lock of his hair and one of Traveller's, a star from his coat collar, the wooden ink stand . . . he used . . . in our war, . . . and the remains of a pound of tea."

259

Since Josephine had been separated from her father for some time, she did not know.

"Well," Lee told her, "I have two good hats, and I don't think a good rebel ought to have two good articles of one kind in these hard times. This was my dress-parade hat. Take it, please, and if your father has not a good hat, give him this one from me."

When the Reverend Stiles got the hat, he refused to wear it, "deeming it too sacred a thing for common use."

Late that afternoon, either June 29 or 30, the Lees boarded the horse-drawn packet for the overnight trip. When it was time for bed, the captain offered Lee the most comfortable berth on the boat. He had always spurned special favors, and now asked that the bed be given to someone else. Since it was a balmy night, he preferred to spend it on deck. Wrapped in his old military overcoat, which he had once said was his "house & bed in the field," he slept under the stars, perhaps for the last time.

The boat docked at the Cocke's landing about sunrise, and Custis, who had ridden Traveller up to Oakland a few days before, was there to meet them.

They stayed a week with Mrs. Cocke. During that time her "head dining-room servant had decided to avail himself of his freedom." He came in "to take his farewell of the assembled family. I well remember the kindness with which the General rose from his seat and, shaking the old servant kindly by the hand, gave him some good advice and asked Heaven to bless him," wrote Mrs. Cocke's sister.

After the demands of Richmond, Lee found the simple life in the cottage "delightful," though he admitted that it was probably "not so exhilarating for the girls." The first week or two, the weather was "so excessively hot" that he had no desire to walk or ride out, but read, wrote letters, and rested in "a quiet so profound that I could number the acorns falling from the splendid oaks that overshadowed the cottage," Mary wrote.

But after a pleasant rain, the weather was cooler and he resumed his daily rides on Traveller. He often stopped for a

260

short visit at Bremo, Belmead, and other houses in the neighborhood; or rode as far as Carter Lee's home, twenty miles away, to talk with him.

One morning, he rode over to Palmore's country store and post office. After he had picked up his mail, he began talking with Mr. Palmore about weather, crops, and other agrarian topics.

Traveller was hitched to the rail under the trees. He was soon recognized, and word that Marse Robert was in the store sped like the wind. Gradually, the store began to fill with people who came to see Lee. He did not notice them at first, but turning around and seeing the press about him, he said:

"Ah, Mr. Palmore, pardon me for keeping you talking about corn and tobacco so long, for I see I am detaining you from your many customers."

"There was nothing whatever to indicate the slightest consciousness that the crowd had pressed in to see him," an observer wrote.

With rest and quiet, Lee began to improve and was soon riding as far as Fluvanna and Albemarle Counties. He found great comfort in the contemplation of nature.

"What a glorious world Almighty God has given us!" a daughter recalled him saying whenever he saw a brilliant sunset sky or a beautiful view.

He decided now that he would write a history of the campaigns in Virginia. To gather material, he sent a circular to all his generals:

I am desirous that the bravery & devotion of the Army of N. Va. be correctly transmitted to posterity. This is the only tribute that can now be paid to the worth of its noble officers & soldiers; and I am anxious to collect the necessary information for the history of its campaigns, including the operations in the Valley & western Virginia, from its organization to its final surrender. . . .

Inspired by Robert's decision, Mary began her reminiscences of the war. Perhaps the recollections were too painful, perhaps Robert discouraged her from dwelling on the past, for she unfortunately ended her account with the first year. Had she continued, she would have contributed an interesting though bitter personal memoir to the annals of the war. Like the rest of the Southern women, she had had to "sit still and endure, while she saw her country ravished and devastated," her people killed and starved. As a Confederate officer wrote:

"Women do not understand that war is a matter of business. I had many friends among the men I fought—splendid brave fellows. Personally, we were friends, and professionally, enemies. Women never get that point of view."

Robert's understanding of human nature led him to believe that the treason charges against him and others would not be pressed.

"I think . . . we may expect procrastination in measures of relief, denunciatory threats, &c.," he told Rooney.

He was right. His pardon was not granted, and the indictment not prosecuted. He realized that these retaliatory acts resulted from the hysteria caused by Lincoln's murder, when "indignation and memorial meetings simply flayed the South alive." At one such gathering in the New York Customs House, before the speaker could finish his harangue, the audience was drowning him out with cries of,

"Hang Lee! The rebels deserve damnation!"

Abraham Lincoln, the true friend of the South who would have wooed and won her with justice and charity, expressed in his homely way as "letting 'em up easy," was gone, and in his place was a man pliable as clay in the hands of the vindictive Radicals.

"Johnson, we have faith in you! By the gods, it will be no trouble now running the government!" Senator Wade told the new President bluntly.

The humiliating and often malignant measures inflicted on the South by these vengeful petty men served to keep alive sectional feeling, and aroused a bitterness more potent and lasting than that which the war had engendered, a bitterness that was carried over through several generations.

Of this travesty of a republican form of government, Lee wrote on September 8, from Derwent, to Captain M. F. Dabney:

262

We have certainly not found our form of government all that was anticipated by its original founders; but that may be partly our fault in expecting too much, & partly in the absence of virtue in the public. As long as virtue was dominant in the Republic, so long was the happiness of the people secure. I cannot however despair of it yet. I look forward to better days, & trust that time & experience, the great teachers of men, under the guidance of an ever merciful God may save us from destruction, & restore us the high hopes & prospects of the past. The thought of abandoning the country & all that must be left in it, is abhorrent to my feelings; & I prefer to struggle for its restoration & share its fate, than to give up all as lost.

"I prefer to struggle for its restoration" is significant in view of his acknowledged desire to find "some humble, but quiet abode" apart from the world.

➤➤➤ III ◄◄◄

A Leader of Youth

(Washington College)

October 2, 1865 ★ October 12, 1870

III. A Leader of Youth

On the evening of August 4, 1865, the remaining four members of Washington College faculty met with its trustees in Lexington, Virginia, to see what might be done to resuscitate the school's fortunes.

When Hunter's raiders reached Lexington in 1864, they had looted the library, destroyed the scientific equipment, and damaged the buildings. According to local tradition, the Lexington ladies kept them from burning it down only by an appeal to their patriotism, proving that George Washington had endowed the college.

At the meeting that night, several names were submitted for the presidency. When the board was about to vote, Colonel Bolivar Christian, a trustee, stood up and said he believed it was his duty to make a statement before the vote was taken, as it might have some bearing on it.

A friend, who also knew Miss Mary Lee, daughter of General Robert E. Lee, had told him that Miss Mary had said that while the Southern people were ready to *give* her father everything he needed, no reasonable offer had been made by which he could *earn* his living.

The board asked the Colonel if he nominated General Lee.

No, he said, he did not want to go that far, but he did want them to know what Miss Mary had said.

After repeated urging, Christian made the nomination, all other names were withdrawn, the roll was called, and Lee was unanimously elected. Then the members sat stunned at their audacity.

"At length a member summoned courage to say that having taken that step, they must go forward, and he moved that a committee . . . be appointed to draft a letter to General Lee." Another member suggested that the letter be delivered personally, and that no one was so well qualified as the college rector,

Judge John W. Brockenbrough, a large, imposing man of courtly manner and eloquent speech.

The Judge thanked the member but said he could not go, for this frayed and shabby suit he wore was his best, and he did not have money to buy another. Mr. Hugh Barclay then offered the loan of his almost new suit of black broadcloth, sent him by a son living in the North. He thought it would "fit pretty well." The Judge thanked him but said there was one more difficulty: the expense of the trip.

But these were resourceful men, not easily daunted. Colonel McLaughlin had the solution: a certain Lexington lady had recently sold a tobacco crop. He was sure she was civic-minded enough to lend the necessary amount.

The letter was written, and Judge Brockenbrough, wearing the borrowed suit, his expenses payed by borrowed money, traveled to Derwent.

What passed at the meeting in the cottage under the oaks neither man recorded, but when the Judge left, he had Lee's promise to consider the offer and let the trustees know. That Lee considered the offer was largely due, no doubt, to George Washington's association with the school.

As a testimonial to Washington's character and public services, the Virginia Legislature presented him with stock in two canal companies—the James River Canal and the Potomac Canal. Washington accepted only on the condition that he be permitted "to turn the destination of the fund vested in me from my private emoluments to objects of a public nature." To what was then called Liberty Hall Academy, he gave in 1798 the one hundred shares of James River Canal stock, enriching the treasury by fifty thousand dollars, a generous endowment for the day. In gratitude, the school changed its name to Washington Academy. When the trustees notified him, Washington replied:

". . . To promote literature in this rising empire and to encourage the arts have ever been amongst the warmest wishes of my heart. . . ."

At this time, the South was the "rising empire," building anew on the ashes and rubble of her culture, and the school's

268

plight was more desperate than any time since its founding.

The salary of fifteen hundred dollars a year plus one-fifth of the tuition fees, which were then seventy-five dollars, would have been satisfactory to Lee, for money considerations were not determining factors with him. With Shakespeare's King John, he had once characterized money as "vile dross."

But the fact that it was customary for the president to teach classes in moral philosophy was a serious objection. The administrative duties would be enough to tax his strength and patience —he could not teach, too. Another objection was that the school was Presbyterian, and he did not want to associate himself with any denominational institution. There was also the question of his status as an unparoled prisoner of war: whether this might not be more damaging to the college than beneficial, especially if they hoped to interest Northern students. And finally, the question of his competency bothered him, and in his dilemma, he rode to Plain Dealing in Albemarle County, to ask advice from a friend, the Episcopal bishop, Joseph P. B. Wilmer.

I was seated at the close of day, in my Virginia home, when I beheld . . . a horseman entering the yard, whom I soon recognized as General Lee. . . . The next morning he placed in my hands the correspondence with the authorities of Washington College. . . . I confess to a momentary feeling of chagrin at the proposed change . . . in his history. The institution was one of local interest, and comparatively unknown to our people. I named others more conspicuous which would welcome him with ardour as their presiding head.

But the Bishop soon found that in Lee's mind "the *cause* gave dignity to the institution, and not the wealth of its endowment or the renown of its scholars . . . and that he only wished to be assured of his competency to fulfil his trust."

Dr. Wilmer gave him this assurance, and discussed with him at length the importance of Christianity in education. He recalled "how feelingly he responded, how *eloquently*, as I never heard him speak before."

On the return ride, Lee decided to accept conditionally. He had heard that if he accepted, the school would become nondenominational. It seemed, he wrote, that this door had been "opened by the hand of Providence." When asked, shortly after he had accepted the Presidency, what had induced him to "undertake that broken-down institution," he said:

"I have a mission to fulfill."

To another friend he spoke at greater length:

No one can have more at heart the welfare of the young men of the country than I have. It is the hope of doing something for the benefit of those at the South that led me to take my present office. My only object is to endeavour to make them see their true interest, to teach them to labour diligently for their improvement, and to prepare themselves for the great work of life.

But there was also a personal consideration which prompted his decision. No intelligent man, however humble and self-effacing, is so totally shorn of pride that he cannot find modest satisfaction in contemplation of a job well done, or of a full and successful life. No man wants to die without having left some good for his years of struggle and endeavor. That Lee reflected on this is proved by a letter written at this time:

"Life is indeed gliding away, & I have nothing of good to shew for mine that is past. I pray that I may be spared to accomplish something for the benefit of mankind & the honour of my God."

"In its broad & comprehensive sense, education embraces the physical, moral & intellectual instruction of a child from infancy to manhood," Lee told Professor John B. Minor of the University of Virginia.

Any system is imperfect which does not combine them all; & that is best which, while it thoroughly develops them, abases the coarse animal emotions of human nature & exalts the higher faculties & feelings. A child has everything to learn & is more readily taught by having before it good example to imitate, than by simple precepts. He should therefore, as far as circumstances will permit, be encouraged to associate with his parents for his heart must be affected, his feelings moved, as well as his mind expanded. He may be taught that it is criminal to steal, sinful to lie, & yet be unable to apply this knowledge to the government of himself; & it will therefore be of no value to him unless the principle is confirmed into habit. . . .

The choice of a profession is not of so much consequence as the manner in which it is pursued. If habits of self-control & self-denial have been acquired during education, the great object has been accomplished. . . .

On August 24, Lee wrote the trustees of Washington College:

". . . The proper education of youth not only requires great ability, but I fear more strength than I now possess, for I do not feel able to undergo the labour of conducting classes in regular courses of instruction. I could not, therefore, undertake more than the general administration of the institution."

He did not want them to forget that he was still unpardoned, and "an object of censure to a portion of the country," making it possible that

occupation of the position of President might draw upon the College a feeling of hostility; & I should therefore cause injury to an Institution, which it would be my highest desire to advance. I think it the duty of every citizen in the present condition of the country, to do all in his power to aid in the restoration of peace & harmony, & in no way to oppose the policy of the State or General Governments directed to that object. It is particularly incumbent on those charged with the instruction of the young to set them an example of submission to authority, & I could not consent to be the cause of animadversion upon the College.

At a trustees' meeting on August 21, they agreed to free the president from instructional duty and wrote Lee that in spite of the objections he had stated, "his connection with the institution would greatly promote its prosperity and advance the general interest of education."

Holding such profound concepts of education as he had stated to John Minor, Lee was well prepared for his position though not exactly reconciled to it. He wrote a friend:

"I accepted . . . in the hope that I might be of some service to the country & the rising generation; & not from any preference of my own. I should have selected a more quiet life & a

271

more remote abode than Lexington, & should have preferred a small farm where I could earn my daily bread."

Riding Traveller, he left Derwent early in the morning of September 15 for the little Blue Ridge town of Lexington. His trunks, a desk and chair, and other small pieces of furniture he shipped by canalboat. As Mary wrote to Emily Mason, Robert was traveling "*en cheval*" because he preferred it, "and besides does not like to part even for a time from his beloved steed, the companion of many hard-fought battles."

The first two days were dusty and hot riding, but on the third day, when he reached the gently rising passes whose thickly wooded slopes were already splashed with the scarlet and gold of maples and oaks, he found it cooler. After he began to climb, he stopped often to enjoy the views across the gorges to the distant ridges veiled in a blue haze so thick that their outlines often fused with the sky.

One o'clock on the first day brought him to Bremo, the home of Dr. Cocke, where he spent the afternoon and night. The next day he was off at sunrise, and by noon had reached Dr. Wilmer's house in Albemarle, staying there for the night. The third day he did not find shelter until midafternoon, when he reached Waynesboro on the crest of the Blue Ridge.

The farmer's wife who answered the door did not recognize him but hospitably offered him dinner and a room. When her husband, who was one of Lee's veterans, returned from town, he could not do enough for the comfort of his old commander.

On the afternoon of the eighteenth, Lee rode into the shabby village of Lexington. "This is a beautiful spot by na-ture—man has done but little for it," he wrote.

Since it was so late in the day, he decided to stay at the hotel rather than go to the house of his host, Colonel Reid, a College trustee. Just as he stopped in front of the hotel, Colonel Reid's son-in-law, Professor James J. White of the school's history department, turned up the main street. He also had been in the army, and recognizing Lee, hurried up and intro-duced himself. Several veterans who were sitting on the hotel porch came up to hold Traveller and help Lee dismount. One of them sped off to spread the news that Marse Robert was in town, and since every able-bodied man in Lexington had been one of his soldiers at some time, a crowd soon gathered and the street rang with cheers.

Professor White convinced Lee that he would not be inconveniencing his father-in-law, as everything was ready for him.

On the nineteenth he toured the college, describing it as "beautifully located," and on the twentieth and twenty-first he met with the trustees. Since the opening of school was postponed until October 2 to allow for completion of the repairs, he decided to spend a few days at the Rockbridge Baths, eleven miles from town, for the benefit of his "rheumatic affection." He took the baths daily, and found them "delightful," but they did not bring relief.

But he found comfort of another sort in the companionship of two cousins from Brandon, Belle Harrison, and Mrs. Anne Leigh and her small children. On Sunday, he rode with them to the top of Jump Mountain where, he wrote, "we had one of the most beautiful views I ever saw." The next day, since there was only one horse for hire, he and Belle rode up the Hays Creek Valley, "which possessed beauties of a different kind."

Not wanting to "trespass," as he said, on his cousins every day, he spent much of his time letter-writing. One letter was to James Green, the Alexandria cabinetmaker, asking him to make furniture for the dining room, parlor, and three bedrooms in the president's house on the campus. This house had been rented to a local doctor, R. L. Madison, and his wife, who agreed to move by the middle of October. After Lee saw the interior of the house, he wrote Mary that it was "in wretched condition."

On September 30, he came back to Lexington, stopping this time at the hotel, a life he disliked more than ever since it brought him too often before the public eye. During his absence, he found that the ladies of Lexington had furnished "the pleasant, good-sized room selected for his office," "very plainly and tastefully" with new carpet from Baltimore, curtains, and fixtures.

He was made very happy when he learned that Custis had been unanimously elected to the chair of civil engineering at

Virginia Military Institute, the West Point of the South, whose campus bordered that of Washington College. Lee was anxious for his company, and wrote to urge Custis to come as soon as possible. He suggested that he come on horseback rather than by boat, and gave him precise directions for the route he had taken.

In keeping with Lee's specific request, a simple and informal inauguration was held on October 2. By nine o'clock in the morning, the trustees, faculty, students, ministers from the local churches, a magistrate, the county clerk, and guests had gathered in the physics classroom.

When Lee, dressed, as the reporter from the *New York Herald* wrote, in a "plain but elegant suit of gray" (this was his uniform shorn of its military insignia), came in with the trustees and was introduced, everyone stood up, bowed, then sat down again. The Reverend W. S. White of the Presbyterian Church said a prayer in which, to the astonishment of the *Herald's* man, he included the President of the United States.

Judge Brockenbrough as rector and chairman of the board, delivered a brief eulogy on Lee, then congratulated the trustees, the college, and the students present and future, for having "obtained one so loved, great, and worthy to preside over the college."

During the speech Lee had remained standing, with his arms folded, "calmly and steadfastly looking into the eyes of the speaker."

The reporter thought Lee seemed to be "enjoying good health—better, I should say, than when he surrendered at Appomattox Court House."

After the speech, the oath of office was taken and the keys to the college were given Lee by the rector. A congratulatory shaking of hands all around ended "the brief but pleasant and memorable ceremony." Lee then went to his office.

"The college opened yesterday," he wrote Mary on October 7, "& a fine set of youths, about fifty, made their appearance in a body. It is supposed that many more will be coming during the month."

As soon as they registered, Lee memorized their names. Then he delicately inquired into their financial condition, their

274

home affairs, and made memoranda of their war records if they had been in the army. His questions were not regarded as prying, but instead made each young man feel that he had in Lee a substitute for an affectionate parent. Several boys thought his manner of receiving them was "almost motherly" in its gentleness.

As the semester advanced he carefully observed each student's disposition and habits, and his associates, and by the system of weekly and monthly reports which he asked of the professors, he soon knew their courses, study habits, progress, and class standing. He was quick to detect any weakness, and as he had done at West Point, was ready to counsel and help the student over his hurdles.

He also watched the progress of each class, was present at least part of the time at all examinations, and tried to inspire his faculty and students to put out their best efforts.

Occasionally he was amused at some boy's struggle to recall the answers during the all-day examinations, and once seeing a lad who simply sat and stared in silence at the professor, he whispered to a visitor who was with him:

"He is trying to *absorb* it from Mr. Humphreys."

But those students who were able to answer correctly during a test and win Lee's smile of approval counted that as their proudest moment, "worth more than the class distinction of the year."

As it had been at West Point, his chief concern was not for the student who excelled:

"Always observe the stage driver's rule," he told a new professor. "Take care of the *poor* horses."

He watched the students' moral and religious development with the same interest as he did their intellectual and scholastic progress, for there was a tendency to lawlessness among the young men of the South, as a natural result of the war.

One morning after prayer service, Lee seemed to be disturbed, and when a faculty member asked what was wrong, he said:

"I was thinking of my responsibility to Almighty God for all these young men."

Another time, he told the Reverend White: "I shall be

275

disappointed, sir—I shall fail in the leading object that brought me here, unless these young men become consistent Christians."

But to the surprise of all and the dismay of some, he abolished compulsory chapel attendance toward the close of his first year. It was one of his fundamental beliefs that young people learn by good example rather than precept, so he went to prayer service each morning before opening his office.

At a faculty meeting, several professors who did not attend chapel regularly were discussing the best means of inducing regular attendance among the students. Lee ended the discussion by saying:

"One of the best ways I know of to induce the students to attend chapel is to be sure that we attend ourselves."

He also abolished Sunday services, preferring each student to attend the church of his own denomination in the village.

During his first year, Lee realized that the chapel would not hold all the students who would be coming to school and would want to go to services, so he suggested to the trustees that a separate chapel be built. This was approved in July, 1866.

Custis selected the design, and General Thomas H. Williamson of Virginia Military Institute made the working drawings and specifications. But Lee chose the site, down the slope facing the main façade, and when construction was started, he supervised it, often going there several times a day.

His attitude toward religion had always been practical. When a new minister allowed morning prayer service to run over into the time set for classes, Lee said to a professor:

"Would it be wrong of me to suggest to Mr. —— that he confine his morning prayers for us poor sinners at college, and pray for the Turks, the Jews, the Chinese . . . some other time?"

When a lady asked his opinion on fasting, he spoke reverently of the church's mandates, but told her:

"The best way for most of us is to fast from our sins and to eat what is good for us."

His understanding of human nature served him well. The

276

Reverend-General Pendleton, new rector of Lexington's Grace Episcopal Church, complained to him one day that the Presbyterian services were drawing most of the students.

"Why, even my son goes to the Presbyterian church. I suppose he is attracted by Dr. Pratt's eloquence."

Lee smiled and said:

"I rather think that the attraction is not so much Dr. Pratt's eloquence as it is Dr. Pratt's *Grace*"—referring to the clergyman's exceptionally pretty daughter.

A testimonial to Lee's powers of attraction is found in the recollections of a former student. Each morning, the boy walked a mile and a half to attend chapel, often going without breakfast to do so. A pious friend met him one morning after service and said accusingly:

"Ah, but I am afraid you were worshipping *Lee* rather than Jehovah!"

"I was!"

2

DURING these first months, Lee was not only making comprehensive plans for improvement of the school's administration, its scholastic scope and standing but also attending in person to its business and correspondence. When enough money was raised for the construction of new buildings and the grading and beautification of the grounds, he drew many of the specifications and laid out the roads and paths. For economy's sake, and because he was thoroughly familiar with the wiles of contractors ("they will generally bear great attention, & then circumvent you," he wrote), he supervised the work.

From his experience in building fortifications, he could just look at a mass of mortar and tell if it contained too much or too little lime; if a steppingstone lay half an inch out of line, he noticed it and called it to the workman's attention.

He astonished the faculty with the range of his knowledge and wisdom, not only in practical matters, but by his familiarity with Latin and Greek, the literary classics, ancient and modern, and with French and Spanish, both language and literature. It seemed to them that his knowledge was universal, for he was conversant in any department.

To the amazement of students of Greek, he would question them in that language to test their knowledge. A young man who had completed a course in Spanish was surprised to find that Lee knew far more of it than he did, and talked with him at some length about the literature of Spain.

Lee had never been a man to parade his knowledge by literary allusions or foreign phrases in his speech or writing, so his scholarship astonished those who thought of him as only a soldier.

The faculty and trustees found his observation "keen, minute and accurate," his memory marvelously retentive, his great store of knowledge at his instant command. His fine attention to detail, his frugality, and his innate sense of beauty and fitness also surprised them. As they grew to know him better, they were astounded by his comprehensive knowledge and understanding of men.

"There was something uncanny in his ability to read other men's thoughts," one of them recalled; and it soon became a common saying in Lexington:

"It is no use trying to throw dust in Marse Robert's eyes!"

Not only did he memorize the students's names and faces, but their class standings and general reputation. At one of his weekly meetings with the mathematics professor, he spoke regretfully that a certain student had fallen so low in that subject. The professor was surprised; the boy was one of his best students, he told Lee.

"Well, he only got fifty-four last month," Lee said.

Reference to the records proved that Lee was right, but an error had been made in setting down the grades.

It was not long until he knew all the names and faces of the children in Lexington and, no less remarkable, all its cows, not from any desire for their acquaintance but because they forced themselves on his notice. In annoyance he would say as he watched them plodding over the newly planted lawn:

278

"I wish Mr. —— and Mr. —— would keep their cows at home!" mentioning each owner by name.

Trees were planted under his direction on the campus, and when asked about their arrangement, he said:

"Not in rows. Nature never plants trees in rows. As far as possible imitate Nature."

When there was finally money enough to put up a rough board fence to keep out the offending cows, and he was asked about the painting of it, he sighed as he said:

"A fence is a blot on any lawn. We must have a fence; but select a color that will render it as inconspicuous as possible: one that will harmonize with the surrounding colors."

The following summer, the college hired a brilliant young man, Edward Clifford Gordon, to serve as proctor, secretary to the faculty, librarian and, during his second year, treasurer. He was also, "a sort of secretary to the president, helping him with his mail, and otherwise in routine matters as he might direct. But I must add that General Lee answered most of his letters with his own hand, and that my duties . . . were chiefly confined to copying letters in an old-fashioned letter-press book."

Gordon was a perceptive and observant person, and left some interesting recollections of his daily contacts with Lee. In spite of the inroads of age, illness, and burdens, Gordon, who had never seen him before, thought him "strikingly handsome" —an opinion shared by faculty and students, who without exception considered him the handsomest man they had ever seen.

In working closely with Lee, Gordon soon found, as others before him had, that vexatious tasks and unwarranted interruptions often brought on outbursts of what he called "a fierce and violent temper, prone to intense expression."

During this time of military occupation and carpetbag invasion, his callers were often intruders: commissions sent to "investigate" charges against the students; vindictive individuals come to insult him; Yankee "schoolmarms" to tell him how to run the school; newspaper reporters to hound him for a

279

statement; salesmen seeking his endorsement of some book or product; and representatives from business houses with proposals for him to lend his name.

He said to one reporter: "If you have come to see me as one gentleman calls on another, I shall be glad to entertain you, sir; but if you have come to report for the newspapers my private conversation, I have nothing further to say."

The man admitted that the latter was his purpose, but he did not leave until Lee got up, and with quiet dignity opened the door and bowed him out.

A salesman peddling a "catchpenny work" on the recent war, said to him:

"I sent you the other day, General, a copy of this book which I am engaged in selling."

"Yes, sir, I received it, and I am very much obliged for your kindness."

Encouraged, the agent then said: "I called this morning to get you to give me a recommendation of the work. A line from you would be worth a great deal to me."

"You must excuse me, sir. I cannot recommend a book which I have not read, and never expect to read."

When a representative from an insurance company, shortly after Lee's arrival at the college, offered him the presidency of his firm at the salary of ten thousand dollars a year, Lee said he was sorry, but he could not give up the position he held, and he could not possibly attend to both.

"Ah, sir, but the use of your name is all that is desired."

"Excuse me sir," Lee said, "I cannot consent to receive pay for services I do not render!"

He customarily received these callers with "scrupulous courtesy," and they managed to escape unscathed—but beware the next person who entered the office! Near the close of the term, when he was especially busy, a committee called at eight o'clock in the morning, just as he opened his office. When they finished their business, they did not have the sense to leave but stayed until nearly noon.

"With them went the last degree of the President's patience," Gordon recalled vividly since he had the misfortune to come in to see Lee right after they had left. He wanted certain information from the letter book which Lee had at home. At Gordon's request, Lee's face flushed and he said harshly:

"I do not want the book; you can come and get it whenever you like!"

"I at once discerned that, to use our college slang, he had been 'sat upon' by that committee, and I hastily beat a retreat," Gordon wrote.

But the next morning as soon as Gordon came into the office, Lee came up and said in his kindest manner:

"Mr. Gordon, here is that memorandum you asked me to make for you."

His attention to little things impressed people. To set broken limestone in the walks, a maul was necessary. But the college had no maul, so Gordon told a workman to make one by sawing off the butt end of a large locust tree that had been felled while the grounds were being graded. When Lee saw the maul, he asked where it had come from and with understandable pride Gordon explained his ingenuity.

"What! cut up one of those locust trees to get a maul! I intended that tree for a gatepost. You might have got a maul from New York, or imported one from Liverpool at less cost."

At a faculty meeting, a professor wanted to refer to a college catalogue and took one from a pile that was ready for mailing. As he started to tear off the wrapper, Lee stopped him and, handing him one that was not yet wrapped, said:

"We must take care of these small matters. Many a man has made his fortune by so doing."

During his first two months, he was also supervising the repairs on his house. Though he had hired carpenters at once to mend the roof and repair the porch, steps, stable, and fences, the lack of lumber kept the work from being started until after the middle of October; then came the first storm of the season, delaying the start another week.

Mr. Green, the cabinetmaker, wrote that though his machinery had been returned, it was so badly damaged (to keep him from turning out war products) that he did not expect to be able to start work until the next year. Lee then sent an order to Renwick of Baltimore for "a dining table & chairs, a sofa, centre table & chairs for the parlour & furniture for two bedrooms viz: a bedstead, bureau, & washstand for each."

He wrote to Cousin Brit asking her to send the curtains and carpets which she and Markie had finally rescued from Arlington. He was determined to get Mary's room furnished—"the rest of us can bivouac," he wrote her. He was also looking for suitable servants.

But with all this attention to minute matters, it was noticed that neither his mind nor vision was cluttered or blurred by details. "All the resources of his opulent knowledge, of his varied experience, of his practical good sense, as well as his incessant industry, were fully used for the advancement of the institution. His wisdom, his ability to adapt means to ends, was unsurpassed." His plans for the college were comprehensive, and greatly in advance of his time.

One of his first amendments was to the rule concerning dormitory living, which he considered as "offering temptations to license." In his belief that young boys needed family life, he found board and lodging for all students in respectable local homes. Previously, only a few older boys had been allowed to board in town. But the results of this startling (to some less flexible minds) experiment soon proved his wisdom. As the student body grew, it was not possible to find homes for all the boys; so the youngest ones retained this privilege.

During his first year, Lee introduced the elective system to supplant the compulsory curriculum, and added five new departments of study in Liberal Arts. In 1866, a law course was started. There was not enough money to establish a department in the college, so an affiliation was made with the Lexington Law School, a private institution headed by Judge Brockenbrough. This same year, the School of Civil and Mining Engineering was also organized; and in 1869, foundations were laid for the future School of Commerce and Business Administration by the establishment of the "Students' Business School," planned along lines previously untried in American colleges. Lee's practical vision is shown in his report to the trustees:

282

In recommending a commercial School, it is proposed, not merely to give instruction in bookkeeping and the forms and details of business, but to teach the principles of Commercial Economy, Trade and Mercantile Law. Such a School may, with great advantage, be added to the Schools of the College, as many students may by its means prepare themselves for business pursuits, while obtaining such scientific and literary culture in the other Schools as time and opportunity may allow.

He was very anxious to have Spanish taught in the Department of Modern Language, since he foresaw closer relations between the United States and her Latin-American neighbors.

He proposed a summer school to remedy deficiencies; he encouraged advanced or graduate study by selecting annually six "resident masters," and urged the establishment of scholarships to allow outstanding young men to attend the college. He started research for public benefit, to be carried on by the faculty or others appointed for the purpose.

In March, 1869, the faculty recommended and he approved a course in journalism and fifty annual scholarships to young men "proposing to make printing or journalism their profession." This was the first time an American college had offered such a course. In 1870, a School of Agriculture, which would include an experimental farm, was also suggested.

Such advanced thinking attracted countrywide notice. The *New York Herald* went so far as to prophecy that Lee's influence in education "was likely to make as great an impression upon our old fogy schools and colleges" as it had "upon our old fogy commanders in the palmy days of the rebellion."

In 1870, the philanthropist, Leander McCormick, a brother of Cyrus, who was a generous benefactor of the college, planned to finance an observatory in Virginia. Lee hoped McCormick might be persuaded to build it at or near Washington College so that it could become affiliated with the school. The trustees approached McCormick with a plan: the college would maintain the observatory, establish a chair of astronomy, and raise an endowment of one hundred thousand dollars. McCormick was disposed to building the observatory in his native county, and came to Lexington to talk with Lee. A campaign was launched to raise the money, and had Lee lived longer, there is little doubt that the plan would have materialized.

Neither Lee's administration nor his form of discipline remotely resembled the military. It seemed, to many people, that he studiously avoided all military concepts and forms.

"Military discipline is, unfortunately, necessary in military education, but it is a most unsuitable training for civil life," he wrote. "For years, I have observed the failure in business pursuits of men who have resigned from the army. It is very rare that any one of them has achieved success."

With remarkable flexibility, he revised his attitudes and concepts to equip young men for civil life. Though a favorite maxim often cited to his students was "Obedience to lawful authority is the foundation of manly character," his discipline took a moral rather than a punitive form. To those new students who asked for a copy of the rules, he would say:

"Young sirs, we have no printed rules. We have but one rule here, and it is that every student must be a gentleman."

He relied on the principles of truth, honor, and courtesy to maintain order.

His knowledge of human nature, his sympathetic tolerance of the foibles of both youth and adult, and above all his sense of humor, gave him the key to almost perfect relationships with students and faculty. To the faculty he seemed like an older brother, "beloved and revered and full of tender sympathy." To the students he was like a gentle father. With new students he always made a tactful appeal:

"Now my friends, I have a way of estimating young men, which does not often fail me. I cannot note the conduct of any one, even for a brief period, without finding out what sort of a mother he had. You all honor your mothers; need I tell you that I know you will have that honor in reverent keeping?"

He did not often express opinions at faculty meetings. When asked for his views, he would usually say:

"Gentlemen, this is a new question to me, I cannot venture an opinion. I prefer to hear what Dr. K. or Colonel A. or

Professor M. has to say about it." In every case, he named the man who was best informed.

But once he had thoroughly investigated a subject, he became "the most dogmatic of men." At no time did he leave any doubt that a master occupied the presidency.

When, in December, 1865, there was agitation among the students for one week's Christmas vacation instead of the one day that had been announced, and a petition was presented to Lee, he denied it on grounds of economy: not a day that could be used for the acquirement of knowledge should be wasted. This was due each parent for the sacrifices made to supply tuition.

The boys were not willing to give in so readily, and a second petition, pledging the signer to stay away from classes during Christmas week, was then circulated. When the faculty seemed disposed to yield, Lee announced that any student whose name appeared on that paper would be "sent home" (his term for expulsion). If every student signed, the college would be closed, and the key put in his pocket!

When one youngster heard this ultimatum, he ran a mile and a half at top speed to get to the campus and scratch out his name. He found that the petition had been destroyed. It was recalled that lectures were well attended during Christmas week.

Occasionally the boys held callithumps, which aside from making the night hideous with its din did little harm. But when Lee heard that a "monster callithump" had been planned for April Fool's Day, he knew such a celebration could get out of hand and was afraid of a clash with the military. He issued one of what his boys called his "General Orders," appealing to their sense of dignity and their pride in maintaining "the fair name of Washington College." That evening came word from student leaders:

"Gentlemen, nothing doing tonight; Marse Robert says not."

Another time, serious trouble threatened with the proposed breaking up of a political meeting, at which, it was rumored,

285

the Radical speaker would slander Lee. He called to his office some twelve or fifteen student ringleaders. They were a diverse group—ex-Confederates, brilliant scholars, leaders in college religious work, and perennial pranksters. He appealed to their reason by reminding them that "under existing conditions it was the duty of all to submit patiently to such evils which only time could cure."

Not a student went, and the meeting "passed off as orderly as a funeral service."

Lee's influence was not confined to the campus. In the spring of 1866, Jonathan Hughes, a horse thief who had been plying his trade successfully in this region was caught, and his victims decided to take the law into their own hands. Word spread quickly on the campus that a crowd intent on lynching Hughes had gathered in front of the jail, and students hurried to the courthouse square.

By the time one student reached the scene, the jailer was standing with his back to the locked door, defying the mob to take the keys which he held high above his head. Suddenly, the young man noticed Lee moving quietly through the crowd, "addressing a few words to each group as he passed," asking them to let the law take its course.

The appeal was effective: every man there had followed Marse Robert's standard for four years, and he was still the commander. Without a word, they mounted their horses and rode out of town.

"Everyone obeyed him not because they feared him, but because they loved him," a student recalled, while another wrote that "he led us all by cords of love." Still, a summons to his office was not relished, and few cases required a second one.

It was the duty of Lewis, the janitor, to issue these unappreciated invitations. He carried a pencil and a long slip of paper on which the names were written, and when he found the desired person with a crowd of his comrades, he seemed to delight in announcing in "his solemn, sepulchral voice":

"Mr. ——, the President wants to see you at the office."

Mr. —— took the pencil and made a cross opposite his name to show that he had received the notice.

286

During these interviews, Lee made an appeal to the boy's pride, honor, or his sense of obligation to his parents for the sacrifices that enabled him to go to college. Often, the wildest boys came out of his office in tears. To the extravagant youth who had run into debt, he would say:

"The money you are squandering represents the sweat of your father's brow. You know our Southern people are very poor, and to send you to college your parents had to economize and deprive themselves of many things."

Sometimes his rebukes took the form of that gentle sarcasm he found so effective with his officers and men. One good student, who had been beguiled into an unexcused absence, he met with a smile as he said:

"Mr. M——, I am glad to see you are better."

"But General, I have not been sick."

"Then I am glad to see that you have better news from home."

"But General, I have had no bad news."

"Ah, I took it for granted that nothing less than sickness or distressing news from home could have kept you away from your duty."

His sense of humor rarely failed him. Another boy who was called in to account for an unexcused absence became so confused in Lee's presence that he blurted out a story about "a violent illness," and then realizing that he appeared the picture of good health, stammered something about having left his boots at the cobbler's.

"Stop, Mr. ——, stop, sir!" Lee interrupted. "One good reason is enough!"

To one lazy young man he said pointedly:

"How *is* your mother? I am sure you must be devoted to her, you are so careful of the health of her son!"

With a student whom he saw staggering through the streets of town he took a subtle approach. Nearly a week passed before the boy's name appeared on the list. Then Lee completely disarmed him by saying:

"Mr. ——, I had occasion to write your mother some time ago and it gave me great pleasure to tell her how well you were getting along in college."

"I trust I may ever live worthy of your commendation," the boy replied.

Looking at him directly, Lee went on in the same kindly tone:

"Mr. ——, did it ever occur to you that when you reach middle life or a time of sickness that you may need a stimulant, and if you have accustomed yourself to taking stimulants in your early life, it will require so much more to have the desired effect when you may need it?"

The boy was never seen drunk again.

There was little hard drinking among the students, although anyone who was habitually intoxicated was expelled. But Lee never took this step without positive proof, for he was slow to condemn. At a faculty meeting, a supposedly habitual drinker who passed all his free time in the saloons was being talked about. Since not a voice was raised in his favor, expulsion seemed impending until Lee asked two questions:

"Have any of you gentlemen *seen* this young man intoxicated?"

"Have any of you *seen* him entering bar-rooms?"

Since the answer to both questions was no, Lee then said:

"We must be very careful how we are influenced by hearsay." He paused for emphasis. "At one time during the war when I was subject to intense physical and mental strain, someone reported to the Executive that I was habitually intoxicated and unfit for duty!"

He later talked with this student, and if the accusations had any foundation in fact, Lee brought about his reform, for there was never so much as a whisper against him again.

Lee had sympathy with the young veteran who suffered from weak eyes, and seemed unable "to get the right grasp on his studies." He asked what exercise he had been taking. The boy said he had been going on long walks. This was fine, but did he think about his studies while walking?

Uncertain as to what answer Lee expected, he said, "Sometimes."

"This will not do. You must cast aside every care, worry, and thought of your work. . . . You will find it difficult, at first, to banish such thoughts and to control the operation of your mind under all circumstances, but the power can be gained by determination and practice."

Lee then recalled his own practices during the war, when he rode Traveller for relaxation and exercise. No matter what battle or movement was pending, no matter what his cares were, he put all such things from his mind, and "made the most of the pleasant thoughts conjured up while riding," returning "refreshed and relieved and in a better and stronger condition. . . . Now, try it, and you will find that even with less exercise . . . you will feel stronger and . . . will be able to manage your tasks with greater satisfaction to yourself. . . ."

He took pains to set the shy boy at ease, and pricked the overconfident youth's ego with gentle barbs. He would often introduce such a student as "the young man who is going to graduate in one session."

Only once is there record of his having lost his temper with a student. M. W. Humphreys, who later became a professor at the college, was damaging his health by overwork, and Lee advised him to ease up.

"Oh, but I am so impatient to make up for the time I lost in the army . . ."

"Mr. Humphreys!" Lee interrupted, "however long you live, and whatever you accomplish, you will find that the time you spent in the Confederate army was the most profitably spent portion of your life. Never again speak of having lost time in the army!"

He had no patience with meanness or persistent falsehood; and with perpetually defiant youths he took swift action, terminating their connection with the school immediately.

But he had infinite patience with most forms of youthful indiscretion, and often when the faculty recommended that a student be "sent home," if he recognized the fundamental character as sound, he would say:

"Gentlemen, don't you think it would be better to bear with him a little longer? Perhaps we may do him some good."

Pranks that did not arise from meanness found in him a lenient judge. The winter of 1866 was especially cold, with

289

eleven successive weeks of snow on the ground. Four students rented a room in the academic building, to study in comfort between recitations, and took turns buying the load of hickory for the stove, keeping the pile in a corner of the room. They began to notice that the wood was disappearing faster than it should and, since the college woodpile was far away and the janitor notably lazy, they had definite suspicions.

One of the boys, John Graham, thought up a plan for discovering the culprit. He bored a large hole in a piece of firewood, filled the hole with black powder, sealed it with clay and, warning the others, put it back on the pile.

Early the next morning there was a terrific explosion in Dr. Joynes' classroom. The stove was blown to pieces, and the room caught fire. Joynes regarded it "as a malicious attempt at a great crime and made a fuss in proportion," a student wrote in his diary that night.

Before chapel the next morning, Lee announced that he would be glad to have anyone who knew about the explosion call at his office during the forenoon. Graham and a companion to bear him witness went to see Lee, and Graham told the story of the missing wood and the trap to ensnare the thief.

"But General, I didn't know it was Professor Joynes!"

Lee laughed, and closed the incident by saying:

"Well, Mr. Graham, your plan to find out who was taking your wood was a good one, but your powder charge was too heavy. The next time use less powder."

In those cases when he felt he needed parental cooperation to help with reform, he wrote tactful letters to the boy's family, just as he had done when he was Superintendent at West Point.

He asked the faculty to "make no needless rules," nor any that they could not enforce. At a meeting, a professor who had appealed to precedent added: "We must not respect persons." Lee reversed this concept by saying:

"In dealing with young men, I always respect persons, and care little for precedent."

It seemed to the faculty and students that he had "a positive aversion" to anything that resembled military regimen, were it superfluous rules or merely forms. They noticed that whenever the Washington College student body marched with the cadets from V.M.I., Lee did not keep step. He walked along in a natural manner at the side of Superintendent Smith. One who watched Lee felt that he must have consciously avoided keeping step, "so uniformly did he fail to plant his foot simultaneously with General Smith or at the beat of the drum."

In his repudiation of things military, he told one professor:

"As a general principle you should not *force* young men to their duty, but let them do it voluntarily and thereby develop their characters." He paused, and then said:

"The greatest mistake of my life was taking a military education."

3

CUSTIS came to Lexington at the beginning of October. But he went to live at the Military Institute shortly after his arrival, and saw his father only at mealtimes when he came to the hotel. They took one Saturday ride together to the Natural Bridge, the greatest charm of which, for Robert, lay in the fact that "all is the work of God."

But Custis did not accept calamity and defeat with his father's philosophic resignation. "He seemed broken and disheartened," a friend observed. His father therefore found less comfort in his company than he had expected, and admitted to his daughters that he felt "very lonely" and was longing for their companionship and that of their friends.

"I have scarcely gotten acquainted with the young ladies," he wrote Mildred, still with her mother at Derwent. "They look very nice in the walks, but I rarely get near them. Traveller is my only companion; I may also say my pleasure. He & I, whenever practicable, wander out in the mountains & enjoy sweet confidence."

Deprived of the social contacts he so enjoyed, he admitted to being "crabbed."

Almost every afternoon, he rode five or six miles, and no

matter how many times the townspeople and students had watched him ride by, they stopped to look again.

"His poise was perfect, and I enjoyed looking at him. I expect I stopped and looked at him hundreds of times," a student wrote.

"Erect, handsome, and grandly heroic" he seemed to them all. He wore his gray uniform, the coat buttoned to the chin. In compliance with the humiliating "Button Order," his Confederate buttons had been replaced by black ones. Since buttons of any kind were so scarce, Southern women took pleasure in covering military buttons with black crêpe and bombazine so that their men appeared in public with their "buttons in mourning."

On one of these rides into the mountains, he was caught in a heavy rain and took shelter in the cabin of one of his old soldiers. With night, the storm increased so Lee asked if he might stay overnight. The veteran was delighted and when it came time to retire, he insisted that Lee take the bed while his wife slept in with the children, and he on the floor. This Lee refused to do, and they at length agreed to sleep together.

The next day after Lee had gone, the soldier went to see his nearest neighbors to tell them that Marse Robert had spent the night at his house.

"And where did he sleep?" they asked.

"Why, he slept with *me*," he said proudly.

"How did it *feel?*"

"I'll tell you, I never closed an eye. I didn't sleep a wink. I might have slept with God!"

Early in November, Mary accepted an invitation from Dr. Cocke to stay at Bremo. After she reached there, Robert sent her a progress report on their future house. Dr. Madison and his wife had been slow to move, which had delayed interior repairs and painting, so it would not be ready until December 1. Mrs. Elizabeth Cocke, their hostess at Derwent, had come to Lexington expressly to furnish Mary's room. Her sister, Mrs. Margaret Preston, a local artist and poetess, had designed the furniture, and Mrs. Cocke had hired Mr. Varner, a one-armed veteran, to make it. Some of the ladies from town had hung the

Arlington curtains and draperies and laid the carpet in the parlor, having to fold it under to fit the smaller room. The only piece of furniture there was a handsomely carved piano, presented by Stieff of Baltimore. Though he appreciated the generosity that had prompted the gift, Lee felt it was "an article of furniture that we might well dispense with under the circumstances."

"Tell Mildred," he wrote in fun, "I shall now insist on her resuming her music, & in addition to her other labours, she must practice *seven* hours a day on the piano, until she becomes sufficiently proficient to play agreeably to herself & others. . . ."

Mildred prided herself not only on her efficient housekeeping but on the management of her brothers. Her father now wrote to suggest that she had better come on and help him arrange the house for her mother.

You know I am a poor hand & can do nothing without your advice. Your brother, too, is wild for want of admonition. Col. Blair is his "fides Achates," & as he is almost as grey as your Papa, & wears the same uniform, *all grey*, he is sometimes mistaken for him by young girls, who consider your brother the most attentive of sons, & giving good promise of making a desirable husband. He will find himself married some of these days before he knows it. You had better be near him.

Traveller, he went on, was paying the price for fame, as the boys were pulling out his tail for souvenirs: "He is presenting the appearance of a plucked chicken."

In letters to Agnes and Mildred, he revived the topic of wives for Custis and Rob, though in Custis' case this was a family joke, for of all the children he was the most silent, reserved, and shy. His indifference to young women was so well known that even Mrs. Jefferson Davis had once punned at his expense. When she heard that at a wartime party, while the girls were preparing supper, Custis had sat down on a gridiron to rest, she asked:

"Was he tender on the gridiron? He has never been known to be so anywhere else."

Agnes now wrote her father for advice: Sally Warwick

had finally made up her mind to settle down and was marrying Major Poor. She wanted Agnes to be a bridesmaid and to come to Richmond and help with the preparations. Agnes did not like to miss going with the family to Lexington; still she wanted to be with Sally. What should she do?

Her father admitted that it was hard to advise her to go away from him, for "you know how much I want to see you & how important you are to me. But in order to help make up your mind, if it will promote your happiness, I will say go."

His attitude toward the marriage ceremony had been untempered by time. Assuming Agnes would go, he told her:

"You may inform Sally from me, however, that no preparations are necessary, & if they were, no one could help her. She has just got to wade through it as if it were an attack of measles or anything else—naturally."

He regretted that Sally had not considered Custis seriously, for he would have liked to count her among his daughters. But this was a young woman's prerogative, and he respected it. He loved her none the less, but he did tease her at every opportunity for having let slip the chance of becoming his daughter-in-law. Knowing that this would make its way to Sally, he affected indifference when he wrote Agnes:

As she would not marry Custis, she may marry whom she chooses. I shall wish her every happiness just the same, for she knows nobody loves her as much as I do. I do not think upon reflection, she will consider it right to refuse my son & take away my daughter. She need not tell me whom she is going to marry. I suppose it is some cross old widower with a dozen children. She will not be satisfied at her sacrifice with less, & I would think that cross would be sufficient.

Sally's sacrifice was clearly not Custis but Lee himself!

Later, he was tempted to send "dear little Sally— for she is dear to me in the broadest, highest sense of the word—the benefit of Jeremy Taylor's opinion on *hasty marriages*," but on reflection he decided not to, for Mary had counseled him:

"When a young woman makes up her mind to get married, you might as well let her alone."

On Saturday morning, December 2, Lee and Custis were

waiting at the Lexington wharf for the arrival of Mary, Rob, and Mildred. They were making the trip from Bremo in the private boat of Colonel Ellis, president of the James River and Kanawha Canal Company, who had loaned it for Mary's comfort. When they reached their new home, they found a delicious breakfast which Professor Nelson's wife had provided.

The furniture from Baltimore had not yet come, so the parlor still had only the piano in it and a few camp stools that Robert had set up; the dining-room furniture was borrowed. Only Mary's room was complete, Mrs. Cocke having seen to every detail for her comfort.

The larder was well stocked through the generosity of the townspeople who had brought staples as well as jellies, pickles, canned fruit, brandied peaches, and preserves. For days and even weeks after they moved in, food was brought by the neighbors and by farmers and mountaineers who walked down from their little places on the slopes to bring bags of potatoes, walnuts, and game.

Aunt Maria Fitzhugh shipped the wines, stores, and pictures which she had kept safely at Ravensworth. The canalboat that was carrying them sank; everything was recovered, but the paintings were damaged by the mud and water and had to be sent to Baltimore for restoration.

When Hunter raided the Valley, the two chests of silver service that had been sent on to Lexington for safekeeping were turned over to the care of the old sergeant at the Military Institute, who had buried them in a place known only to himself. Now, Rob went with him to dig them up. The chests were safe but the silver was black from the damp, and temporarily useless. With obvious delight, Lee opened his camp chest and brought out the faithful tinware.

To Rob, his father appeared "bright and even gay." It made him very happy to have Mary and his "little children" with him again. Since Rob was still suffering from malaria, contracted when working with Rooney on his farm, his father gave him the nickname of "Robertus Sickus."

Good servants were impossible to find, so Lee encouraged Mildred, and later Daughter and Agnes when they came home, to cook, sew, and do the marketing. He was amused at their failures in the kitchen.

"You are all very helpless," he laughed. "I don't know what you'll do when I am gone."

But there was praise for their successes, and "he would admire the calico dresses we made with our unskilled fingers," Mildred wrote.

As soon as winter was over, he planted vegetables, fruit and shade trees, a lawn, roses, jasmine, and other flowers, in an effort to make his womankind content with "the small life of poverty . . . the ugly, meanly built little house with its ordinary surroundings . . . and . . . the provincial society," as Mildred described it.

After life at Arlington and even the unsettled war years, this existence seemed small and dull to the girls, accounting for their frequent and long stays in places where they could take part in unlimited social activities.

One daughter at least was able to laugh at their plight. When walking back from market one day with a basket of fine pears, she met a friend who remarked on their quality.

"Yes," she told him, "they are nice and I would offer you one, but I have just enough for my dessert tomorrow."

She smiled, and then said: "I want this inscribed on my tombstone:

> " 'Although on pleasure she was bent,
>   She had a frugal mind.' "

Only for the first half year of his presidency was the "small life of poverty" a necessity. With the collapse of the Confederacy, Lee lost around $20,000 invested in government bonds, but he had enough sound securities to yield around $3600 interest per annum. After the first semester his salary was raised to $3000, which with his share of the tuition, gave him an income of $4,756 in 1866–67.

Though it was written of him that he was "fond of elegance of every sort; fine houses, furniture, plate, clothing, ornaments, horses, equipage," to have lived opulently in these times would have been against his principles. He had shared

296

Virginia's prosperity, and he would share her poverty and set an example of self-denial. He was content to occupy a small whitewashed room adjoining Mary's. Here he had his camp bed, a single chair, and two battered trunks. The only ornament was a group of dress swords in elaborate sheaths, hung on the wall. Two of them had belonged to Washington, one to his father, and the others were his own.

Though Mary was thankful for the asylum and the kindness of the people, she admitted to a close friend that she often longed for a sight of the James or the Potomac, and was oppressed by the feeling that the mountains shut her off from all that she formerly knew and loved. She never relinquished the hope that Arlington would be returned to them, and that they could resume the old way of life.

After the Lees were settled, faculty members and their wives, students, professors from the Military Institute, cadets, and townspeople called. It was not long until the President's house, described as "the abode of real old 'Virginia hospitality,' " became the center of Lexington social life.

To distinguish the younger students who called from the "Confeds," Lee originated the title "yearling," and from this sobriquet he came to call a professor "a leader of the herd," terminology which became standard in his household.

One afternoon, a large number of visitors came "with a sort of exalted reverence to pay their formal respects to the General and Mrs. Lee." Among them was the artist, Margaret Preston, and her young son. When she was ready to leave, she found that the boy had misplaced his cap.

"What was my surprise," she wrote, "to hear Mrs. Lee interrupt her husband in his animated talk with some distinguished gentleman present—not to ask him to summon a servant to do her errand, but to say:

" 'Robert, Herbert Preston has lost his cap; will you go into the back parlor and see if he has left it there?' "

Robert went in search of Herbert's cap. "We were not used to hear the leader of our armies bidden to wait on a child," Mrs. Preston wrote.

One evening, a student brought to the house an old deaf

kinsman who was determined to meet Lee. He was so hard of hearing no one tried to talk with him long, but Robert took a chair at his side, and kept up a lively conversation with apparent ease—relieving the embarrassment of the young man, and completely charming the old gentleman.

Those callers who came to see the Lee girls were expected to spend some time with their parents. When the guests were all young people, the parlor was given over to them. In the dining room, Robert would read aloud while Mary mended or knitted. But when ten o'clock struck, Lee would shut the book, get up, and close the shutters slowly and carefully. If this hint were not taken, he would say:

"Good night, young gentlemen."

When he saw some boy too absorbed in a *tête-à-tête* with one of his daughters or a friend to notice his gentle reminders of the hour, he would take a chair beside him and start a general conversation. The girl would then excuse herself and join Mary in the dining room, and the young man, brought to his senses, would depart.

A frequent caller at the house was told one day that General Lee had referred to him as "a fine young man."

"Do you know why?" he asked. "It is because I have never been caught in the parlor at ten o'clock. I came very near to it last night, but got out into the porch before the General shut the first blind!"

4

IN January, 1866, Lee and Bolivar Christian went to Richmond to appear before the Committee on Education, then meeting with the state legislature. Christian presented the financial plight of Washington College, which had been for years dependent for part of its support on the interest from eighty-eight thousand dollars invested in state bonds. This income had stopped with the Confederacy's fall.

What Lee had to say added little to the Colonel's remarks but his presence counted. When his name was read in the

House of Delegates, "it was received with cheers on all sides" and the members voted a short recess to pay their respects to him.

He stayed in Richmond almost a week, doing a bit of effective lobbying in behalf of a bill to benefit colleges throughout the state, visiting, and shopping for Mary. Agnes was still there, but she was looking so poorly he urged her to accept an invitation from the Selden family in Norfolk, rather than expose herself to the severe mountain winter in Lexington. But he teased her about going so far away. From Norfolk, he told her, she could easily get to New York, where she would find steamers leaving daily for Europe.

"Let us know when you sail," he joked.

On arriving home, he found the family "as usual," he wrote Agnes. "Your mother is a great sufferer, but is as quiet & uncomplaining as ever. Mildred is active & cheerful, & Custis & I silent as our wont."

Shortly after his return, he received a New Year's present given by twenty-four admirers from Greenway, near Rockbridge Baths. "As a slight token of our esteem" they brought four hams, two shoulders, one turkey, thirty pounds of buckwheat flour, one barrel of white flour, ten bushels of corn, half a bushel of dried peaches, a crock of quince butter, and one of apple butter. Two of the farmers had donated the use of their wagons and teams to collect the food.

He was deeply touched by such evidence of his people's love, and by the veneration and interest of such men as Lord Acton, Philip Stanhope Worsley, and George Long.

In January, 1866, Maria Dalberg Acton wrote Mary enclosing a lecture recently given by her husband, the noted historian, John Emerich Edward Dalberg, first Baron Acton. It was, she said, "to add to the many testimonies which you must have received of the sympathy and veneration which have been inspired in Europe by the illustrious career of General Lee. . . ."

Mary replied, and the following November, Lord Acton wrote Lee, hoping he would not "resent as an intrusion a letter from an earnest and passionate lover of the cause whose glory and whose strength you were." Acton wanted Lee to tell him "the light in which you would wish the current politics of America to be understood," for he had been "requested to furnish private counsel in American affairs for the guidance of the editors of a weekly Review which . . . will be conducted by men who are followers of Mr. Gladstone. You are aware, no doubt, that Mr. Gladstone was in the minority of Lord Palmerston's cabinet who wished to accept the French Emperor's proposal to mediate in the American war."

Because Lee was hopeful that some benefit might arise from a proper understanding of the issues, knowing that "the influence of current opinion in Europe upon the current politics of America must always be salutary," he discussed with unaccustomed freedom those subjects he usually avoided.

Amid the conflicting statements and sentiments in both countries, it will be no easy task to discover the truth, or to relieve it from the mass of prejudice and passion, with which it has been covered by party spirit [he told Acton]. I am conscious of the compliment conveyed in your request for my opinion . . . and had I the ability, I have not the time to enter upon a discussion, which was commenced by the founders of the Constitution and has been continued to this present day. I can only say that while I have considered the preservation of the constitutional power of the General Government to be the foundation of our peace and safety at home and abroad, I yet believe that the maintenance of the rights and authority reserved to the States and to the people, not only essential to the adjustment and balance of the general system, but a safeguard to the continuance of a free Government. I consider it the chief source of stability to our political system, whereas the consolidation of the States into one vast Republic, sure to be aggressive abroad and despotic at home, will be the certain precursor of that ruin which has overwhelmed all those that have preceded it.

Discussing the question of sovereignty and independence of state action, he wrote:

If, therefore, the result of the war is to be considered as having decided that the union of the States is inviolable & perpetual under the Constitution, it naturally follows that it is as incompetent for the general Government to impair its integrity by the exclusion of a State, as for the States to do so by secession; and that the existence and rights of a State by the Constitution are as indestructible as the Union itself. . . . The South has contended only for the supremacy of the Constitution, and the just administration of the laws made in pursuance of it. Virginia to the last made great efforts to save the Union, and urged harmony and compromise.

Speaking for himself and other rational Southerners, he said:

Although the South would have preferred any honourable compromise to the fratricidal war . . . she now accepts in good faith its constitutional results, and receives without reserve the amendment which has already been made to the Constitution for the extinction of slavery. This is an event that has long been sought, though in a different way, and by none has it been more earnestly sought than by the citizens of Virginia.

Lord Acton asked about Lee's progress with his narrative of the campaigns in Virginia, and he told him: "I regret to state that I progress slowly in the collection of the necessary documents for its completion. I particularly feel the loss of the official returns showing the small numbers with which the battles were fought."

When the British poet and scholar, Philip Stanhope Worsley, was translating the *Iliad*, he compared Lee's career with Hector's.

"He is the hero, like Hector . . . of the most glorious cause for which men can fight, and some of the grandest passages in the poem come to me with yet more affecting power when I remember his lofty character and undeserved misfortune," Worsley wrote to Lee's nephew, Edward Lee Childe. On the flyleaf of the copy of the *Iliad* that Worsley sent on to Lexington, he inscribed:

> "To General Lee,
> The most stainless of living commanders,
> And, excepting in fortune, the greatest. . . ."

This was followed by a dedicatory poem of five stanzas.

When Lee thanked him for this unusual and touching

301

tribute, he disclosed his familiarity with the *Iliad*'s Greek form:

". . . Its perusal has been my evening's recreation, & I have never more enjoyed the beauty & grandeur of the poem than as recited by you. The translation is as truthful as powerful, & faithfully represents the imagery & rhythm of the bold original."

Modestly, he refused to accept the dedication for himself: "The undeserved compliment in prose & verse, on the first leaves of the volume, I received as your tribute to the merit of my countrymen, who struggled for constitutional government."

The following March, when he learned through Edward Childe that Worsley was seriously ill, he wrote him:

So great is my interest in your welfare that I cannot refrain, even at the risk of intruding upon your sickroom, from expressing my sincere sympathy. . . . Like many of your tastes & pursuits, I fear you may confine yourself too closely to your reading. Less mental labour & more of the fresh air of Heaven might bring to you more comfort, & to your friends more enjoyment, even in the way in which you now delight them. Should a visit to this distracted country promise any recreation, I hope I need not assure you how happy I should be to see you in Lexington. I can give you a quiet room, & careful nursing, & a horse that would delight to carry you over our beautiful mountains. . . .

After reading aloud the *Iliad*, Lee borrowed from the library of the Franklin Society, of which he was a member, Goldsmith's *Rome*, a work dealing with the overthrow of the Republic. The next book withdrawn was the Duchess D'Abrantes' *Memoirs*. Not long after that, Lee began to prepare his father's book for a new edition, so the third volume charged to him was Jared Sparks' biography of Washington.

The works from which he read aloud were varied: a two-volume biography of Goethe, followed by *Faust;* Shakespeare; Macaulay's *England; The Vicar of Wakefield; The Pilgrim's Progress; Bleak House;* Dr. Elisha Kent Kane's *Arctic Expeditions;* many anthologies of English poetry; Hood's *Poems; Leo the Tenth;* and always, issues of current literary magazines.

During the winter of 1865, he read Thomas à Kempis'

Imitation of Christ, which Markie had sent to him. When thanking her, he said:

I have read some of your favourite chapters, & hope I may derive from the perusal of the book, the good you desire. I prefer the Bible to any other book. There is enough in that, to satisfy the most ardent thirst for knowledge, to open the way to true wisdom, & to teach the only road to salvation & eternal happiness. It is not above human comprehension, & is sufficient to satisfy all its desires.

When a group of English admirers sent him a handsome edition of the Bible, he wrote the spokesman, the Hon. A. W. Beresford Hope: "The Bible is a book in comparison with which all others in my eyes are of minor importance, & which in all my perplexities has never failed to give me light & strength."

When another English scholar, George Long, translated the meditations of Marcus Aurelius, the first edition of his work was pirated by an American publisher who dedicated it to Emerson. Long was indignant, and immediately issued a second edition which contained this explanatory note:

I never dedicated a book to any man, and if I dedicated this, I should choose a man whose name seemed to me most worthy to be joined to that Roman soldier and philosopher. . . . I would dedicate it to him who led the Confederate armies against the powerful invader, and retired from an unequal contest defeated, but not dishonoured; to the noble Virginian soldier whose talents and virtues place him by the side of the best and wisest man who sat the throne of the imperial Caesars.

Lee was disheartened by the vindictive course of the Federal government, dominated by the Radicals who overruled the temperate policies of the President. He wrote frankly to his Northern admirer and champion, Senator Reverdy Johnson:

"To pursue a policy which will continue the prostration of one-half the country, & alienate the affections of its inhabitants from the Government, & which must eventually result in injury to the country & the American people, appears to me so manifestly injudicious that I do not see how those responsible can tolerate it."

Mary's bitterness over these proceedings distressed him, for he felt it was injurious to her health. She had become an assiduous newspaper reader, a practice which brought on fits of anger.

"It is bad enough to be the victims of tyranny, but when it is wielded by such cowards and base men as Butler, Thaddeus & Turner it is indeed intolerable," she wrote Mrs. Chilton. "The country that allows such scum to rule them must be fast going to destruction and we shall care little if we are not involved in the crash."

She still grieved and fretted over Arlington's loss. Efforts were being made to have it restored, and when asked by a friend what she would do about all the "Yankee graves" if she returned there, she said:

"My dear, I would smooth them off and plant my flowers."

Robert made every effort to divert her mind and keep her cheered. When with her he was sprightly; he waited on her, pushed her rollingchair, and tried to keep conversation away from current politics. As soon as he came into house, he would call out brightly:

"Where is my little Miss Mildred? She is my light-bearer; the house is never dark if she is in it."

And when he came into the parlor or dining room, he would tell Mary about some amusing incident at the college or give details of his afternoon's ride—whom he had met and talked with on his way through town; which road he took; what wild flowers he saw; and describe the views and evening skies.

Often, he had some interesting or touching happening to tell. One afternoon when he passed a little cabin on the slopes, a young country woman had recognized him and run out to beg him to come in. As he was dismounting, she blew a long blast on a tin horn, and from every direction a crowd of ragged children came running.

"Oh, General, these are my little children. Please give every one of them your blessing."

He knew that a change of scene was helpful to Mary and, always hoping that the mineral waters might benefit her, arranged for her to spend several months each summer at one of the springs. To spare her discomfort and the hazard of climbing in and out of the baths, he devised a special chair that could be raised and lowered into the water, by means of pulleys.

In December, 1865, Congress formed the Reconstruction Committee to investigate conditions in the former Confederate states, and "report whether they . . . are entitled to be represented in either house of Congress."

In February, 1866, Lee was called as a witness before this committee, and an honorary staff of young men from Lexington volunteered to go with him to Washington. Word of his presence in the capital soon spread, and multitudes called at his rooms in the Metropolitan Hotel. His staff managed to keep out those who had no claim on his time and strength, but he was still nearly overwhelmed.

One old Confederate came time and again to see Lee, but having no just claim, he was turned away. When he came to the door once more, begging for just a sight of his old commander, it was felt no harm would be done by letting him in. He was introduced, and Lee shook his hand, but as he was about to be led off, to the horror of the staff, he drew himself up and addressed Lee in a loud voice:

"General, I have always thought that if I ever had the honor of meeting you face to face, and there was opportunity allowed me, I would like to ask you a question which nobody but you can answer. I seem to have that opportunity now. . . . What was the reason you failed to gain the victory at Gettysburg?"

Most men would have given this ill-timed question a curt rejoinder, but Lee took the old rebel by the hand and said kindly:

"My dear sir, that would be a long story, and would require more time than you see I can possibly command at the present; so we will have to defer the matter to another occasion."

Lee's chief interrogator, when he appeared before the committee, was Senator Jacob M. Howard of Michigan. Though

305

the Senator was always civil, his questions were frequently irrelevant. More interesting than Lee's answers—which were invariably direct, terse, and temperate—was his remarkable restraint, patience, and lack of rancor. Though he was in an intensely hostile atmosphere, he remained outwardly calm and replied to all questions with the same courtesy he would have shown toward guests in his home.

Whatever the committee hoped to accomplish by calling Lee—whether to add to its fund of information or to humiliate him—they did not succeed. His answers were so general and cautious, they contributed nothing, and his nobility and magnetic presence caused even his bitterest foes to speak favorably of him.

This visit to Washington was not a happy one. "The changed times & circumstances did recall sad thoughts; but I rejoiced to think, that those who were so prominent in my thoughts, at former periods when returning from long & distant excursions, & whose welcome was so grateful, were now above all human influences, & enjoying eternal peace & rest."

He made a few calls in the city, but as he explained to a cousin:

"I am considered now such a monster, that I hesitate to darken with my shadow the doors of those I love best lest I should bring upon them misfortune."

In the hope of seeing Markie—"knowing how our Merciful God mixes in the cup he gives us to drink in this world, the sweet with the bitter"—he drove out to Tudor Place in Georgetown. But Markie, still trying to escape her great grief over Orton's death, was with friends in Philadelphia. He had no wish, he wrote, to approach Arlington "nearer than the railway which leads to the city. I know very well how things are there."

Shortly after he reached home, he received a letter from Amanda Parks, a former house servant at Arlington. She had called at his hotel when he was not in and was sorry to have missed seeing him. On March 9, Lee replied:

"I . . . regret very much that I did not see you when I was in Washington . . . for I wished to learn how you were, & how all the people from Arlington were getting on in the world. My interest in them is as great now as it ever was, & I sincerely wish for their happiness & prosperity. . . ."

Mrs. Jefferson Davis also wrote to call his attention to a speech in which Schuyler Colfax had attacked him maliciously. He knew nothing about it, he told her, for he avoided reading the newspapers and all other controversial matter.

Had it, however, come under my notice, I doubt whether I should have thought proper to reply. *I have thought, from the cessation of hostilities, that silence and patience on the part of the South was the true course;* and I think so still. *Controversy of all kinds* will, in my opinion, only serve to continue excitement & passion, & will prevent the public mind from acknowledgment & acceptance of truth. These considerations have kept me from replying to accusations made against myself, & induced me to recommend the same to others.

He wrote in a similar manner to General Early, who had gone to Mexico. Early had written him about the defamation of Jefferson Davis. Lee also regretted it, but believed that "the reflecting or informed portion of the country" would be little influenced by it. As to the accusations against himself, which Early had also mentioned, he said he was content to ignore them.

"I have not thought proper to notice, or even correct misrepresentations of my words or acts. We shall have to be patient, & suffer for a while at least. . . . At present the public mind is not prepared to receive the truth."

Only once, when his honor was besmirched, did he come to his own defense. Senator Simon Cameron, who had been Secretary of War at the time of Lee's resignation from the United States Army, stated during a debate in Congress that Lee had verbally accepted the command of Federal troops, then under guise of returning to Virginia to settle his business, had "deserted under false pretenses."

Senator Reverdy Johnson challenged this statement, asking Cameron if he had heard Lee's verbal acceptance. Cameron admitted that he had not; that the acceptance had been made to a third party, "a gentleman who had my confidence and in whom I relied thoroughly."

307

"That is another matter," Johnson said. "The statement was not made to the honorable member."

"I have no doubt of its truth," Cameron replied.

"I doubt very much its truth. It is not in keeping with the character of Lee," Johnson told him.

Mary brought the controversy to Robert's attention, and he wrote to Johnson to thank him for his bold defense.

"I never intimated to any one that I desired the command of the United States Army; nor did I ever have a conversation with but one gentleman, Mr. Francis Preston Blair, on the subject, which was at his invitation, & as I understood, at the instance of President Lincoln," Lee wrote.

He told Johnson how, after listening to Blair's remarks, he had declined, "stating as candidly & as courteously as I could, that, though opposed to secession & deprecating war, I could take no part in an invasion of the Southern States."

Whenever there was an opportunity, he urged patience and silence. He said to one woman who had lost her husband in battle, and was talking bitterly:

"Madam, do not train up your children in hostility to the government of the United States. Remember, we are one country now. Dismiss from your mind all sectional feeling, and bring them up to be Americans."

To a friend who was preserving as a reminder of the war the shattered trunk of a tree felled by Federal fire, he said:

"Cut it down, my dear Madam, and forget it!"

Overhearing a clergyman talking harshly about the Northerners, he told him:

"Doctor, there is a good old book which I read from and you preach from, which says, 'Love your enemies, bless them that curse you, do good to them that hate you, and pray for them which despitefully use you and persecute you.'" After the minister had apologized, Lee said:

"I have fought against the people of the North because I believed they were seeking to wrest from the South her dearest rights, but I have never seen the day when I did not pray for them."

He practiced patient resignation and forgiveness whenever

possible. One day, a needy man came to his door. His ragged appearance and his inability to find work aroused Lee's sympathy, and he fitted the man out with some clothing, and gave him some money.

Mary saw Robert go by with the clothes over his arm, and asked who was at the door.

"An old soldier," he said evasively.

"Of whose command?"

"General Sherman's—but we must not remember that against him now."

5

"I HOPE you do not feel obliged to reply to all these letters," Margaret Preston said to Lee one day as she looked at the stacks of mail piled neatly on the round pedestal table which he used as a desk in his office.

"I certainly do. Think of those poor people! It is a great deal of trouble for them to write; why should I not be willing to take the trouble to answer them? And as that is all I can give most of them, I give it ungrudgingly."

And so he sent a courteous refusal to the young man from Oxford, Mississippi, who asked for a recommendation so that he could teach fencing. For the spiritualist who wanted Lee's opinion on a military movement of von Moltke's, there was gentle sarcasm:

Theirs was a question on which military experts would differ, and his own judgment would be poor at best. Since they had the power to consult, through their mediums, such men as Caesar, Alexander, Napoleon, and Wellington, he could not think of obtruding his opinion in such illustrious company.

A distressed young woman wrote that her lover had been in either "Mr. Lee's or Mr. Johnston's army." She had not heard from him since the war, and though his family reported him dead, she thought this was a ruse to keep her from marrying him. If Mr. Lee could not find him, would he write for her to Mr. Johnston?

He took great pains "to relieve the poor woman," and when his efforts proved fruitless, he wrote her sympathetically.

For Miss Mattie Ward, who sent "two photographic copies" of her painting of Stratford, there was a nostalgic note of appreciation:

"Your picture vividly recalls scenes of my earliest recollections & happiest days. Though unseen for years, every feature of the house is familiar to me."

To an artist who wanted to sell him a painting of the old house on the White House plantation, he wrote in regret:

"I am now unable to purchase works of art of any kind." His recollections of the house would have to serve him.

There was a gracious note of thanks to a man who had returned "three articles taken from Arlington by U. S. soldiers"; and a detailed letter to a Baltimore man whose son had bought a ring and pin from a Federal soldier. They had been identified as belonging to Lee, and the man wanted to return them.

The pin and ring, Lee wrote, each contained locks of General and Mrs. Washington's hair; he had packed them himself in a French rosewood dressing case in which he had put other family pieces, among them an antique ring with the bust of Socrates on it. His daughter, Mary, had taken the case to Cedar Grove and left it there when she went to Richmond. Though the house had been visited by many Federals, the case was unmolested until the fall of '64, when Merritt raided Fauquier County; then it had been carried off.

"I shall consider it a great favour if you will allow me to refund the sum paid the soldier by your son."

He wrote a polite refusal to the editor of the *Southern Review*, who asked him to review Hozier's *Seven Weeks' War*, for he had not time to study the campaigns properly. To another editor who wanted him to criticize a book on the recent war, he wrote:

"I have felt so little desire to recall the events of the war since the cessation of hostilities, that I have not read a single work that has been published on the subject."

To a man who believed he had two of Light-Horse Harry

310

Lee's swords, Robert said he doubted if he could identify them, as he had not seen them since childhood.

To "Messrs. Styll & Davis," he wrote a courteous note of thanks for a comfortable armchair; and another to an admirer in Wyoming who had sent him a beaver robe.

He said to the piano manufacturer in Baltimore who wanted to call his latest composition "The Washington College Galop":

"The College I am sure will appreciate the compliment of your selection of the name of your musicial composition."

There was a note addressed to "Messrs. Jms. M. Heinnich & Bro.," also of Baltimore, thanking them for the offer of a new hat:

"I have a very good hat, which will answer my purpose the whole year, & would therefore prefer you to give to others what I really do not require."

He replied modestly to Julia Balch, who wanted to visit him to procure material for a biography:

"I should be happy to see you in Lexington, but not on the errand you propose, for I know nothing good I could tell you of myself & I fear I should not like to say any evil. The few incidents of interest in which I have been engaged, are as well known to others as to myself & I know of nothing to say in addition."

He received many requests for autographic letters of General Washington. There were none to spare, but to those whose requests he felt were justified he sent signatures which he cut from Washington's account books.

When General Gordon, who had become president of the Southern Life Insurance Company in Atlanta, asked Lee to become a director, he replied:

"It would be a great pleasure to me to be associated with you, Hampton, Ben. H. Hill & other good men whose names I see are on your list of Directors, but I feel I ought not to abandon the position I hold at Washington College at this time or as long as I can be of use to it."

He gave this same reason to dozens of other men who offered him more lucrative employment in business firms and

311

at other universities. The only business which he helped and lent his name to was the Valley Railroad, and this was because the College would benefit by a railway into Lexington.

The most flattering proposal of all came in February, 1867, when Robert Ould, Virginia state senator, asked if he would accept nomination for governor of Virginia.

Mary was anxious for him to accept, as she felt this was a fitting climax to his career. But to Robert there was never a question of personal satisfaction or pride, and in his letter of refusal, he said:

> I think it important, in selecting a Chief Magistrate of the Commonwealth, for the citizens to choose one capable of fulfilling its highest trust, and at the same time not liable to the misconstruction which their choice of one objectionable to the General Government would be sure to create, and thereby increase the evils under which the State at present labours.
>
> I have no means of knowing . . . whether my election as Governor . . . would be personally injurious to me or not. . . . But I believe it would be used by the dominant party to excite hostility toward the State, and to injure the people in the eyes of the country; and I therefore cannot consent to become an instrument of bringing distress upon those whose prosperity and happiness are so dear to me. If *my* disfranchisement and privation of civil rights would secure the citizens of the State the enjoyment of civil liberty and equal rights under the Constitution, I would willingly accept them in their stead.

When William Preston Johnston sent, from San Francisco, a collection of minerals for the college, Lee responded with a warm letter:

> Notwithstanding their long journey from the Pacific, they were so well packed that they arrived in perfect order, & are among the most valuable specimens in our cabinet. . . . As a contribution to Washington College by the son of my friend & comrade General Albert Sidney Johnston—one of the bravest, truest, & noblest men I have ever known—they are particularly prized.

Two years later, young Johnston was elected to the Chair of History and Literature at Washington College.

To one little namesake (there were hundreds at this time),

young Robert Lee Mooty of La Grange, Georgia, he wrote this typical letter:

My dear young friend:

I have become acquainted with you through a letter from your father & hasten to express the pleasure this knowledge gives me.

I shall watch your future career with great interest & pray that it may be one of great usefulness to your friends & your country.

That it may be, listen to the teachings of your parents; obey their precepts, & from childhood to the grave, pursue unswervingly the path of honour & of truth. Above all things, learn at once to worship your Creator & do his will, as revealed in His Holy book.

With much affection, I am your sincere friend,

R E Lee

General Fitz John Porter, U. S. A., wrote to ask:

"What would have been the probable result of an attack upon Longstreet after 12 M. (29 Aug. '62) with about 12,000 men? If repulsed what would have been the effect upon the fortunes of that day, so far as Pope's position is concerned? Also its effect upon Jackson's safety, if the attack had been made after 5 P.M.?"

Lee replied: ". . . in my opinion the probable result . . . would have been a repulse . . . and would have insured Jackson's safety."

To the man who perhaps hoped to embarrass Lee by suggesting that he invite Grant to visit Washington College, he wrote:

I am much obliged to you for your letter . . . which I am sure has been prompted by the best motives. I shall be glad if General Grant would visit Washington College. But if I were to [invite him], it might not be agreeable to him, & I fear at this time my motives might be misunderstood, both by himself & others, & that evil would result instead of good. . . ."

For Messrs. Lippincott & Co., Philadelphia, who had sent a recent publication for his approval, there were rare words of praise, since it was not his practice to recommend books:

313

Gentn:

I have been able to give the first six parts of your Pronouncing Dictionary of Biography & Mythology only a cursory examination, but I think that its general arrangement is good, its pronounciation clear & correct, & the typography distinct & plain. It is the most valuable work of the kind in English that I have seen.

Very respy

Your obt. Svt.

R E Lee

He received hundreds of applications from former officers and men—for recommendations, for advice, for records of their service—and an equally large number of requests for autographs and pictures, from all over the land. There was also a heavy correspondence concerning his personal business. He was trying to unfreeze his investments, and bring about the return of Arlington and those furnishings removed by the Federals and placed in the U. S. Patent Office in Washington. He had also started a suit to regain Smith's Island. Finally, there were letters relative to college business, letters to parents, and letters of thanks for donations of money and equipment— and even furnishings.

When Miss Anne Upshur Jones of New York broke up housekeeping, she decided to send the contents of her home to "the greatest living man" for his own use or for the college. In thanking her, he wrote:

The books were arranged in the library on their arrival, the globes in the philosophical department, while the furniture, carpets, sofas, chairs, &c., have been applied to the furnishing of the dais of the audience-room of the new chapel, to the comfort & ornament of which they are a great addition. I have yet made no disposition of the plate & tableware, & they are still in the boxes in which they came.

He invited her to visit Lexington at graduation, when he would show her "the successful operation of the college."

Since no other use was found for the silver and dishes, he finally agreed to accept them for his home.

In addition to all these other letters, there was his personal correspondence with Markie; Norvell Caskie; Charlotte Haxall, a new favorite just blooming into "belleship"; his daughters, one or more of whom were always away; the Stuart girls; and Eliza Stiles, though on December 21, 1867, she died, leaving, as he wrote sadly, "one less earthly tie to bind me."

It is no wonder that he looked forward to a ride on Traveller every afternoon, and allowed nothing except a heavy storm to keep him home. As soon as he was out of town, he would let the gray run full speed up the hills, for unless ridden regularly and hard he became restive, and had "a very disagreeable, fretful trot." After a good run, he was content to proceed quietly.

Quite often, Lee would ride over to see his friends Andrew Cameron and Colonel Ross, both prosperous farmers near Lexington, and talk with them about crops, cattle, and horses, subjects he found relaxing.

Since times were so unsettled, and thieves abounded, Ross kept a pack of vicious dogs. These were customarily locked up during the day, but one afternoon the Colonel heard them barking in the front yard. Hurrying out, he saw Lee standing with his back to the gate, confronted by several big dogs, the largest and fiercest of which stood on his hind feet with his front feet on the General's shoulders, their noses not six inches apart. "The General stood like a statue calmly looking into the dog's eyes." Ross called off the dogs, and apologized. He was amazed to find Lee "entirely unruffled" and ready to chide him playfully for not keeping his dogs tied up.

Another favorite ride was the wooded road leading to the Rockbridge Baths. One afternoon, he met in these woods a plain old soldier who, as soon as he recognized Lee, reined up and said:

"General Lee, I am powerful glad to see you and I feel like cheering you!"

Lee pointed out that there was little call for cheering, but the veteran was not convinced. Waving his hat above his head, he shouted "in a ringing voice that awoke the echoes":

"Hurrah for General Lee! Hurrah for General Lee!" keeping it up until Lee was out of sight.

Traveller, it was conceded by all, was the privileged character at the President's house. Regardless of flowers and shrubbery, he was permitted to browse on the front lawn. Whenever he saw Lee, he would greet him with a toss of the head, a form of military salute and an expression of affection, the students liked to think. When Lee came in the front gate, he would walk across the grass and pass a few minutes with Traveller, patting him, talking to him, and frequently feeding him a sugar lump. The great love between master and mount was obvious to those who stopped to watch.

One day when Robert escorted a guest to the canalboat, he tied Traveller to a post while he took the young lady aboard. As he was talking to her on deck, someone called out that Traveller was loose, and Lee saw the gray increasing his speed as a number of men and boys started after him. Coming ashore, Lee asked the crowd to be still. Then he whistled a peculiar, low whistle. At the sound, Traveller stopped and pricked up his ears. On hearing it a second time, he gave a whinny, turned around, and trotted back to Lee, who patted and talked with him for a few minutes before tying him again.

A bystander expressed surprise at such docility, and Lee told him that he did not understand how "any man could ride a horse for any length of time without a perfect understanding being established between them."

Mr. Seseney, the Lexington blacksmith, recalled that Lee always stood beside Traveller when he was being shod, talking to him quietly, and that he asked the smith to have patience:

"He was made nervous by the bursting of bombs around him during the war," he explained.

When a new house for the President was finished in 1869, at the back of the lot near the street was a large comfortable brick stable connected to the house by a covered passageway. Lee found this arrangement pleasing, and was often heard to say how happy he was to be "living under the same roof with Traveller."

On one occasion when he had to be away from him for some while, Robert wrote his secretary:

"How is Traveller? Tell him I miss him dreadfully, & have repented of our separation but once—and that is the whole time since we parted."

316

He liked to think of him as a member of the family, and would often link his name with someone in the household:

"Traveller & Custis are both well, & pursue their usual dignified gait & habits, & are not led astray by the frivolous entertainments of lectures & concerts."

When they moved to Lexington, Robert planned to keep horses for his daughters, but for economy's sake and because of the shortage of hired help, he gave up this idea.

"Horses do not live on air here, nor do they wait on themselves," he wrote.

When Rob came up from Romancoke, where he was now farming, to spend Christmas, 1866, he brought with him the mare, Lucy Long, who had been either stolen or claimed by a soldier after the surrender. She was not with Lee at the time but had been sent to the rear to recuperate. Eventually, she came into the hands of a man in Essex County, where someone recognized her as Lee's mare. The owner described her in a letter, and offered her return. Lee asked Rob to go and identify her.

After Lucy came, Mildred often went with her father on his rides. She recalled that in passing through the streets of town, her father always had a "pleasant word of greeting for everyone," and stopped frequently to chat. But once in the country, he would then indulge in boyish spirits.

Nothing seemed to rest him like these rides, and he would laugh & tease me & let Traveller out to his fullest speed, leaving me far behind on slow little Lucy,—then wait for me at the top of the next hill—his eyes sparkling with fun. If I was silent he would often say,

"Life, tell me something—tell me about those schoolmates whom Robertus Sickus says have experienced every calamity but matrimony!"

She remembered that he liked to quote Rob, or at least ascribe words to him. He talked to the horses as though they were people, always speaking of the mare as "Miss Lucy." While he waited for them to catch up, he would turn in the saddle and call out gaily:

"Come along, Miss Lucy, Miss Lucy, Lucy Long!" parody-

317

ing the old song, "Oh! Take your time Miss Lucy, take your time Miss Lucy Long."

He would often scold Traveller for refusing to walk, and once lost his temper and gave him a whipping, much to Traveller's surprise.

In June, 1867, he and Mildred took a horseback trip to the Peaks of Otter. Mildred recalled that as they set out at daybreak, her father was "in the gayest humour, laughing and joking with me as I paced along by his side on quiet 'Miss Lucy.' "

"At midday we dismounted, and, tying our horses while resting on the soft grass under a wild-plum hedge by the roadside, ate our lunch."

Around nine o'clock that night, they reached the little mountain inn at the foot of the Peaks, and after a hearty supper, country style, retired to a loft to sleep soundly in deep feather beds. At dawn, they left with the innkeeper for the climb up to the top. They went as far as they could by horse, then tied their mounts, "and climbed the rest of the way to the summit on foot. When the top was reached, we sat for a long time on a great rock, gazing down on the glorious prospect below."

Her father said little and seemed to Mildred "very sad." He did not say what was on his mind, and she did not question him.

When they reached the valley again, they said good-by to the innkeeper and rode on. They had gone only a short distance when a thunder shower overtook them, and they turned and galloped back to a log cabin they had passed.

"Papa lifted me off Lucy and, dripping with water I rushed in, while he led the horses under an adjacent shed. The woman of the house looked dark and glum on seeing the pools of water . . . on her freshly scoured floor, and when Papa came in with his muddy boots her expression was more forbidding and gloomy."

Lee mollified her with apologies and praise of her nice floor. When the rain stopped, Lee went out for the horses, and

Mildred told the woman who he was. She was stunned, and kept repeating:

"What will Joe say? What will Joe say!" Her husband, like nearly every man in the country, had been a soldier in Lee's army.

After riding ten miles, they came to the town of Liberty and went to see their cousins, the Burwells, at Avenel. That night, Mildred amused her father by appearing in crinoline: with foresight, she had squeezed her hoops into her saddlebags.

On Monday, they rode on to Captain Buford's, where Mary, Daughter, and Agnes had spent several months during the sad summer of 1863. The Captain's candor and originality tickled Lee, and he quoted him for weeks afterward. He especially relished telling how, when on the night of their arrival he asked the Captain at what hour they should be ready for breakfast, Buford had said:

"Well, General, as you have been riding hard, and as you are company, we will not have breakfast tomorrow before sunup." In those long June days this meant considerably before five o'clock.

On the return trip, they stopped to see the Natural Bridge and reached home that same night, after a forty-mile ride.

Not long after their return, Captain Buford sent Mildred, whom he called "a real chunk of a gal," a Jersey cow. She was to get up early each morning and milk her, and send him part of the butter she made. This cow soon won a favored place in Robert's heart.

"She stands next in my affections to Traveller," he wrote. When later she took sick and died, he wrote feelingly of her death:

"Her troubles are all over now, & I am grateful to her for what she has done for us. I hope that we did our duty by her."

Soon after the move to Lexington, the family acquired cats. In December of their first year, Robert was writing an absent daughter:

"Our feline companions are flourishing. Young Baxter is

growing in gracefulness & favour, & gives cat-like evidences of future worth. He possesses the fashionable colour of 'moonlight on the water'. . . & is strictly aristocratic in appearance & conduct."

He had called his own kitten "Tom, surnamed 'The Nipper,' from the manner in which he slaughters our enemies the rats & mice."

In the fall of 1866, Markie had come to Lexington, bringing with her several small nieces. After her return home, Robert wrote to tell her that her stay had brought him "unalloyed pleasure." He asked her to be sure to tell the little girls that "I have advanced my cat from the stable to the house, & that he is in great favour with their Cousins Mary, Agnes & Mildred. The latter pronounces him as sweet as Arlington Tom. Having been bred up with Traveller, he is accustomed to good society & charms all visitors by his manners."

There were also pet chickens—"Laura Chilton," "Mildred," and "Don Ella McKay"—which Mildred had brought from Derwent; and during the last year of his life, Robert began looking for a dog as well. General Bier, a kinsman in Maryland, offered him a Newfoundland puppy, while Fitz Lee had for him a full-grown dog, also of large breed. He accepted both, though he explained to Fitz:

"It is not my purpose to put my dog to towing Canal boats or hauling dirt carts, but want him to play the part of a friend & protector. His disposition is therefore of vital importance to me & he ought not to be too old to contract a friendship for me, neither is his size so important to me as a perfect form."

He was worried how this "mammoth dog," as he called him, could be sent. The pup could come by stage, but Fitz's dog would have to be shipped by rail to Lynchburg, then transferred to the packet.

"The expressman must request the Captain in my name to take charge of him," he told Fitz. "I shall be very glad to get the Dog & hope that he may reach me safely."

Whenever Mildred could not ride with her father, he would ask Professor White to join him. They became very close, though in later years when White was asked if he had not been a confidential friend of Lee, his invariable answer would be:

"No, sir, no man was great enough to be *intimate* with General Lee!"

This suggests that the awe with which he had come to be regarded presented a barrier to most of his adult relationships, as had happened to George Washington after he achieved fame. White's own account of one ride when darkness overtook them and they had to spend the night at a farmhouse and share a bed confirms this. He "would as soon thought of sleeping with the Archangel Gabriel as with General Lee," and "lay on the very edge of the bed" and "did not sleep a wink," he told a friend.

It was this awe that caused so many people who met him now to speak of him as grave and unapproachable, and a lonely man who gave himself to no one. He had always been reserved in crowds of strangers, but never with individuals, particularly those he singled out for friendship.

But he still drew children to him as easily as ever. They found him warm, approachable, and as candid and simple as themselves. He could penetrate the reserve of the shyest child.

One little girl who often came to the house would talk with every other member of the family but Lee. One day when he was in his bedroom, she tiptoed to the door and peeped in. He asked her to enter but she shook her head. However, she stayed in the door, looking carefully at everything in the room. When she saw a penwiper in the shape of a man, hanging on the wall, she forgot her shyness and asked:

"Is that your doll-baby?"

"Yes," Lee said. She was delighted, and came in to talk about the little man. This marked the beginning of a fast friendship.

At chapel, little Carter Jones, son of a former chaplain, made a habit of slipping away from his mother to sit by Lee. Once during graduation ceremonies, he crept up onto the platform and fell asleep leaning against Lee's knees.

321

One afternoon, Robert came on two of his professors' small daughters riding a sleepy old horse up and down a back street. Knowing them well, he called:

"Come with me, and I will show you a beautiful ride." He took them on one of his favorite roads out beyond the fairgrounds where there was a grand "stretch of mountain scenery."

One little girl was just getting over the mumps and still had her face tied up. This gave Lee grounds for much pretended alarm over Traveller's health, and he kept saying:

"I do hope you won't give Traveller the mumps!" and,

"What shall I do if Traveller gets the mumps?"

Another day, he found his god-daughter, Virginia Lee Letcher, age six, sitting by the road with her small sister, Fannie. Virginia was in a pet because Fannie had tagged along uninvited and, in spite of coaxing and commanding, refused to go home. When Lee came up, she appealed to him:

"Oh, General Lee, won't you *please* make this child go home to her mother?"

He leaned from the saddle and took Fannie in his lap. When they reached home, Mrs. Letcher asked Virginia why she had put the General to so much trouble. She said naïvely:

"I couldn't make Fan go home, and I thought *he* could do anything."

Occasionally, he was powerless to control children. His favorite story concerned a time when he took shelter from a thunder shower at the house of friends who were away for the day. Their children were in the parlor playing marbles with several companions. Lee told them to go on with the game while he sat and watched.

Suddenly, one of the boys accused a girl of cheating, and her brother angrily collared her accuser and started pounding him. The young lady then burst into tears and appealed to Lee to stop the fight.

"My good fellows," he said, grasping each by the shoulder, "there is some better way to settle your quarrels than with your fists."

But they were immune to reason.

"I argued, I remonstrated, I commanded, but they were like two young mastiffs, and never in all my military service had I to own myself so perfectly powerless. I retired beaten from the field, and let the little fellows fight it out."

6

SOCIAL life in Presbyterian Lexington was restricted. The townspeople generally did not approve of cards, dancing, or merrymaking, and the few social activities sanctioned seemed to the Lee girls "provincial." A professor who called on them soon after they came was taken into their confidence.

"They don't seem to like Lexington much; think the people stiff & formal, which is very much the case," he wrote.

They were determined to enliven the society, but because of the temper of the community, had to proceed cautiously. Their first effort was a Reading Club.

"As far as I can judge," their father wrote in amusement, "it is a great institution for the discussion of apples & chestnuts, but is quite innocent of the pleasures of literature." But he was sympathetic with its purpose, and admitted:

"Still, it . . . brings the young people together, & promotes sociability & conversation."

During the winter, the Lee girls skated on the North River above the dam. It was not long until other young ladies were also skating. One night, Agnes and Daughter went sleigh riding with two bachelor professors.

"In the evening we astonished the natives by a genuine old-fashioned sleighing party," one of them wrote. "We drove out about 6 miles into the country & got back about 8 o'clock P.M. We all enjoyed it very much."

Then these young professors took the courage to entertain the Reading Club with a ball—in the recollection of Lexington's oldest inhabitant, the first ever held in the town. It was described as "delightful," so delightful that the dancing was kept up until three o'clock in the morning, and even then the ladies were so unwilling to go home that the hosts had to have

323

"the reel played and . . . the music sent away." Though the Lee girls wanted to ask for the polka or waltz, they did not yet dare, and had to be content with lancers, quadrille, and reels. Their parents were greatly amused that these innocent pleasures should so shock the townspeople.

Because of "this dearth of pleasure," as Robert called it, he encouraged his daughters to accept invitations to gayer centers, and in the summer urged Mary to select one of the more popular spas where they would be certain to meet relatives and old friends.

Around the first of July, 1867, after the trip to the Peaks of Otter, Mary, with Agnes and her friend, Mary Pendleton (Mildred was now off visiting), and Custis as escort, took the long trip to the White Sulphur Springs. The choice had been influenced by Mary's desire to try the waters again after fifteen years, while Agnes and Mary Pendleton were anxious to take part in the gay season at the famed resort. Lee and Professor White set out a day in advance, on horseback.

The "Harrison Cottage" in Baltimore Row had been reserved for the Lees, and soon became a social center. One day, a pompous man from the Deep South came to the door. Assuming a theatrical pose, he said:

Do I behold the honored roof that shelters the head of him before whose name the luster of Napoleon's pales into shadow? Do I see the walls within which sits the most adored of men? Dare I tread the floor which she who is scion of the patriotic house of the revered Washington condescends to hallow with her presence? Is this the portico that trails its vines over the noble pair? . . .

"Yes," Mary interrupted, "this is our cabin. Will you take a seat upon the bench?"

It became Lee's habit to visit his friends in the hotel parlor right after breakfast, then ride Traveller into the mountains. In the late afternoon, he rode out again, this time as escort for a party of girls who, to the chagrin of the younger men, preferred Lee's company. Whenever he appeared, he was always surrounded by these girls, and at night when the large dining room was converted into a ballroom, he would bring a group in with him, introduce the new arrivals to one another, see that they all found partners, and then, with the prettiest on his arm, join the promenade. He no longer danced, apparently, but sat and watched, following with obvious pleasure the progress of many an incipient love affair.

One evening, he noticed a number of new guests who were taking no part in the promenade or dancing. When he learned they were from the North, he asked his young companions if they had introduced themselves. They had not, and were not anxious to.

"Well, then I shall now introduce myself, and shall be glad to present any of you who will accompany me."

No one volunteered. Then Christiana Bond of Baltimore spoke up:

"I will go under your orders."

"Not under my orders, but it will gratify me deeply to have your assistance."

As he and Christiana walked across the room he said to her:

"When you go home, I want you to take a message to your young friends. Tell them from me that it is unworthy of them as young women, and especially as Christian women, to cherish feelings of resentment against the North. Tell them that it grieves me inexpressibly to know that such a state of things exists, and that I implore them to do their part to heal our country's wounds."

He introduced Miss Bond and himself to the Northerners, and accepting seats, chatted with them pleasantly.

When a noted Union sympathizer from West Virginia and his beautiful and fashionable daughter came to the hotel the young women, once again, were distant; and though the men were eager to meet the daughter, they were afraid of the women's censure. As Lee was walking to the ballroom one night, he noticed the girl sitting off in a corner of the parlor, reading a book. He introduced himself and asked to take her in to the dance. They joined the promenade, and afterward, when he led her to her seat, there was a general rush for introductions. She soon became one of the season's belles.

325

Not since long before the war had Lee been able, as he wrote Markie, to have "nothing else to do than see our friends & drink the water & bathe." The gaiety visibly raised his spirits, but he did regret the absence of his other children. During the war, he had looked forward to a time when he could gather his "little children" about him and enjoy their company. So far, this had not been realized.

The first Christmas in Lexington, he had hoped for a reunion, but Daughter had preferred to stay on with the Goldsboroughs at Ashly, in Maryland; Agnes was with Sally Warwick; Rob was unable to leave his farm; and Rooney was building a house on his plantation, with a view to asking Mary Tabb Bolling of Petersburg to share it.

He was pleased at the prospect of Rooney's marriage, and urged Rob to "get a nice wife," too. "I do not like you being so lonely. I fear you will fall in love with celibacy," he wrote him from the White Sulphur.

Custis' continued resistance to the charms of the opposite sex, and his refusal to take part in the social life of the resort, both amused and worried his father. There is little doubt that Custis had been in love with Sally Warwick, and that her frivolity had embittered him. Though by nature reserved, he was made more so through fear of being ensnared again.

His father tried by various means to interest him in some nice girl, but failed in every attempt. When he promised to introduce Custis to the prettiest of his favorites, Custis did not appear; and after Lee had persuaded him to join the promenade and introduced him to the chosen girl, Custis dutifully took up his post beside her chair, and reported each day thereafter, "usually silent and erect as if on guard."

One night when he had stood for what seemed hours in silent attention beside the chair, Christiana Bond asked him:

"General Custis, why do you not sit down?"

With a trace of humor he replied: "I am a modest man, and for a modest man to have his hands and feet on his mind at the same time is too much; when I stand, my feet are off my mind and I have only my hands to attend to."

Only once did he voluntarily interest himself in a girl—a

326

shy, plain, freckled girl with a dumpy figure. But her father had done some kind service when Custis' command was taken prisoner, and Custis now passed the word to the other young men at the resort that this girl should be shown all the attention of a reining belle.

When it came time to retire that night, Custis was still hard at work showing the young woman a good time.

"Let us go," his father finally said to him. Then turning to a group of girls beside him he said:

"I know my son Custis; he will never fail in his duty. We may return tomorrow and find him still promenading here."

Robert was told one day that a number of his old soldiers had come down from their mountain farms to see him. He found about twenty waiting for him in the parlor. "The General came in, and shaking hands, greeted them all in his genial way. Not one spoke, but all regarded him with devouring eyes in which the tears glistened."

Two Englishmen staying at the springs were introduced, and after that always strolled with Robert about the grounds. Lee usually liked English people, but these men were prone to public exhibitions of hero worship which were embarrassing. A friend asked if he did not find them something of a trial, and he said:

"Yes, they trouble me a little, but I think I get even with them. When they join me in my walks, I always take them down to the springs and make them drink the water. They are too polite to refuse when I hand them the glasses, and I fill them up with the nauseous water, and thus have my revenge."

When the manager of a circus in the neighboring village of Dry Creek came to the Springs to sell tickets, he called at Lee's cottage and offered to leave complimentary tickets and to send carriages for the General and any friends he might like to take to the show. Lee refused the free tickets but bought many to give to children staying at the resort.

The next morning, he rode to Dry Creek "where crowds of country people, many of them his old soldiers, feasted their eyes on him to the neglect of the circus." He did not go to the performance but invited a large party to come to the cottage

327

afterward to share a sixty-pound watermelon, sent to him by a farmer from Mobile.

It was customary to spend several weeks at the "White" and then move on to the Old Sweet Springs. At the end of three weeks, Lee and his party went to the Old Sweet, where one of the smaller parlors in the hotel was converted into a bedroom for Mary; this arrangement allowed her chair to be pushed onto the verandah or into the ballroom.

At the end of August, Lee took cold. "It seems to me if all the sickness I ever had in all my life was put together, it would not equal the attack I experienced," he wrote Markie. Beyond this, there is no knowing whether, in addition to the virus, he also suffered from his heart ailment.

One morning, when his condition was most serious and it was necessary that he not be disturbed, Mary Pendleton happened to see an old farmer cautiously opening the shutters.

"Go away!" she said sharply. "That is General Lee's room."

Sighing deeply, the man stepped back, and said mournfully:

"I only wanted to see him."

Because of his feebleness, which lasted for many weeks, he made the trip home in easy stages, going by way of the Hot Springs, the Healing, and the Rockbridge Alum. Traveller seemed to sense his condition, and "was considerate of my weakness & suited his gait to my debility," Robert wrote. At the Healing, he was detained two or three days by a slight relapse, and doubted if he could make the twenty-nine-mile ride to the Alum in one day.

When he reached home, he found that Mary (who had preceded him) had a letter from Rooney formally announcing his engagement to Mary Bolling. Robert was unable to send his congratulations right away, for he was so weak he could not attend to "all the pressing business connected with the College," so his personal correspondence had to suffer. When he did write, he said:

I have the most pleasing recollections of "Miss Tabb," & of her kindness to me, & now that she has consented to be my daughter

328

the measure of my gratitude is filled to overflowing. I hope she will not delay the consummation, for I want to see her very much, & I fear she will not come to see me until then. You must present her my warm love, & you both must accept my earnest prayers & most fervent wishes for your future happiness & prosperity.

Rooney wrote that the date had been set for November 28; that the wedding would be held in Petersburg, and that they expected him to come.

He did not answer for nearly a month, for he was not well and was uncertain about accepting the invitation. When he did write, he said he did not think his presence "could add to the enjoyment of anyone." He supposed the ceremony would be in the church, "according to the present fashion," and he would therefore see little of Tabb and Rooney. He suggested that, instead of going to the White House, they come up to Lexington after the wedding.

"I suppose the pretty bride will want to see her old father & mother & what kind of people her sisters are. At any rate I want to see her very much & I should be unable to do so in Petersburg, as she would be surrounded by all her old beaux & companions."

Instead of writing, Rooney went to Lexington and before he left he had his father's promise to come to the wedding.

Mildred had been invited to visit Norvell Caskie, so Rooney took her to Richmond, where he planned to stay until the wedding day. In his pocket, he carried instructions and measurements to be given to the tailor for the making of a black broadcloth suit for his father.

Both Lee and Custis were called as witnesses at Jefferson Davis' preliminary trial for treason, set for November 26, in Richmond. They reached the capital on the afternoon of the twenty-fifth and took rooms at the Exchange Hotel where Rooney was staying.

Since Judge Salmon Chase was absent on the twenty-sixth, all that could be done was impanel the jury. That afternoon, Robert bought the necklace he gave to Tabb "to remind her, hereafter, of her Papa," as he said.

The next afternoon at two o'clock, he appeared before what he called "the august court," and submitted to two hours of questioning by the United States counsel, who tried to force Lee to exculpate himself by seeking to make Jefferson Davis responsible for the war and Lee's conduct of it. Seeing through the design, Lee admitted that Davis was the commander in chief of the Confederate army and was often consulted by him and other officers.

"But I am responsible for what I did; and I cannot now recall any important movement I made which I would not have made had I acted entirely on my own responsibility."

His testimony brought little satisfaction or information, so he was excused.

At this time, he was asked for his opinion of Davis' role during the war.

"If my opinion is worth anything, you can *always* say that few people could have done better than Mr. Davis. I knew of none that could have done as well."

On the afternoon of the twenty-eighth, Lee, wearing his new suit, boarded the special car attached to the train for Petersburg. With him were his three sons, Mildred, his nephew Fitz (a groomsman), cousin Williams Wickham and daughter Annie, Charlotte Haxall, Miss Giles, Miss Enders, and a bevy of other young girl friends of the bride. Agnes had stayed in Lexington to care for a small cousin who had come to live with them, and Daughter, who seemed to be living in self-imposed exile, was still with the Goldsboroughs.

Lee's reluctance to go to the wedding arose chiefly from his dread of returning to war-ravished Petersburg.

"When our armies were in front of Petersburg, I suffered so much in body & mind on account of the good townspeople, especially on that gloomy night when I was forced to abandon them, that I always reverted to them in sadness & sorrow," he wrote.

His children noticed that he took no part in the gaiety of the bridal party on the train, and seemed "sad and depressed." Actually, his mind was far away, reliving the anguish. As he said later,

330

"All my old feelings returned to me."

The Washington Street depot in Petersburg was packed with admirers. As soon as Lee appeared on the train steps, he was cheered, and a band struck up "Dixie." The throngs opened their ranks, and he walked to the street where his host, General Mahone, was waiting with a carriage and four white horses. After he was seated, a number of men tried to take out the horses and pull the carriage themselves, but Lee told them that if they did so, he would have to get out and help them.

The band then played "The Bonnie Blue Flag," the crowd cheered, and filling the street, refused to part until Lee had stood up, removed his hat, and bowed.

When he reached the Mahone house on the corner of Sycamore and Marshall Streets, it was three o'clock. He found a note there from Tabb, asking him to come and see her. He walked across the street to the Bollings', and gave the necklace to the radiant and statuesque Tabb. He did not stay long, for this was no time to intrude, but went on to the Banister home, where he found the girls all excited, for Mollie, an older daughter, was one of her Cousin Tabb's ten bridesmaids, and his favorite, Anne, just turned sixteen, was going to wear her first long party gown. Taking her hand, he patted it fondly, and said:

"Remember, my dear, I am to have the honor of taking you in to supper. Ask your escort to lend you to me."

"I was so happy I literally danced all around him in my delight," Anne recalled.

That night, Grace Episcopal Church was crowded beyond capacity. Robert was the first of the family to enter; he was escorting a Mrs. Carr. Characteristically, he stopped just inside the door to kiss a small girl who smiled up at him sweetly.

Behind him came the Mahones, then Mildred, "all life, in white & curls," as her father wrote, escorted by Custis, "very composed"; then Rob (suffering from chills), with Charlotte Haxall. Rooney, it seemed to his father, "shone in his happiness" while "the bride looked lovely & was, in every way, captivating."

After breakfast the next morning, Lee rode out to the

331

neighborhood of the Turnbull house, where he had his final headquarters, to call on an old lady who had sent him many presents of eggs and butter during the seige. He had lunch at the Bollings' and afterward held an informal reception to which the whole town came.

That night there was a party in Tabb's honor at the home of the William Johnsons. "He enjoyed the evening very much and expressed his feeling of relief at seeing everyone so bright and cheerful."

Rooney and Tabb were going to leave for Baltimore on the thirtieth, so Lee made his plans to leave for Richmond that day, too. But when they changed their minds and decided not to leave until the second, he wrote in disappointment:

"If I had known that they would remain till Monday, as is now their intention, I should have made my arrangements to stay."

He had enjoyed himself thoroughly and was as reluctant to go as he had been to come. But he never changed such plans and so left on Saturday, Custis, Rob, and Fitz going with him.

When it was known that he was leaving, the people came out to cheer him, and the band escorted him to the depot.

He was in a festive mood when he reached Richmond and took Rob on a round of visits—to the Tripletts, the Branders, the Peebles, the Dunlops, and the Andersons. He was happy to find everyone cheerful here, too, and hard at work rebuilding their city and their future.

"People have got to work now," he wrote. "It is creditable to them to do so; their bodies & minds are benefitted by it."

On Monday, December 2, Custis and Rob went with him down the James to Lower Brandon. When he had met Belle Harrison at the White Sulphur, she had made him promise that he would visit her when he was next in Richmond. As the steamer passed Chaffin's Bluff and City Point, where he had opposed first McClellan and then Grant, he was evidently thinking of those times, for his sons found him "depressed," though what little he had to say did not concern the war, but the gracious old plantations along the shores.

He regretted there was not time to stop at Shirley and

332

passed it each time "with a heavy heart," he later told Hill Carter.

He spent just one day at Brandon. The Harrisons begged him to stay, but he did not think that he could in conscience be away any longer from the college.

He passed one more day in Richmond and another at Hickory Hill, a visit that gave him, he said, "pleasant thoughts for the rest of my life." He reached Lexington on Saturday, December 7, the exact day he had scheduled for his return.

At eight o'clock on Monday morning, the ninth, he was in his office, ready to start work with renewed spirit. Everywhere he had been—Richmond, Petersburg, Brandon, Hickory Hill —he had seen new life emerging from the rubble of shattered hopes and a crumbled civilization. Like the fabled phoenix, his people, endowed anew with youth, vigor, and beauty, were rising from the ashes. When he saw this, he wrote, there was lifted from his heart that "load of sorrow which had been pressing upon me for years."

7

THAT Christmas, Agnes and Custis were the only children home, for after Rooney's wedding, Mildred had stayed in Richmond to be a bridesmaid for her classmate, Lizzie Triplett; Daughter was still in Maryland, and Rob was spending the holidays with the family of his future wife, Charlotte Haxall.

Smith had recently written Robert that since his daughters were such "gads," they would make excellent wives for his sons. "As you both find it so agreeable to be from home," Robert wrote an absent daughter, "you could then live a true Bohemian life & have a happy time generally."

The domestic circle had been enlarged that fall when three of Carter Lee's children came to Lexington. Two sons, Henry and George Taylor, enrolled in the college, and a young daughter, Mildred, lived with the family and attended a local school. The house was not big enough to accommodate the nephews (Custis lived at the Institute for this reason), but they gathered there for meals. To avoid confusion, and because he always enjoyed giving nicknames, Robert was soon calling the new Mildred "Powhattie," derived from her native county of Powhatan.

After the new year, Rob escorted his sister, Mildred, home and spent a few days with his parents. He found his father especially bright and cheerful, playful, and always ready to tease Powhattie, his newest favorite.

As soon as Precious Life arrived, Agnes left for Baltimore and Life took over the management of the household, taking in considerable territory, according to her father:

> She . . . considers herself now a great character. She rules her brother & my nephews with an iron rod, & scatters her advice broadcast among the young men of the College. I hope it may yield an abundant harvest. The young mothers of Lexington ought to be extremely grateful to her for her suggestions to them as to the proper mode of rearing their children, & though she finds many unable to appreciate her system, she is nothing daunted by their obtuseness of vision, but takes every opportunity to enlighten them as to its benefits.

His nephew, George, found him always ready to make some joke or pun. Once when there was a very charming and petite house guest, a Miss Long visiting the Lee girls, someone spoke of a certain young man who was coming to see her at least once a day and sometimes oftener.

"Yes, he is different from most men," Lee said with a twinkle in his eye. "He wants but little here below, but he wants that little Long!"

One afternoon as he was riding through town, Robert met two of Lexington's prettiest girls. When he stopped to talk with them, Traveller was restive. He pawed and pranced and afforded Lee an opportunity to show off his superb horsemanship. A man who had paused across the street to admire the sight noticed after a moment that this exhibition of equestrian skill was provoked by Lee's "dextrous and coquettish use of the spur."

334

But as is natural in all sensitive persons, his spirits were not always buoyant. His letters of this period often reveal undertones of sadness and expressions of longing to lay aside his burdens for all time.

"My only pleasure is in my solitary evening rides, which give me abundant time for quiet thought," he wrote Tabb, while to Markie he admitted:

"I look . . . forward with joy to the time, which is fast approaching, that I will lay down & rest."

This winter was an especially severe one, and both he and Mary took heavy colds, while little Powhattie had chills and fever. The weather intensified Mary's pains, though to Robert she seemed stronger and looked better than she had for a long time. On clear days, she went out into the garden after the snows were gone, moving about on her crutches to look for the first crocus, snowdrops, and violets; sometimes she would go with Robert to inspect his vegetable plot.

In January, Mr. Washington, a descendant of that branch of the family which had formerly owned Audley, braved the snow and came to Lexington from his New York studio to paint Lee's portrait. Robert had consented to his coming chiefly to please Mary, and to help the artist, who had told him that such a commission would be an asset.

"My suffering is over," he wrote in relief to Markie, when the sittings were finished. He enclosed in this letter some early violets:

"I . . . hope when you inhale their sweet perfume it may remind you of other days that are gone & that their breath may speak the words that I would utter if within your reach," he said tenderly.

This was not the first portrait since the war. Right after Lee reached Lexington, Mary wrote to him from Derwent that both the sculptor, Edward V. Valentine, and the painter, John Adams Elder, at Mr. Caskie's suggestion, would like sittings.

"I have no desire to sit either to Mr. Valentine or Elder, but if it will gratify them, or Mr. Caskie, I will submit. They can come any time that is convenient to them. All times will be irksome to me."

Elder came, but for financial reasons, Valentine deferred his trip.

Lee felt that Washington's portrait was "better than those taken since the war." Still, he told Markie, who had also painted his picture:

"I did not feel that confidence in him that I had in you, & his brush brought not that soothing repose which yours infused. If you had only been as successful with Traveller as you were with his rider, I should have been permanently content."

On May 1, Lee went to Richmond to testify in the trial of Jefferson Davis, but found that the case had been postponed until June. He sympathized with Davis' plight:

"As long as this trial is hanging over him, of course he can do nothing. He can apply his mind to nothing, nor could he acquire the confidence of the business community in anything he might undertake, from the apprehension of being interrupted in the midst of it."

As he had been anxious for some time to visit the White House and Romancoke, this delay offered an ideal opportunity. He was afraid that things might not be as rosy as Rooney pictured them, and that Tabb might be suffering hardships. So he was relieved to find that his son had built a comfortable house, and that the farm was prospering, "looking better than I had imagined."

Rob had been equally industrious, but his house was so "forlorn" as to be hardly habitable. It was "too uncomfortable for a fair occupant, so he will have to wait until he can provide a suitable bower for the lady who is to grace his establishment," he wrote. After his return home, he drew plans for a new house and offered to loan Rob thirty-five hundred dollars without interest.

Mary had become extremely nervous and irritable of late. "She . . . broods over her troubles so much that I fear it increases her sufferings," Robert wrote a son. "I am therefore the more anxious to give her new scenes & new thoughts." He believed that she had been improved by her stay at the White Sulphur the previous summer, and wanted her to try those waters again.

336

But she refused to go there, perhaps because the trip was long and strenuous, perhaps it was her whimsicality. So it was decided that she should try the Warm Springs in Bath County; if after two weeks she found no benefit, Robert would then take her to the Hot. He planned to pass several weeks at the White Sulphur to drink the water. Mildred wanted to go with her father; and Agnes, who had returned, decided to stay with her mother.

On the morning of July 14, the stage was at the door, but Lee's womenkind were not ready, so while he waited, he wrote to Charlotte Haxall—"My Beautiful Lottie"—asking her to meet him at Covington and go with him to the White Sulphur. His spirits were high, as they always were when addressing a lovely girl, and he sketched a charming word picture of the scene:

Mildred is quite well again, & is flying about this morning with great activity. Agnes is following with slower steps. Mrs. Lee is giving last minute injunctions to Sam & Eliza. Letitia [a maid] is looking on in wonder at the preparations, & trying to get a right conception of the place to which she is going, which she seems to think is something between a steel-trap & a spring-gun. Custis is waiting to help his mother into the stage, & you see how patient I am. To add interest to the scene, Dr. Barton has arrived to bid adieu & to give Mildred an opportunity of looking her best. I believe he is the last rose of summer. The others, with their fragrance & thorns, have all departed. . . .

They reached the Warm Springs that night, and were settled comfortably in the Brockenbrough Cottage. A few days later, Mildred came down with typhoid fever.

"As she seems more accessible to reason from me, I have come to be her chief nurse," her father wrote.

Mildred insisted that she could not sleep unless her father held her hand, and she did not want him ever to leave the room. Night after night, he sat patiently by her bed, gently caressing her hand until she fell into a restless sleep; he would then doze in his chair or on a cot in the corner, always near to comfort her in wakeful moments.

On August 14, she was considered convalescent, though

337

still too weak to speak. A week later, she had improved enough to be allowed to go with her father to the White Sulphur.

He was disappointed to find that the guests this season were principally Confederate officers and civil servants. The air was surcharged with talk of the war and politics, both distasteful to him. Then General Rosecrans, his old adversary on Sewell Mountain and now manager of the Democratic Party, arrived. He knew that this spa was popular with prominent Southerners, and wanted to get from them a statement concerning their willingness to accept the results of the war and the Negro in his new status. With this he intended to refute Republican statements that all Southerners were "unreconstructable," and that their attitude toward the freedman was "hostile."

He was pleased to find Lee there, and asked him for a statement. But Lee refused to become spokesman for the South, though in the interest of clearing up misunderstandings between the sections, he agreed to call a meeting at his cottage.

Rosecrans learned from this representative gathering that the Southern people earnestly desired peace. As to the Negro: "They have grown up in our midst, and we have been accustomed since childhood to look upon them with kindness. The change in the relations of the two races has wrought no change in our feelings toward them."

Rosecrans then sent Lee a letter asking him to join with the others in a formal statement of these sentiments. Lee gave the letter to Alexander Stuart, a Virginia lawyer also staying at the Springs, and asked him to draft a reply.

He approved Stuart's letter, for it expressed his own attitude exactly:

. . . The people earnestly desire tranquility and restoration of the Union. They deplore disorder and excitement as the most serious obstacle to their prosperity. They ask restoration of their rights under the Constitution. They desire relief from oppressive misrule. Above all, they would appeal to their countrymen for the re-establishment, in the Southern States, of that which has been justly regarded as the birthright of every American, the right of

338

self-government. Establish these on a firm basis, and we can safely promise, on behalf of the Southern people, that they will faithfully obey the Constitution and laws of the United States, treat the Negro population with kindness and humanity and fulfil every duty incumbent on peaceful citizens. . . .

Lee and thirty-one other prominent Southerners at the Springs signed the letter on August 26, 1868.

Robert was worn out by the weeks of nursing Mildred. This and the uncongenial atmosphere brought on a mood of depression.

"All are gay, & only I solitary," he wrote. "I am all alone."

Early in September, he and Mildred went on to the Hot Springs, finding Mary and Agnes improved and ready to go home. In October, a visit from his nephew, Edward Lee Childe, brought him pleasure, and by the end of that month his spirits were restored.

With Colonel William Allan, the professor of Applied Mathematics, he rode to Staunton on business, arriving there during the County Fair. They visited the exhibits and Lee was received by the people with enthusiasm. A Washington College student who watched one of these ovations said waggishly to his companion:

"I don't see why the Staunton people make all this to-do over General Lee. Why, in Lexington, he sends for *me* to come to see him!"

Over Lee's protests that the money should be applied to some more worthy cause, the trustees voted to build a new and roomier house for the president. But when he found that the board was determined, Lee agreed to the plan, and according to Rob, "at once commenced designing a new 'President's House.'" Because of the demands on his time, he may not have drawn the entire plan but only made changes and additions to a basic one of his selection. But with his usual interest in such matters, he supervised the construction and inspected progress daily. The house was being built on the same slope as the old one but closer to the street.

In the winter of 1868, it was nearly finished, and while Rob

339

was in Lexington, his father took him to see what he always called the "new President's house"—never *my* house or *our* house, explaining all the details of the plan.

Christmas, 1868, all the children except Rooney were there for the first time since Arlington days. Beside each plate on Christmas morning there were several presents, but at Mildred's place there was a mound. During her recent convalescence, she had one day listed for her father all the things she would like to have—and there they were, not one forgotten.

Lee and Rob paid New Year's calls together and attended "the mild festivities" of the neighborhood. To Rob, his father seemed in the best of health and "almost gay."

On December 25, there came appropriately a general amnesty proclamation, and on February 15, 1869, the indictments against Lee, Custis, Rooney, and Fitz Lee, as well as fourteen other Confederate general officers, were formally withdrawn.

Lee did not, as has so often been stated, die a paroled prisoner of war, nor was he disfranchised, for he could have qualified to vote when the new state constitution was ratified and the test-oath abolished in May of this same year. That he did not do so probably arose from his desire to keep apart from the unjust legislation of the time. He was disbarred from holding public office, though this right could have been restored by a two-thirds vote of Congress.

But of more interest to him, perhaps, was the birth of his grandson and namesake on February 11.

"I wonder what he will think of his grandpa," he ventured, and tried to plan a visit to the White House. He was unable to set a time because "the dilatoriness of the workmen in finishing the house, & the necessity of my attending to it, getting the grounds enclosed & preparing the garden, will prevent me. I will also have to superintend the moving. In fact, it never seems convenient for me to go away," he told Rooney.

Captain James May, whom Lee had first known in St. Louis, was trying to have returned to Mrs. Lee those objects taken by the Federals from Arlington to Washington for safekeeping. The items—a pair of breeches, a waistcoat, a candlestick, washstand and mirror, and a set of dishes—were purely of sentimental value because of their association with George Washington. Captain May had been officially assured that President Johnson would be willing to restore the articles, and suggested that Mary apply to the President for their return.

She wrote the letter, and everything was going smoothly until the press heard about it, and with that unfortunate proclivity of newspapers for inaccuracy, stated that Lee had made the application, that the objects had been taken from "General Lee's estate" and were to be returned to him.

This angered General John Logan, member of the House, who demanded "by what right the Secretary of the Interior surrenders the articles so cherished as once the property of the Father of his Country to the rebel general-in-chief."

This was all that was necessary to spark opposition and prevent their return.

It embittered Mary further, and distressed Lee on this account. "But as the country desires them, she must give them up. I hope their presence at the capital will keep in the remembrance of all Americans the principles & virtues of Washington," he wrote.

In 1903, these objects were restored to the family, by the order of President McKinley.

In April, Robert took another bad cold, the effects of which he felt for over a month. Mary also had a cold, Agnes was unwell, and Custis was described by his father as only "so-so." Mildred only was holding her own:

"Both of her cats have fresh broods of kittens, & the world wags cheerily with her," he wrote.

Though far from well by April 22, Lee consented to go with a delegation of prominent men to Baltimore to raise money for the Valley Railroad Company. He had insisted that his presence would be of no value, but, as he wrote a son, "they have made such a point of it that it would look ill-mannered & unkind to refuse."

He was still weak and easily tired, and wanted to avoid all public demonstrations in his honor. But everywhere he went, he received an ovation. As soon as he came on the floor of the Corn and Flour Exchange for a meeting of businessmen, he

341

was greeted with cheers and applause. When the delegation appeared before the city council meeting in the High School, the hall was jammed with spectators, many of them women, come to see him and cheer. Here, he listened with an expression "as impassive as the Sphinx" to a long laudatory speech about himself.

Sunday morning, he went to St. Paul's Church on Charles Street, and after the service a crowd collected to see him come out. As soon as he appeared, "all heads were uncovered and kept so until he had passed through the long lines extending down the street." Among his admirers were many Negroes who had known him when he lived in Baltimore. They came up to his carriage and, in what Lee described as "the most affectionate manner," put their hands in the window to shake his hand. He felt this was significant, particularly since the Northern press continued to insist that the South had been fighting to perpetuate slavery. This was evidence, he told the Reverend John Leyburn, that they did not consider him hostile to their race. "They would hardly have received him in that way, he thought, had they looked upon him as fresh from a war intended for their oppression and injury," Leyburn wrote.

Leyburn, a Baltimore minister, called on Lee when he was a guest at the Samuel Tagart home and later wrote an account of their talk. He found Lee "not only indignant but hurt" at the attitude of the Northern press.

So far from engaging in a war to perpetuate slavery, I am rejoiced that slavery is abolished [Leyburn recalled him saying]. I believe it will be greatly for the interests of the South. So fully satisfied am I of this, as regards Virginia, especially, that I would cheerfully have lost all I have lost by the war, and have suffered all I have suffered, to have this object attained.

He spoke at length on the misrepresentations of Southern attitudes and concepts by Northern writers, adding warmly:

"Doctor, I think some of you gentlemen that use the pen should see that justice is done us."

The Tagarts gave a reception for him. "There his old friends crowded to see him, and the greatest affection and

342

deference were shown him," a reporter wrote. He went to see his Carter cousins at Goodwood in Prince George County, happy to find Ella Carter George, an old favorite, there; and visited nearby Lynwood, the home of Washington Peter, a Custis connection.

Rooney came to Baltimore on business, and he and his father called on the McKims, Glenns, Marshalls, Bonds, Bakers, and Sally Warwick Poor, and her babies. He wished only that Mary had been there to share the pleasure of revisiting their old friends, for changes of scene were always good for her spirits.

As he thought about it, he believed that she would be less likely to brood and have fits of nervous irritability if she were able to get about more in Lexington. With this in mind, he bought her "a little carriage," the best he could find. "I hope this will enable you to take some pleasant rides," he wrote.

He had heard on good authority that Grant, now President, would like to see him. On Saturday, May 1, he took an early train to Washington and called at the White House.

Grant received him cordially, and introduced him to John Motley, the newly appointed Minister to England, and to his secretary, young Robert Douglas, son of Stephen A. Douglas. When Grant asked Lee to take a chair, both Motley and Douglas withdrew, so no one was there to record what passed at the meeting.

Douglas wrote afterward that the visit "was merely one of courtesy, and did not last long," and Rob wrote that it was a meeting of "no political importance whatever, but simply a call of courtesy. . . . The interview lasted about fifteen minutes, and neither General Lee nor the President spoke a word on political matters."

Rob's authority came from his father, so it must be accepted as accurate. It has been claimed that they talked of railroads, which is not unlikely. Lee probably told Grant his reason for coming to Baltimore.

After leaving the White House, Lee drove to Tudor Place where he stayed with Cousin Brit until Tuesday.

On Sunday, he had dinner with Mildred de Podestad

(daughter of his half sister, Lucy Grymes) and her husband, who was Secretary of the Spanish Legation. On Monday, at Mary's request, he had his picture taken by Alexander Gardner, Mathew Brady's partner; he considered the results better than any others taken since the war.

He took the steamer to Alexandria on Tuesday, and as he walked from the landing up the familiar cobbled streets to his Cousin Anna's town house, he was greeted along the way with cheers. As he neared the house, he heard someone calling:

"Marse Robert! Marse Robert!" Turning, he saw an old Negro woman, her face wreathed in smiles, hurrying toward him.

"I am Eugenia, one of the Arlington slaves," she said as they shook hands. She told him how happy she was to see him again and asked all about the family. Lee, in turn, inquired about her present situation, for he was still concerned over the fate of these people.

"I wonder if you would like to have my picture, Eugenia?" he asked as he left her.

" 'Deed I would, Marse Robert!" Later she received it by mail.

He found Sis Nanie and Fitz at Mrs. Fitzhugh's, and later in the day, Smith rode up from Richmond, his farm on the Potomac, near Acquia Creek. This was their first meeting since parting in Richmond right after the war, and it was fitting that it should take place in the house that had been second home during boyhood, in the city whose markets, streets, and wharves they had explored together as children.

"There is no community to which my affections more strongly cling, than to Alexa composed of my earliest & oldest friends, my kind school-fellows & faithful neighbours," Robert wrote.

So many of these "kind school-fellows & faithful neighbours" came to see him that an informal reception was held at Green's Mansion House, a hotel on North Fairfax Street. There, for three hours, a steady procession shook hands and said a few words to him. The *Gazette* reported the next day:

"It was more like a family meeting than anything else, for

344

we regard General Lee as one of our Alexandria boys. . . . We have never seen a more lovely exhibition of the grateful and unbought homage of the heart to worth and high character than was exhibited last evening."

On the morning of May 7, he took the train for Staunton, where he met Agnes and their cousin, Virginia Peyton.

When he reached home, his family asked if he had enjoyed himself, and he said:

"Very much; but they would make too much fuss over an old rebel!"

His only regret was that there had not been time to visit Rooney and see his grandson. "That pleasure, I trust, is preserved for a future day."

Soon after his return, he asked Agnes and Virginia Peyton to take a walk with him. They accepted, but as he was putting on his hat, Agnes complained that it was shabby.

"What! you do not like my hat? Why, I have seen a whole cityful come out to admire it!"

Virginia recalled that there were no sluggards in that household; everyone was expected to be at the breakfast table by seven o'clock, when Robert would come into the dining room with a dewy rosebud for each lady. She also remembered that he read aloud to them at night from Irving's *Life of Washington*.

Another visitor at this time was Christiana Bond of Baltimore. One afternoon, Robert was sorting the contents of his trunks in preparation for moving into the new house. Mary had her wheel chair drawn up to a table covered with old letters and miniatures of the Washington family, all discolored and molded from damp. She believed she could restore the paintings but felt the letters were hopeless. From time to time, Lee would come into the room with something of interest to show them. Once he held up a richly ornamented saddle blanket with the words, "To Our Deliverer" embroidered on it in gold.

"They thought I would ride through the city with *that* on my horse," he said with a laugh.

He showed Christiana Washington's swords, one that had belonged to his father, and "The Sword of the Confederacy."

345

He took this one out of its sheath and read the inscription of presentation. The sword that he had worn at the surrender he held up "almost reluctantly, and the gravity of his manner forbade questions," Miss Bond recalled.

He gave her a little memento—a velvet watchcase embroidered in gold.

"It was under my pillow every night during the war, when I *had* a pillow. Let it now be under yours," he said.

8

THE move to the new house was made around June 1. Mary's room was on the first floor, and opened onto a verandah that ran along three sides. Every fine day she sat there reading, sewing, knitting, or painting, for she had taken to her art work with renewed interest. In her lap or perched on her shoulder or even her head, were her favorite cats, "Mrs. Rufnor" and "Love."

Robert soon found that his favorite spot in the house was a deep window in the dining room. From there, he could look at the distant wooded slopes, veiled at times in blue, at others distinct and splashed with autumnal scarlet and gold or clothed in the soft green of spring. Since the war, he had been taking a short nap right after dinner (he called it his "siesta") while seated in his chair. In the new house, he turned his chair to face the view and while his hands were rubbed (this was now considered a great privilege) by his daughters, niece, or other kinswoman, he would doze for ten minutes and wake refreshed.

He was delighted with the conveniences of the new place— the large sunny stable for Traveller and Lucy Long; the barn for the cow; the woodshed, greenhouse, elevated water tank that provided a pressure system of running water for the house, and even a special outbuilding for Mildred's cats, which she kept by the dozen.

Anticipating their roomier quarters, Mildred and Agnes had invited most of their friends to come to the graduation that June. They were just settled when the Misses Haxall, Jones,

346

Kirkland, Albert, Burwell, and Wickham arrived. There were beds for them all, but the others who were coming were going to have to sleep somewhere else. Picnics with the students and cadets, riding parties into the mountains, boating in the Lee skiff on the North River, suppers, and dancing were their entertainments.

Lee was trying to fit into his crowded schedule a summer visit with Rob and Rooney, to see his grandson, and help Rob plan his house. But he was so "occupied with examinations, visitors, arrangements, &c." that he wondered how he could find time. All college officers were new, and since they were to start work on July 1, he felt he should stay until they understood their duties. Then the Educational Association of Virginia was meeting in Lexington on the fifteenth, and although he had never gone to any of their councils and was not anxious to, he did not want to leave while they were in session; it might seem as if he were avoiding them. After the convention, he planned to take Mary to the Rockbridge Baths and then go with Agnes and Mildred to the White Sulphur for a month. Markie and her nieces would come to one of the resorts (she had not decided which, yet), and he was planning to meet her and bring them all back to Lexington for a visit. He wondered if he would even live through the coming week.

For the first time in his life, he wrote: "I am now obliged to consider my health," and at the end of this exhausting month he suggested that his sons come to see him, and offered as special inducement for his grandson a puppy and kitten to play with.

"It is delightfully quiet here now. Both Institutions have closed & all are off enjoying their holyday. I should like to remain here if I could," he wrote Charlotte Haxall. But this was not to be. On July 20, he took Mary to the Baths, and just as he had seen to her comfort and was planning to go on to the White Sulphur, he received a telegram telling him of his brother Smith's unexpected death. He left at once for Alexandria, but reached there too late for the funeral.

"After seeing all that remains to us of our dear brother deposited in its last earthly home, & mingling my sorrow for a brief season with that of his dear wife & children, I shall return

347

to you. May God bless us all & preserve us for the time when we too, must part, the one from the other, which is now close at hand," he wrote Mary.

For years, he and Smith had been separated by far-off assignments, but they had remained "devoted to each other, having always kept warm their boyish love. . . . It was delightful to see them together and listen to their stories of the happy long ago they would tell about each other," Smith's nephew wrote.

From Alexandria, Lee and Rob, who had come to the funeral, went to Ravensworth. Lee's spirits did not revive during his stay, and once when passing the room in which his mother had died he stopped at the door, and in a voice husky with emotion said:

"Forty years ago I stood in this room by my mother's deathbed! It seems but yesterday."

To divert his mind, Rob persuaded him to return home by way of the White House so he could see his grandson. He found neither Tabb nor the little boy, who was just recovering from whooping cough, looking well. Believing that the mountain air would restore them both, he convinced Tabb that she should go with him to the Rockbridge Baths.

Impressed by the transitory quality of life, they decided to have the little boy christened while they were all together, so that his grandfather might stand as his godfather. Custis came down from Richmond, and the next Sunday the ceremony was performed in the old colonial church of St. Peter's, just a few miles away, where according to one tradition, the blooming Martha Custis married George Washington.

Leaving Tabb and the baby with Mary at the Baths, he, Agnes, and Mildred went to the White Sulphur. The resort was crowded and very gay—almost every night there was some gala affair: one night, a concert for the benefit of Lexington's Grace Church; another, a ball in honor of the philanthropist, George Peabody; and still another, a raffle at which the prize was a wreath made from Lee's, Mary's, and Mildred's hair.

He was pleased that the concert netted $605 for their church, increased to $805 by donations of $100 apiece from

Mr. Peabody and W. W. Corcoran, the financier, but admitted: "I should prefer more quiet."

But Agnes and Mildred were at once in the vortex, and he saw little of them. "Foot-free" was his term for them. They would send love, he wrote Mary—"if I could find them."

"They are always busy at something, but never ready," he complained.

The third edition of Light-Horse Harry Lee's *Memoirs* was now in the hands of the University Publishing Company of New York. Besides his editorial work, Robert had written a biographical sketch of his father containing a charming nostalgic word picture of Stratford Hall, and had prepared a genealogy based on one compiled by William Lee in 1771.

A letter from Mr. Richardson, the publisher, reached him at the Springs. He wanted Lee to include his picture in the book. He explained that this was at the suggestion "of many mutual friends" who felt that his picture would give additional interest, and thereby increase the sales.

"That may or may not be so & at any rate I differ from them," Robert wrote Mary. "Besides there is no good portrait accessible to him, & the engraving in the 'Lee Family' I think would be an injury to any book."

He left the final decision to Mary, who agreed with Mr. Richardson and the "many mutual friends." Robert did not intend to keep the profits from the work for himself, but wanted to give them to Carter, the impecunious member of the family.

When asked about his history of the campaigns in Virginia, he said that he had still not had time to put the material into form.

Lee found no benefit from "assiduously drinking the waters" and the girls were tired of the company, so they left for home on August 30. Once there, Robert had to find servants while the girls readied the house for their mother, Tabb and the baby, and Daughter; Cousin Julia Stuart; Markie and her nieces, and a friend, Mrs. de Gomez; and Edward Lee Childe and his wife, Blanche, who were coming from Paris. When everything was prepared, he planned to ride to the Baths and escort Mary and her party home, then go back and meet Markie either at Alleghany Station or Covington, whichever suited her best.

Financial prospects for the college were better this semester. Cyrus McCormick, elected a trustee, had pledged five thousand dollars to the endowment (he had given ten thousand dollars in June, 1866). Also, George Peabody became interested in the school after meeting Lee and transferred to it a claim he had for one hundred and twenty-five thousand dollars against the State of Virginia. The gift of one thousand dollars to the presidential chair, by General William Harney, U.S.A., and a prospective ten thousand dollars to be subscribed to the chair of Applied Chemistry by a group of Missourians also brightened the fiscal outlook.

When Lee heard of General Harney's contribution, he was touched and wrote him:

"This information recalls so vividly the kind acts extended to me in former years, that I hope you will allow me, in thanking you in the name of the College . . . to express . . . my individual thanks for the manner in which it has been bestowed."

No longer was there any mention in Lee's letters of that "obscure retreat" he had envisioned for so many years. As he replied to one business firm that offered highly lucrative employment in New York:

"I am grateful, but I have a self-imposed task which I must accomplish. I have led the young men of the South in battle; I have seen many of them die on the field; I shall devote my remaining energies to training young men to do their duty in life."

The previous year when writing to General Ewell, he was hopeful that Ewell's health had improved now that his "toils" were over. He then added significantly:

"For my own part, I much enjoy the charms of civil life, & find too late that I have wasted the best years of my existence."

The "little carriage" was in use almost every day during the beautiful autumn weather, with Lucy Long in the traces and Lee at the reins. Mary's thoughts were diverted by the opportunity the carriage afforded her to get into the country.

One afternoon, Robert and Tabb went by themselves to see

350

William Preston Johnston (the son of Albert Sidney), who lived two miles down the North River. In climbing the long steep drive to the front door, Lucy Long fell down, unconscious. Lee jumped out and quickly unfastened the harness, seeing as he did so that she had been choked by a tight collar. He was very disturbed and, as the mare began to revive, petted her and apologized for his oversight in not checking the harness before setting out. He took himself severely to task for such treatment after all her years of faithful service.

Another guest that fall was William Johnston's sister, Margaret. As a little girl, she had sat in Lee's lap and had been carried in his arms when he stayed with her parents at Fort Mason, Texas. "He was the very perfection of a host, exquisitely thoughtful and courteous to all, and showing me in addition the tenderness a soldier always feels for the child of a dead comrade," she wrote. "If he was grand in prosperity, in adversity he was sublime."

Late in October, he took another bad cold which lasted for over a month. On November 27, he wrote Markie that he was better than when she left, "& generally able to attend to my duties, though still in the hands of the Drs." A week later he wrote Rooney:

"The Drs. still have me in hand, but I fear can do no good."

Rapid exercise produced severe pain and difficulty in breathing. By mid-December, he was well enough to ride but admitted: "Traveller's trot is harder to me that it used to be & fatigues me."

It was obvious to him that his ailment was serious, and perhaps even fatal. There were frequent premonitions of the approaching end. He sent a message to a young woman who had been unable to visit him that fall but promised to come next summer:

"Tell her she should have come now; next summer will be too late, I shall not be here."

When the girl who was the messenger protested, he said wearily:

"My child, I think I am the very oldest man you have ever seen."

But with Mary and his children and with young people

351

generally, these depressed moods were rare; he made every attempt to keep cheerful and even gay.

"We are all as usual—the women of the family very fierce & the men very mild," he wrote a son; and to Mildred, who had gone to Richmond, he wrote a spirited account of the family's perplexities over unintelligible passages in her last letter:

We held a family council over it. It was passed from eager hand to hand & attracted wondering eyes & mysterious looks. It produced few words but a deal of thinking, & the conclusion arrived at, I believe unanimously, was that there was a fund of amusement & information in it if it could be extracted. I have therefore determined to put it carefully away till your return, seize a leisure day, & get you to interpret it. Your mother's commentary, in a suppressed soliloquy, was that you had succeeded in writing a wretched hand. Agnes thought that it would keep this cold weather —her thoughts running on jellies & oysters in the storeroom; but I, indignant at such aspersions upon your accomplishment, retained your epistle & read in an elevated tone an interesting narrative of travels in sundry countries, describing gorgeous scenery, hairbreadth escapes, & a series of remarkable events by flood & field, not a word of which they declared was in your letter. Your return, I hope, will prove the correctness of my version of your annals.

This letter vied in spirit with any of those to Jack Mackay or Andrew Talcott.

When telling Mildred about the town's social life, he said:

"Gaiety continues. Last night there was a cadet hop. Night before, a party at Colonel Johnston's. The night preceding, a College *conversazione* at your mother's. . . . You know how agreeable I am on such occasions, but on this, I am told, I surpassed myself."

By early February, Lee wrote that he was feeling much "stronger," though he could walk no farther than the college without being tired, nor was he ever free from pain while walking. But he was encouraged when he found he could ride without discomfort.

His doctors were unwilling for him to risk taking more cold during the harsh month of March and advised that he go where it was warmer. At first he refused to consider the suggestion, but when the faculty wrote him a joint letter urging that he take a vacation for his health, and his family and friends added their pleas, he agreed. He had little hope of recovery and even expressed doubt that he would survive a trip.

I think I should do better here, & am very reluctant to leave home in my present condition . . . [he wrote Mildred] but the Drs. & others think I had better go South. . . . They seem so interested in my recovery & so persuasive in their uneasiness, that I should appear obstinate, if not perverse, if I resisted longer. I therefore consented to go, & will take Agnes to Savannah, as she seems anxious to visit that city, or perhaps, she will take me.

One place he wanted to visit was Annie's grave, "where I have always promised myself to go, & I think if I am to accomplish it, I have no time to lose."

On Thursday, March 24, 1870, he and Agnes took the packet boat to Lynchburg and the train to Richmond. The canal trip and the train ride had been "trying, but I survived it."

On the twenty-sixth, he had a two-hour physical examination by Doctors Huston, Cunningham, and McCaw. He believed he felt stronger than when he left home, he wrote Mary, but "a little feverish," which he did not know whether to attibute to the trip "or to the toddies Agnes administers." Still, he did not feel well enough to pay any calls, to buy the groceries Mary had asked him to, or even go to church.

Sunday afternoon, he and Agnes met Colonel Mosby, who was shocked to see Lee "so pale and haggard," looking not at all "like the Apollo I had known in the army." Later in the day, Mosby called at Lee's rooms. Though the conversation was limited to "current topics," the Colonel "felt oppressed by the great memories his presence revived, and while both of us were thinking about the war, neither of us referred to it."

Another friend who called was Colonel James Corley, former chief quartermaster for the Army of Northern Virginia. He asked about their trip and how far south they planned to go. This, Lee told him, depended on how strong he felt. The

353

Colonel then insisted on serving as escort; he would arrange to leave his affairs and meet them at Charlotte, North Carolina.

At two o'clock on the afternoon of March 28, Lee and Agnes left Richmond. At 10 P.M., the train stopped at Warren Plains, North Carolina. Captain William J. White, miller, merchant, politician, and veteran, was at the depot to meet his sister, who was returning from Petersburg. He did not see her as she walked toward him, for he was looking intently at someone else who had come off the train. Could it be Marse Robert? It was.

Will introduced himself (Agnes had met his family at the time of Annie's death), and invited them to be guests at Ingleside, his parents' home. Lee accepted.

The next morning, Mrs. White gathered an armful of white hyacinths, Will loaned his carriage and horses, and, unattended, Lee and Agnes drove to the cemetery where Annie was buried. Agnes had brought from home some Spanish moss which Kitty Stiles had once sent. She twined this around the base of the monument and spread the hyacinths over the grave. Her father wrote afterward that the visit was "mournful, yet soothing to my feelings."

After leaving the cemetery, they drove to the farm of the Mrs. Jones, who had suggested the monument to Annie's memory and had been instrumental in getting it. She and her husband insisted that they stay for the noon dinner, a meal made lively by the presence of eleven Jones children, "and numberless others," Agnes wrote her mother. Then they called on another Mrs. Jones and her daughters, who had given them much help and comfort during Annie's illness.

When they returned to Ingleside, the townspeople called. Lee was pleased, he told Mary, to be able to thank all those "kind friends for their care of her [Annie] while living & their attention to her since death. I saw most of the ladies of the committee who undertook the preparation of the monument & the inclosure of the cemetery."

That evening, they took the train and spent their first night in a "sleeping-car," which Agnes described as "very handsome & comfortable." The novelty made them both wakeful.

354

Word of Lee's coming raced ahead of him, and when they reached Raleigh, enthusiastic crowds were there to cheer "vociferously" and call out, "Lee! Lee!" But as Agnes wrote: "We were locked up and 'mum.'"

The next day, the triumphal tour began in earnest. As he said, he would have preferred more quiet but the ovations which greeted him at every way station and depot were a revelation. Lee had not known how generally he was looked on as a hero. He was touched and awed.

"Indeed, I wish you could travel with Papa, to see the affection & feeling shown toward him everywhere," Agnes wrote her mother.

At Charlotte, Colonel Corley joined them. Throngs had come out to see Lee, and there was a band to serenade. There were cheers (and a good many rebel yells), Godspeeds, handshakes, flowers—and tears. Whenever the train stopped, coffee and food were sent to his compartment and veterans who were aboard brought fruit to him. Agnes was afraid they would die from eating.

At Columbia, there was a fifteen-minute stop. Here was another crowd of veterans and townspeople, with Colonel Alexander Haskell acting as master of ceremonies. He asked Lee to appear on the rear platform of the train so that he could introduce him.

"Why should they care to see me?" he asked the Colonel. "Why should they care to see me? I am only a poor old Confederate."

But he went, and as soon as they saw him, the band struck up, the people cheered, and little girls tossed him bouquets. He bowed his acknowledgments.

General E. Porter Alexander elbowed his way up to the train to shake hands, ask after the rest of the family, and lift up his small daughter for Lee to hold.

Namesakes of all sizes appeared along the way; the little ones were held up to see and be seen. "I hope they will all come to good," he said. Old ladies stretched their heads into the car window, and then withdrew them to say to one another:

"He is mightily like his pictures!"

355

Wednesday night, they reached Augusta, where they planned to spend the night and go on to Savannah the next morning. Mayor Allen, members of the council, and a committee of distinguished citizens were at the station to receive them. Lee was put in the first carriage with the Mayor, a Miss Russell whose father and sisters he had met at the White Sulphur, and Mr. Stoval, a councilman. Agnes rode in the second carriage with Colonel Corley, General Lafayette McLaws, Colonel Rains, and Major Branch. According to her account, they were "whirled" off to the Planter's Hotel, where others were waiting to greet them.

The next morning, Lee was tired and decided to stay until Friday. But there was no rest. All of Thursday morning was given over to a formal reception at which Miss Russell, "tall & handsome . . . superb in a white lace moiré-antique with a train," stood in the receiving line.

"Crowds came. Wounded soldiers, servants, working-men even," Agnes wrote. "The sweetest little children—namesakes —dressed to their eyes, with bouquets of japonica—or tiny cards in their little fat hands—with their names."

James Ryder Randall, Robert Burwell, Generals McLaws, Wright, and Gardner also came, and a thirteen-year-old boy, Woodrow Wilson, who had to squeeze through the throng to gaze on Lee "in reverence."

The Branch brothers were most attentive to Agnes. In the afternoon, Melville, who had been a cadet at V.M.I., took her on a tour of the city, driving, as she wrote, "at the rate of a mile a minute." At night, the Major took her to a skating rink where she saw for the first time "young men & maidens with *rollers* fastened to skates darting around the room."

Friday morning, far from rested, they were "whirled" back to the station, and as Lee climbed on the private car, a crowd of veterans gave the rebel yell, which he acknowledged with a bow.

But not even inside the train was he safe from his admirers. The door suddenly opened, and Will Fleming, a boy of fourteen, rushed in to hand him a rose he had picked in his mother's garden. He recalled that Lee "laid aside his paper, rose from his seat, bowed with the grace of a Chesterfield, took the rose and said:

" 'Thank you, my son, and now with your permission I will present it to my daughter.' "

At Savannah, they were met by the largest crowd yet and had trouble walking through to the open barouche waiting at the curb. There were more huzzas, rebel yells, flowers, and music.

They drove to General Lawton's house on the corner of York and Lincoln Streets, where Agnes was to stay. At bedtime, Andrew Low, the British cotton factor who had married Eliza Stiles' daughter, Mary, sent his carriage to bring Lee to his stately mansion facing beautiful Lafayette Square.

Lee would have preferred to stay with Agnes, but this proved a happy arrangement, for since his wife's death Low had been keeping house alone, and as there were no other guests, it proved quiet and restful.

It was generally believed that Lee was staying with the Lawtons, so that night, after he had gone, the Saxe Horn Band and the Washington Comet Band serenaded alternately with old favorites. A crowd gathered and called for Lee. General Lawton went out, thanked the musicians, and excused Lee from appearing by saying that he was tired from his trip and had already gone to bed. The bands then struck up "The Bonnie Blue Flag" in unison, and went off to serenade General Joe Johnston, who was now in the insurance business in Savannah.

"Papa has borne the journey & the crowds far better than I thought he would & seems stronger," Agnes wrote. But from her father's pen came a different picture:

"I have had a tedious journey upon the whole, & have more than ever regretted that I undertook it." A few days later, he wrote:

"I don't think travelling in this way procures me much quiet & repose. I wish I was back."

He did find that he walked more easily but thought this might be owing to Savannah's better streets.

The morning after his arrival ("rather cool & raw, with an

357

easterly wind"), Agnes and Corinne Lawton took him for a short drive around the city. On the way back, they stopped to see "Mrs. Dr. Elliott" (the former Margaret Mackay), Mrs. Gordon, Mrs. Gilmer, Mrs. Anderson, and Mrs. Owen. When he came back to his quarters, he found that Andrew Low had asked Joe Johnston, Generals Lawton and Gilmer, and Colonel Corley for dinner.

Agnes was having her share of attention: "Crowds of persons have been coming to see me ever since I came," she told her mother. She was entertained by all of her father's old friends, and driven to scenic spots about the city. But she became overtired and took cold, delaying the trip to Florida by several days.

At Robert's first meeting with Kitty Stiles, he asked her to write Eliza's sisters, Kate and Sarah Mackay, then at Etowah Cliffs, and tell them that "the old man" would like to see them but did not feel up to coming out to their country home. They came and opened up the old house on Broughton Street where he visited with them. He found them "looking very well."

He called on Joe Johnston and his wife and, probably at her suggestion, the two old warriors had their pictures taken together. The results show Lee "wan and haggard," and old beyond his years.

The weather turned warm, and Robert's back pains were lessened. "But I perceive no change in the stricture in my chest. If I attempt to walk beyond a very slow gait, the pain is always there. . . . I . . . fear that nothing will relieve my complaint, which is fixed & old. I must bear it."

A little more than a week later, he wrote that the pain in his chest was there occasionally even when he was inactive—a new symptom.

He wanted to visit his father's grave again, so on Tuesday, April 12, he and Agnes took the steamer *Nick King*. Andrew Low, thinking, as Robert wrote Mary, that "Agnes & I were unable to take care of ourselves," went with them. At Brunswick, William Nightingale, a grandson of General Greene, joined the party and escorted it to Cumberland Island. Dungeness had been burned and the island devastated by the Federals, but the cemetery was undamaged. Agnes decorated her grandfather's grave with spring flowers.

"I presume it is the last time I shall be able to pay to it my tribute of respect," Lee wrote simply.

From Cumberland, the *Nick King* went to Jacksonville, Florida, where a delegation of prominent citizens came on board to welcome Lee. In the upper saloon, he held a reception for the townspeople. For several hours, they filed by. By then, Lee was visibly tired yet there were crowds still waiting on the dock. So as not to tire himself further, it was suggested that he step on deck where all could see him.

When he did, "an awed silence settled on the crowd." There was not a cheer but "the very silence of the multitude spoke a deeper feeling than the loudest huzzas could have expressed."

Because his Savannah friends were concerned about his health, Lee agreed on his return to be examined by Doctors Arnold and Reed. "They concur in the opinion of the other physicians, & think it pretty certain that my trouble arises from some adhesion of the parts, not from any injury of the lungs & heart, but that the pericardium may not be implicated, & the adhesion may be between the pleura & ——, I have forgotten the name."

He and Agnes decided to vary the return trip by going along the coast. At Charleston, South Carolina, they were the guests of W. Jefferson Bennett, who had two sons at Washington College. Mr. Bennett gave a reception for Confederate officers only, as Lee had asked to be excused from holding a general reception. But still there were so many friends who wanted to see him that, with his permission, the Bennetts held two invitational receptions at their home. Between the receptions was "a grand dinner party."

According to the *Courier*, to both receptions came

the old and young, the gray beards and the sages of the country, the noble, pure, honorable, poor and wealthy . . . glad to do him honor. Stately dames of the old school, grandmothers of seventy, and a long train of granddaughters, all flocked around our noble old chief, glad of a smile, of a shake of the hand; and happy was

359

the girl of twelve, or fourteen, who carried away on her lips, the parting kiss of the grand old soldier.

As soon as Lee stepped off the train at Portsmouth, Virginia, cannon boomed, fireworks and skyrockets popped and hissed, and that "maniacal maelstrom of sound," the rebel yell, swelled the din. Walter Taylor was there to escort them on the ferry across the river to Norfolk, where a carriage was waiting to drive them to Dr. Selden's beautiful home overlooking the river.

William E. Taylor gave an elaborate dinner in Lee's honor, and Dr. Selden held a reception. Because of the heavy rain, he did not go with Agnes and Mrs. Selden to the house of Richard Page, where he had hoped to see his faithful mess steward, Bryan, again. Agnes brought back love and "kindly inquiries" after himself and Mary from "everyone down to Bryan."

From Norfolk, he and Agnes went to Lower Brandon, the first of the Harrison houses on the James, where his favorite Belle lived with her widowed mother. He wrote from there:

"I am better, I trust; am getting fat, but am still rigid & painful in my back." The old plantation was "very beautiful" and it was "refreshing to look at the river. The garden is filled with flowers & abounds in roses. The yellow jasmine is still in bloom & perfumes the atmosphere."

But not even here did he take any rest. On the day of his coming, he rode "to the other Brandons [Middle and Upper] & saw all the inhabitants." The next morning, he and Agnes called on the Warrenton Carters. Everything around them looked "comfortable & flourishing. They have a nice house, & as far as I could see, everything is prospering."

That night, they went to Middle Brandon to see a tableau put on by George Harrison's children. Until Tuesday, May 10, when he and Agnes moved on to Shirley, they were entertained each day at one of the Brandons, and spare time was, as he wrote, "a scarce commodity."

At Shirley, "all the country came out to see him" and Hill Carter held a large dinner in his honor. The company of Hill's daughters was very pleasing to him.

"He liked to have us tickle his hands," one of the girls wrote,

360

"but when Cousin Agnes came to sit by him that seemed to be her privilege. We regarded him with the greatest veneration. We had heard of God, but here was General Lee!"

Mary finally fulfilled a long-cherished ambition to visit Rooney and his family. Markie came to Lexington in April, and early in May they went to the White House. On the trip, Mary found "the woods lovely with wild flowers & dogwood blossoms & with all the fragrance of early spring, the dark holly & pine intermingling with the delicate leaves just brought out by the genial season, daisies, wild violets, & heart's-ease. I have not seen so many wild flowers since I left Arlington."

On Thursday, May 12, Agnes and her father arrived at the White House.

"He looks fatter, but I do not like his complexion, & he seems stiff," Mary wrote to Mildred, who had stayed in Lexington.

Rob came up to see his parents and persuaded his father to visit Romancoke. It had always been a dependency of the White House and managed by an overseer. Since taking over the property in 1866, Rob had been keeping bachelor hall in the overseer's house. On Lee's first visit, he had described Rob's house as "forlorn" but he was unprepared to find that it had meanwhile become such a shambles, and that Rob's equipment for living was so makeshift.

"His self-control was great and his emotions were not on the surface, but when he entered and looked around . . . he appeared really much shocked," Rob recalled.

But on the farm, he found everything prospering. They walked and drove over it, discussing plans for its improvement, selecting a site for the new house and locating the proper places for barns, icehouse, and other buildings. It was evident to Rob that he enjoyed his stay and felt "refreshed by the rest and quiet."

On May 23, Lee and Agnes took the train to Richmond, where shortly after his arrival he wrote Mildred: "I came up . . . this morning with Agnes, but she threatens to divorce herself from me, & we have already separated. She is at Dr. Fairfax's & I am at Mr. McFarland's. She promises however, to see me occasionally, & if I can restore our travelling relations even at costly sacrifice I shall be happy to take her along with me."

He spent four days in Richmond. Part of the time was passed in further examinations by the doctors. The first day, he saw Dr. Huston, who told a colleague that the symptoms pointed to "chronic pericarditis." Robert had never had much faith in doctors: "I am to have a great medicine talk tomorrow," he wrote Mildred. He submitted to the examinations only to satisfy his family and friends.

Lee made a few calls in town and went shopping to buy Rob a set of silver-plated forks and knives.

In 1865, the sculptor, Edward Valentine, had wanted to model Lee and though Lee had agreed reluctantly to sit for him, Valentine had not come to Lexington. Now he called on Lee and talked again about the bust. Robert was agreeable, and made an appointment for May 25 to call at his studio on Main Street between 12th and 13th to look at some of his work and to let Valentine take measurements of his face.

As the artist worked he talked, to set them both at ease, and found unsuspected humor in his model. When he mentioned his own change in fortune since the war, he was surprised to hear Lee say,

"An artist ought not to have too much money."

Lee then told him that "misfortune nobly borne is good fortune," an epigram Valentine thought original until he found it in the writings of Marcus Aurelius.

When they parted, Valentine said that he could come to Lexington then or in the fall, whichever suited Lee better. Lee said that although there would be more time in the autumn, he had better come now.

It was the artist's feeling that Lee was aware of the proximity of his death.

9

THE day he reached Lexington, Lee read the trustees' minutes to post himself on the latest business. He found that at their April 19 meeting, to lighten his burdens, they had appointed

Professor White his confidential secretary; that they had passed a resolution to deed the President's house to Mrs. Lee, and agreed to seetle on her an annuity of three thousand dollars in case of Lee's disability or death.

But Lee wanted all money to be "devoted to the purposes of education," and would accept neither the house nor annuity: "I am unwilling that my family should become a tax to the College," he wrote.

When the trustees received his letter, they politely ignored it, had the deed recorded, and went ahead with plans for the annuity.

During the first week in June, Edward Valentine came to Lexington, having traveled on money loaned by a relative. Lee received him cordially and invited him to use a downstairs room as a studio, but the sculptor, still greatly in awe of "the grand idol of the South," was unwilling to inconvenience the family. So they walked into town to see where the artist might be accommodated.

Lee's sprightly manner as he joked with several acquaintances whom they met on the way reassured Valentine, who, though he had been told of Lee's "noble simplicity" and "gentle and kindly bearing," admitted to a feeling of "dread" at the thought of being closeted so long with this "great man."

They found a vacant store on the ground floor of the hotel on the main street, and Valentine prepared it for the sittings. He screened the front windows from the public gaze, set up a low platform with a comfortable chair, and built a fire to remove the dampness.

They had a tacit agreement that there would be no audience, an arrangement that suited Valentine perfectly. Lee specified that only Custis and Professor White were to be admitted.

Valentine wrote his sister that the first sitting took place on June 7: "He is very patient, and we have quite a conversation while I work."

Lee enjoyed talking about his boyhood, of swimming in the Potomac and riding across the fields at Stratford. He spoke of his years at West Point, both as a cadet and as superintendent, and of his friendship with the painter, Robert Weir. He talked of the Mexican War and Texas. But his conversation was not limited to the past: he made many comments "on persons and things of a more recent date."

As they grew better acquainted, the topics became more personal, and one day Valentine told him of the effect of lime-stone water on his system. He had consulted Dr. Graham, who had prescribed "Dovers' Powders," which had relieved him. A day or two later, Lee said to him jokingly:

"I think you work much better when you have the dysentery on you. I must tell your doctor to keep it up!"

Valentine appreciated Lee's jokes, and in turn told some himself.

He was anxious to have a memento of the occasion in the form of apparel, which he could use later in case he modeled a complete figure. He had in mind a pair of military boots, and approached Lee by telling the story of the office seeker who asked President Jackson for the post of Minister to England. On being told that it was already filled, he then asked to be appointed Secretary of the Legation. When told that there was no vacancy there either, he asked to be made vice-consul. Again Jackson had to tell him there was no opening.

"Well, then, Mr. President, would you give me a pair of your old boots!"

When Lee laughed, Valentine added: "That is what I would like to have you do for me, General."

"I think there is a pair at home that you can have," he said. The next day, June 10, he brought the dress boots, size 4½C, that he had worn as a cadet. On the lining was written: "R. E. Lee, U.S.A."

Valentine could detect no difference in Lee's manner from his ordinary bearing as he sat for the bust (a time when most people try to look their best), and he felt that if asked to name Lee's most characteristic trait, he would say:

"A complete lack of the melodramatic in all that he said and did."

Later, he expanded his notes: "An artist, above all other men, is quick to observe the faintest suggestion of posing; the slightest indication of a movement or expression which smacks

364

of vanity he is sure to detect. Such weaknesses . . . were totally lacking in General Lee."

In the little diary Valentine kept while in Lexington, he noted that Lee parted his hair behind, and was his own barber. One day he wrote:

"The General told me his height was 5 ft. 11 inches."

He also noted that Lee often put his hand to his breast as though in pain—an indication, the artist felt, of "heart trouble" though Lee did not talk about his health.

Mary, Markie, and Agnes had by now returned to Lexington, and since Mary could not go to the studio to see the bust, Valentine hired a Mr. Berniecker to take it up to the house in a cart. She had invited friends to view it, so the parlor was full when Valentine arrived.

He sensed that it was an "ordeal" for Lee to be turned this way and that "by the good wife" as she compared the bust with the original and asked Markie and Margaret Preston for their opinions. But he noted that he submitted patiently "without a murmur." When it was over, Mary had two minor objections: the middle of the moustache did not seem quite right, and the left ear might be more delicate.

Valentine asked Lee to have photographs taken from various angles, and with these as guides, the artist was ready to return to Richmond to make the cast. When he came to the house to say good-by, he found Lee, wearing a white linen sack, in the parlor with two ladies and a man. Just as Valentine came in, he heard Lee say:

"I feel I have an incurable disease coming on me—old age. I would like to go to some quiet place in the country and rest."

But rest and quiet were just a dream. It was again time for the final examinations, and to plan the commencement. The Reverend W. T. Brantly of Atlanta was to give the baccalaureate sermon, and Lee had asked him and his daughter to stay at the house. Agnes and Mildred had invited the usual number of friends for the closing exercises, which now lasted a week and ended in a ball, the climax of the Lexington social season.

At the trustees' meeting after graduation, it was decided to

365

reorganize the business school, to adopt a regular curriculum for the schools of Commerce and Agriculture, and to make provisions for the law department under Judge Brockenbrough to become a regular school of the college.

As soon as the college business was finished, Lee went to Baltimore to consult the noted doctor, Thomas H. Buckler. He reached the city at nine-fifteen on the night of July 1, finding his host, Samuel Tagart, waiting for him at the depot.

"It was the hottest day I ever experienced, or I was in the hottest position I ever occupied both on board the packet & in the railroad cars, or I was less able to stand it, for I never recollect having suffered so," he wrote.

The next morning, Dr. Buckler came to the house and examined Lee for two hours, finding the lungs "working well" though "the action of the heart a little diffused, but nothing to injure." He had a "rheumatic constitution" and must guard against taking cold. He advised outdoor exercise and prescribed lemon juice, and a "blister" to relieve the pains in the shoulders and chest.

The company of the attractive Mrs. Tagart revived him, and in spite of fatigue, heat, rain, and the "medicine talk," he wrote Mary that his host had been waiting for him for over an hour at the depot, "thanks to his having a punctual wife, who regulates everything for him, so that he had plenty of time for reflection."

When the rain stopped, he went to see Washington Peter, and then to Goodwood, where he stayed for over a week. From there, he went on to Alexandria, which he found so "piping hot" he gave up his plans to visit Sis Nanie, and Rooney and Tabb. "I am unable to bear heat now," he explained.

He caught another cold, spent a restless night in his stifling room at the Mansion House, and wakened in the morning "full of pains." Still, he went to see his attorney, Francis L. Smith, who invited him to stay at his house where Lee might be cooler.

Among other matters, they discussed the possibility of recovering Arlington. "The prospect is not promising," he wrote Mary, though he would not give up hope until he had talked to Cousin Cassius.

366

Mr. Smith held a reception for him, a final review, as it would prove. Among the callers was Colonel Mosby. When he came to say good-by, Lee looked at him earnestly and said:

"Colonel, I hope we shall have no more wars."

He stayed several days with Cassius Lee. One afternoon, they talked about Robert's recent trip south, and he told his cousin of a meeting with their old teacher, William B. Leary. In 1866, Mr. Leary had come to Lexington to see him, and now during the southern tour, in spite of age and infirmities, he had attended a reception in Lee's honor.

This of course recalled their school days and boyhood exploits and adventures. Then the talk switched to the war. With Cassius he had never been reluctant to discuss the subject, but on this day, he seemed even less so.

He spoke of Jackson's delay in getting on McClellan's flank, and told how it had precipitated the unexpected battle at Mechanicsville.

But Jackson had later redeemed himself, and Lee felt that if Stonewall had been at Gettysburg, there would have been a great victory.

Cassius asked why he did not go on to Washington after Second Manassas, and Robert said simply:

"Because my men had nothing to eat."

Pointing to the ruins of Fort Wade beyond the house, he said:

"I could not tell my men to take that fort when they had had nothing to eat for three days. I went to Maryland to feed my army."

This brought up the subject of the mismanagement of the commissary, and Lee cited many examples of the curtailment of his operations on account of it. Doubtless he spoke of the failure to send supplies to Amelia Court House, a blunder he was slow to forgive.

The Southern newspapers were included in his censure. They were ignorant of the definition of *patriotism*, he told Cassius: time and again they had published army movements, frustrating his plans when the enemy read of them.

Cassius then asked which Federal general he had considered the most capable. Without any hesitation, he said:

367

"McClellan by all odds."

"Ah, Robert," Cassius then said, "I gave up hope after Stonewall Jackson fell!"

At this, Lee sprang up and exclaimed:

"Cassius, do you suppose General Jackson went about the country fighting battles without orders!"

While staying with his cousin, he went to see Bishop Johns, who had confirmed him, and General Samuel Cooper, whose financial distress he had tried to relieve while in Savannah. One afternoon, a neighbor saw him gazing wistfully over the fence into the garden where he used to play.

"I am looking," he explained, "to see if the old snowball trees are still there. I should have been sorry to have missed them."

He next went to Ravensworth, where he hoped the heat might be more bearable, but described it as "almost insupportable"; at six in the evening the thermometer in the hall read 86°. Aside from rheumatism, Cousin Anna was otherwise well.

Because of the continued heat, he gave up all thoughts of visiting Richland or "the boys on the Pamunkey." He did not even have the energy to write to them and make his excuses, but asked Mary to say for him:

"It is too hot & . . . I am too painful."

Later, he wrote Custis, visiting at the White House, to tell him of his disappointment at not being able to see him, and his "farmer sons, my sweet daughter Tabb & my G^rdson all together, & to have been thereby in a measure rejuvenated. . . . I feel that my opportunities of enjoying your company are becoming daily more precarious."

He was back in Lexington by July 27, and submitted to yet another examination by the local doctors, Barton and Madison, who recommended the Hot Springs for his rheumatic pains.

Before leaving, he wrote to Dr. Buckler and thanked him for inviting him to go with him to Paris, where he and his family had been living since 1866:

"There is no one whom I would prefer to have as a companion on the voyage, nor is there one . . . who would take better

368

care of me. But I cannot impose myself upon you . . . you must cure me on this side of the Atlantic."

He also wrote to General Cooper, enclosing three hundred dollars contributed by friends in Savannah and one hundred dollars of his own. He regretted the sum was not larger, but hoped it might at least "supply some immediate want & prevent you from taxing your strength too much."

He was so busy right up to the day of departure, August 9, that there was not time to say good-by to the neighbors. After he reached the Hot Springs, he asked Mary to apologize for this lapse.

He and Professor White started out by train, but passing through the beautiful countryside, they were so overcome by memories of their rides through these mountains that they decided to follow their old route by stage.

When they reached the Hot Springs, they found "quite a company" there, among them friends from Baltimore—Mrs. Walker, wife of the Confederate Secretary of War, and William Washington, the painter, making sketches of the scenery.

Lee consulted Dr. Cabell, the resident physician, who recommended that he start with what was called the "Hot Spout" and alternate with another called the "Boiler," virtually guaranteeing him a cure if he persisted, a prospect Lee found "tedious."

The weather was not good: when the sun shone, which was not often, it was too hot; and when it rained, which was "the usual condition," it was cold. He thought the picturesque was more easily obtainable in this country than health, he wrote, with William Washington in mind.

Nor was he happy in the baths, for "the society has a rather solemn appearance, & conversation runs mostly on personal ailments, baths, & damp weather. . . . I have a merry time with my cronies, tell Mildred. I am getting too heavy for them now. They soon drop me."

But there was one pleasure in store, one he had been looking forward to: the formal engagement of Rob and Charlotte Haxall. When he got the news, he wrote his "Beautiful Lottie" at once to tell her of "the happiness you have given us & my

369

gratitude at your consent to enter our family." But there was an underlying note of sadness in the presentiment that there was little time left for him to enjoy her company:

"I already love you as a daughter. I can do nothing more than beg you quickly to become so, for I have little time to wait, & now want to see you more than ever."

He urged her to come and see them in September, when Rob planned a visit.

When he wrote to Rob that same day, he again stressed the time element:

I hope . . . that your marriage will not be deferred so long. You will have to hasten with your work. . . . I shall be ready to help you in any way that I can & you must let me know what I can do for you & when. . . . When you come up in September you must tell me all your plans & I think the best thing she can do is to accompany you & stay with her Papa till you build her a house.

Poetically he concluded:

"You must make more wheat, put more lime on the land, & cast over the fields the sweet smiles of your wife."

After submitting to the Spout for five days and the Boiler for four, he found little benefit:

"Hot bathing is not agreeable to me . . . in its operations or effects, but I see daily evidences of its good results in others."

After two weeks, he wrote gloomily: "I hope that I am better, but am aware of no material change, except that I am weaker. I am very anxious to get back. It is very wearying at these public places & the benefit hardly worth the cost. I do not think I can even stand Lexington long."

But he was looking forward to the company of Rob and Charlotte, Rooney and Tabb, his niece Mildred de Podestad and her husband, Charles Carter of Goodwood, and daughters Ella and Mildred, and wrote Mary to prepare for their arrival. Since there were already guests, he said:

"The girls will have to prepare my room for some of the visitors, & put me anywhere. I can be very comfortable in the library. Tell the little creatures they must work like beavers &

get a supply of eggs & chickens. Recollect there is flour at Leyburn's mill when you want it."

He suggested that she send for Traveller and Lucy Long, at pasture on Andrew Cameron's farm, so that the girls could "scour the country" for supplies. But he cautioned her to see that Henry, the hired man, took proper care of the horses. He must be "particularly gentle & kind to them, or the gray will give him great trouble. He must wash them clean, & not pull out their manes & tails."

On August 27, he wrote that he felt better in the last few days than during his entire stay, and wished only that he might stay longer but he had to attend a stockholders' meeting of the Valley Railroad in Staunton.

"Possibly the little improvement now felt will continue. If not, I shall have to bear my malady."

Two days later, he left for the meeting. He was unanimously elected president of the company. Normally, he would have declined but he had been convinced by the other stockholders that his name would lend confidence, particularly when money was to be raised.

After his return to Lexington, the faculty noticed that he set to work "with that quiet zeal and noiseless energy that marked all his actions, and an unusual elation was felt by those about him at the increased prospect that long years of usefulness and honour would yet be added to his glorious life."

"I am better," he wrote Samuel Tagart. "In fact, I suppose I am as well as I shall be. I am still following Dr. B.'s directions, & in time I may improve still more."

He looked forward to a visit with the Tagarts that fall when he went to Baltimore in behalf of the Valley Railroad.

Although Rob, Charlotte, Rooney, and Tabb had all been delayed in paying their promised visit, they were coming for sure in October, a prospect that made him very happy.

On Wednesday, September 28, he spent the morning with his correspondence and other business, and refused all offers of help from the faculty.

Just as he closed his office door to go home to dinner, he met Percy Davidson, a sophomore, who wanted him to auto-

371

graph a picture. Davidson suggested that he return at a more convenient time, but Lee said:

"No, I will go right back and do it now."

He returned to the round table, took up his pen, and signed his name—as it happened, for the last time.

After his midafternoon dinner, he took his customary nap in his armchair in the bow window, looking out on the hills that were veiled in rain. Agnes rubbed his hands, while in the next room Mildred practiced on the piano. As he closed his eyes he heard the familiar strains of Mendelssohn's "Song Without Words."

After ten minutes he woke up, refreshed. Since there was to be a vestry meeting at Grace Church to discuss plans for a new building and means to raise the rector's salary, he prepared to go.

When he came into the parlor, he wore his military cape and had his hat in his hand. Mildred was still at the piano, and still at Mendelssohn, now playing "The Funeral March."

"Life," he said, "that is a doleful piece you are playing!"

Then he kissed her, as he did whenever he came in or left the house, and said:

"I wish I did not have to go and listen to all that pow-wow."

He walked to the front door and stood there for a few moments, looking out at the rain. Then he walked to the red-brick church just down the slope from his house.

The church was cold and damp, and it was noticed that he kept his cape on as he talked with the other vestrymen before the meeting, telling "with marked cheerfulness of manner" some anecdotes of Bishop Meade and John Marshall.

When the meeting came to order, he acted as chairman and as usual listened to all the others speak before he gave an opinion. The discussion was lengthy and before it was over Lee appeared tired. In spite of the cold room, he was noticeably flushed.

About seven o'clock, he brought the meeting to a close with a characteristic act—his last public act. The amount pledged for Dr. Pendleton's salary was still lacking fifty-five dollars.

"I will give that sum," he said quietly.

372

It was close to seven-thirty when he left the church and walked through the heavy rain to his house. He went directly to his room, as was his habit, to hang up his coat and hat. When he came downstairs, he heard Mildred talking and laughing with some young man in the parlor, probably a "yearling." Since he was already late for tea, he did not stop to speak to Mildred's guest, but hurried into the dining room.

Since Mary had been waiting for more than half an hour, it was her turn to rally him for being tardy:

"You have kept us waiting a long time. Where have you been?"

He did not reply, but took his place in front of his chair and stood there as if to say grace. When he tried to speak, the familiar words did not come, but with that self-mastery which was present to the very end, he took his seat quietly, showing neither agitation nor alarm.

"You look very tired. Let me pour you a cup of tea," Mary said.

Again the words failed, but he straightened in his chair, and as his wife and Agnes turned anxious eyes on him, it seemed to them that his face wore "a sublime air of resignation" as if aware "that his hour had come."

Mary became alarmed and called Custis, who asked him if he wanted anything and, on his failing to reply, sent for the doctors.

Mildred was called from the parlor. She saw her father seated with his head bowed; he was speaking now, but the words were incoherent.

Within fifteen minutes, Doctors Madison and Barton, who had also been at the vestry meeting, came. When they took off his coat, he said distinctly:

"You hurt my arm," and pointed to the shoulder that had been paining him.

He was aware of all that was happening, and even helped pull off his clothing. Examination revealed no paralysis, and no apparent inflammation of the brain, but his consciousness was slightly impaired, there was a marked debility, and a tendency to drowsiness. The doctors diagnosed it as a "venous conges-

373

tion" and ordered him put to bed with cold compresses on his head and hot ones applied to his feet.

Mildred suggested that his bed—"a small low single bed"—be brought from upstairs and set in front of his favorite window in the dining room. Once in bed, he slipped off into a peaceful sleep, and the doctors predicted that he would be much improved by morning.

He did waken somewhat better, though still drowsy. He slept most of that day and for many days afterward, though he always roused easily and was completely conscious of all who were in the room. He understood everything that was said to him, answered questions clearly but briefly, generally nodding his head or responding with the monosyllables he tended to use when sick.

Mildred fixed his meals and sat with him during the day. When she came into the room each morning, she recalled, "his beautiful sad eyes always gave me a look of love and recognition." One day as she sat stroking his hand, he took hers up and kissed it. Another time she heard him call her "Precious baby," and again, heard him murmur,

"I am so weary!"

Whenever Mary came up to him, he greeted her with "an outstretched hand and kindly pressure."

How it rained that first night, Mildred remembered, and for eight days afterward, causing roads, bridges, houses, men, and cattle to wash away. For a time, all communication with the little town was suspended, and no word could be sent to Daughter, Rooney, or Rob.

"Nature seemed to grieve with convulsive throbs and the windows of Heaven to be opened," Mary wrote.

A fire was kept going in the sickroom to keep out the damp, and as Lee "lay straight & motionless" he would gaze "with that solemn unalterable look, into the flames that played on the hearth. . . ." Hour after hour, Mildred and Agnes sat "rubbing his dear hands in the old way he used to like," never saying a word, "for words were frozen in our mouths," while their mother, helpless to add to his comfort, sat beside him and prayed.

Agnes, "her face set and pale like death itself" from the

374

strain of the long hours, gave him his medicines around the clock, while Custis and one professor from the college kept the vigil.

Soon, everyone in town knew of his illness and came to the house to offer sympathy and help. The village churches were filled with those who went to pray for him.

For a time, he seemed to respond favorably to cupping and stimulants. He ate with apparent relish, and grew strong enough to turn over in bed and sit up for his meals. This gave everyone hope. Only he seemed to have neither the expectation nor the desire to recover.

One morning when Dr. Madison found him looking better, he asked:

"How do you feel today, General?"

In replying, Lee enunciated each word slowly and distinctly:

"I . . . feel . . . better."

"You must make haste and get well; Traveller has been standing so long in the stable he needs exercise," the doctor said cheerfully.

Lee only shook his head sadly and closed his eyes.

When on another day Custis spoke of his recovery, he shook his head and pointed upward. Several times after that he put aside his medicine, saying to Agnes:

"It is no use."

On Monday, October 10, there was a marked change for the worse. He seemed to be suffering and when he tried to speak, words failed him. He could only look beseechingly at those around his couch.

"Ever and always those glorious dark eyes . . . speaking with imploring, heart rending tones!" Mildred wrote. "Oh, the horror of being helpless when he needed help!"

Outside, the rain pelted the panes and the wind lashed the trees. Doctors Madison and Barton, who had been called, hurried into the room. After one look at the patient, they quietly asked the family to leave. Through her tears, Mildred could see Agnes, "so calm and despairing," Custis, "worried," and "Mama so patient, being able only to pray."

During the afternoon, his pulse became feeble and rapid

and his breathing short and labored. Around midnight, he was siezed with spasms of shivering, and Dr. Barton announced the seriousness of his condition.

Tuesday morning in coming down very early, Mildred saw "an agonized expression" on her father's face. He was turning uneasily and trying to get over on his right side. He refused breakfast, nor would he take any medicine except from the doctors' hands. He was less observant, though he still recognized everyone who approached him.

Sometime during that day he slipped off into partial delirium and his mind "wandered to those dreadful battlefields," Mary recalled.

"Tell Hill he *must* come up!" he cried out once in ringing tones.

At other times, the words were mumbled or whispered but those who leaned close heard commands and generals' names.

That night Mildred went to bed exhausted. Toward midnight, Agnes came in and gently waked her. Her face told the story. Hand in hand, the two girls returned to the sickroom. The Reverend General Pendleton was there to read the prayers for the dying. The children knelt by their father's bed while the two doctors and Professor Harris, a watcher, stood aside.

Mildred could hear her father's heavy breathing punctuating the prayers; he appeared unconscious.

When Dr. Pendleton finished, he and the others who were not family members went out, leaving Mary with Robert's hand in hers while Agnes moistened his lips and fanned him, and Mildred wept silently. She noticed that the wind had died and the rain stopped, but she could hear the distant roar of the creeks and river.

Morning found them still clustered about the bed. Mildred looked out. How blue was the sky! "How scarlet were the berries in the hedge—how soft and magical was the October sunshine!"

But to Mary it seemed only "to mock our grief."

At nine o'clock, her father appeared to be struggling and Mildred ran out for Dr. Madison. When he came, he looked at Lee and then with bowed head turned away.

"Never was more beautifully displayed how a long and severe education of mind and character enables the soul to pass with equal step through this supreme ordeal," wrote William Preston Johnston, a watcher by the deathbed. ". . . all the massive grandeur of his form, and face, and brow remained; and death seemed to lose its terrors, and to borrow a grace and dignity in sublime keeping with the life that was ebbing away. The great mind sank to its last repose, almost with the equal poise of health."

Outside the window, a bird chirped in the hedge. In the village, the clock chimed the half hour. The watchers in the room were startled to hear a voice, strong, deep, musical, and resonant—the voice of Robert Lee—call out:

"Strike the tent!"

Then, with one last deep-drawn sigh, he passed gently to his final rest.

Epilogue

Epilogue

AFTER Mary Custis Lee had returned to her own room on the morning of October 12, she gave way to her emotions for the first time during the long ordeal. Putting her arms around Mildred, she drew her close and murmured through her tears:

"Do be kind to me now!"

They wept together while Agnes, pale and silent, made preparations for the funeral.

Since it was supposed at first that Lee would recover, none of the absent children was sent for until his condition became grave. Then, due to the temporary suspension in the mail service, the letters were slow in reaching them. Once they all started out for Lexington, there were further delays because of floods. Rooney and Rob arrived on the morning of the twelfth, but too late to find him alive. With Mildred they stood in the darkened room where their father lay on his bier, dressed in the suit of black broadcloth he had worn to Rooney's wedding.

Word of his death spread quickly. First the chapel bell began to toll, then those of other churches in the village. Schools were closed and all business suspended until the following week. Every building front and door was draped in black and hung with wreaths of cypress and immortelles.

When the news reached Richmond on the thirteenth, a day of mourning was declared. The streets were soon deserted and by ten o'clock that morning, nearly every store on Main, Broad, and Cary Streets had closed. On their doors also hung badges of mourning. Shop windows were stripped of their wares and showed instead photographs and portraits of Lee, draped in black. Most houses displayed wreaths of laurel and cypress, intertwined with crêpe.

The public offices of the State were closed for the day, and the bells in the old Bell Tower in Capitol Square and in the churches and police stations all over the city tolled until sunset. Throughout Virginia and the South, flags were at half-mast, bells tolled, and people wept and prayed.

381

No man since George Washington had so captured the hearts of the people, not only in the South, but in the North, in Canada, England, and on the Continent.

Charles A. Dana and Horace Greeley paid him tribute as a soldier and Christian, as did the editors of the *New York Herald* and the *Cincinnati Enquirer*. The *Montreal Telegraph*, in writing of his military genius, predicted:

"Posterity will rank Lee above Wellington or Napoleon, before Saxe or Turenne, above Marlborough or Frederick, before Alexander, or Caesar. . . . In fact, the greatest general of this or any other age. He has made his own name, and the Confederacy he served, immortal."

The *London Standard* wrote: ". . . the fatherlands of Sidney and of Bayard never produced a nobler soldier, gentleman, and Christian than General Robert E. Lee."

In Germany and France, he shared the glory of Frederick and Napoleon and was placed on the pedestal beside George Washington, for like him, Lee was characterized "un grand citoyen." England's Lord Wolseley, recalling his wartime visit with Lee, wrote:

I shall never forget his sweet, winning smile, nor his clear, honest eyes that seemed to look into your heart while they searched your brain. . . . He is stamped upon my memory as being apart and superior to all others in every way, a man with whom none I ever knew and few of whom I have read are worthy to be classed. . . . When Americans can review the history of their last great war with calm impartiality, I believe all will admit that General Lee towered far above all men on either side in that struggle. I believe he will be regarded not only as the most prominent figure of the Confederacy, but as the greatest American of the nineteenth century. . . ."

As Mary Lee told a friend: "If he had succeeded in gaining by his sword all the South expected & hoped for, he could not have been more honoured & lamented."

Gamaliel Bradford has written: "Success is the idol of the world and the world's idols have been successful. . . . Who shall say just how far that element of success enters into their greatness?"

Then, speaking of Lee, he continued:

Here was a man who remains great, although he failed. . . .
Here is a man who failed grandly, a man who said that "human
virtue should be equal to human calamity," and showed that it
could be equal to it, and so, without pretense, without display,
without self-consciousness, left an example that future Americans
may study with profit as long as there is an America.

At one-thirty on Friday afternoon, October 14, a procession
formed in front of the President's house to escort Lee's body to
the college chapel. Professor White, the companion of many an
afternoon's jaunt and summer excursion, was the chief marshal. The escort of honor was made up of Confederate veterans; the twelve pallbearers represented the trustees, faculty,
and students of the College and V.M.I., and citizens of Lexington. Behind the hearse came Traveller, led by two soldiers, his
bridle and empty saddle covered with crêpe.

The body was laid in state on the chapel dais and an honor
guard of students, selected by themselves, kept watch until ten
o'clock the next morning.

Saturday dawned cloudless and bright, the air, pure and
bracing. Many felt this was a fitting close to Lee's "splendid
and unsullied career."

Precisely at ten, the funeral procession left the President's
house, and filed over to the hotel where it was joined by digni-
taries of the State. With the escort of honor, consisting of
veterans (among them Walter Taylor and Charles Venable,
who had defied floods to come), the clergy, attending physicians, trustees and faculty, students and cadets, visitors, townspeople, and Traveller, it moved off slowly up the hill to the
chapel.

Leaving Mary seated in her wheel chair reading over some
old letters from Robert, the family walked down the slope to
attend the service. Through her tears and heavy veil, Mildred
could see the metallic coffin covered with flowers and symbolic
crosses of evergreen and immortelles. Before a congregation
that filled the church and overflowed into the grounds, Dr.
Pendleton read the Episcopal service for the dead. This was

all. Mary had specified that there was to be no sermon, no eulogium, no pageantry or public exhibition of grief. This was the way he would have wanted it to be.

Illness had kept Lee from going to George Peabody's funeral in March. After he read the accounts of "the protracted parade and lingering ceremony which was practiced on the occasion, so opposed to my feelings of sorrow & resignation," he had regretted less his inability to attend. He had once told his Cousin Anna that only joy was for others to see and share.

Then the family accompanied the body to the basement where the casket was set in the vault, "while on the green bank outside hundreds of voices sang the hymn my mother had chosen as his favorite: 'How Firm a Foundation Ye Saints of the Lord.'"

Mary was anxious for her old friend, Emily Mason, to write a biography of the General, and asked his cousins Cassius, Edmund, and Sally Lee for their recollections of his boyhood. She then began to sort Robert's letters for that purpose.

Her spirits were raised by reading the world's tributes to Lee, and she kept up a vast correspondence with strangers from the South, the North, and Europe, who wrote her of their veneration and affection for him.

When Edward Valentine was commissioned to model a recumbent statue of Lee for the college chapel, she was greatly interested in his proposed designs, and loaned one of Robert's uniform coats for the model to wear.

In early spring, she took the packet to the White House, to visit her favorite son and his family. She stayed for Rob's wedding—destined to end tragically the next year with the untimely death of the lovely Charlotte Haxall.

But, as more and more of her earthly ties loosened, Mary's interest in life waned. "Now that the light of my existence has disappeared from my horizon the prospect is drear & gloomey. . . . I know that my loss is his gain. He needed rest from all the toils & cares of his eventful life—the glorious rest of heaven. . . . A few more years & I shall go to him."

Sensing her approaching end, she did not feel that she

could die content until she had seen Arlington once more, and while on a visit at Ravensworth, she drove out to her loved old home. It was an unfortunate decision, for, as she said sorrowfully afterward:

"I could not realize that it was Arlington!"

"Take me away!" she said to the driver when she saw the green hill covered with graves.

On October 15, 1873, she suffered a shock from which she never recovered. On that day, Agnes died suddenly at the age of thirty-two. Just before the funeral, Mildred walked into the garden and picked two late roses from a bush their father had planted. She laid them on Agnes' breast. It was impossible for Mary to find consolation for the loss of this favorite daughter. Again and again she would say through her tears:

"To think that I have outlived her!"

But it was not for long. Near midnight on November 5, less than a month after Agnes' death, Mary Anne Randolph Custis Lee passed on to that "glorious rest of heaven."

* * *

On the twenty-eighth of October, 1870, the trustees of Washington College met and "called to the presidency" Custis Lee, who accepted and took office on February 1 the following year. By then, the General Assembly of Virginia had authorized the school to be called Washington and Lee University, thus linking those two illustrious names. In spite of poor health —Custis suffered from what was called "rheumatic gout"—he served for twenty-six years.

Shortly after his mother's death, he began legal action for the return of Arlington, his inheritance, eventually carrying the case to the United States Supreme Court, which decided in his favor in 1882. However, since the grounds had been converted into a national cemetery and thousands of soldiers were already buried there, he decided to accept the government's offer of one hundred and fifty thousand dollars for the property. He never married, and when he retired in 1897, he went to Ravensworth to live with Rooney's family. Here he remained quietly until his death in February, 1913, at the age of eighty-one.

By 1874, Anna Maria Fitzhugh had also died, and Ravensworth passed to Rooney, who moved there with his family, which by then included another son, George Bolling. He continued to farm and to take part in national politics. He was elected to Congress three times, his final term cut short by his unexpected death.

October seemed a strangely fateful month for the Lees. On October 15, 1891, the exact day on which Agnes had died nineteen years before (Annie had died on October 20, twenty-nine years before), Rooney succumbed to some malady. Mildred was with him, and recalling those other October deaths, wrote in her journal the next morning:

"Fitzhugh died yesterday. The same golden sunshine—changing foliage—the same tears & pain at parting!"

Rob stayed at Romancoke until 1890, when he moved to Washington to engage in business. In 1892, he married Juliet Carter, the daughter of Thomas Hill Carter at whose home, Pampatike, his father had spent those restful days in June, 1865. By this marriage he had two daughters, Anne Carter, and Mary Custis. Rob died in 1916, at the age of seventy-three.

Mary (Daughter), the second oldest child, outlived the other members of her family; she died in November, 1918, at the age of eighty-three. At the time of her father's death, she was forty-five years old and a confirmed spinster. Her life pattern was so well established that she could contentedly round out her days in constant travel here and abroad, where, as the daughter of Robert E. Lee and his last surviving child, she was honored and feted by royalty and other distinguished members of British and European society.

Mildred also passed most of her time in travel abroad, but she was keenly aware of the vacuity of her life, which ended in 1905. The final words in her journal are poignantly revealing:

"Most women when they lose such a Father, replace it by husband & children—I have had nothing."

386

Notes & Sources Consulted & Quoted

THE largest and most important collection of primary source material on Robert E. Lee and his immediate family is the R. E. Lee Papers, housed in The Library of Congress. This not only contains most of Lee's letters to his wife, children, and other kindred for the years 1832 to 1870, but includes memoranda books kept while in Texas, letters to superior officers, and personal correspondence with friends and strangers over this same period. Here also are letters and papers of R. E. Lee's father; Mrs. R. E. Lee, and their seven children; cousins Edmund, Cassius, and Sally Lee; George Washington Parke Custis and his wife; Anna Maria Fitzhugh, Martha Custis Williams, and letters of interest to the Lees. Of great importance are the journals of the Lee daughters.

Careful reading of this material has brought to light many items of interest and importance, has corrected errors and misconceptions of long standing, and furnished letters and papers never before published.

The letters of Charles Carter Lee, eldest brother of R. E. Lee, to their half brother, Henry Lee, are a new and highly important collection of primary source material, in The Virginia State Library. These relate details of Robert's activities, establish such important dates as his engagement to Mary Custis, and reveal much that is new concerning Robert and the immediate family.

Another valuable primary source, released from restrictions, is the collection of thirty-two letters from R. E. Lee to his friend and assistant, Henry Kayser of St. Louis. These letters, written between July 26, 1838, and November 25, 1843, give details of Lee's work on the Mississippi River, his social activities, movements, opinions, and glimpses of family life. They also correct a number of errors.

Still another new and interesting collection of Lee family letters is the George Bolling Lee Papers, Virginia Historical Society, although the student is hampered by the restrictions that no part may be copied or quoted.

The Pierpont Morgan Library collection of R. E. Lee—Martha Custis Williams letters was another new and valuable source.

The Mackay Family Papers, Georgia Historical Society, proved most helpful in filling in details of Lee's lifelong friendship with this unusual family.

"The Friendship of Gen. R. E. Lee and Dr. Wm. Beaumont," by Ruth Musser and John C. Krantz, *Bulletin of the Institute of the History of Medicine*, vol. vi, May, 1938, was another new source, as was "Recollections of West Point in 1853," by An Officer's Wife, printed in *The Association of Graduates of the United States Military*

387

Academy, 1903, Bulletin No. 3, which gave a charming picture of social life at the Academy and glimpses of Lee.

Note: All sources are listed in order of their use in each chapter. Unless otherwise identified, all letters are from the R. E. Lee Papers, The Library of Congress.

I. In Defense of Virginia, April 19, 1861, to April 9, 1865

1, pages 3–14.

Robert Stiles, *Four Years Under Marse Robert* (Washington, 1903) gives a description of war-frenzied Richmond at this time. John Janney's speech and Lee's reply in Robert E. Lee, Jr., *Recollections and Letters of General Robert E. Lee* (New York, 1924). Alexander H. Stephens, *A Constitutional View of the War Between the States*, vol. 2 (Philadelphia, 1868) for opinion of Lee. Letters of Cassius Lee and Dr. May quoted in William E. Brooks, *Lee of Virginia* (Indianapolis, 1932). Lee to Andrew Talcott, 30 April, 1861, Virginia Historical Society. Unfavorable opinions of Lee quoted in Mary Boykin Chesnut, *A Diary From Dixie*, ed. by Ben Ames Williams (Boston, 1949). Armistead L. Long, in *Memoirs of Robert E. Lee* (New York, 1886), described Lee's unpretentious headquarters and his personal appearance as did George Cary Eggleston, *A Rebel's Recollections* (New York, 1875). Walter H. Taylor, *Gen. Lee, His Campaigns in Virginia, 1861–1865, with Personal Reminiscences* (Norfolk, 1906), is a valuable source for observations by the sensitive and brilliant young man who worked closely with Lee for four years. Williams C. Wickham's observations on secession quoted in Charles Minor Blackford, *Letters From Lee's Army*, ed. Charles Minor Blackford III (New York, 1947).

2, pages 14–20.

Varina Howell Davis, *Jefferson Davis* (New York, 1890). Clifford Gordon in Franklin P. Riley, *General Robert E. Lee After Appomattox* (New York, 1922), recalled Lee's reputation as a "bear." William Gilmore Beymer, "Williams, C.S.A.," *Harper's Monthly Magazine*, Sept., 1909, for details of Orton Williams. John Beauchamp Jones, *A Rebel War Clerk's Diary at the Confederate States Capital* (Philadelphia, 1866), is an excellent source for Davis' relations with his subordinates, his comments, speeches, etc; serves as an insight on Davis' character. Also contains recollections of Lee. Henry Kyd Douglas in *I Rode With Stonewall* (Chapel Hill, N. C., 1940) remembered the christening of "Stonewall" Jackson. Charles Minor Blackford and his brother William Willis Blackford, who wrote *War Years With Jeb Stuart* (New York, 1945), recalled the flight and pursuit. Mrs. Chesnut recorded that Beauregard and Johnston were compared with Eugene and Marlborough.

3, pages 20–32.

Long was on W. W. Loring's staff and gave firsthand accounts of the western Virginia campaign. Taylor's *General Lee* is another reliable source. Rust's report in *The War of the Rebellion: A Compilation of the Official Records of the Union and Confederate Armies* (Washington, 1880–1901). *Confederate Veteran*, July, 1898, for history of Traveller. Jefferson Davis, "Robert E. Lee," *North American Review*, Jan., 1890, and George Cary Eggleston consulted.

4, pages 32–45.

Long. Eggleston. Charles H. Ohlmstead, *Memoirs*, edited by Lilla Mills Hawes, in *Collections of the Georgia Historical Society*, vol. xiv (Savannah, 1964). Alexander A. Lawrence, *A Present for Mr. Lincoln* (Macon, Ga., 1961); both works record Lee's stay in Georgia; Lawrence gives anecdotes of Lee's visit to Savannah, St. Simon's Island, and Brunswick; Ohlmstead tells of the visit to Cockspur. John Preston's observation of Lee's dissatisfaction with Charleston's defenses, in Mrs. Chesnut. Paul Hamilton Hayne quoted in J. William Jones, *Personal Reminiscences, Anecdotes and Letters of General Robert E. Lee* (New York, 1874). Taylor in *General Lee*, and Long, both wrote of the Charleston fire. Lee to Charlotte Lee, and to Daughter, 25 December, 1861, both in Jones, *Reminiscences*. Lee to Custis Lee, 4 Jan., 1862, Duke University Library. Jeb Stuart quoted in Eggleston.

5, pages 45–65.

Mary C. Lee to Eliza Mackay Stiles, 11 March, 1862, Charles F. Mills collection, Robert E. Lee Memorial Foundation, Inc. J. B. Jones gives an excellent account of the official feuds in Richmond. Charles Marshall, *An Aide-de-Camp of Lee*, edited by Sir Frederick Maurice (Boston, 1927), gives an excellent exposition of Lee's position at this time. Lee to Albert Sidney Johnston, 26 March, 1862, Mrs. Mason Barret Collection, Tulane University Library. John Esten Cooke, *A Life of Gen. Robert E. Lee* (New York, 1875), quotes Mrs. Lee's note to Northern soldiers. Cooke was on Jeb Stuart's staff, and had many contacts with Lee whom he observed closely. Dr. George Lyman, "Some Aspects of the Medical Service in the Armies of the United States During the War of the Rebellion," Papers of the Military Historical Society of Mass., Vol. 13, for account of interview with Mrs. Lee. Major W. Roy Mason in *Battles and Leaders of the Civil War* (New York, 1887–88). Long recalled Johnston's refusal to cooperate with Davis and Lee. Jefferson Davis consulted, and J. B. Jones. Colonel Ives' opinion of Lee quoted in E. Porter Alexander, *Military Memoirs of a Confederate* (New York, 1907). Eggleston recalled the typical Southern soldier. Constance Cary Harrison, *Recollections Grave and Gay* (Richmond, 1911), for anecdote of Lee and Davis on the field. J. B. Jones told of Davis' brush with death in the farmhouse. J. W. Jones, *Reminiscences*, for anecdote of Lee and surgeon. Alexander recalled the fight. William W. Blackford told about Stuart's ruse and the feast at the White House. Mary C. Lee to Eliza Stiles, 5 July, 1862, Georgia Historical Society. Robert Stiles was present at Lee's interview with Jackson. J. W. Jones in *Reminiscences* told of Magruder and evacuation of Golding's.

6, pages 65–82.

Mason, *Battles and Leaders*, for Longstreet's remarks. John Goode, *Recollections of a Lifetime* (Washington, 1906), quoted Lee to Early. Douglas described the battlefield after Malvern Hill, and was also in the Poindexter house during the meeting and in the room after it. J. B. Jones, John Esten Cooke, and Mrs. Chesnut all recorded the people's enthusiasm for Lee. Gen. Pope quoted in Alexander. Charles Minor Blackford saw Lee for the first time when he left Pres. Davis' house. Lee to Charlotte Lee, 22 June, 1862, in Jones, *Reminiscences*. Mary C. Lee to Eliza Stiles, 5 July, 1862, Georgia Historical Society. Lee explained the principles which guided his conduct in battle to Justus Scheibert, *Der Bürgerkrieg in dem Nordamerikanischen Staaten: Militarisch Beleuchtet für den deutschen Offizier . . .* (Berlin, 1874). Gen. R. F. Hoke quoted in George Taylor Lee, "Reminiscences of Robert E. Lee, 1865–68," *South Atlantic Quarterly*, April, 1927. Long was with Lee when he barely escaped capture near Orleans, and when he comforted the ladies near Salem. R. E. Lee, Jr., for account of his meeting with his father. F. G. de Fontaine, *Marginalia, or Gleanings from an Army Note-Book* (Columbia, S. C., 1864), for Lee and the straggler. Long and Douglas for account of Lee's accident. Constance Cary Harrison for R. E. Lee, Jr., and request for new boots. Leighton Parks, "What a Boy Saw of the Civil War," *Century Magazine*, June, 1905, watched Lee's army first on its way into Maryland and later when it was going to Pennsylvania. Charles Minor Blackford described the crossing. Emily Mason, *Popular Life of General Robert Edward Lee* (Baltimore, 1872), for Lee and the teacher. G. F. R. Henderson, *Stonewall Jackson and the American Civil War* (London, New York, 1898), for Lee after Sharpsburg. Garnet Wolseley, "A Month's Visit to the Confederate Headquarters," *Blackwood's Edinburgh Magazine*, Jan.–June, 1863. William W. Blackford, John Esten Cooke, and *A Virginia Girl in the Civil War*, edited by Myrta Lockett Avary (New York, 1903), all described Stuart and his musicians. Cooke recorded the people's veneration for Lee; Eggleston and Stiles, the soldiers' veneration.

7, pages 82–101.

Walter H. Taylor, *Four Years with General Lee* (New York, 1877). Harrison and R. E. Lee, Jr., for anecdotes. Dabney H. Maury, *Recollections of a Virginian in the Mexican, Indian, and Civil Wars* (New York, 1897), for story of the roast beef; Long for anecdotes and headquarters hen. Cooke recalled the visitors at headquarters and their veneration for Lee. William W. Blackford noted the foreign visitors. Ella Lonn, *Foreigners in the Confederacy* (Chapel Hill, S. C., 1940), told of Lee's kindness to Schiebert. Douglas also knew the Corbins, and was present whenever Lee was there. Douglas described the Christmas dinner. Beymer for account of Orton Williams. Mildred Lee recalled her father's attitude toward their suitors, in R. E. Lee Papers. Varina Howell Davis. Lee to James A. Seddon, 10 Jan., 1863, *Official Records*. Carleton McCarthy, *Detailed Minutiæ of Soldier Life in the Army of Northern Virginia, 1861–65* (Richmond, 1882), for recollections of Lee and army life. Eggleston described Northrup. Lee to Custis Lee, 5 Jan., 1863, Duke. Lee to Custis Lee, 7 Aug., 1863, Duke. Walter Taylor's *Four Years* and Giles Cooke in *Confederate Veteran*, Vol. 35, 1916, for recollections of Lee's temper. John Esten Cooke recalled Lee's daily rides and recounted anecdotes.

8, pages 102–115.

Lee to Davis, 6 July, 1864, Duke. Charles Minor Blackford wrote of the snow battle. *Confederate Veteran*, October, 1909, for description of rebel yell. John B. Hood, *Advance and Retreat* (New Orleans, 1880). John Dooley, *Confederate Soldier: His War Journal*, edited by Joseph Durkin (Washington, 1945), for religious revival; also J. W. Jones, "Lee as a Christian," in Franklin P. Riley. Warren Lee Goss, *Recollections of a Private* (New York, 1890), a Northern soldier who distinctly remembered the mud march. Lee to Custis Lee, 5 Jan. and 28 Feb., 1863, Duke. Douglas remembered Mr. Minnis coming into camp. Lee called the photographer Mr. "Cowle," whereas Douglas called him Minnis. Minnis and Cowell were partners. I have relied on Lee's letter in which he tells about the photographer rather than Douglas' recollection of the incident. Both gave a similar account, differing only in the name. Alexander for details of battles. James Powers Smith in *Battles and Leaders*. Long. Wilbourn in John Esten Cooke. George Taylor Lee. Stiles and Marshall. W. D. Pender in *Confederate Military History*, edited by Clement A. Evans (Atlanta, 1899).

9, pages 115–133.

Ella Lonn. Maury wrote of the garland for Stuart's horse. John Esten Cooke, *Wearing of the Gray* (New York, 1867), for account of review. R. E. Lee, Jr., Lee to Charlotte Lee, 11 June, 1863. Jones, *Reminiscences*. F. W. Dawson, *Confederate Reminiscences* (Charleston, S. C., 1882), remembered the committee of ladies. Charles Minor Blackford also wrote of the crossing into Maryland. Arthur J. L. Fremantle, *Three Months in the Southern States*, April–June, 1863 (New York, 1864). W. H. Stewart, *A Pair of Blankets* (New York, 1901), for anecdotes of the entry into Maryland. Mrs. McLellan quoted in Jacob Hoke, *The Great Invasion of 1863: Or, Gen. Lee in Pennsylvania* (Dayton, Ohio, 1887). Reference to Marshall. Anderson quoted in Longstreet. Lee to Carroll in J. William Jones, *Life and Letters of Robert Edward Lee, Soldier and Man* (Washington, 1906). Hood, Scheibert, John Esten Cooke, and Alexander all observed Lee closely at Gettysburg. Hooker quoted in Alexander. John B. Imboden in *Battles and Leaders*.

10, pages 133–154.

Napier Bartlett, *A Soldier's Story of the War* (New Orleans, 1874), recalled the soldiers' reaction to Gettysburg. Charles Minor Blackford commented on Lee's address and the retreat. Susan P. Lee, *Memoirs of William Nelson Pendleton* (Phila., 1893), Lee's attempt to keep up morale. G. Moxley Sorrel, *Recollections of a Confederate Staff Officer* (New York, 1917), recalled the pontoon bridge, as did Blackford.

Cooke, *Life;* Jones, *Reminiscences,* for anecdotes. Marshall. Lee to Eliza Stiles, 25 July, 1863, Collection of Charles F. Mills, in Robert E. Lee Memorial Foundation, Inc. Beymer for details of Orton Williams. Lee to Custis Lee, 7 Aug., 1863, Duke; 26 July, 1863, Jones, *Reminiscences.* William H. Palmer remembered Lee's statement about Wright, and told it to both Richard Cunningham and D. S. Freeman. Davis to Lee, 28 July, 1863, *Official Records.* Lee to Davis, 8 Aug., 1863, and Davis to Lee, 10 Aug., 1863, *Official Records.* Sorrel for anecdote of Lee and the handkerchief. Lee to Caroline and Margaret Stuart, printed in "Lee and the Ladies," by D. S. Freeman, *Scribner's Magazine,* Oct., 1925. Cooke and Long, for anecdotes. Account of Lee at the review in *The Grayjackets* by A Confederate (Richmond, 1867), and R. E. Lee, Jr. William W. Blackford took part in "Buckland Races."

11, pages 154–167.

Lee quoted in Cooke, *Life.* Lee to Gen. Cooper, Report of Mine Run, *Official Records.* J. B. Jones recorded the people's despondency. Lee to Davis, 3 Dec., 1863, *Official Records.* Lee to Stuart, 9 Dec., 1863, Duke. Mrs. Chesnut remembered Lee in church; also women's admiration of him. Lee and Sen. Hill quoted in Long. Walter Taylor to Miss Saunders, Taylor Mss., Miss Janet Fauntleroy Taylor. Lee to Northrup, 5 Jan., 1864, *Official Records;* also Lee to Seddon, 22 Jan., 1864, and 6 March, 1864. Lee to the Richmond City Council in Long. Sally Nelson Robbins in A. R. Brock, editor, *General Robert Edward Lee, Soldier, Citizen, and Patriot* (Richmond, 1897), for anecdotes. Lee to Seddon, 6 March, 1864, *Official Records.*

12, pages 167–181.

Lee to Rooney Lee, 24 April, 1864, Jones, *Reminiscences.* U. S. Grant, *Personal Memoirs,* 2 vols. (New York, 1886). Lee to Seddon, 12 April, 1864, *Official Records.* Lee to Davis, same date, Virginia Historical. Mrs. Chesnut for Lee's stormy interview with Hampton. Longstreet's remarks to Sorrel in Charles Minor Blackford. Alexander wrote of the review, as did F. M. Mixon, *Reminiscences of a Private* (Columbia, S. C., 1910). Lee to Custis Lee, 29 March, 1864, Duke. Taylor, *Four Years.* A. R. H. Ranson, "Gen. Lee As I Knew Him," *Harper's Monthly Magazine,* Feb., 1911. Long for Grant's crossing. Fitzhugh Lee, *General Lee* (New York, 1894). Alexander wrote about Lee and McGowan. Lee in the Wilderness described by "R. C." in *The Land We Love,* vol. 5, 1868; and William C. Oates, *The War Between the Union and the Confederacy* (Washington, 1905). Long described the woods. John B. Gordon, *Reminiscences of the Civil War* (New York, 1903). Randolph H. McKim, *The Soul of Lee* (New York, 1918), a sensitive interpretation. W. Gordon McCabe in R. E. Lee, Jr., for Lee's reaction to news that Stuart was dying. John Esten Cooke came into Lee's tent after Stuart's death.

13, pages 181–199.

William Blackford and John H. Worsham, *One of Jackson's Foot Cavalry* (New York, 1912), and Cooke, *Life,* for anecdotes. Walter H.

Taylor to Gen. Anderson, 31 May, 1864, *Official Records. The Life and Letters of Emory Upton*, edited by Peter Michie (New York, 1885); Upton wrote his horror at Grant's methods of warfare, as did Warren Lee Goss. Anne Banister (Pryor), "Incidents in the Life of a Civil War Child," Mss. in Virginia State Library, wrote of the repulse of Grant at Petersburg. Jones, *Reminiscences* for anecdotes. Charles Blackford. Cooke, *Life*. A. R. H. Ranson, "General Lee As I Knew Him," *Harper's Monthly*, Feb., 1911. Taylor, *Four Years*. Sara Rice Pryor, *My Day: Reminiscences of a Long Life* (New York, 1909). John S. Mosby, "Recollections of General Lee," *Munsey's Magazine*, April, 1911.

14, pages 199–216.

J. B. Jones. John B. Gordon, *Reminiscences of the Civil War* (New York, 1904). Lee to Seddon, 27 Jan., 1864, Duke. Eggleston for agitation against Davis. Lee to Davis and Davis to Lee, quoted in Cooke, *Life*. Charles S. Venable to Walter H. Taylor, 29 March, 1878, Taylor Mss., recounts Lee's threatened break with Davis. Lee to Davis, 19 Jan., 1865, Virginia State Library. Douglas was present at the review. Pendleton and Taylor recalled that Lee was in church when he was notified of the crossing. John A. Sloan, *Reminiscences of the Guildford Grays* (Washington, 1883), for Lee's meeting with the recruits. Lee to Seddon, 8 Feb., 1865, *Official Records*. John J. Craven, *The Prison Life of Jefferson Davis* (New York and London, 1866), contains Davis' letter in regard to Lee's attitude toward Northrup. Lee's general order, 9 Feb., 1865, *Official Records*. Taylor, *General Lee*, for account of Longstreet's meeting with Ord. Stanton to Grant, 3 March, 1865, *Official Records*. George Taylor Lee. Pryor, *Reminiscences of Peace and War*. Taylor, *Four Years*, for Lee's reaction to Hill's death. Lee to Breckinridge, 2 April, 1865, *Official Records*. Charles Blackford was in St. Paul's Church when Davis received the message. Lee to Davis and Breckinridge, 2 April, 1865, *Official Records*. "A Virginia Girl in the Civil War" wrote about Taylor's wedding plans. Cooke, in *Life*, observed Lee closely at this time. Douglas took part in the serenade for Agnes Lee. Kate Virginia Cox Logan, *My Confederate Girlhood*, edited by Lily Logan Morrell (Richmond, 1932), recorded Lee's visit. Cooke in *Life* described Lee at Amelia Courthouse. Lee to Rooney Lee, quoted in Long. Cooke in *Life* told about Lee starting to lead the troops.

15, pages 216–232.

Taylor, *Four Years*. George Taylor Lee. William N. Pendleton, "Personal Recollections of General Lee," *Southern Magazine*, vol. 15, 1874. Correspondence of Lee and Grant, *Official Records*. Charles Marshall, *Appomattox* (Baltimore, 1894). Marshall, *An Aide-de-Camp*. Taylor, *General Lee*. Alexander, Cooke, *Life*, Pendleton, and Gordon, all described Lee on morning of April 9. Consulted Grant for Federal details, and his own appearance. Arthur C. Parker, *The Life of Gen. Ely S. Parker* (New York, 1919). Horace Porter, "Campaigning with Grant," in *Battles and Leaders*. Jones, *Reminiscences*, for anecdote of Lee and visiting clergyman. George A. Forsyth, "The Closing Scene at Appomattox Court House," *Harper's Monthly*, April, 1898, and Seth M. Flint, "I Saw Lee Surrender," *Sat. Eve. Post*, 6 April, 1940, were consulted for composite picture.

16, pages 232–243.

Ranson and William Blackford were eyewitnesses to Lee's return from the meeting with Grant. Blackford recalled the soldiers' gloom the next day. Douglas remembered Marshall writing the final order. Theodore Lyman, *Meade's Headquarters, 1863–65*, edited by George Agassiz (Boston, 1922), recalled meeting of Lee and Meade. F. M. Mixon, *Reminiscences of a Private* (Columbia, S. C., 1910), for ancedote of Meade and flag. Hunt quoted in Long. Douglas was present at the stacking of arms. R. E. Lee, Jr., was in the room when Davis received Lee's letter of April 12. Taylor in *General Lee* wrote of the return to Richmond; also Ranson and Cooke, *Life*. Recollections of D. C. Richardson and Polly Gilliam appear in Southern Historical Society Papers, Virginia Historical Society. Carleton McCarthy was one of the soldiers waiting for a meal when Lee and party arrived. William E. Hatcher, *Along the Trail of the Friendly Years* (Chicago, 1910). Charles Marshall Graves, "Recollections of Gen. Robert E. Lee," *Harper's Weekly*, 2 Feb., 1905, wrote of Lee's arrival in Richmond, as did Julia Page Pleasants in Minnie Kendall Lowther, *Mount Vernon, Its Children, Its Romances, Its Allied Families and Mansions* (New York, 1930). Myrta Lockett Avary, *Dixie After the War* (New York, 1906), told of Lee's parting with Will McCaw. Mrs. Pleasants watched Lee arrive at 707 East Franklin St.

II. A Private Citizen, April 15, 1865, to October 2, 1865

Pages 247–263.

R. E. Lee, Jr. Avary told of the meeting of Emily Mason and Gen. Weitzel. Mildred Lee told about her mother's courage on evacuation day in Richmond. Lee's advice about taking the oath in Avary. J. B. Jones recorded the reaction to Mrs. Lee serving breakfast to the guard. Lee to Markie, 2 May, 1865, Huntington Library. Lee's interview with the *Herald's* reporter, Avary. Sally Nelson Robbins in Brock recalled Lee's first days at home. George A. Townsend interviewed Mathew Brady, *New York World*, 12 April, 1891. A Brady interview in *Chicago Evening Post*, 11 Feb., 1893. Channing Smith in *Confederate Veteran*, Vol. 35. Lee's meetings with his veterans in Jones, *Reminiscences*, Mason, and from Mildred Lee to W. W. Estill, quoted in Franklin Riley. Clement Sullivane, in *Confederate Veteran*, Vol. 28, wrote of Lee and Texas veteran. Thomas Hill Carter wrote of Lee's stay at *Pampatike* in R. E. Lee, Jr. Lee to Beauregard, 3 Oct., 1865, Jones, *Life*. Grant to his wife quoted in Avary. Lee to Markie, 24 June, 1865, Huntington. Stiles. Margaret J. Preston, "General Lee After the War," *Century Magazine*, June, 1889, told of Lee and Mrs. Cocke's dining-room servant; also story of Lee in Palmore's store. Avary quoted the Confederate officer on Southern women's attitude toward the war; Miss Avary also described the "indignation meetings."

III. A Leader of Youth (Washington College), October 2, 1865, to October 12, 1870

1, pages 267–277.

Alexander L. Nelson, "How Lee Became a College President" in Riley. Henry A. White, in *Robert E. Lee and the Southern Confederacy* (New York, 1897), gave a history of Washington College, as did Information Services, Washington and Lee University. Bishop Wilmer in R. E. Lee, Jr. Lee to Trustees, R. E. Lee Papers, Virginia State Library. Mary C. Lee to Emily Mason quoted in Avary. C. A. Graves, "Gen. Lee at Lexington" in Riley, told of Lee's arrival in town. M. W. Humphreys, in *Richmond Times Dispatch*, Jan., 1907, recollections of Lee. Lee to Prof. Graves quoted in Riley. Edward S. Joynes, gave details of Lee's reforms in Jones, *Reminiscences.* Information concerning the planning and building of the chapel supplied the writer by Gene B. Hansley, former Assistant Director of Information Services, Washington and Lee University. Richard W. Rogers and W. Strother Jones; student recollections of Lee in Riley.

2, pages 277–291.

E. C. Gordon in Riley for details of Lee's improvement of the grounds, attention to detail, and broad general knowledge; also D. Gardiner Tyler, Edward S. Joynes, "Robert E. Lee as College President," M. W. Humphreys, and J. W. Ewing, all in Riley. Thomas Nelson Page, *Robert E. Lee, Man and Soldier* (New York, 1922), a student, recalled his contacts with Lee. Jones *Reminiscences* is an excellent source for Lee's trials and problems during the Reconstruction; also details of the demands on Lee's time. Joynes, in Jones *Reminiscences*, gave Lee's scholastic improvements. R. E. Lee, Jr. for anecdotes. James R. Winchester, in Riley, also gave recollections of Lee.

3, pages 291–298.

Christiana Bond, *Memories of Gen. Robert E. Lee* (Baltimore, 1926), for recollections of Custis Lee. W. W. Estill in Riley, recalled the sight of Lee on Traveller. Avary for the "Button Order." Jones, *Reminiscences,* for Lee sleeping with his old soldier. R. E. Lee, Jr., described the arrival of the family at Lexington. Margaret Preston. R. E. Lee, Jr., and Gordon gave Lee's methods of dismissing guests.

4, pages 298–309.

Lee to Lord Acton, 15 Dec. 1866, in *Selections from the Correspondence Of John Emerich Edward Dahlberg Acton* (London, 1917). R. E. Lee, Jr., for Lee reading the *Iliad.* Franklin P. Riley in Riley, for "What Gen. Lee Read After the War." Lee to Markie, 20 Dec., 1865, Huntington. R. E. Lee, Jr., for Lee's reply to Hope, and George Long's note. Mary C. Lee to Mrs. R. H. Chilton, 10 March,

ROBERT E. LEE *THE COMPLETE MAN*

1866, Chilton Papers, Confederate Museum, Richmond, Va. Preston for Lee's visit to Washington. Lee to Markie, 7 April, 1866, Huntington. Lee to Amanda Parks and Mrs. Jefferson Davis in R. E. Lee, Jr. Lee to Reverdy Johnson, 25 Feb., 1868, R. E. Lee, Jr. Jones, *Reminiscences*, for Lee's advice to his people, and anecdote of Sherman's soldier.

5, pages 309–323.

Miss Anne Upshur Jones' gift in R. E. Lee, Jr. Gordon in Riley told about Lee and vicious dogs. Mildred's recollections in R. E. Lee Papers and R. E. Lee, Jr. Lee to Fitzhugh Lee, 19 Sept., 1870, R. E. Lee Papers, Virginia State Library. Edward V. Valentine, in Riley for anecdote of Lee sleeping with Professor White. Mrs. Angus McDonald in Hunter McDonald, "General Lee After Appomattox," *Tenn. Historical Magazine*, Jan., 1926, for the shy child. Story of Virginia Lee Letcher in R. E. Lee, Jr. Margaret Preston remembered Lee and the quarreling boys.

6, pages 323–333.

Mrs. Preston recorded the bombastic man from the Deep South. R. E. Lee, Jr., and Christiana Bond for Lee's stay at the White Sulphur. Ranson recalled the English hero-worshipers. R. E. Lee, Jr., recalled his father on the train to Petersburg. *The Petersburg Express*, 29 Nov., 1867, for Lee's reception. Anne Banister. R. E. Lee, Jr., recorded the stay in Petersburg and the trip to Lower Brandon.

7, pages 333–346.

Mary C. Lee to Mrs. Chilton, 6 May, 1867, Chilton Papers, Confederate Museum, told about their nephews. R. E. Lee, Jr., for "Powhattie." George Taylor Lee remembered his uncle's puns and jokes. Anecdote of Lee's horsemanship in Gamaliel Bradford, *Lee the American* (Boston, 1927), in preface to revised edition. Lee to Markie, 7 April, 1866, Huntington. Lee to Markie, 5 Feb., 1869, Pierpont Morgan Library. Alexander F. Robertson, *Alexander Hugh Holmes Stuart, 1807–1891* (Richmond, 1925), consulted. R. E. Lee, Jr., for ovation at Staunton; also the new President's house. Jones, *Reminiscences*, for work of Capt. May to have Arlington returned. Lee's conversation with Dr. John Leyburn in *Century Magazine*, Vol. 30, 1888. Mary G. Powell re: servant Eugenia, quoted in Douglas Southall Freeman, *R. E. Lee*, 4 vols. (New York, 1936). Berlin in Riley, authority for Lee preferring the Gardner photograph. *Alexandria Gazette*, 5 May, 1869. R. E. Lee, Jr., for anecdote of old hat.

8, pages 346–362.

Mildred Lee's recollections of her mother. Margaret Johnston Pritchard, in *Confederate Veteran*, Aug., 1903. Lee told Miss Bond that he was the oldest man she had ever seen. Lee's visit to Warren Plains in "Lee's Visit," printed in *The State*, 27 Oct., 1962. Woodrow Wilson, *Robert E. Lee, An Interpretation* (New York, 1924). William H.

Fleming in *The Augusta Herald*, 14 Sept., 1930. *The Jacksonville Union* quoted in *Savannah Republican*, 16 April, 1870; also *Charleston Courier*, 26, 28 of April, 1870, for account of Lee's reception. Some newspaper accounts were inaccurate, and all were carefully compared with the letters of R. E. Lee and Agnes. Edward V. Valentine in Riley. Location of Valentine's studio furnished by The Valentine Museum, Richmond, Va.

9, pages 362–377.

Valentine in Riley, and Valentine's Mss. journal, in The Valentine Museum. Mary G. Powell, in *History of Old Alexandria* (Richmond, 1928), had recollections of Lee looking into his old garden. Lee's conversation with Cassius Lee in R. E. Lee, Jr. Account of Lee and Percy Davidson in *Washington and Lee Alumni Magazine*, Jan., 1929. Mildred Lee's journal for details of her father's illness and death. William Preston Johnston, and Mary C. Lee to Mrs. Chilton quoted in R. E. Lee, Jr., and Jones, *Reminiscences*.

Epilogue, *pages 381–386.*

Mildred Lee's journal. Description of Richmond on Oct. 13, in *Walks About Richmond* (Anonymous), printed in Richmond, 1870. Eulogies in Jones, *Life*. The German opinion of Lee in Alexander C. Niven, "Robert E. Lee—A German Appraisement," in *The American-German Review*, April–May 1960. Details of funeral in William A. Anderson, "General Lee as a Man," in Riley. Long told about Mary Lee's final visit to Arlington. Information concerning Custis Lee's tenure, and changing of the name of Washington College, supplied by Washington and Lee University Information Services. Edmund Jennings Lee, *Lee of Virginia, 1642–1892* (Philadelphia, 1895), for some family details.

Complete Bibliography

(Covering all sources cited for *Robert E. Lee: A Portrait* as well as for the present volume.)

Primary Sources, Manuscript

Anne A. Banister (Mrs. A. Campbell Pryor), "Incidents in the Life of a Civil War Child," Virginia State Library, Richmond

Chilton Papers, Confederate Museum, Richmond

C. C. Lee Papers, Virginia State Library

Custis and Lee Family Papers, The Library of Congress

George Bolling Lee Papers, Virginia Historical Society, Richmond

Gen. Henry Lee Papers, The Library of Congress and Virginia State Library

Letter of Maj. Henry Lee to Richard T. Brown, The Library of Congress

Maj. Henry Lee Papers, The Library of Congress

Miscellaneous Lee family letters and papers, Robert E. Lee Memorial Foundation, Inc., Stratford Hall, Virginia

Richard Bland Lee Papers, The Library of Congress

R. E. Lee Papers, personal letters, and official wartime dispatches and correspondence, Duke University Library

R. E. Lee Papers, The Library of Congress

R. E. Lee letters, Manuscript Division, New York Public Library

R. E. Lee Papers, personal letters, and official wartime correspondence, Virginia Historical Society

R. E. Lee Papers, personal letters, and official wartime correspondence, Virginia State Library

R. E. Lee Memoranda Books (3), kept while in U. S. Army, The Library of Congress

R. E. Lee–Jerome Bonaparte Family letters, McCormick Library, Washington and Lee University

R. E. Lee letters and dispatches to John C. Breckinridge, Official Records, War of the Rebellion, National Archives and Records

R. E. Lee letters and dispatches to Jefferson Davis, Official Records, War of the Rebellion, National Archives and Records

R. E. Lee–Henry Kayser letters, Missouri Historical Society, St. Louis

R. E. Lee–Mackay Family letters (typed copies), Georgia Historical Society, Savannah

R. E. Lee–Mackay Family letters (originals), Fort Pulaski National Monument, Savannah Beach, Ga.

R. E. Lee–John Mackay letters (originals), owned by Ralston B. Lattimore and Karl Derst of Savannah; and Lucius S. Ruder of Clearwater, Fla.

R. E. Lee–Mercer Family letters, Mercer Papers, Georgia Historical Society

R. E. Lee–Albert Sidney Johnston letters, Mrs. Mason Barret Collection, Tulane University Library

R. E. Lee letters and dispatches to James A. Seddon, Official Records, War of the Rebellion, National Archives and Records

R. E. Lee–Talcott Family letters, Talcott Papers, Virginia Historical Society

R. E. Lee–Talcott Family letters, Virginia State Library

R. E. Lee–Andrew Talcott letters (photostat copies), Virginia State Library

R. E. Lee's Letterbook while Superintendent of West Point (photostat copy), Virginia State Library

R. E. Lee's will (photostat copy), Virginia State Library

R. E. Lee–Martha Custis Williams letters, The Pierpont Morgan Library, New York

Letters of William Henry Fitzhugh, William B. Leary, C. C. Lee, and Henry Lee, Jr., to John C. Calhoun, National Archives and Records

Edward V. Valentine Papers, The Valentine Museum, Richmond

Primary Sources, Printed

Craven, Avery, editor, *"To Markie": The Letters of Robert E. Lee to Martha Custis Williams* (Cambridge, 1933). Originals are in the Huntington Library, San Marino, Calif.

Cuthbert, Norman B., "To Molly: Five early letters from Robert E. Lee to His Wife," *Huntington Library Quarterly*, Vol. 15, May, 1952. Originals are in the Huntington Library.

Drumm, Stella M., editor, "Glimpses of the Past," twenty-eight letters of R. E. Lee to Henry Kayser, *Missouri Historical Society Publication*, Vol. III, Nos. 1–2, Jan.–Feb., 1936. Originals in Missouri Historical Society.

Freeman, Douglas Southall, "Lee and the Ladies," *Scribner's Magazine*, October, 1925, contains letters to Julia, Margaret, and Caroline Stuart, and Norvell Caskie.

Jones, J. William, *Life and Letters of Robert Edward Lee, Soldier and Man* (Washington, 1906), contains several R. E. Lee letters not to be found in manuscript.

Jones, J. William, *Personal Reminiscences, Anecdotes and Letters of General Robert E. Lee* (New York, 1874), contains a few R. E. Lee letters not to be found in manuscript.

Lee, Fitzhugh, *General Lee* (New York, 1894), contains some R. E. Lee letters not to be found in manuscript.

Lee, Henry, *Memoirs of the War in the Southern Department of the United States* (New York, 1869), contains letters from "Light-Horse Harry" Lee to his son, Carter.

Lee, Robert E., Jr., *Recollections and Letters of General Robert E. Lee* (New York, 1924), contains several R. E. Lee letters not to be found in manuscript.

Printed Material Relating to
R. E. Lee's Ancestry, Youth, and
Career up to the Civil War

Adams, Henry, *The Education of Henry Adams* (Boston, 1908)

Anderson, Charles, *Texas Before and on the Eve of the Rebellion* (Cincinnati, 1884)

Andrews, Marietta, *Scraps of Paper* (New York, 1929)

Armes, Ethel, *Stratford Hall, the Great House of the Lees* (Richmond, 1936)

Armes, Ethel, "Stratford on the Potomac" (pamphlet, Richmond, 1928)

Blackford, L. Minor, *Mine Eyes Have Seen the Glory* (Cambridge, Mass., 1944)

Boyd, Thomas, *Light-Horse Harry Lee* (New York, 1931)

Brock, A. R., editor, *General Robert Edward Lee, Soldier, Citizen and Patriot* (Richmond, 1897)

Cosby, George B., "With General Lee in the Old Army," *Confederate Veteran*, April, 1905

Crane, John, and James F. Kieley, *West Point* (New York, 1947)

Cullum, George W., *Biographical Register of the Officers and Graduates of the United States Military Academy, West Point, New York* (New York, 1868)

Darby, John F., *Personal Recollections* (St. Louis, 1880)

Darrow, Mrs. Caroline, in *Battles and Leaders of the Civil War* (New York, 1887–88)

Davis, Jefferson, "Robert E. Lee," *North American Review*, January, 1890

D'Ormieulx, Mrs. Theophile, "Recollections of West Point in 1853," *The Association of Graduates of the United States Military Academy, Bulletin No. 3*, 1903

Douglas, Henry Kyd, *I Rode With Stonewall* (Chapel Hill, N. C., 1940)

Drumm, Stella M., "Robert E. Lee and the Improvement of the Mississippi River," *Missouri Historical Quarterly*, Vol. 6, 1929

Dupuy, R. Ernest, *Where They Have Trod* (New York, 1940)

Fithian, Philip, *The Journal and Letters of Philip Fithian* (Williamsburg, 1957)

Ford, John Salmon, *Rip Ford's Texas*, edited by Stephen B. Oates (Austin, Tex., 1963)

Ford, Paul Leicester, *The True George Washington* (Philadelphia, 1896)

Forman, Sidney, *West Point: A History of the United States Military Academy* (New York, 1950)

Hallowell, Benjamin, *Autobiography of Benjamin Hallowell* (Philadelphia, 1883)

Harrison, Constance Cary, *Recollections Grave and Gay* (Richmond, 1911)

Hartridge, W. C., *The Letters of Robert Mackay to His Wife, 1795–1816* (Athens, Ga., 1949)

Hendrick, Burton J., *The Lees of Virginia* (Boston, 1935)

Herman, Lewis, *This Is West Point* (New York, 1950)

Hitchcock, Ethan Allen, *Fifty Years in Camp and Field* (New York, 1909)

Hood, John B., *Advance and Retreat* (New Orleans, 1880)

Hughes, Rupert, *George Washington; The Human Being and the Hero, 1732–1762*, Vol. I (New York, 1926)

Hunt, Henry J., quoted in Armistead L. Long, *Memoirs of Robert E. Lee* (New York, 1886)

Jett, Dora Chin, *In Tidewater Virginia* (Richmond, 1924)

Johnson, R. W., *A Soldier's Recollections in Peace and War* (New York, 1887)

Johnston, Eliza, "The Diary of Eliza (Mrs. Albert Sidney) Johnston," edited by Charles P. Roland and Richard C. Robbins, *Southwestern Historical Quarterly*, April, 1957

Johnston, Joseph E., quoted in Armistead L. Long, *Memoirs of Robert E. Lee* (New York, 1886)

Jones, Charles C., Jr., *Reminiscences of the Last Days, Death, and Burial of Gen. Henry Lee* (New York, 1870)

Jones, Katherine M., *The Plantation South* (Indianapolis, 1957)

Keyes, Erasmus D., *Fifty Years' Observation of Men and Events, Civil and Military* (New York, 1884)

Kimball, Marie G., *Jefferson, the Road to Glory, 1743–1776* (New York, 1943)

Lee, Cazenove G., Jr., *Lee Chronicle* (New York, 1957)

Lee, Edmund J., *Lee of Virginia, 1642–1892* (Philadelphia, 1895)

Lee, Fitzhugh, *General Lee* (New York, 1894)

Lee, Gen. Henry, *A Correct Account of the Conduct of the Baltimore Mob* (Winchester, Va., 1814)

Lee, Lucinda, *Journal of a Young Lady of Virginia*, edited by Emily V. Mason (Baltimore, 1871)

Lee, Robert E., Jr., *Recollections and Letters of General Robert E. Lee* (New York, 1924)

Leech, Samuel V., *The Raid of John Brown at Harper's Ferry As I Saw It* (New York, 1909)

Lindsey, Mary, *Historic Homes and Landmarks of Alexandria, Virginia* (Alexandria, 1962)

Lomax, Elizabeth Lindsay, *Leaves From An Old Washington Diary* (New York, 1943)

Long, Armistead L., *Memoirs of Robert E. Lee* (New York, 1886)

Lowther, Minnie Kendall, *Mount Vernon, Its Children, Its Romances, Its Allied Families and Mansions* (New York, 1930)

Mason, Emily V., *Popular Life of General Robert Edward Lee* (Baltimore, 1872)

Maurois, André, *Adrienne, The Life of the Marquise de La Fayette* (New York, 1961)

Maury, Dabney H., *Recollections of a Virginian in the Mexican, Indian, and Civil Wars* (New York, 1897)

Musser, Ruth, and John C. Krantz, Jr., "The Friendship of Gen. R. E. Lee and Dr. Wm. Beaumont," *Bulletin of the Institute of the History of Medicine*, Vol. VI, May, 1938

Oswandel, Jacob J., *Notes on the Mexican War, 1846–47–48* (Philadelphia, 1885)

Owens, Hamilton, *Baltimore on the Chesapeake* (New York, 1949)

Packard, Joseph, *Recollections of a Long Life* (Washington, 1902)

Pearson, Hesketh, *The Man Whistler* (New York, 1952)

Powell, Mary G., *History of Old Alexandria* (Richmond, 1928)

Rhodes, Charles Dudley, *Robert E. Lee the West Pointer* (Richmond, 1932)

Sanborn, Franklin Benjamin, *Recollections of Seventy Years*, 2 vols. (Boston, 1907)

Scott, Winfield, *Memoirs*, Vol. II (New York, 1864)

Semmes, Raphael, *Service Afloat and Ashore During the Mexican War* (Cincinnati, 1851)

Shackelford, George Green, "Stratford Hall, Architectural Mystery," *Northern Neck of Virginia Historical Magazine*, December, 1958

Stephenson, Nathaniel W., *Texas and the Mexican War* (New Haven, Conn., 1921)

Strong, George, *Cadet Life at West Point* (Boston, 1862)

Turner, Marietta Fauntleroy, quoted in Marietta Andrews, *Scraps of Paper* (New York, 1929)

Villard, Oswald Garrison, *John Brown* (Boston, 1911)

Wilson, Woodrow, *George Washington* (New York, 1929)

Wise, Henry A., *Seven Decades of the Union* (Richmond, 1881)

Lee During the Civil War, as
Seen by His Contemporaries

A Confederate, *The Grayjackets* (Richmond, 1867)

Adams, Charles Francis, *Lee at Appomattox* (Boston, 1902)

Alexander, E. Porter, *Military Memoirs of a Confederate* (New York, 1907)

Alexander, E. Porter, "Pickett's Charge," *Century Magazine*, January, 1887

Blackford, Charles Minor, *Letters From Lee's Army*, edited by Charles Minor Blackford III (New York, 1947)

Blackford, William W., *War Years With Jeb Stuart* (New York, 1945)

Bowen, J. J., *The Strategy of Robert E. Lee* (New York, 1914)

Chesnut, Mary Boykin, *A Diary From Dixie*, edited by Ben Ames Williams (Boston, 1949)

Cooke, John Esten, *Wearing of the Gray* (New York, 1867)

Cooke, John Esten, *A Life of General Robert E. Lee* (New York, 1875)

Daly, Maria Lydig, *Diary of a Union Lady*, edited by Harold Earl Hammond (New York, 1962)

Davis, Jefferson, *The Rise and Fall of the Confederate Government*, 2 vols. (New York, 1881)

Davis, Jefferson, "Robert E. Lee," *North American Review*, January, 1890

Dawson, Francis W., *Reminiscences of Confederate Service* (Charleston, S. C., 1882)

De Fontaine, F. G., *Marginalia, or Gleanings From an Army Notebook* (Columbia, S. C., 1864)

Douglas, Henry Kyd, *I Rode With Stonewall* (Chapel Hill, N. C., 1940)

Dunn, Nellie P., "Grant's Petersburg Progress," *South Atlantic Quarterly*, Vol. 12, 1913

Eggleston, George Cary, *A Rebel's Recollections* (New York, 1879)

Flint, Seth M., "I Saw Lee Surrender," *Saturday Evening Post*, April 6, 1940

Forsyth, George A., "The Closing Scene at Appomattox Court House," *Harper's Monthly*, April, 1898

Fremantle, Arthur J. L., *Three Months in the Southern States, April–June, 1863* (New York, 1864)

Goode, John, *Recollections of a Lifetime* (Washington, 1906)

Gordon, John B., *Reminiscences of the Civil War* (New York, 1904)

Goss, Warren Lee, *Recollections of a Private* (New York, 1890)

Grant, U. S., *Personal Memoirs*, 2 vols. (New York, 1886)

Graves, Charles Marshall, "Recollections of General Robert E. Lee," *Harper's Weekly*, Vol. 15, February 2, 1907

Harrison, Constance Cary, *Recollections Grave and Gay* (Richmond, 1911)

Hatcher, William E., *Along the Trail of the Friendly Years* (Chicago, 1910)

Hoke, Jacob, *The Great Invasion of 1863: Or, Gen. Lee in Pennsylvania* (Dayton, Ohio, 1887)

Hood, John B., *Advance and Retreat* (New Orleans, 1880)

Hunt, Henry J., quoted in Armistead L. Long, *Memoirs of Robert E. Lee* (New York, 1886)

Hunton, Eppa, *Autobiography* (Richmond, 1933)

Imboden, John B., in *Battles and Leaders of the Civil War* (New York, 1887–88)

Ives, Joseph C., quoted in E. Porter Alexander, *Military Memoirs of a Confederate* (New York, 1907)

Jones, J. B., *A Rebel War Clerk's Diary at the Confederate States Capital* (Philadelphia, 1866)

Jones, J. William, *Personal Reminiscences, Anecdotes, and Letters of General Robert E. Lee* (New York, 1873)

Jones, J. William, *Life and Letters of Robert Edward Lee, Soldier and Man* (Washington, 1906)

Keyes, Erasmus D., *Fifty Years' Observation of Men and Events, Civil and Military* (New York, 1884)

Lawrence, Alexander A., *A Present for Mr. Lincoln* (Macon, Ga., 1961)

Lee, Fitzhugh, *General Lee* (New York, 1894)

Lee, George Taylor, "Reminiscences of General Robert E. Lee, 1865–68," *South Atlantic Quarterly*, Vol. xxv, April, 1927

Lee, Robert E., Jr., *Recollections and Letters of General Robert E. Lee* (New York, 1924)

Logan, Kate Virginia Cox, *My Confederate Girlhood*, edited by Lily Logan Morrell (Richmond, 1932)

Long, Armistead L., *Memoirs of Robert E. Lee* (New York, 1886)

Longstreet, James, *From Manassas to Appomattox* (Philadelphia, 1896)

Lyman, Theodore, *Meade's Headquarters, 1863–65*, edited by George Agassiz (Boston, 1922)

Marshall, Charles, *Appomattox* (Baltimore, 1894)

Marshall, Charles, *An Aide-de-Camp of Lee*, edited by Sir Frederick Maurice (Boston, 1927)

Mason, W. Roy, in *Battles and Leaders of the Civil War* (New York, 1887–88)

Maury, Dabney H., *Recollections of a Virginian in the Mexican, Indian, and Civil Wars* (New York, 1897)

McCarthy, Carlton, *Detailed Minutiæ of Soldier Life in the Army of Northern Virginia, 1861–1865* (Richmond, 1882)

McKim, Randolph H., *The Soul of Lee* (New York, 1918)

McKim, Randolph H., *A Soldier's Recollections* (New York, 1921)

McLellan, Mrs. Ellen, quoted in Jacob Hoke, *The Great Invasion of 1863: Or, Gen. Lee in Pennsylvania* (Dayton, Ohio, 1887)

Mixon, F. M., *Reminiscences of a Private* (Columbia, S. C., 1910)

Mosby, John S., *War Reminiscences* (Boston, 1887)

Mosby, John S., "Recollections of General Lee," *Munsey's Magazine*, April, 1911

Oates, William C., *The War Between the Union and the Confederacy* (Washington, 1905)

Ohlmstead, Charles H., *Memoirs*, edited by Lilla Mills Hawes, in *Collections of the Georgia Historical Society*, Vol. XIV (Savannah, 1964)

Page, Thomas Nelson, *Robert E. Lee, Man and Soldier* (New York, 1911)

Page, Thomas Nelson, *Robert E. Lee the Southerner* (New York, 1909)

Parker, Arthur C., *The Life of Gen. Ely S. Parker* (New York, 1919)

Parks, Leighton, "What a Boy Saw of the Civil War," *Century Magazine*, June, 1905

Pendleton, William N., "Personal Recollections of General Lee," *Southern Magazine*, Vol. XV, 1874

Pleasants, Julia Page, quoted in Minnie Kendall Lowther, *Mount Vernon, Its Children, Its Romances, Its Allied Families, and Mansions* (New York, 1930)

Porter, Horace, "Campaigning with Grant," in *Battles and Leaders of the Civil War* (New York, 1887–88)

Pryor, Mrs. Roger A., *Reminiscences of Peace and War* (New York, 1904)

Pryor, Mrs. Roger A., *My Day: Reminiscences of a Long Life* (New York, 1909)

Ranson, A. R. H., "General Lee As I Knew Him," *Harper's Monthly*, February, 1911

Ranson, A. R. H., "New Stories of Lee and Jackson," *South Atlantic Quarterly*, October, 1913

"R. C." (of Hood's Texas Brigade), in *The Land We Love*, V, 1868

Robbins, Sally Nelson, in A. R. Brock, editor, *General Robert Edward Lee, Soldier, Citizen and Patriot* (Richmond, 1897)

Royall, William L., *Some Reminiscences* (Washington, 1909)

Scheibert, Justus, *Der Bürgerkrieg in den Nordamerikanischen Staaten* (Berlin, 1874)

Sloan, John A., *Reminiscences of the Guilford Grays* (Washington, 1883)

Smith, Henry Hunter, in *Confederate Veteran*, February, 1898

Smith, James Powers, in *Battles and Leaders of the Civil War* (New York, 1887–88)

Sorrel, G. Moxley, *Recollections of a Confederate Staff Officer* (New York, 1917)

Stephens, Alexander H., *A Constitutional View of the War Between the States*, Vol. 2, (Philadelphia, 1868)

Stiles, Robert, *Four Years Under Marse Robert* (Washington, 1903)

Taylor, Walter H., *Four Years With General Lee* (New York, 1877)

Taylor, Walter H., *General Lee: His Campaigns in Virginia, 1861–1865, With Personal Reminiscences* (Norfolk, 1906)

Watson, William, *Life in the Confederate Army* (London, 1887)

Wise, John S., *The End of an Era* (Boston, 1899)

Wolseley, Garnet, "A Month's Visit to the Confederate Headquarters," *Blackwood's Edinburgh Magazine*, January–June, 1863)

Worsham, John H., *One of Jackson's Foot Cavalry* (New York, 1912)

Lee After the Civil War

Avary, Myrta Lockett, *Dixie After the War* (New York, 1906)

Bond, Christiana, *Memories of General Robert E. Lee* (Baltimore, 1906)

Gaines, Dr. Francis Pendleton, "Lee: The Final Achievement, 1865–1870," address in pamphlet form; no date

Graves, Charles Marshall, "Recollections of General Robert E. Lee," *Harper's Weekly*, Vol. 15, February 2, 1907

Jones, J. William, *Personal Reminiscences, Anecdotes and Letters of General Robert E. Lee* (New York, 1874)

Joynes, Edward S., quoted in J. William Jones (above)

Lee, George Taylor, "Reminiscences of General Robert E. Lee, 1865–68," *South Atlantic Quarterly*, Vol. XXV, April, 1927

Lee, Robert E., Jr., *Recollections and Letters of General Robert E. Lee* (New York, 1924)

McDonald, Hunter, "General Lee After Appomattox," *Tennessee Historical Magazine*, January, 1926

Mason, Emily V., *Popular Life of General Robert Edward Lee* (Baltimore, 1872)

Mosby, John S., "Recollections of General Lee," *Munsey's Magazine*, April, 1911

Page, Thomas Nelson, *Robert E. Lee, Man and Soldier* (New York, 1911)

Preston, Margaret J., "General Lee After the War," *Century Magazine*, June, 1889

Pritchard, Margaret Johnston, in *Confederate Veteran*, August, 1903

Ranson, A. R. H., "New Stories of Lee and Jackson," *South Atlantic Quarterly*, October, 1913

Riley, Franklin P., *General Robert E. Lee After Appomattox* (New York, 1922)

Robbins, Sally Nelson, in A. R. Brock, editor, *General Robert*

Edward Lee, Soldier, Citizen, and Patriot (Richmond, 1897)

Smith, Channing, in *Confederate Veteran*, Vol. 35

Other Biographies and Appraisals of Lee

Bradford, Gamaliel, *Lee the American* (Boston, 1912)

Brooks, William E., *Lee of Virginia* (Indianapolis, 1932)

Davis, Burke, *Gray Fox* (New York, 1956)

Freeman, Douglas Southall, *R. E. Lee: A Biography*, 4 vols. (New York, 1936)

Maurice, Sir Frederick, *Robert E. Lee the Soldier* (Boston, 1925)

The Southerner, "Lincoln and Lee," *South Atlantic Quarterly*, January, 1927

White, Henry A., *Robert E. Lee and the Southern Confederacy* (New York, 1897)

Winston, Robert W., *Robert E. Lee* (New York, 1934)

General Background

Anonymous, *Walks About Richmond* (Richmond, 1870)

Avary, Myrta Lockett, editor, *A Virginia Girl in the Civil War, 1861–1865, Being a Record of the Actual Experiences of the Wife of a Confederate Officer* (New York, 1903)

Bartlett, Napier, *A Soldier's Story of the War* (New Orleans, 1874)

Beatty, John, *Memoirs of a Volunteer, 1861–1863* (New York, 1946)

Bryan, J., III, *The Sword Over the Mantel* (New York, 1960)

Chamberlain, Samuel E., *My Confession*, edited by Roger Butterfield (New York, 1956)

Davis, Burke, *Jeb Stuart: Last Cavalier* (New York, 1958)

Davis, Charles E., Jr., *Three Years in the Army, the Story of the Thirteenth Massachusetts Volunteers* (Boston, 1894)

Davis, Varina Howell, *Jefferson Davis*, 2 vols. (New York, 1890)

De Leon, T. C., *Belles, Beaux and Brains of the 60's* (New York, 1907)

Figg, Royall W., *Where Men Only Dare to Go* (Richmond, 1885)

Gilmor, Harry, *Four Years in the Saddle* (New York, 1866)

Henderson, G. F. R., *Stonewall Jackson and the American Civil War*, 2 vols. (London, 1898)

Henry, Ralph S., *The Story of the Confederacy* (Indianapolis, 1931)

Hill, A. F., *Our Boys; The Personal Experiences of a Soldier in the Army of the Potomac* (Philadelphia, 1866)

Holmes, Oliver Wendell, *Touched With Fire* (Cambridge, Mass., 1940)

Huffman, James, *Ups and Downs of a Confederate Soldier* (New York, 1940)

Jones, Virgil Carrington, *Ranger Mosby* (Chapel Hill, N. C., 1944)

Jones, J. W., *Christ in Camp, or Religion in Lee's Army* (Richmond, 1887)

Johnson, Rossiter, *Campfire and Battlefield* (New York, 1894)

Law, E. M., "Round Top and the Confederate Right at Gettysburg," *Century Magazine*, December, 1886

Le Conte, Emma, *When the World Ended, The Diary of Emma Le Conte*, edited by Earl Schenck Miers (New York, 1957)

Le Conte, Joseph, *'Ware Sherman* (Berkeley, Calif., 1938)

Livermore, Thomas, *Days and Events* (Boston, 1920)

Longstreet, James, "Lee's Invasion of Pennsylvania," *Century Magazine*, February, 1887

Lonn, Ella, *Foreigners in the Confederacy* (Chapel Hill, N. C., 1940)

McDonald, Rose M. E., *Mrs. Robert E. Lee* (Boston, 1939)

Marcus Aurelius Antoninus, *Meditations* (New York, 1957)

Meredith, Roy, *Mr. Lincoln's Camera Man* (New York, 1946)

Meredith, Roy, *The Face of Robert E. Lee in Life and Legend* (New York, 1947)

Mixon, Frank, *Reminiscences of a Private* (Columbia, 1910)

Nicholay, John G., *Abraham Lincoln* (New York, 1902)

Nicholay, John G., and John Hay, "Abraham Lincoln: A History," *Century Magazine*, November, 1886, through April, 1887

Pember, Phoebe Yates, *A Southern Woman's Story* (New York, 1879)

Quaife, Milo M., editor, "The John Askin Papers (Volume I,

1747–1795)," *Burton Historical Records*, I (Detroit, Detroit Library Commission, 1928)

Russell, William Howard, *My Diary North and South* (New York, 1954)

Sandburg, Carl, *Abraham Lincoln: The War Years* (New York, 1940)

Small, Abner R., *The Road to Richmond* (Berkeley, Calif., 1931)

Smith, William Ernest, *The Francis Preston Blair Family in Politics*, Vol. 2 (New York, 1933)

Snow, William Parker, *Southern Generals, Their Lives and Campaigns* (New York, 1866)

Taylor, Richard, *Destruction and Reconstruction* (New York, 1879)

Thomas, Benjamin, *Abraham Lincoln* (New York, 1952)

Weber, Latham B., "The Early History of Washington and Lee University," *Southern Association Quarterly*, August, 1941

Welch, Spencer Glasgow, *A Confederate Surgeon's Letters to His Wife* (Washington, 1911)

Wiley, Bell I., *The Life of Johnny Reb* (Indianapolis, 1943)

Wiley, Bell I., *The Life of Billy Yank* (Indianapolis, 1952)

Wright, Mrs. D. Giraud, *A Southern Girl in '61* (New York, 1906)

List of Names

NOTE: Since most of Robert E. Lee's seven children either had nicknames or were called by their middle or even third names (which applies to several of the Lees' relatives who were close to the family), it is believed that the reader will find this alphabetical list helpful in identifying them.

Agnes: Eleanor Agnes Lee, third daughter of R. E. Lee.

Annie: Ann Carter Lee, second daughter of R. E. Lee.

Aunt Maria: Mrs. Anna Maria Goldsborough Fitzhugh, Mrs. R. E. Lee's aunt by marriage (and R. E. Lee's cousin).

Carter: Charles Carter Lee, R. E. Lee's eldest brother.

"Chass": Charlotte Wickham Lee, first wife of R. E. Lee's second son, W. H. F. ("Rooney") Lee.

Cousin Anna: Mrs. Anna Maria Goldsborough Fitzhugh, R. E. Lee's cousin (and Mrs. R. E. Lee's aunt by marriage).

Cousin Brit: Mrs. Britannia Peter Kennon, cousin of Mrs. R. E. Lee.

Custis: George Washington Custis Lee, oldest son of R. E. Lee.

Daughter: Mary Custis Lee, oldest daughter of R. E. Lee.

Fitz: Fitzhugh Lee, nephew of R. E. Lee.

Fitzhugh: William Henry Fitzhugh Lee, second son of R. E. Lee, known best as "Rooney."

Lottie: Charlotte Haxall, fiancée of Robert E. Lee, Jr.

"Markie": Martha Custis Williams, cousin of Mrs. R. E. Lee.

"Nanie": Mrs. Anna Maria Mason Lee, wife of R. E. Lee's brother Smith Lee.

"Powhattie": Mildred Lee, niece of R. E. Lee.

"Precious Life" or "Life": Mildred Childe Lee, youngest daughter of R. E. Lee.

Rob or Robertus: Robert E. Lee, Jr., R. E. Lee's youngest son.

"Rooney": William Henry Fitzhugh Lee, R. E. Lee's second son.

Tabb: Mary Tabb Bolling Lee, second wife of "Rooney" Lee.

Index

419

Robert E. Lee in 1869